GOD
— and —
FREE WILL

TRUE STORIES OF SINS, FAITH, AND REDEMPTION

JOHN L. FONTANA

Copyright © 2023 John L. Fontana.

All rights reserved. No part of this book may be reproduced, stored, or transmitted by any means—whether auditory, graphic, mechanical, or electronic—without written permission of both publisher and author, except in the case of brief excerpts used in critical articles and reviews. Unauthorized reproduction of any part of this work is illegal and is punishable by law.

ISBN: 979-8-89031-661-5 (sc)
ISBN: 979-8-89031-662-2 (hc)
ISBN: 979-8-89031-663-9 (e)

Because of the dynamic nature of the Internet, any web addresses or links contained in this book may have changed since publication and may no longer be valid. The views expressed in this work are solely those of the author and do not necessarily reflect the views of the publisher, and the publisher hereby disclaims any responsibility for them.

One Galleria Blvd., Suite 1900, Metairie, LA 70001
(504) 702-6708

To Blessed Mother Mary and Saint Pio

To my wife, Joni

To our children—Alissa, Dominic, Liz, Alex, and John

CONTENTS

Introduction vii
Chapter 1   It's about Choice 1
Chapter 2   Free Will 16
Chapter 3   God Is Calling You 38
Chapter 4   The Dark Side 67
Chapter 5   Lizard Man and Rocky Balboa 96
Chapter 6   Wound Care 104
Chapter 7   Hurricane Katrina 120
Chapter 8   Miracles 136
Chapter 9   So Much Love, So Much Suffering 153
Chapter 10   Failure Is Not an Option 177
Chapter 11   Titles 195
Chapter 12   Ten Commandments 218
Chapter 13   Change the World 245
Chapter 14   Mighty Mouse 257
Chapter 15   As You Wish 265
Chapter 16   PFLT 278
Chapter 17   Superstar 311
Chapter 18   Open Door Policy 340
Chapter 19   Oh Yeah, a Conclusion 348
God and Free Will Bibliography 357
About the Author 379

INTRODUCTION

God was silent but not Satan. For months I was hearing the voice of Satan and ignoring him, but this time was different. This night I was listening to the soft whispers of the serpent, and he was making sense! The hour was late into the night, and it was raining. I was alone, and Satan entered my thoughts and came at me with everything he had! He reminded me of all the sins I committed, told me I was worthless, insignificant, inconsequential, and unimportant. Yes, I had failed again and again, and I would continue to fail; I was a loser. I had destroyed the lives of innocent people: my wife and my two children. No one was going to forgive me for that! Friends I believed to have had abandoned me. They would not miss me. They would be happy that I would be gone. They did not need me nor had time to listen to my cries. I had no job, no income to sustain me, for I had just been laid off from my medical sales job. My house was repossessed and in the process of being sold at a sheriff auction. I had no money to help with my children's tuition, and other activities and the lack of funds always produced arguments with my ex-wife. I just closed my failed wound clinic. I had no girlfriend, and my faithful husky recently died. I am in constant lower-back and upper neck pain that I sustained when my car was totaled after being hit from behind while sitting at a red light. What I do have is painful loneliness, debt, and lawsuits.

There was a large bottle of bourbon next to me. The taste of the substance felt like a sponge of sour wine at the end of a reed stick. The glass was half full. I had been drinking for several hours now, and I was contemplating my options; none of which looked very promising or rewarding. Over and over I agreed; I was going to do what the seducer suggested. I knew it would be several days before anyone found me, for no one neither called to check on me nor visited my home. The pain of my sorrow and loneliness was unbearable to subdue anymore. I had failed God, or rather God had failed me. I begged for salvation and to be rescued from years of torment and mental anguish. I looked to the Son for deliverance, but He too was still. At times throughout my life, I often spoke to anyone listening, that if you can't find the Son, then seek His mother. Nonetheless, just as the Father and the Son were unmoved, I believed my *mother* was also unyielding.

Raised Catholic, I knew and felt the love of Jesus and had always tried to emulate His teaching into my life and those of others. I tried to follow my earthly father's meek and humble ways of life, and I often took solace sitting in my father's bedroom rocking chair, softly speaking with him in his bed while my mother, the bride of my father, lay in slumber next to him. Confidence in my spiritual faith, I pledged my life to Christ during my junior year in high school. One night with my buddies, we attended our weekly "Come, Lord Jesus" session held in the rectory of Saint Mary Magdalene Parish Church. I can recall that very night I naively told God, "Give me a challenge to my faith!" How stupid was that? God would honor my request, but not in my time, but in God's time—thirty years later.

Never have I stood in judgment to those unfortunate individuals standing at the side of a road holding that cardboard sign simply stating "Hungry." I gave all I had from my wallet, for I remembered my father's words: "Jesus asked us to feed His people, not judge them." At LSU (Louisiana State University) and in nursing school, I started the "Come, Lord Jesus" program I had learned in high school and invited everyone I befriended to attend. Once on a date with my future bride-to-be, I asked her to join me at a spiritual retreat that was going to be held at Camp Abby; she laughed and invited me to take a puff of weed. A champion of the cross, I had so much going for myself. However, unbeknown to me lay a sleeping beast waiting to stir at just the right place and time. Many years earlier in my simple innocent childhood, a seed was planted

INTRODUCTION

that one day would explode with all the roar of a hungry lion. How did I fall from grace and fall so low?

The gun was a .40 S&W (Smith & Wesson, .40 caliber). It was black, cold, and made of steel. In the drawer where I kept the gun was a box of hollow-point bullets, twenty rounds in all. But all I needed for this night was one. As I consumed more of my liquid poison, I thought about the best spot to put that bullet for maximum impact. Was it the frontal lobe, the temple, the cerebellum, or directly into the heart? As a former trauma nurse who had seen my shares of gunshot wounds, I knew the damage a hollowpoint bullet could do to the human body. With only one friend inside my head, I had only one thought—it was time to end it. I felt nothing. Well, I did think about the shock that maybe my ex-wife would feel upon hearing about my untimely death, and that gave Satan and me a laugh. One more drink and a toast to the world with a shout-out of "Kiss my ass!" and it would all be over. "FU" to my childhood sex abuser! "FU" to my ex-wife! "FU" to my so-called friends! "FU" to everyone! Now or never! It was my choice and my choice alone. After all, I had free will.

It must have been the booze, for I woke up late in the afternoon with a pounding headache. Feeling hung over, I stumbled to the bathroom after getting off the sofa. What a night! What a terrible nightmare! What…the hell? The gun was nearby, the chamber loaded! I quickly showered, packed the unloaded gun into my car, and drove two hours straight to my brother's law office. Entering his office, I handed him the gun and told him to take it away from me. "It's speaking to me!" This story really did happen.

Free will is about free and unrestricted choices and repercussions. That afternoon before I left for my brother's office, I read this passage from the book *The Dolorous Passion*, recalled by the visions of Saint Anne Catherine Emmerich, which provided me with a renewal of faith, hope, and strength:

> *I saw Jesus still praying in the grotto, struggling against the repugnance to suffering which belonged to human nature, and abandoning himself wholly to the will of His external father. Here*

the abyss opened before Him, and He had a vision of the first part of Limbo. He saw Adam and Eve, the patriarchs, prophets, and just men, the parents of his Mother, and John the Baptist, awaiting his arrival in the lower world with such intense longing, that the sight strengthened and gave fresh courage to his loving heart. His death was to open Heaven to these captives —his deaths was to deliver out of that prison in which they were languishing in eager hope! When Jesus had, with deep emotion, looked upon these saints of future ages, who, joining their labors to the merits of his Passion, were, through Him, to be united to His heavenly Father. Most beautiful and consoling was this vision, in which He beheld salvation and sanctification flowing forth in ceaseless streams from the fountain of redemption opened by his death. The apostles, disciples, virgins and holy women, the martyrs, confessors, hermits, popes and bishops, and large bands of religious of both sexes—in one word the entire army of the blessed—appeared before Him. All bore on their heads triumphed crowns differed in color, in form, in odor, and in perfection, according to the difference of suffering, labors and victories that had procured them eternal glory. Their whole life, and all their actions, merits, and power, as well as all the glory of their triumph, came solely from their union with the merits of Jesus Christ.

But the consoling visions faded away, and the angels displayed before Him the scenes of his Passion quite close to the earth, because it was near at hand. Jesus having freely accepted the chalice of suffering, and received new strength, remained some minutes longer in the grotto, absorbed in calm meditation, and returning thanks to His Heavenly Father. He was still in deep affliction of spirit, but supernaturally comforted to such a degree as to be able to go to his disciples without tottering as walked or bending beneath the weight of his suffering. When Jesus came to his disciples, they were lying as before, against the wall of the terrace, asleep, and with their heads covered. Our Lord told them that then was not the time for sleep, but that they should arise and pray: "Behold the hour is at hand."[1]

Maybe God was listening to my prayers after all. I should have been dead! Again, that day, like I did in high school, I rededicated my life to Christ. I freely chose to recapture that lost soul I once knew. I chose Christ! Free will is about choice:

> *The choice is always whether to trust in the Lord or do it yourself. The decision is being made constantly and not always consciously. Throughout each day we encounter decisions, actions, and recourses to incidents impacting our lives. Even our perceptions determine our attitudes and behavior. To rely upon our own strength and wisdom makes us vulnerable to temptations and susceptible to influences that are contrary to God's will. The wicked that lie in wait to attack may not be blatantly evil but simply things that cause us to choose our own will. Self-serving motives and gratification of the flesh may be what robs us of victory. There are only two choices in every situations—submission to the lordship of Christ or going our own way.*[2]

Jesus Christ forces himself on no one. In him, God purposely limits his omnipotence in order to respect human freedom. He gives countless signs and indications that he is to be trusted, that he is who he says he is, but he refuses to give any evidence that will eliminate the need for trust and faith. He invites; does not compel. He is a Lord who wages his wars by appealing to the heart, by showing love, and by speaking the truth, but if we refuse his advances, he will leave us free to go our own way. He wants followers who are friends, not slaves—a kingdom of freedom, not bondage.[3]

---

[1] Anne Catherine Emmerich, *The Dolorous Passion of Our Lord Jesus Christ* (El Sobrante, CA: North Bay Books, 2003), pp. 43–53.
[2] Jerry Rankin, *In the Secret Place* (Nashville, TN: B&H Books, 2009), pp. 28–29.
[3] Father John Bartunek, *The Better Part* (Hamden, CT: Circle Press, 2007), p. 393.

This freedom to accept or deny God did not start with Jesus. On the contrary. It started at the very beginning. Even before Adam and Eve. It started with the angels; read *Ezekiel 28:12–19* and *Isaiah 14:12–15*. These are two scripture quotes describing the reason Satan fell out of grace with God. "I could no longer sympathize with Lucifer, for I saw that he cast himself down by his own free will."[4] Human freedom did begin with Adam and Eve.

As the father of two children (Alissa, age thirty-one; Dominic, age twenty-four), I want nothing but the very best for my kids. As toddlers, their mother and I began teaching them the values, principles, morals, and ethical ideals that were taught to us and, now as adults, we still believe in. We taught them about love, manners, kindness, values, morals, principles, ethics, beliefs, traditions, virtues, respect, the Ten Commandments, the difference between right and wrong, and the love and salvation of God. We love them so much that we hope and dream that what was passed on to them, lessons instilled from our parents, will help shape their character and guide them to live a loving and blessed life with God in the center. We had help in this endeavor.

As nurses, my former wife and I encouraged our daughter to become a nurse, believing that her love and compassion for people would be a good and wise career move for her. Nursing is always a profession in demand that pays well and would allow our daughter independence and the ability to support herself financially. So, when she switched her major in her second year at LSU to journalism, I had many questions. I encouraged her to get her nursing degree so that she has a well-paying job to fall back upon. "Nursing is in such demand you can work anywhere. It would be your backup plan." "No!" she said. "I don't like nursing. I want to major in mass communication and get a journalism degree." Her mind was made up. Although I tried to steer her in the direction of what I believed was in her best interests, she made her freewill choice and switched her college major. As her loving father, I respected her freewill choice.

---

[4] Blessed Anne Catherine Emmerich, *The Life of Jesus Christ and Biblical Revelations* (Charlotte, NC: Tan Books, 2004), p. 2.

INTRODUCTION

As I began to write this book, it was 2008, and my twenty-year-old daughter was boarding a plane to fly and study in Italy for five weeks. She is such a shy girl that I wonder how she is going to survive the trip. Only yesterday at dinner, the day before she left for Italy, she asked me to tell the waiter that she wanted an iced tea. "Are you kidding me? You have to ask me to ask the waiter, and you're going alone to Italy for five weeks? Who are you going to get to ask the Italian waiter?" She is a bright, intelligent, and beautiful girl, and we taught her well, but does she really know the difference between right and wrong? I think so. I hope so. I pray so! Just before she kissed me goodbye, I gave her some final fatherly advice. She better not get pregnant, thrown in jail, or have to be hospitalized for drugs. I do not want to see her in a Girls Gone Wild video. If she is kidnapped, we do not have the money to pay for her ransom; and if sold into the sex slave industry, I will not be able to rescue her like James Bond or Liam Neeson in the movie *Taken* (her grandmother actually took her to see this movie before she left for Italy). My daughter's decisions in Italy will be her own, right or wrong, good or bad. Despite the love, wants, concerns, and wishes of her parents, our daughter will be traveling the Italian countryside expressing her free will. All I can do is hope for the best and pray to offset the worst.

Today people go through life taking every gift for granted. Over the years I have talked to many individuals that feel so resentful for not having more. People are never satisfied with their lives—always complaining. The first time I became unemployed, I would go on job interviews in the morning and then sunbathe at the local health club in the afternoon while scanning the newspaper (way before the internet was invested) for a new job opportunity. For an entire week, I sat near the same ten ladies sunbathing next to me and listened to their loud complaints about their husbands, children, maids, tennis team members, vacation plans, pets, friends and family, etc. These women were very wealthy and did not have to work. After a week of listening to them complaining, I could not take it anymore and told them to stop being so grouchy and do something about their so-called hard life—change it!

GOD AND FREE WILL

God gave us existence, but we are the ones responsible for our choices in this life. Our life is based on what we have decided it to be. Right or wrong in the eyes of God, our decisions are entirely established on free will. Established by God, free will is the ability to make our own choices independently without force or coercion. But, with free will comes accountability and responsibility. We tend to forget to ask God for guidance in life, and when things don't work to our satisfaction, we get mad at Him, or we make Him responsible for what is happing to us. We avoid responsibility and shift the blame to someone else, all the while making excuses for why we did not achieve the dream or goal. I hope and pray that you, the reader, will utilize my hard lessons learned to help you make positive and righteous decisions and selections in life. If you do make unfortunate choices, remember to forgive yourself, try to learn from the mistake, and become a wiser and better person—change the behavior. Do not give up on yourself, and keep God in the mixture.

God is ruler and king over all of us whether we choose to believe that or not, and one day we will be called before Him to give account of our earthly life. The consequences of our choices made in this life will determine our judgment. Therefore, it is essential to live for God rather than for what this fallen and material world tells us otherwise. There are a billion things in this world competing to take our focus off from God. Every day we are being tested to choose those things that glorify God or those things that are contradictory to God's will. In my short sixty years of life, I have made some good and righteous decisions, but I have also made some devastating and bad choices that have had enormous repercussions on my family and those that I love dearly. The outcome of my choices that were contrary to God's will has placed me in a desired outcome not what I had in mind.

You will derive from my writings that this book recounts an inspirational journey that starts with a life of lies and ends with confidence, tranquility, and a stronger sense of purpose after overcoming desperation, depression, suicide temptations, sexual abuse, evil, and a dark seduction. *Free Will* has true-life stories that have many forms of debauchery known to man: sex, drugs, adultery, embezzlement, bribe, kickbacks, shakedown, theft, forgery, felony, sex abuse, failures, murders, divorce, lies, seduction, hate, envy, rage, anger, and frustration. It also includes real-life lessons learned from surviving a category 5 hurricane and the aftermath that followed: about a rescue, a lesson learned at a snowball stand, hope, faith, preservation, redemption, salvation, trust, forgiveness, triumph, and the love of God. The core of this book is a true-life account of my own struggles in the center of a raging storm and my fall from God's grace to the return of a prodigal son episode.

While my writing is not on the same disparity as the deep theologian philosophers such as Scott Hahn, Emmet Fox, Laurie Beth Jones, Rick Warren, Jonathan Kirsch, Eric Metaxas, and Bishop Fulton Sheen, I am able to present my thoughts, ideas, and reflections in a logical, balanced, and simple approach. I wanted my method to reflect the simple but serious tone of the teachings of Christ to correspond into easy reading with entertaining stories. I also poke fun at a few good friends as well as myself. Using some of my favorite movie quotes, music lyrics, and true-life stories, I hope that this book will enable you, the reader, to stop and reflect on your life and evaluate whether you are going on the right path. Are you choosing the goodness of God's graces or the destruction from the thousands of temptations this fallen world has to offer? Are you like me dabbling in life's richness but struggling with the many enticement of depravity? Do you value what you have and thank God for His mercy and kindness? Is He the center of your life, or does He revolve around you? Describing *free will* to someone is like listening to the words of the Southwest Airline commercial: "You are now free to move about the cabin."

CHAPTER 1

IT'S ABOUT CHOICE

As mentioned in the introduction, my daughter spent the summer of 2008 in Italy to take some journalism classes. Though she did take some classes, she surely played a lot. Arriving in Rome for her first day of the program, Alissa met her new classmates at the airport. They then traveled to their hotel where the entire group stayed for a few days to bond while seeing the sites. The day she spent touring the Vatican, the Roman Forum, and the Coliseum, I knew she was going to call me later in the evening to tell me about her visits. Having viewed Rome five years earlier and loved all of it, I was so excited waiting for that call to hear all about what she saw. When the phone rang, I excitedly began asking her questions of her tours. This is how the conversation went down:

Father: So, how was the Vatican? Did you like it? Did you see the Sistine Chapel? Did you go to the grotto? Did you climb to the top of Saint Peter and go on the roof? What did you think of Michelangelo's paintings?

Alissa: Yeah, it was nice, but let me tell you about this ice bar!

Father: How was the Roman Forum? What did you think of it? Did you see the spot where Caesar was killed? What about the Senate building? Did you get to go to the bathhouse?

Alissa: I liked it, but, Dad, this bar was built out of ice!

Father: Was the Coliseum awe-inspiring and moving? Where you able to go beneath the walkway to the gladiator's pit?

Alissa: Yeah, we did that…but will you listen to me? We went into an ice bar! It was like ten below freezing. We had to put on fur coats. The bar, the chairs, and the glasses were all made of ice. It was so awesome!

Father: Alissa! [I yelled into the phone.] You are surrounded by four thousand-years plus of history, and the greatest part of the day was the ice bar?

Alissa: Yeah, Dad, it was the coolest thing I've ever saw. We had a blast inside shooting shots!

Wow! Did we make the wrong choice sending her abroad to study? Ice bars over the Vatican? Where did we go wrong? Was it the divorce? Her mother and I believed it would be in her best interest to apply to nursing school, but her mind was made up. Respectfully, we did not try to force our input upon her. Out of love, we honored her freewill decision. Six months after her trip to Italy, an event she witnessed changed her mind, and she submitted this letter to LSU Health Science Department. In it she admits that she had to "work through the process…to come to her own conclusion."

> *Throughout my life I have always been surrounded by nursing. At a young age, I saw nursing was a way to help people who were not capable of helping themselves. I saw nursing give job stability even when the economy was not at its best. Finally, I saw nursing could change a person's entire life. My parents met in 1981 at Charity Hospital School of Nursing in New Orleans. Today my dad is a Wound Care Certified Nurse and my mom is a Certified Nurse Anesthetist. Most of my childhood memories involve going to work with my dad or watching my mom study for anesthesia school.*

Nursing was the reason my brother and I grew up in a loving family, in a safe town, and attended wonderful school.

Different reasons brought my mother and father in the field of nursing. My dad taught me compassion at a young age. He went on several medical missions' trips to Guatemala as a nurse, and he and I went on a mission trip to Mexico together. He wanted me to know helping others is what life is really all about. Today, I know that helping others is the only life worth living. Nursing allows a person to help others every single day. I watched my dad work in the recovery room, medical sales, and hyperbaric and diving medicine and work in the home health care industry. I also watched him get laid off from the medical sales industry, but he always managed to get a new nursing job. However, in the end, financial reasons tore my family apart.

When times got tough, it was my mom who worked the extra hours to pull us out of the financial rut we found ourselves in. My mother's career as a CRNA allowed her to always have a great job. Growing up, my mom always told me I needed to be able to take care of myself, and that I should never depend on another person. It wasn't until my parent's divorce I realize what she meant. My mother's job saved our family and gave her the opportunity to stabilize our family's financial situation.

I watched nursing provide amazing opportunities while growing up, but I had yet to be fully convinced it was the career choice for me. When I enrolled as a freshman at LSU I declared pre-nursing as my major because it was the familiar thing. However, I soon learned that was not a reason to choose nursing. I needed to figure out what I wanted to do for myself.

In December 2008, my grandfather was diagnosed with multiple myeloma. He was in and out of the hospital for three weeks when he decided he wanted to go home. The nurse told us he would only make it until the end of the week. My family stayed by his side; however, it was my mother who took care of him. My grandfather seemed so helpless as opposed to the strong man I knew. Now, he depended on my mom to help him. She knew exactly what to do in every situation that occurred. It was in this one week, as I watched my mom care for the person she loved most in the world, I knew 100 percent I wanted to become a nurse. I want to be able to care for the helpless and comfort the suffering. I want to be a nurse so that I can go on to work in pediatric oncology and help suffering children the way my mother helped my suffering grandfather.

I have been at LSU for three years now, and I would love for it to be one day my alma mater. LSU Health Science School of Nursing gives me the chance to keep my loyalty at LSU. LSUHSC values loyalty as a part of the core value integrity. Also, being based in New Orleans keeps me close to home allowing me to give back to my community as stated in LSUHSC's mission statement. It is at LSUHSC where I will be prepared to deliver the best form of health care as my mother and father always have, and given the chance to advance in any practice, such as pediatrics.

LSUHSC School of Nursing vision statement states the school produces local, national, and international leaders. As a nurse I hope to embark on worldwide medical mission trips and become a traveling nurse. This enables a person to help out anywhere they end up in life. It allows a person to experience diversity, and I am part of a generation where diversity is a positive thing. As a nurse you become part of a group, and at LSUHSC the students work together to becoming a family. The students are not an average group but the best. As a nurse, I never want to be average but always excel when helping others. I want to be challenged each day and learn the responsibilities that come with being a nurse LSUHSC School of Nursing values respect, excellence, and professionalism as core values just as my parents taught me.

> *Caring is the core value I believe in most. I believe compassion is the key to humanity and without it we are not truly human. LSUHSC is based on valor meaning "to be worth" and no life is worth living if we never give back. The core value at LSUHSC reflects a life worth living by joining together and helping others. These values are something I was taught at a young age and something I wish to never forget.*[5]

My daughter, on her own and with the guidance of God's wisdom, worked through her struggle; and in the end, she chose to serve the sick. On May 1, 2010, my daughter received her acceptance letter to the LSU School of Nursing program. Like my daughter, everybody has trials and struggles that must be worked through. Some choices may be minor while others will be difficult. Choices and options are not always easy and viewed in black and white. Many times, God will present to us choices that seem to have no outcomes. We may also feel that our family and friends have neither answers nor any solutions. God too may seem to have deserted us. This is called desolation (the absence of feelings). Desolation may be intense and painful emptiness with absolutely no thoughts of excitement, pleasure, or spiritual fulfillment. One may feel as if he is parched and dry as a desert. Still, God is always nearby and watching you work through the struggle for His glory. Listen for His whispers. The outcome of your choice depends on your faith—to believe or not believe, to trust or not to trust.

Today my son Dominic Joseph Fontana is twenty-three years old. However, back in August 2014, Dominic was eighteen years old and entering his first semester at Roosevelt University in Chicago. Dominic was accepted to Chicago College of Performing Arts. When he was in the third grade, and without any influence from his sister, friends, and his parents, Dominic made a freewill choice that, so far, he has not deviated from that decision. With only eight years of life experiences, I've never seen anyone in my life so focused and determined to achieve a goal. Back in third grade, after watching his older sister in her dance

---

[5] Alissa Fontana, LSU Health Science application letter, 2010.

classes and recitals, Dominic asked if he too could take dance lessons. Can you imagine that? Being the manly man I was, I tried talking him out of that request. I told him that his name would sound so very cool being announced repeatedly in front of ninety thousand people in Tiger Stadium at LSU. His mother tried another approach by offering him violin lessons. She said, "Dominic, if you learn to play the violin, you are going to get all the classy babes." "No!" he said. He wanted dance lessons because he wanted to become an actor. Well, his mother and I never thought he would stick with it, but he proved us wrong. It turned out that the Lord has blessed that boy with a gift. Not only does he love dancing and performing, he is superb at it. As a sophomore in high school, he auditioned and was accepted into New Orleans Center for Creative Arts' Musical Theater program, where he excelled and had leading roles in many performances. As a junior in high school, he was accepted into Columbia University summer program "Cap 21." In his senior year, Dominic was hired as a dancer for the music video "Blackmail" by Kara Mann.

A few weeks prior to leaving for Chicago to pursue his lifelong dream, I had a talk with Dominic. I said, "We need to discuss your backup plan." He replied, "I'm not having a backup plan. Backup plans indicate failure." So, I said, "Okay. Let's discuss your 'reality plan.'" Once again, with confidence, he said, "No reality plan! Reality plans are for failure. Dad, I know it's a long shot and a long struggle, but that is what I want to do. I will be a famous actor one day. Trust me! So, either you support my choice or not?" His mother's talk was very different from mine. She said, "Dominic, if you get a girl pregnant, I will cut off your penis and beat you to death with it!" Ha ha. Now, that is great advice!

Dominic has successfully graduated from college. In those four years of school, his training and practice have dramatically improved. His voice, dance, and his acting have advanced so much that when I now watch him perform, I have that awe and wow moment. In the spring of 2017, Dominic had the leading role in *Cabaret*. His performance made me cry! At Senior Showcase, it should have been called the Dominic Showcase, for he was in most of the acts. We should all be so focused like Dominic. Dominic has not taken his focus from his dream. He knows what he wants, and he is going after it. Dominic resides in LA and has released his first CD called *Blueboy*. He is currently working on his second CD and a music video. However, he is still on the payroll, but he assured me that one day, we don't know when, he will be off the payroll! The moral of this story is that we should also chase God with the same drive and focus as Dominic chases his dream.

Father John Bartunek agrees. In his book *The Better Part*, he writes the following:

> *We see that every day the great men and women of the world, the CEOs, the athletes, the movie stars, the political leaders—many of them are exemplary in their tenacity, their determination, and their astuteness. They set a goal and let nothing stop them from achieving it. They turn everything into an opportunity to advance their cause. No sacrifice is too great. Imagine how different the Church (and the world) would be if everybody pursued holiness as energetically as most people pursue pleasure, honor, and wealth.*

New York Times best-selling author Erick Metaxas sums up trusting in God from his book *Everything You Always Wanted to Know about God but Were Afraid to Ask*:

> *Jesus knew what was in a man. It means that Jesus knew that apart from God—we are inclined toward sin and selfishness and destruction and death, to put it bluntly. He knew that apart from God-we cannot really be trusted. For one thing, He knew that in a short time, the same folks who were celebrating Him and saying He was the Messiah would be shouting "Crucify Him"! He knew the fickleness and depravity of the human heart. We must know and trust God. If we don't know God—if we have not turned our lives over to Him—then God is scary. But He wants us to know Him and to trust Him, not to be afraid of Him and to run from Him. If we know God—if we have turned our lives over to Him and know Him, as He wants us to know him—then we know that He loves us and that we have nothing to fear from Him. If you believe*

in Jesus it can mean nothing or it can mean everything. But if you really believe in Him, you will trust Him with your whole life, and you will obey Him—because if you really trust Him, you know He would never steer you wrong.[6]

An incredible story about struggling with a life decision choice can be found in the book *Where Men Win Glory* by Jon Krakauer. This story is about Pat Tillman, a professional football player with the Arizona Cardinals, who has a change of heart regarding his life after the 9/11 attack on the World Trade Center in New York City. For over a year, Pat contemplated leaving a comfortable, secured, and profitable life for hardship and possibly death by serving his country in the Armed Forces. Pat weighed all the pros and cons. He was getting married, had family and friends who loved him, and he was getting publicity in a game that he loved to play. The Cardinals offered him a $3.6 million contract to stay with them for the next three years. On pages 137–138 of Jon Krakauer's book, Pat records his thoughts.

Many decisions are made in our lifetime, most relatively insignificant while others life altering. Tonight's topic…the latter. It must be said that my mind, for the most part, is made up. More to the point, I know what decision I must make. It seems that more often than not we know the right decision long before it's actually made. Somewhere inside, we hear a voice, and intuitively know the answer to any problem or situation we encounter. Our voice leads us in the direction of the person we wish to become, but it is up to us whether or not to follow. More times than not we are pointed in a predictable, straightforward, and seemingly positive direction. However, occasionally we are directed down a different path entirely. Not necessarily a bad path, but a more difficult one. In my case, a path that many will disagree with, and more significantly, one that may cause a great deal of inconveniences to those I love.

---

[6] Erick Metaxas, *Everything You Always Wanted to Know about God (but Were Afraid to Ask)*.

IT'S ABOUT CHOICE

My life at this point is relatively easy. It is my belief that I could continue to play football for the next seven or eight years and create a very comfortable lifestyle for not only Marie and myself but be afforded the luxury of helping out family and friends should a need arise. The coaches and players I work with treat me well and the environment had become familiar and pleasing. My job is challenging, enjoyable, and stroke my vanity enough to fool me into thinking it's important. This all aside from the fact that I only work six months a year, the rest of the time is mine. For more reasons than I care to list, my job is remarkable.

On a personal note, Marie and I are getting married a month from today. We have friends and family we care a great deal about and the time and means to see them regularly. In the last couple of months, we've been skiing in Tahoe, ice climbing in Utah, perusing through Santa Fe, visiting in California, and will be sipping Mai Tais in Bora Bora in a little over a month. We are both able to pursue any interests that strike our fancy and down the road, any vocation or calling. We even have two cats that make our house feel like a home. In short, we have a great life with nothing to look forward to but more of the same.

However, it is not enough. For much of my life I've tried to follow a path I believed important. Sports embodied many of the qualities I deemed meaningful: courage, toughness, strength, etc. while at the same time, the attention I received reinforced its seeming importance. In the pursuit of athletics, I have picked up a college degree, learned invaluable lessons, met incredible people, and made my journey much more valuable than any destination. However, these last few years, and especially after recent events, I've come to appreciate just how shallow and insignificant my role is. I'm no longer satisfied with the path I've been following…its no longer important. I'm not sure where this new direction will take my life though I am positive it will include share of sacrifice and difficulty, most of which falling squarely on Marie's shoulder. Despite this, however, I am equally positive that this new direction will, in the end, make our lives fuller, richer, and more meaningful. My voice is calling me in a different direction. It is up to me whether or not to listen.[7]

When I think of the decision Pat made during his struggle, I am reminded of John 3:16, "For God so loved the world that He gave His only begotten Son, that whoever believes in Him should not perish."[8]

On April 22, 2004, at the very young age of twenty-eight, Pat was killed by friendly fire while serving his country in Afghanistan.

Even Jesus had to work through His struggles as He became troubled and distressed that very night in the Agony in the Garden of Gethsemane. When Jesus needed the support of God and His disciples the most, he was truly in desolation. As a man, fully capable of feeling bodily pain, Jesus slumps to the ground tormented with visions of his passion to come. His body shakes violently as to reject the anticipation of all the horrible inflictions He will sustain. (Jesus appeared to St. Bridget of Sweden and reveled to her that he received 5,480 blows.) As a man, Jesus was inconsolable with all that physically awaited Him: torture, the crown of thorns, flagellation, stumbling under the heavy cross, impaling of the nails, and succumbing to death with outstretched arms. As a man, Jesus was pondering if all this suffering would be worthwhile. However, this was nothing in comparison to the spiritual assault Satan made. To truly understand the spiritual and emotional impact of Satan's attack upon our Lord, one must go back and quote from the visions of Saint Anne Catherine Emmerich in the book *The Dolorous Passion of Our Lord Jesus Christ*.

When Jesus left His disciple, I saw a number of frightful figures surrounding him in an ever-narrowing circle. His sorrow and anguish of soul continued to increase, and He was trembling all over when he entered the grotto to pray. Atlas, this small cavern appeared to contain the awful picture of all the sins that had been

---

[7] Jon Krakauer, Where Men Win Glory, pp. 137–138.
[8] National Conferences of Bishops, the New American Bible (Wichita, KS: Devore & Sons, 1981), p. 1141.

or were to be committed from the fall of Adam to the end of the world. Satan, who was enthroned amid all these horrors, and even filled with diabolical joy at the sight of them, let loose his fury against Jesus and displayed before the eyes of his soul increasingly awful visions. Satan brought forward innumerable temptations as He had formerly done in the desert to Him. Then he laid to the charge of our Lord a host of imaginary crimes. He reproached Jesus with having been the cause of the massacre of the Innocents, as well as of the suffering of his parents in Egypt and not having saved John the Baptist from death. Jesus soul became terrified at the sight of the innumerable crimes of men, and of their ingratitude towards God, and His anguish was so great that He trembled and shuddered as He exclaimed: Father, if possible, let this chalice pass from me.' I saw the cavern in which He was kneeling filled with frightful figures; I saw all the sins, wickedness, vices and ingratitude of mankind torturing and crushing Him to earth; the horror of death and terror which He felt as man at the sight of the expiatory sufferings about to come upon him surrounded and assailed His person under the forms of hideous specters.

His Body was covered with a cold sweat, and He trembled and shuddered. He then arose but His knees were shaking and apparently scarcely able to support Him; His countenance was pale, and quite altered in appearance, His lips white and His hair standing on end. The tempter was permitted to do to Him what he does to all men who desire to sacrifice themselves in a holy cause. Satan played before the eyes of our Lord the enormity of that debt of sin that he was going to pay and was even bold and malicious to seek faults in the very works of our savior himself as he asked the tremendous question: "and what good will result from this sacrifice?" Then a most awful picture of the future was displayed before his eyes and overwhelmed His tender heart with anguish. So violent was the struggle which then took place between his human will and his repugnance to suffer so much for such an ungrateful race that from every poor of his sacred body there bust forth large drops of blood *which felled to the ground. In his bitter agony, he looked around, as though seeking help, and appeared to take Heaven, earth, and the stars of the firmament to witness his suffering.*[9]

As God incarnate, Jesus fully understood that God wanted to demonstrate to the world that man's atonement of sin can only be redeemed by God Himself. Sacrificing His only Son shows the immense love God has for man. The prediction of *Hebrews 12:4* clearly indicates Jesus will struggle to shed his blood: "In your struggle against sin you have not yet resisted to the point of shedding your blood."[10] At any time during this horrific conflict, Jesus could have changed His mind, for He too had free will. As God incarnate, Jesus could have called twelve legions of heavenly angels to rescue Him from this hellish nightmare, but He did not! As God incarnate and for the love of man, Jesus freely and voluntarily accepted the chalice His father offered in Gethsemane. In *John 12:27*, Jesus says, "For this purpose I have come to this hour."[11] In *Mark 14:41–42*, Jesus approaches His disciples and says, "Are you still sleeping and taking rest? It is enough. The hour has come. Behold, the Son of Man is to be handed over to sinners. Get up, let us go. See, my betrayer is at hand."[12] Jesus becomes the new Adam with His humiliating death at Calvary. His obedience to God reversed the disobedience of Adam and Eve. Jesus came to serve and not be served, as He demonstrates in *John 13:4–16*:

He rose from supper and took off his outer garments. He took a towel and tied it to his waist. Then he poured water into a basin and began to wash the disciples' feet and dry them with the towel around his waist. Peter said to him; "Master, are you going to wash my feet"? Jesus answered and said to him: "What I am doing, you

---

[9] Anne Catherine Emmerich, *The Dolorous Passion of Our Lord Jesus Christ* (El Sobrante, CA: North Bay Books, 2003), pp. 43–53.

[10] National Conferences of Bishops, the New American Bible (Wichita, KS: Devore & Sons, 1981), p. 1337.

[11] Ibid., p. 1156.

[12] Ibid., p. 1085.

do not understand now but you will understand later." Peter said, "You will never wash my feet." Jesus answered him; "Unless I wash you, you will have no inheritance with me." Simon Peter said to him, "Master, then not only my feet but my head and hands as well." Jesus replied to him: "Whoever has bathed has no need except to have his feet washed for he is cleaned all over. Do you realize what I have done for you? You call me teacher and master and rightly so, for indeed I am. If I, therefore, the master and teacher, have washed your feet, you ought to wash one another's feet. I have given you a model to follow, so that as I have done for you, you should also do. No slave is greater than his master nor any messenger greater than the one who sent him."[13]

Jesus wants us to grow in virtue and not in selfishness. He invites everyone to His kingdom. However, out of love for us, Jesus will never force or coerce man into loving God. However, open to the will of God, one will eventually conclude that our earthly plan has no meaning unless it has meaning and glory for God. Saint Ignatius of Loyola sums it up like this:

Man is created to praise, reverence, and serve God our Lord, and by this means to save his soul. All other things on the face of the earth are created for man to help him fulfill the end for which he is created. From this it follows that man is to use these things to the extent that they will help him to attain his end. Likewise, he must rid himself of them in so far as they prevent him from attaining it. Therefore, we must make ourselves indifferent to all created things, in so far as it is left to the choice of our free will and is not forbidden. Acting accordingly, for our part, we should not prefer health to sickness, riches to poverty, honor to dishonor, a long life to a short one. And so, in all things we should desire and choose only those things that will best help us attain the end for which we are created.

---

[13] Ibid., p. 1157.

GOD AND FREE WILL

> *All power and dominion belong to Him, and we can either choose to serve Him and live for Him or ourselves. Paul speaks of our bodies being the temple of the Holy Spirit living within us. We are to glorify God in our bodies by avoiding anything that would defile the temple of God. This has always been a deterrent to me from indulging in sexual impurity, smoking, drinking, and anything that would not glorify God in the temple of my body. We should be reminded that his eyes are always upon us, observing and judging the sons of men.*[14]

We can live our lives like the bad thief hanging on the cross, filled with sin, rage, and bitter resentments rejecting God; or we can be like the good thief saying, "Jesus, remember me when you come into your kingdom."[15] The reward of righteous choices in this life is the assurance of hearing Jesus say, "Amen, I say to you, today you will be with me in Paradise."[16]

> *God made us one way, and we've made ourselves, in virtue of our freedom, another way. God wrote the drama, we changed the plot. We are free to abuse our freedom, but we are not to blame God. God has established a law of free choices. When you purchase a car it come with a set of instructions telling you how to set your tire pressure, the kind of oil it muse use, the kind of gas you must put in the tank etc. The manufacturer really wants to be helpful when he gives you instructions. He wants you to get the maximum utility of your car. However, you can take his advice or discord it and do as you please. The same is with God. God has nothing against us when He gives us commandments it's just that God is anxious for us to get the maximum amount of happiness out of life. However, God will not be a dictator and He will not abolish evil by destroying human free will.*[17]

---

[14] Eric Metaxas, *Everything You Always Wanted to Know about God (but Were Afraid to Ask)*.

[15] National Conferences of Bishops, the New American Bible (Wichita, KS: Devore & Sons, 1981), p. 1129.

[16] Ibid., p. 1132.

[17] Bishop Fulton L. Sheen, *Your Life Is Worth Living* (Schnecksville, PA: St. Andrew's Press, 2014), pp. 166–167.

The choice is ours to make.

Things to contemplate alone or with a group:

- What about this story that caught your attention, and why?
- What types of choices are you constantly making: bad or good?
- Are your choices repeated over and over?
- How can you avoid making bad choices?
- What are the external/internal factors that influence your choices?
- What is required of you to live a righteous life and do the will of God?

CHAPTER 2

FREE WILL

Bruce: How do you make so many people love you without affecting free will?

God (snorts): Heh, welcome to My world, son. If you come up with an answer to that one, let me know.[18]

Hanging on the walls of each of my children's bedroom is a framed relic that I cherish dearly. To me, these relics are worth more than gold. Each time I view these vestiges, I am filled with immense joy and happiness as they remind me of the great love that I have for my children. At the same time, I marvel at the love God has for man, and I am brought back to the story of the creation of Adam and Eve. You see, inside of these framed relics is the hospital scrub shirt I was wearing at the time of my children's birth along with three pictures of them taken shortly after their births. The cool part about these framed shirts is the imprint upon them. Each shirt has the small stamped footprints of each of my kids' just minutes after I witnessed their births. When my daughter Alissa was born in 1988, I began taking pictures of her as she was being cleaned and cared for by the OB nurse. I was viewing Alissa through the camera lens and taking

---

[18] Steve Koren, Mark O'Keefe, Steve Oedekevk, *Bruce Almighty* (Universal Pictures, 2003).

pictures of her as the OB nurse was taking measurements, weighing her, and placing her ink-stained feet and hands on to a chart for the purpose of recording her new life. While I continue to snap away with my camera, the nurse said to me to move closer to her. As I moved in reach of the nurse, she turned toward me holding Alissa; and suddenly, she pressed Alissa's ink-stained feet against my scrubs, forever imprinting her stamp of life. I framed that stamped scrub along with three baby pictures. When it came time for the birth of Dominic, I had the OB nurse repeat the same event that has taken place with Alissa eight years earlier. One day I will give Alissa's and Dominic's record of life to them. But for now, whenever I am feeling nostalgic for that day, I quietly stare at those tiny feet, and I am in awe of the love I have for them. Staring at those tiny feet, I often ponder this thought: If I feel this incredible love for them, I can only try to imagine how God, who breathed their souls unto them, feel and love them as well. Alissa's great-grandmother practically raised her. When we told Mimi (Alissa's great-grandmother) that Alissa was going to have a brother, Mimi exclaimed, "I don't have enough love to love another baby." Ha ha! That didn't last long! One look at baby Dominic, and she was hooked.

One of the greatest gifts that God has given to mankind is the gift of love and creating life from love of one another. Creating life is such a thrill that I cannot adequately describe the excitement, joy, and love I felt the day my wife told me she was pregnant. To me, it must be the closest emotion on earth to what it must feel like to touch the soul and face of God. Creating life is a nine-month journey that is jointly undertaken and is filled with a roller-coaster ride of emotions and anticipations: seeing that urine dipstick changing colors indicating she is pregnant; telling your spouse, friends, and parents; viewing the ultrasound for the first time; hearing the heartbeat for the first time; feeling her belly when the baby kicks, has the hiccups, and flips over; trying to determine if that is a head or a foot; imagining what the baby will look like; will it have her eyes or your nose; picking out names and wondering if it is a boy or a girl; picking out baby clothes and furniture and setting up the crib that once belonged to her great-grandmother. There were so many times that I was in such awe of what I had a part in that at night it moved me to just stare and watch as the extension of our love lay asleep in that little bed covered with a blanket embroidered with a lamb. Looking at my sleeping babies filled me with wonderful aspirations, dreams, and plans for them.

Having children to love is much more a bigger responsibility than I ever could imagine. I am also charged with the responsibility of their souls. It is my Christian duty to instruct, guide, and nurture my children in the ways of Jesus's to keep them on the straight and narrow road to God's kingdom. I must provide them with all the tools necessary for them to make righteous and virtuous choices. God did the same thing for man. He gave us the prophets, the Bible, and his only Son to keep all of us on the same straight and narrow path. However, just as young birds leave the nest and never to return, I too am fully aware that my children will leave their protected nest to enter a world filled with billions of options competing to remove their focus from God's will. No matter what I tried to instill into their souls, they will one day decide for themselves; they will have the freedom (free will) to accept or not all my teachings, values, and training was for their best interests. Putting things into perspective, I guess this is the same way God felt about Adam and Eve. To fully grasp the concept of free will, it is important to study and understand the story of Adam and Eve. But before we can look at this story, what is free will anyway? *Webster*'s definition of *free will*: "is a voluntary choice or decision; freedom of humans to make choices that are not determine by prior causes or divine interventions."

So, when did God offer free will? Many theologians will debate that free will did not start with Adam and Eve but rather with the angels. How else can one explain the fallen angels? However, the Bible's first book, the book of Genesis, begins with the creation of man, not angels. So how can it be that the angels had free will first? The only thing about the fall of the angels is found in the last book of the Bible, Revelation 12:7–9:

> *Then war broke out on heaven. Michael and his angles battled against the dragon. The dragon and its angels fought back, but they did not prevail and there was no longer any place for them in*

heaven. *The huge dragon, the ancient serpent, which is called the Devil and Satan, who deceived the whole world, was thrown down to earth and its angels were thrown down with it.*[19]

This passage does not say anything about free will but that only there was a battle amongst the angels and that some of them no longer held a place in heaven and were cast down to earth. So, what gives? Many theologians debate about what would cause a war in heaven among the angles. It is widely accepted that God provided the angels with free will, and that in a prefallen state, the angels must have had some perception of humans and the love connection to God. One popular theory speaks about the angels being aware that humans would be superior to them, and this greatly upset Lucifer, who believed he was vastly more superior to a mere human. A proud and arrogant angel, it is widely taught that Lucifer would never accept man, much less God incarnate as man whose act of obedience on the cross redeems salvation. An angry Lucifer then rebels against God.

In his book *Your Life Is Worth Living*, Bishop Fulton J. Sheen has this to say about angels:

> *God created a myriad of angels who are just pure minds and bodiless spirits. They are dependent upon God and endowed with freedom. Because they are free, they also have the possibility of denying dependence on God. The gifts the angels received were to be confirmed and made permanent only on condition that they would pass the test of love. Their sin was an abuse of freedom. It was a son of pride. They wanted to be free and likened to God. They could not sin by sex for they had no bodies. They could not sin by avarice because they had no pockets, not even in their wings. They sinned only by and undue exaltation of their intellect, in other words, "I'm going to be independent of God, I'm going to be a god myself." The truth is they wanted to be like the uncreated, though they were created. The leader of them all, Lucifer, fought his battle*

---

[19] National Conferences of Bishops, the New American Bible (Wichita, KS: Devore & Sons, 1981), p. 1384.

cry, "Non servian": I will not serve! They were guilty because they did not love so they lost all the blessings they received and one third of them fell and became what are known as fallen angels, the devils. The prophet Isaiah spoke of the angels as follow: "What fallen from heavens thou Lucifer that once did herald the dawn. I will scale the heavens, such was thy thought, I will set my throne higher than God's stars, the rival, the most high."[20]

Again, from his book, *Everything You Always Wanted to Know about God (but Were Afraid to Ask)*, Erick Metaxas places emphasis with the fallen angel story according to biblical tradition.

Satan was originally an angel named Lucifer. He was the most beautiful angel, very close to God Himself. But he essentially fell in love with himself and his own wonderfulness, and he decided he didn't want to be under God's thumb anymore. So, he rebelled. But it's so ironic and so tragic, the idea of rebellion against God. It's rebellion against love itself. Since Lucifer is damned for all eternity and there is no hope for him unless he is remorseful, which he is not, he has decided to take the humans with him! He wanted to hurt God, so he set out to get us—the human race—on his side. To take us to hell with him! God made the whole universe for us, created us in His image and put us in paradise, and Satan figured that if he could tempt us to go with him, he would hurt God very badly. As John Milton explained in his poem "Paradise Lost," "Satan declared it was better to reign in Hell than serve in Heaven; better to be the top dog in hell than be subservient to God in Heaven."

It is important to know about the fallen angels because God has mercy for Adam and Eve after being deceived by Lucifer. I must make a very strong point here before we go any further—God has mercy for Satan also. Yes, you read it right. If Satan would be remorseful and repent, God would forgive him. But, hate and pride is Satan's downfall.

---

[20] Bishop Fulton L. Sheen, *Your Life Is Worth Living* (Schnecksville, PA: St. Andrew's Press, 2014), pp. 154–155.

Bishop Sheen states that "angels can't be forgiven. When an angel decides anything, it sees all the consequences of its acts with perfect clarity. Man cannot do the same. So, when an angel chose to rebel against God, to make itself God, to deny love, it made pardon forever impossible. Without the clarity of the angels, man's mind is darkened, and intellect is weakened, and the will is poor in its resolution, God allows man pardon."[21]

Eric Metaxas interjects,

Pride rejects the idea of forgiveness, of the concept that we need forgiveness. Pride—is the idea that I can get to heaven on my own; the idea that I don't need God and I don't need God's forgiveness. Ironically, it's the idea that I don't need forgiveness for my sins that proves I need forgiveness for my sins. It's just the kind of self-righteous pride that marks me as someone who needs God's forgiveness desperately. Pride is so bad that it's the root of all sin! It's the absolute antithesis of the truth about who we are. The idea to think that we can get into heaven without God is just insane. But it is tempting to think that we can. Notice that as Satan tempted Eve, he appealed to her sense of pride and self-sufficiency—she and Adam could be "as gods." It's the ultimate temptation—that we can be like God, and therefore we simply don't need Him.[22]

So as we come to understand, there is no salvation for Lucifer and his fallen angels. So, in other words, it sounds as if the first sin ever committed from a creation of God was by a certain group of angels refusing to worship their Creator; is this not so?

A very interesting paper regarding this very topic is written by Dr. Lorraine Day: "What Was God's Purpose in Creating Humanity?" The paper begins like this:

---

[21] Ibid., pp. 154–155.
[22] Eric Metaxas, *Everything You Always Wanted to Know about God (but Were Afraid to Ask)*.

Why did God create the human race? The answer often given by Christians is that God wanted friends. But God had millions and millions of friends when he created the angels. Why did he create an entirely different order of being: humanity? And why did God create humanity into a universe already heavily contaminated with sin? The human race is not responsible for sin. Sin was already present in the universe when God created Adam and Eve. Satan and his evil angels had been sinning for some period of time, maybe a very long time, before Adam and eve were created. Why didn't God solve the "SIN" problem with the angels? After all, that's where the sin problem started. Why was the human race drawn into this mess? We didn't' ask to be here. Not a single one of us asked to be born. And we certainly didn't ask to be born sinners, as the bible says in Romans 3:23 all have sinned. Why did God created Adam and Eve perfect and then put Satan right in their neighborhood? IF God really didn't want Adam and Eve to sin, why did God place the tree of Knowledge of Good and Evil right in their living room where they had to pass by it every day? Also, why did God create a single tree that contained the knowledge of both good and evil? In other words, why did God combine good and evil in the same tree. Before Adam and Eve sinned, is there any Biblical record that they ever praised God? The answer is—no! Before they sinned, did Adam and Eve understand what a magnificent garden God had given them for their home? How could they, they never experienced anything else? Before they sinned, did Adam and Eve understand what good health was? How could they, they had never been sick. They had never seen disease nor death in anything—not in humanity. Adam and Eve could not appreciate any of these things because they had never known anything other than perfection.[23]

All very good questions to answers we do not know; we can only speculate. Maybe the creations of the angels were a trial base before

---

[23] Dr. Lorraine Day, "What Was God's Purpose in Creating Humanity?" *Why Did God Create Human Beings into a Universe Already Heavily Contaminated with Sin* (2006).

the creation of the human race. In any case, what we do know is the creation of humanity is an entirely different and separate creation from the angels. Man was created in the image of God, and the angels—the celestial's wonders— are not. Humans—in other words, only *man* is created in the image of God.

> *The God said: Let us make man in our image, after our likeness. Let them have dominion over the fish of the sea, the birds of the air, and the cattle, and over all the wild animals and all the creatures that crawl on the ground. God created man in his image: in the divine image he created him; male and female he created them.*[24]

Before we move on, I want to give you some trivia. Did you notice in the above verse it begins with God saying "Let *us* make"? Who is the *us* part in God? To find that answer, we must look at the word *Elohim*, the Hebrew word for *God*. *Elohim* is the plural form, just as Christians believe in the Trinity, also a plural form. Who is the second person of the Trinity? Jesus is! Where did salvation come from? Jesus dying on the cross! Okay, moving on! Let's get back to the subject regarding Dr. Day's paper. If the angles failed and God is omnipotent, He surely knows that this new species, man, will also fail. Right? The answer can be found in *Isaiah 43:7*.

> *Everyone who is named as mine, whom I created for my glory, who I have formed and made.*[25]

"For His glory," does this mean that we are created to make God more glorious than He already is? Not at all! It is because of His glory that mortal man should humble himself with the knowledge that God has always existed. By creating mere man out of nothing, God is displaying and sharing His glory with man. Our love and worship for God only exhilarate His glory. "For His glory" also implies everything

---

[24] Genesis 1:26–27, National Conferences of Bishops, the New American Bible (Wichita, KS: Devore & Sons, 1981), p. 9.
[25] Ibid., pp. 782.

that is good about God: love, power, majesty, wisdom, mercy, etc. This passage is also letting us know that we can count on God for everything. What God does for us is proof of His colossal love for us. You can count on Him to provide you with all you need, in good and bad. God's love is always unconditional.

When we look at all of God's earthy creation, we find "God looked at everything he had made and found it very good." However, what is the distinction from the animals, the fish of the seas, the birds of the air, the cattle and all other creatures, and man? God made man with a body to house the soul. "The lord God blew into his nostrils the breath of life, and so man became a living [soul] being."[26]

Unlike the angels who are spirits, man has a body, a temple to house the soul of life.

> *The soul is what makes every individual person a man: his spiritual life-principle and inmost being. The soul causes the material body to be a living human body. Through his soul man is a creature who can say I and stand before God as an irreplaceable individual. Although the soul's existence cannot be proved scientifically, man cannot be understood as a spiritual or intellectual being without accepting this spiritual principal that transcends matter.*[27]

The creation of man is unmistakably set apart from the creation of all other things God has made. Our bodies therefore do not belong to us but rather it belongs to God. The body is required for the soul to dwell in. God also gave man a heart, capable of feeling emotions, feeling love and giving love; a *spirit* [mind] to understand reasons, to develop friendship and walk with God; and *free will*, the ability to choose his own destiny, his own path. Unlike the animals, man is a living person capable of understanding to decide for himself to serve for or against love.

---

[26] Ibid., Genesis 2:7, p. 9.
[27] Rev. John Trigilio Jr., PhD, and Rev. Kenneth Brighenti, PhD., *Youth Catechism of the Catholic Church* (San Francisco, CA: Ignatius Press, 2010), p. 45.

I will again interject Eric Metaxas from his book *Everything You Always Wanted to Know about God (but Were Afraid to Ask)* for some clarification:

The bible says that He made Adam out of the dust of the ground. The Hebrew word "Adamah" means just that—"soil" or "earth." Before God breathed life into Adam, Adam was not alive; he was just clay. So, the breath of God was what was what gave him life. And when you realize that that's who we are— since we are all Adam's descendants—you see that we, too, are made of "the dust of the earth" and that it's God breath that gives us life. So apart from God we are dead! It's the breath of God that fills us and makes us alive.

Man is now a very special creation of God. So much so that God has given special emphasis, status, or recognition to him. He has domain over all the other creations of God. Continuing onward with the Genesis story, we find Adam and Eve living in the greatest garden ever cultivated. "The Lord settled him in the garden of Eden to cultivate and to care for it."[28]

The first couples are now given responsibilities: to take care of this paradise on earth. So far in this story, we have no mention of free will. All we have is God joining communion with Adam and Eve. He walks with them in the garden "at the breezy time of day," in the cool of the breeze; they know his footsteps. Up until this point, God is enjoying fellowship with His creation. When God created man, He had wonderful plans, ideas, dreams, and aspirations for man. Because He loves man so much, God wants man to share in His endless joy. God will live in man and have man live in Him—to have man know His glory. Walking with God is forming intimacy, a bond. Notice that God is not walking in front of them, rather He is walking side by side as friends do. There is a healthy respect and love between God and His creation. God is not forcing anything upon them. To do so would not be free will. God could have made man whereupon he automatically

---

[28] Genesis 2:17, Genesis 1:26–27, National Conferences of Bishops, the New American Bible (Wichita, KS: Devore & Sons, 1981), p. 9.

follows His will, but that is not love, and love never forces anything. To force free will is not love, and God is pure love. Therefore, God does not force his love upon Adam and Eve.

In the center of Adam and Eve's dwelling place are two trees: the tree of life and the tree of knowledge of good and bad. To stay in union with God, He permitted Adam and Eve to eat from the tree of life but not from the tree of knowledge of good and bad. The Lord God gave man this order:

> *You are free to eat from any trees of the garden except from the tree of knowledge of good and bad. From that tree you shall not eat; the moment you eat from it surely you will die.*[29]

Simply, you can make your own conclusion, but if you eat from that tree of knowledge of good and bad, there will be consequences. With free will comes an enormous responsibility. Regardless of the choice made, actions do have consequences. Genesis does not tell us how long our first parents lived in the garden. Whether it was a day or many years, we just do not know. Genesis does not indicate what types of fruit were on the two trees. One tree, the tree of life, could be eaten from and live for eternity; and the other tree, the tree of knowledge of good and bad, would result in death as soon as you ate from it. I wonder what was on the tree of life that you could eat and live forever (eternally)? Was it the food of the angels, manna from heaven or the Eucharist? Genesis does not indicate that Adam and Eve ever partook from the tree of life. All that we can acquire from this part of the story is that God gave a very stern warning to them regarding the tree of knowledge: "surely you will die." This is the very first warning label. It's very ironic that in the year 2019, man still needs instructions and warnings to protect him from harm. Just look at the entire manufacture products' inserted instructions and warning packages.

Remember *Webster*'s definition of *free will*? It's the "freedom of humans to make choices that are not determined by prior causes or

---

[29] Ibid., Genesis 2:16, p. 9.

divine interventions." Adam and Eve surely could have used some divine intervention at the next stage in the story of Genesis. It is here that Eve meets the most cunning of all the animals that God has ever created. In Genesis 3:1–6, we find that Eve is alone, and the serpent, the devil, is lurking by and trying to deceive her and take her focus off God. Where is Adam? We do not know the answer to that question, but Eve is vulnerable, and her "free will" is being put to the test: up until this point, life has been perfect, and she has no reason to suspect or know that there is any danger.

> *Now the serpent was the most cunning of all the animals that the Lord God had made. The Serpent asked the women, "Did God really tell you not to eat from any of these trees in the garden?" The woman answered the serpent: "We may eat of the fruit of the trees in the garden; it is only about the fruit of the tree in the middle of the garden that God said, 'You shall not eat it or touch it least you die.'"*[30]

So far so good! Eve stood her ground. She spoke the truth. But the slick serpent is crafty and smooth, and he then plants doubt in Eve's head. He told her something so unbelievable. Something she has never heard before—a lie! Adam and Eve never had to doubt the words of God, for God always spoke the truth. But a lie—that was unheard-of and dishonest. That is how Satan appeals to man. He can't do it on honest reasons. After all, he is the most cunning of all of God's creation. Satan introduced the bait and switch method.

> *No, God knows you will certainly not die! No, God knows well that the moment you eat of it your eyes will be opened and you will be like gods who know what is good and what is bad.*[31]

At this point, Eve should have bolted and run for the safety nest of God. She should have yelled for Adam. She should have done a

---

[30] Ibid., 3:1–6, p. 10.
[31] Ibid., 3:4.

thousand things at this point, but she did not. The seed of doubt was planted, and Eve exercised her free will. Eve may have been thinking that there was something extremely special that the tree of knowledge of good and bad had, but God was keeping it away from her. Whatever Eve was thinking, she lost focus of God and lost paradise after Satan appealed to her sense of pride. From Mr. Metaxas:

> *It was so tempting that Eve took the bait and so did Adam; and here we are, no longer in paradise. Think about the painful irony of it! We were free and didn't know it, and now we're no longer free. We believed the lie—the lie of all lies—and now we're dealing with it in every aspect of our existence. We jumped on board with a liar and to this day most of us are still in denial about it even when God reaches out to us in His grace and love and forgiveness, trying to win us back, trying to bring us back into paradise where we belong.*[32]

> *The woman saw that the tree was good for food, pleasing to the eyes, and desirable for gaining wisdom. So, she took some of its fruit and ate it.*[33]

What about this tree that was so alluring? Was it really the tree, or was it the way the serpent presented it to Eve? Did Eve really have faith in God and walked with Him, or was her faith truly lacking, for she knew of nothing else—as Dr. Day explained in her paper. For example, in Eve's defenses, Dr. Day elucidates it this way:

> *It's impossible to know what good health is unless you've been sick or have seen sickness in someone else. It's impossible to be appropriately grateful for all you have if you have never been*

---

[32] Eric Metaxas, *Everything You Always Wanted to Know about God (but Were Afraid to Ask)* (Ventura, CA: Regal, 1973), p. 153.
[33] Genesis 3:16, National Conferences of Bishops, the New American Bible (Wichita, KS: Devore & Sons, 1981), p. 9.

without. It's impossible to know "good" unless you have known the opposite: evil. In other words, did Eve ever experience evil?[34]

The book of Genesis does not indicate that she did? What about a talking snake? Did any of the other animals speak? Again, Genesis does not indicate this to be. Instead of finding God and asking Him about this, Eve finds her husband, Adam, and gave some of the fruit to him: "And she gave some to her husband, who was with her, and he ate it."[35]

By all account, I assume from that statement Adam was with her all the time! So, he too must have heard the same words the serpent spoke to Eve. However, we do not know this. All Genesis denotes is that at the time Eve ate the fruit and Adam was with her. Why did he not stop Eve from this tragic moment? Why did he follow Eve's advice? Why did Adam not man up and get into the serpent's face? We do not know. All we know is that Adam also expressed his free will and succumbed to the fruit of the tree of knowledge of good and bad. A lot has happened in these past six verses. Now that the serpent has gotten what he wanted, he disappears from the rest of the story. It's very noticeable that the serpent is gone; he is no longer in the story! That is how he does things, subtle and placing doubts; taking the focus off God, and he is gone. It's important to point out right here some important facts about God and Satan. God will always speak to man about his kingdom and all the benefits man's actions of loyalty will earn him. God will never abandon man, even when he has doubts and confusion. God's love is unconditional. On the contrary, Satan does not and will not speak about the benefits of his kingdom, for anyone with wisdom knows that his kingdom is filled with death and destruction. All Satan needs is a nanosecond to switch and bait and to take your focus off God. Then—sin is committed.

Bishop Sheen says Satan has three steeps in his diabolical approach to tempting man.

---

[34] Dr. Lorraine Day, "What Was God's Purpose in Creating Humanity," *Why Did God Create Human Beings into a Universe Already Heavily Contaminated with Sin* (2006).

[35] Genesis 3:6, National Conferences of Bishops, the New American Bible (Wichita, KS: Devore & Sons, 1981), p. 9.

First he aroused a doubt. "Why did God command you? God's restriction is unjust. Be Free! Can't you see that this commandment is a restriction of liberty and your constitutional rights? Satan will try to unsettle the mind. Look back on any temptations you've ever had. Has it not begun with a why?" An inner voice seems to be talking to us. "Why don't you use your sex instincts? Didn't God give them to you? Why not make all the money you can? Isn't that why you're here? Why does the Church say you should not marry again while the first spouse is living? "Why" is the question that is happening everyday in the world. Satan second step is to remove all fear of the consequences of sin. He ridiculed punishment and said, "You will surely not die." Satan always contradicts God and minimizes sin. "Go ahead and do it, No one will no!" "Have that affair. She wants you." "Don't be silly, there is no hell." Finally, Satan gives false promises: "You will be like God knowing good and evil."[36]

As soon as our first parents ate the forbidden fruit, something happened inside of them. They were not the same spiritually as they were just a nanosecond ago. Spiritually they died, and they were ashamed and wanted to hide, for they were naked.

Their nakedness was a picture of our nakedness before God. In fact, we suddenly know that something is wrong, and we innately feel a need to cover it up—to hide from Him—and we somehow think that our fig-leaf effort will solve the problem. But it does not! Our sin is much worse than we seem to think. And God isn't fooled. Dealing with sin is simply not something that we can do. We're not able to do it. We can't solve the problem. In fact, the bible says that "the wages of sin is death."[37]

---

[36] Bishop Fulton L. Sheen, *Your Life Is Worth Living* (Schnecksville, PA: St. Andrew's Press, 2014), pp. 160–161.

[37] Erick Metaxas, *Everything You Always Wanted to Know about God (but Were Afraid to Ask)* (Ventura, CA: Regal, 1981), pp. 155–159.

Then, the eyes of both of them were opened, and they realized they were naked; so, they sewed fig leaves together and made loincloths for themselves.[38]

Their innocence caused a betrayal, and their innocence caused a rift with God. Yes, they were innocent, and that is more of the reason that they should have gone back to God with the situation at hand. They had deceived God by not trusting in His goodness, His friendship, and the harmonious relationship that had been established. The repercussion of their disloyal act caused sin, and sin is anything that produces a separation from God's love; and that is death. Their intimacy with God is now filled with fear and shame. At this point in this story, I always reflect on those stories of children being convicted of committing a horrible crime. Often the parents of the guilty party are quoted as saying, "He is guilty of the crime, but I will never stop loving him/her as my own." I somehow believe this is how God was feeling toward Adam and Eve. Hate the sin but love the sinner! The repercussion of Adam and Eve's freewill choice was punishment from God. God ejected them from the garden. Still, one must continue to read the story, for God does not abandon His children in times of trouble just as a parent will not abandon one's own children in times of trouble. Adam and Eve rightly deserved punishment and were removed from paradise, but God is still with them and continues to provide for them, as we read in *Genesis 3:21–24*:

The Lord God made leather garments, with which he clothed them. And when he expelled the man, he settled him east of the Garden of Eden.[39]

Before we continue, this very important passage cannot be overlooked. It's the first time in the Bible that the spilling of innocent blood is implied. For leather garments to be made by God, innocent

---

[38] Genesis 3:7, National Conferences of Bishops, the New American Bible (Wichita, KS: Devore & Sons, 1981), p. 9.
[39] Ibid., Genesis 3:21–24, p. 11.

animals were killed and/or sacrificed so that the sins (nakedness) of Adam and Eve could be covered by God. God fixes the problem with blood just as He will send His only Son to spill His blood to rectify (cover or fix) the problem of man's salvation back to God. This passage is foreshadowing that only God has the answer to man's demise. "Jesus coming to earth is God's way of fixing the problem and it was not an easy thing to fix. God—in the form of Jesus— had to leave heaven and set aside his divinity. He had to become a real human being, and He had to leave heaven and come to a place full of sin, sickness, suffering and death. And then He voluntarily took those things upon Himself in order to free us of them. He defeated sin, sickness, suffering and death, and His resurrection from the dead was the final proof of that," said Eric Metaxas. In simpler words, for man to reap the benefits, Jesus will pay the price with His life—His spilled blood.

This may sound like a raw deal for God, but on the contrary, this shows God's great mercy and love for His children. Again, man is God's greatest creation, and He wants us to succeed. Throughout the Bible, God shows that He is slow to anger and gives man ample opportunities to correct his behavior and go back to God. Just read the story of the Hebrews wandering in the desert for forty years. So, God provides clothing for our parents and finds suitable living arrangement for them, He does not abandon them in time of their troubles. Nonetheless, God is still mighty mad at them and rightly justified. As a father who loves his children, I too was disappointed when my children broke my trust. A broken trust resulted in punishment and a stern lecture to my children. God does the same thing with His children in *Genesis 3:16–19*.

> *To the woman he said: I will intensify the pangs of your childbearing; in pain you shall bring forth children. Yet your urge shall be for your husband and he shall be your master. To the man he said: Because you listened to your wife and ate from the tree of which I had forbidden you to eat cursed be the ground because of you! In toil shall you eat its yield all the day of your life. Thorns and thistles shall it bring forth to you as you eat of the plants of the field. By the sweet of your face you shall get bread to eat, until you return*

to the ground from which you were taken; for you are dirt and to dirt you shall return.[40]

By the way, just because the serpent is out of the story does not mean that God has let him off the hook. This is what God tells His creation the serpent:

Because you have done this you shall be banned from all the animals and from all the wild creatures. On your belly shall you crawl, and dirt shall you eat all the days of your life. I will put enmity between you and the woman and between your offsprings and hers: He will strike at your head while you strike at his heel.[41]

The story of Adam and Eve shows that God had something very special He wanted to give and share with man. Man is God's greatest accomplishment. God's goal for man was eternal life. Free will allowed Adam and Eve to choose independence from God, to obey or not obey. Independence from God is sin, and sin is evil. Their sin altered God's desired outcome and caused man to fall out of grace with Him. The path that God wanted was not the path that Adam and Eve chose. Therefore, the consequences of that decision has resulted in the children of Adam and Eve living in a world of dichotomies: love and hate, wealth and poverty, peace and war, famine and food, disease and health, crime and justice, democracy and communism, dictators and freely elected presidents/prime minister, life and death, salvation and damnation, pride and humility, greed and generosity, sloth and motivation, etc. Due to Adam and Eve's disobedience, man inherited a sinful nature. From the moment of our conception, this sinful nature is present, passed on to generations from the loins of Adam and Eve. When they first sinned, all mankind sinned. Sin causes death. Living in paradise, Adam and Eve were not subjected to death; their sin changed that outcome, and death is passed on to all mankind as well. From the very beginning, man was not created sinful, but righteous, sacred, and holy.

---

[40] Ibid., Genesis 3:16–19, p. 10.
[41] Ibid., Genesis 3:14–15, p. 10.

GOD AND FREE WILL

By forging an intimate friendship with God, man can be fulfilled through God's love. "God wants us to have life and have it more abundantly."[42] Accepting God's invitation is filled with a plethora of rewards. Rebelling against His invitation causes sin, and it's a crime against God. "Rather, it is your crimes that separate you from God; it is your sins that make him hide His face from you."[43] There is no pressure placed upon man to choose for or against God. That is why it is called free will. The choice is yours and yours alone. But beware, your freewill choice will be duly noted in heaven and on earth as recorded in Deuteronomy 30:19.

> *I call heaven and earth to record this day against you that I have set before your life and death, blessing and cursing: therefore choose life that both thou and thy seed may live.*[44]

Adam and Eve were adorned in grace. Most likely they were created immortal with complete integrity of their soul. Grace is a gift from God; grace is God Himself. "And now I commend you to God and to the world of His grace, which is able to build you up and to give you the inheritance among all those who are sanctified"[45] (Acts 20:32). Grace is the real expression of God in the Trinity, and Adam and Eve were in a state of natural grace with God. Up until Satan entered the story, Adam and Eve only knew and experienced peace, tranquility, goodness, and love. Nevertheless, they were very capable of deciding for themselves and not relying and trusting in God.

> *If it does not please you to serve the LORD, decide today whom you will serve; the gods which your fathers served beyond the river or the gods of the Amorites, in whose country you are dwelling. As for me and my household, we will serve the LORD.*[46]

---

[42] Ibid., John 10:10, p. 1152.
[43] Ibid., Isaiah 59:2, p. 796.
[44] Ibid., Deuteronomy 30:19, p. 189.
[45] Ibid., 1 Acts 20:32, p. 1197.
[46] Ibid., Joshua 24:15, p. 215.

Although Adam and Eve were somewhat deceived, they did not rely on God's love and trust, and they were cut off from the presence of God. Losing God's presence is death—spiritually and physically: "You are dust and to dust you shall return."[47] The spiritual death of Adam and Eve resulted in sin, and that sin, known as original sin, stains the soul of all born into a fallen world. Wounded by sin, the children of Adam have a will that is weakened; there is a will to desire God, but man has many struggles resisting enticements to sin. Although man searches for truth, that truth is blocked by sin. While man is created for goodness, sin propels man toward evil. The desire for sin (evil) is called *concupiscence*, a Latin word meaning "to long for."

God, so full of love and mercy, gives humans a second chance at redemption; but the gate to heaven is closed. So, man falls from God's grace, becomes mortal, and will now experience every vice of sin that sin has to offer. Tough love by God is enforced, and the sons and daughters of Adam repent to prove their worthiness. For a very long time, man offered animal sacrifices to appease God. By slaying the selected animal, they would then atone for their sinful ways with the burnt blood offering. They knew that if the smoke rose up into the heavens, God accepted the offering, but if the smoke stayed around the ground, the offering was denied. This would suffice until the second person of the Trinity, Jesus, became Man incarnate. As man, Jesus led a sinless life, and with His free will, He would freely submit and substitute His precious blood as the sacrificed lamb for the salvation of man. Communion with God is now reestablished! *Romans 5:12–19* stipulates that one man's obedience will make all things right with God:

> *Therefore as sin came into the world through one man and death through sin, and so death spread to all men because all men sinned.... For as by one man's disobedience many were made sinners, so by one man's obedience many will be made righteous.*[48]

---

[47] Ibid., Genesis 3:19, p. 10.
[48] Ibid., Romans 5:12–19.

> *"Our pilgrim life on earth cannot be without temptation, for it is through temptation that we make progress and it is only by being tempted that we come to know ourselves."*[49] *In other words "it is impossible to know good without knowing evil; it is impossible to learn right without understanding what is wrong, and that often takes personal experience in wrong-doing. It is impossible to build character without having trials and tribulations. The only way we change is by having trouble. If everything is going fine, we will 'never' change. It takes troubles, catastrophes, illness, financial upsets, severe loneliness, heartbreak, to force us to change our directions, to turn to God."*[50]

Although Jesus was divine, He was also man, capable of feeling and experiencing all things mortal men go through. It is recorded twice in the Bible where Jesus—at His weakest point, alone and without His support group—is tested and tempted. From the Gospel of *Luke 4:1–12*, three times Satan tempts Jesus while He is in the desert, fasting and praying for forty days. Staying true to His Father and trusting in God, Jesus exercises His free will and replies to Satan, "It also says that you shall not put the Lord God, to the test. When the devil had finished every temptation, he departed from him for a time."[51] Satan may leave, but rest assured, Satan will again return. In *Luke 22:39–46*, Jesus is undergoing enormous stress during the Agony in the Garden:

> *He said to his disciples: Pray that you may not undergo the test. Withdrawing a stone throw away from them and kneeling he prayed: Father if you are willing take this cup away from me; still, not my will but yours.*[52]

---

[49] St. Augustine.
[50] Dr. Lorraine Day, "What Was God's Purpose in Creating Humanity," *Why Did God Create Human Beings into a Universe Already Heavily Contaminated with Sin* (2006).
[51] Luke 4:1–12, National Conferences of Bishops, the New American Bible (Wichita, KS: Devore & Sons, 1981), p. 1099.
[52] Ibid., Luke 22:32–39, p. 1130.

Jesus was in such agony, and He prayed so fervently that His sweat became like drops of blood falling on the ground. And to strengthen Him, an angel from heaven appeared to Him. It is universally understood that during this time of Jesus's agony, Satan put the full-court press on Him to get Jesus to fall and not take the cup His father was offering. Did Jesus have free will to change His mind? Yes. Did He change His mind? No. His love for God and man's salvation kept him on the right path. He trusted in God more than He trusted His mortal thoughts and feelings and chose the cup that God handed to Him. Jesus's freewill choice to succumb and die upon the cross reestablished communion back with God.

So, there we are. We are free to make our own independent choices without God's interfering. We can obey or deny, say yes or no, worship or rebel. We can ask God to intervene, or we can tell Him to butt out. Nonetheless, choice without consequences is worthless freedom.

Things to contemplate alone or with a group:

- What about this story that caught your attention, and why?
- Did God test Adam and Eve?
- Did the angels commit the first sin?
- If the angels committed a sin, were Adam and Eve also destined to sin?
- Did Adam and Eve pass or fail the test, and why?
- What will you do when tested by God and/or the devil?
- Is sin really a bad thing?
- Why is sin so evil, and what does it mean to you that sin will cause you to die?

CHAPTER 3

GOD IS CALLING YOU

God invites each one of us to serve our fellow man and to spread the good news while supporting our brothers on that straight and narrow path to heaven. Sometimes God's calling is very dramatic, like when He called Saul to serve:

> *As he was nearing Damascus, a light from the sky suddenly flashed around him. He fell to the ground and heard a voice saying to him, "Saul, Saul, why are you persecuting me?" Saul replied, "Who are you, sir?" "I am Jesus whom you are persecuting."*[53]

To get Moses's attention, God "spoke through a burning bush."[54] Now that would freak me out! But most of the time, God calls us by a whisper, a thought, by witnessing something, hearing a homily, reading an inspiring passage or book, or experiencing a tragic or near-death experience. Throughout the Bible, there are many passages where God is calling man to serve His purpose and for His glory. Those that speak to me include Isaiah 49:1, "Before I was born the Lord called me"; 1 Samuel 3:8–9, "The Lord called Samuel a third time. Samuel, Samuel! Samuel answered; speak for your Servant is listening"; Matthew 4:18–21, "To Peter and his brothers he said to them. Come after me

---

[53] Ibid., Acts 9:3–5, p. 1181.
[54] Ibid., Exodus 3:2–6, p. 60.

and I will make you fishers of men"; Matthew 9:9, "As Jesus passed on from there, he saw a man named Matthew sitting at the customs post. He said to him 'follow me.' And he got up and followed."[55]

Best-selling author Rick Warren writes in his book *The Purpose Driven Life* about God calling ordinary people:

> *If you're not involved in any service or ministry, what excuse have you been using? Abraham was old, Jacob was insecure, Leah was unattractive, Joseph was abused, Moses stuttered, Gideon was poor, Samson was codependent, Rahab was immoral, David was a murderer and an adulterous, Elijah was suicidal, Jeremiah was depressed, Johan was reluctant, Naomi was a widow, John the Baptist was eccentric, Peter was impulsive and hot-tempered, Martha worried a lot, the Samaritan woman had several failed marriages, Zacchaeus was unpopular, Thomas had doubts, Paul had poor health and Timothy was timid. That is quite a variety of misfits, but God used each of them in His services. He will use you, too, if you stop making excuses.*

In my view, Rick Warren missed the one person that was called by God and helped start the history of the New Testament—Mary, the mother of God! Mary holds no great position like Zechariah, and though she is most likely poor, and though as she is an unmarried woman, she occupies a lowly state in society. Mary says yes. Notice that she does so in absolute freedom. No one coerces her. And she was free to say no. Mary also makes her decision without appealing to a man. She doesn't ask Joseph for permission. Nor does she tell the angel she must consult with her father. The young woman living in a patriarchal time decides about the coming king. Someone with little power agrees to bring the powerful one into the world. "Let it be with me according to your word,"[56] she replies to the angel. Mary said yes!

One day I received an unmarked email titled "Mary Said Yes." I do not know where this source is from, and here is what it said:

---

[55] Ibid.
[56] James Martin, SJ, *Jesus* (New York City, NY: Harper One, 2014), p. 39.

Mary could have said no. She was promised in marriage to Joseph. To become pregnant by another would dishonor her and risk her life in the community.

Mary could have said no. Herod plotted to kill her child. Simeon prophesied that her heart would be pierced. Her young Son was lost for three days in the temple.

Mary could have said no, to avoid the sorrow of her Son's humiliation and crucifixion, the anguish of cradling his broken body in her arms, and the despair of witnessing her Savior seemingly lost forever.

But Mary said Yes! For God who is mighty has done great things for me.

Mary said yes, and through her faith salvation came to a world starved for love.

In the July 2009 issue of *Sports Illustrated*, there is even a wonderful story about a football player hearing the call of God. On page 56, you can read an article by Austin Murphy regarding Tim Tebow, a Heisman Trophy winner and a two-time national champion with the University of Florida. In the article, Tim reveals to prison inmates at the Lawtey Correctional Institution

that as a young boy he cared more about sports than about his Savior. I told myself, I don't need Jesus, he says. I was full of pride. It was about all about me. Then he asks the convicts a question: If you were to die right now, where would you be? For me, he says I have an answer to that question. I am one hundred percent certain that I am going to go to heaven because I have Jesus Christ in my life.

From this article, you have a wonderful insight into a young college man developing his relationship with God. In addition, you are surprised that time is more than football. In his spare time from the Florida Gators, Tim works with his father's ministry, the Bob Tebow

Evangelistic Association, which has preached the Gospel to over 15 million people and helped start 10 thousand churches.

Tim has played professional football for the New York Jets and the Denver Broncos, and he has received criticism for his faith. Many fans proudly display his jersey with the name *Jesus* on the back while other fans' feathers are ruffled. In addition, Tim's faith has also ruffled the feathers of ex-Broncos quarterback Jake Plummer. Jake was gripping about Tim in a 2011 radio interview, saying,

"I wish Tim would shut up about God! I wish he'd just shut up after a game and go hug his teammates. Tim's continued proclamation of thanks to God after every good play and winning games are all too much, and that everyone already knows that his religion is important to him."

Responding to Jake's quote, Tim handled it with grace and style. Tim said: "Any time I get an opportunity to tell Him (God) I love him or give an opportunity to shout Him out on national TV, I'm gonna take that opportunity. If you're married, and you have a wife, and you really love your wife, is it good enough to only say to your wife, I love her the day you get married? Or should you tell her every single day when you wake up and every opportunity. And that's how I feel about my relationship with Jesus Christ and he is the most important thing in my life."

In a 2011 online article regarding Tim Tebow titled "God's Quarterback," writer Patton Dodd begins by describing how Tim is off target in his game and he is ineffective while playing. While obnoxious fans are heckling and cursing Tim, one loyal Tebow fan shouts out:

"Just wait until the end of the fourth quarter," he said. "That's Tebow time."

And when the shouting was over, Mr. Tebow did what he always does—he pointed skyward and took a knee in prayer.

> *Mr. Tebow's habit of taking one knee in prayer on the field has given rise to an Internet memo called "Tebowing."*

Fans have posted pictures of themselves praying on one knee while doing everything from surfing and fighting fires to touring China and going into battle. Raised in the Jewish faith, Jared Kleinstien was so moved and inspired by Tim's sideline act of praying that he developed the Internet website *Tebowing*. This site receives millions of hits per day with pictures of people all over the world posting pictures performing the "Tebowing."
Mr. Kleinstien says,

> *People found hope through a gesture noting a muchdiscussed picture of a young boy with an IV attached to his arm who wrote that he was Tebowing while chemoing. It has made prayer in public something to not be ashamed of he says. I think that crosses all religious boundaries.*

Although Mr. Dodd's article sings praises of Tim Tebow, he then switches to a different point of view to show that man is still dubious of goodness and sincerity.

> *In communities across America, whether religious or secular, fields of play are often seen as workshops of character. Parents and coaches get kids involved with sports because they care about encouraging them to be better people. At the national level, however, big-time sports are big business, with billions of dollars at stake, and Americans tend to be cynical about the whole show. In this world, Mr. Tebow's frequent profession of faith can come across as a discordant note, equal parts overearnestness and naïveté. It's hard to resist the thought that, eventually, a darken reality will show through. Mr. Tebow may indeed turn out to be a hypocrite, like other high-profile Christians in recent memory. Some of us might even want that to happen, because moral failure is something we understand. We know how to deal with disappointed expectations,*

to turn our songs of praises into condemnation. *What we are far less sure how to do is to take seriously a public figure's seemingly admirable character and professions of higher purpose. We don't know how to trust goodness.*

Hey, Tim, you are in great company. They thought the same about Jesus's goodness.

In September 2013, theblaze.com posted an article by Jason Howerton regarding a legendary rock star eviscerating the media in bold defense of Tim Tebow.

Gene Simmons, the legendary rock star and front man of KISS, came to Tim's defense saying the press has treated him unfairly because of his religious beliefs. "He's got a passion, as well as he should, we're in America. He's proud to be a Christian, what's wrong with that? And yet, with sports media and pop culture media they make fun of his religion. Really? In America? If he was wearing a burqa, they wouldn't dare say anything. But if you're a Christian, you get to be picked on? The guy's got family values. I never saw the media picking on Michael Vick for torturing dogs. Or this other football player, who's alleged to have killed, committed murder. That's cool! But a guy who's religious and has got family values isn't cool? He's cools to me!"

Six years later, Tim's tradition continues in other players both professionally and at the college level. Oftentimes I will see football athletes pointing up to the sky in reference to God after performing an excellent play or scoring a touchdown. Before and after the game is ended, it is not unusual to see players from both team huddle together in the middle of the field praying and giving thanks to God.

Man has heard God's calling in some of the most unique locations: in the desert, on a mountain, on a beach, in a bedroom, and while collecting taxes. I heard God's calling at a Hibachi Grill and Sushi Bar! It's true. In 2007 while sitting around a hibachi grill with my children, I struck up a conversation with a young woman named Linda, who was also sitting there with her family. Inquiring of her profession, she said she was the coordinator of religious education at Our Lady of the Lake Catholic Church. This is the same church I attend. Linda also said she oversaw the CCD program. So, there we are, the two of us talking about God and her need for teachers for the CCD classes—around a hibachi grill. I told Linda that I once thought about volunteering, and that was all she needed to hear. For the next several months until class began, Linda was very persistent in recruiting me to teach tenth graders. Okay, okay! I hear you loud and clear, Linda! And I'm almost deaf in my right ear. I taught CCD for the next seven years.

Another time I heard God's calling was from the parish priest in our church. He was speaking about a mission trip to Mexico for high school students. It was time to show my fifteen-year-old, know-it-all daughter the other side of life. So, one day I said to her, "I spoke to Mom about you and me, and she agreed that you and I need some quality time together. So, we are going to Mexico." Needless to say, she was thrilled. "What city are we going to?" she excitedly asked. "Arteaga," I said. "What airline are we flying?" I said, "We are going to take a bus." "A bus?" she said. "Yes, and it's going to take twenty-one hours." Now she has that look on her face we all know—that sourpuss one! "What hotel are we staying in?" she asked. I replied, "We will be staying in a retreat center at the local church." Angrily she screamed, "You signed me up for that mission trip!" "Not only did I sign you up, I also talked the parents of your two best friends into letting their daughters go along, and I am going as the nurse." Boy, was she peeved.

Even though she knew there would be fifty boys on the trip, she tried everything to get out of it. The day we boarded the bus with her friends and the other ninety-six students on the trip, she was not talking to me. By the end of the second day, she came up to me and said that she was having fun. By the fourth day, she said that she wanted to come back the following year. In my group, I had twenty students: ten boys and ten girls. Our work site was close enough so that we could walk to the church where we were building a sidewalk and a public restroom. Although the walk to the site took about thirty minutes, I wanted the students to see the village and have the village see the students. This way, the students would get a different perspective of the village and the people, rather than looking at the villagers through a window on a bus. Once we arrived at the church, I led them in prayer and then talked to them for about fifteen minutes about whatever subject the Lord had decided to pop into my head. Then we would begin our job for the day. The students flirted with each other more than they worked. Regardless, we were having fun.

One evening stands out in my memory. I was listening to the girls of my group talking about this and that when one of the girls made a comment about her father. There it was! The key I was looking for to join in the group's conversation. I asked them to tell me about their parents, and the words flew: "My father is stupid." "My mother is clueless." "My dad is a jerk." "My parents are jackasses." and "My mother is a bitch." This went on for about twenty minutes. My daughter, however, did not say a word. I did ask her if she had anything to add to the conversation, but she just laughed while shaking her head no. I then proceeded to explain what goes through parents' heads while they are sleeping.

I said, "While you are comfortably and safely sleeping in your bed, your parents are talking to each other about how they are going to pay for the school tuition, the mortgage, the car, electric bill, food, and the insurance. They are wondering if they will have a job in this struggling economy. They worry if they should let their child attend that function in the city with all the crime that occurs there. They struggle with thoughts about telling you they cannot afford that new dress, computer, cell phone, car, and iPod that you keep badgering them about." I told the girls how much their parents love them and how much they worry. After my speech, I left them alone with their thoughts.

About an hour had passed when all the girls approached me clinging on to Clair, who was hysterically crying. Clair said to me, "I always thought my father was a jackass, but now I realize I'm the jackass." Several weeks after that trip ended, I had parents of these teenage girls approach me and ask me what I did to their children. "What do you mean?" I replied. "Well, when I asked my kid what the best part was of the trip, he/she would reply—Mr. Fontana!" How far-out is that!

Another time I heard God beckoning me was the year 2004. I was attending a fundraising event for the church. There I met a quiet and petite woman with a beautiful smile who was showing some pictures. All she said to me when I stopped by her booth was "Do you want to come?" "Not really," I said. I was with my wife, and this was the year before we divorced. This lady smiled and said, "Well, perhaps another time." The following year I ran into her, and again she repeated her offer: "Can you come?" How could I refuse those beautiful brown eyes? Now that my wife was divorcing me, what else did I have to do? "Yes, count me in. I will come with you."

The lady I met is Dr. Alma Levy, a neonatologist at the hospital where I work part-time. Her persistent invitation was to partake as a member of a medical team traveling on a mission trip to Escuintla, Guatemala. The cost was $500 plus the airfare and any medical supplies we could bring. The morning the ten of us left Covington on our way to New Orleans to catch a 7:00 a.m. flight to Guatemala, I overslept. I woke up as they were boarding the flight in Houston, Texas. Frantically, I reached Dr. Levy on her cell phone. I told her I overslept, but I was keeping my promise. I was still coming but on a later flight. She said someone would pick me up at the airport in Guatemala City. "They better! I'm arriving at 10:00 p.m., and I don't speak Spanish," I nervously shouted back. "Don't worry!" she said.

Don't worry, ha! Let's recap: I missed my flight. I had to purchase another ticket because the airline told me that since I did not show up for the first flight, my ticked was invalid (I did not have the money for one ticket much less a second one). I was going to a foreign country I'd never been to, where I know no one, much less speak the language; and I was hoping someone who never met me will recognize that I am the idiot that they are looking for. And, I'm arriving at night! So, don't worry, she said.

As the airplane was making its landing approach, I was searching the ground for familiar landmarks. Ah, there is one: the Hilton Hotel. As the airplane was taxiing, I was developing my game plan. If no one approaches me, then I would get a cab and go to the Hilton for the night and try to track down Dr. Levy in the morning. After all, it was about 11:00 p.m. As I walked into the empty terminal with the other passengers, I was scanning all over the place for a sign, any sign. And there it was: a man standing with a sign that said "Fontana." I knew it all along! I was not one bit concerned. Yeah, right! I was a little more than nervous to say the least. Dr. Levy kept her word. The following morning, I met the medical team about 6:00 a.m. as they made their way to the chapel for morning prayers.

We were forty trained medical volunteers from all over the world with different medical specialties and religions. Fast Eddie, a dentist from Cleveland, was making his fifth trip along with Dan, also a dentist, from Montana, and he too was on his fifth trip. Paula was a nurse from Columbia; Hyatt, a Muslim dentist, on her first trip; Ann, a nurse from New York; while Tammy, Katie, and Marie were nurses from Covington. Also attending was Dr. Heintz, a general surgeon from Covington. There was a pediatric heart surgeon from South Carolina, a general surgeon from Mexico City, and a Hindu anesthesiologist from San Francisco. After breakfast, the hospital team went to their locations, and I boarded the bus for our two-hour ride to the clinic in the mountain.

I was unprepared for what I saw. The center of this village had a simple church that was the focal point of the village. The houses were very small with dry dirt floors; some homes have no doors and maybe a light bulb hanging from the ceiling. There is no sewage system. The water came out of a pipe located outside, and they cooked on wood-burning stoves. All the laundry was washed by hand and hung dry. The animals they raised to eat sat in the raw sewage. The average wage was about $2 a day, with the majority of the population (roughly seventeen thousand people in the surrounding countryside) working on the banana farms. The hospital was too far a drive for most of the villagers. Unless it was a life-or-death situation, the villagers did not seek medical treatment.

Prior to our arrival, the only priest from the only Catholic Church in the vicinity informed the villagers we were coming. And they came too! We saw about four hundred plus people a day. The dental team was just as busy. Because the water is so unfit to drink, the townsfolk drink soda instead; therefore, everyone had cavities and multiple dental disorders. The medical issues were no different than those we see in any US hospital. The wealthy Catholics of Guatemala City sent their children to us every day to serve as our interpreters. They were such a joy to be around as they were full of life and excitement. They too were happy to assist the poor. I have never seen poverty like I witnessed in Escuintla, or even in Mexico. In my opinion, the people of Escuintla were worse off. But amazingly these people were a proud and happy race. Many came to our clinic dressed in their Sunday best, colorful Mayan Indian outfits. They waited patiently in the heat for hours. They were so grateful for our presence that they wanted to give us what little they had. When I made my daily visits to their homes, I found that most of the homes had only one chair inside, but the villagers were happy to have me in their shack and proud to offer me that one chair.

One day a man whom I treated for a leg ulcer insisted that I be paid for my service. I called his bluff and said, "How are you going to pay me since you have no money?" After a brief pause, he pulled out a flute from his bag and offered to play for me. I have never ever been thanked in such a beautiful manner before or since. While these people have nothing, what they lack in material value, they make up in spiritual. These people are very happy and faithful to God. If they made it to the time, they could rest their heads on a pillow, it was a good day. Their faith was and is so aweinspiring. I was humbled by their faith, humiliated by the lack of mine, while inspired by their simple way of life and their love for one another. To survive, they need one another, and they ask for help. Vanity is not a concern in this community.

Prior to the medical mission of this group, the villagers' children were dying on average of one to three per month from parasites. Since the medical team started treating the villagers, no child has died from parasites in five years. I fell in love with the country, the villagers, and the medical team. I returned the following year, and I brought my niece Claire, a pediatric Spanish-speaking nurse from Seattle, with me. I was unable to participate in 2009, but I returned with them in 2010.

In January 2010, a 7.0 earthquake hit the small island of Haiti, killing hundreds of thousands and leaving the island inhabitants devastated. The call for help was heard worldwide. I too heard the call. I contacted every relief agency I could find to inquire about volunteering. My family is friends with a Catholic priest that runs a mission in Haiti for over twenty years. One of my sisters-in-law even works in the mission's Louisiana office as his administrator. I contacted her and told her the dates that I could go to his mission and help provide medical care. From what I knew of this mission, it was located about three miles from a hospital. That was perfect for me! I could stay at the mission and work at the hospital. I sent Father Glen several emails and even called him on his satellite phone. To my surprise, he never returned any of my calls or my emails. Every time I thought about going to Haiti, I would hear a small whisper in my head telling me to go to Guatemala. I would reply to the voice, "I don't want to go to Guatemala. I want to go to Haiti." This went on for weeks. Running into Dr. Levy at the hospital one day, she asked me, "Are you coming to Guatemala?" "If the Lord is willing and the creek does not rise, I told her." This was always my standard answer to her. "I'm trying to go to Haiti," I replied. "What are the days?" When she told me March 12 through 20, I had a cold chill run through my spine! Those were the days that I requested off from the recovery room to go to Haiti.

I continued to argue with the voice in my head. Every time I heard the voice tell me to go to Guatemala, I would reply by saying I don't want to go to Guatemala, I want to go to Haiti. I have been to Guatemala twice already, and I really wanted to visit a different country. Finally, two weeks before the trips, I was praying in church, and I asked God to tell me which country I could give Him the greatest glory, and I will go to that country. He whispered in my head—Guatemala. The next day I called Dr. Levy and informed her that I had purchased a plane ticket to Guatemala and that I would be joining her team for the ten-day medical trip.

On the third day in Guatemala, I realized why He wanted me there. The medical team was divided into small groups, and we were sent into separate parts of the town meeting the villagers and inviting them to join us in prayers and witnessing. The first house my team visited had an elderly man who was very sick. He was the head of the family. After doing a head-to-toe assessment on him, I noticed he had a dressing on his right foot. As I began to unwrap the dressing, I smelled a familiar pungent odor indicating I was going to view a rotten foot. Lo and behold, this man had one of the worst diabetic foot infections I have seen in a very long time. To save his life, I knew he needed an amputation, but he absolutely was refusing my advice to go to the hospital. I explained to him that his only option was an amputation because his foot was too infected to salvage. He refused the amputation stating he would rather die wholesome than die without his leg. So, what was my option? Sharp debriding his foot would still not save his life. He needed a BKA (below-the-knee amputation). He stuck to his views as I tried to reason with him what I thought was his best intentions. I thought to myself, how is this situation going to give God glory? This man may not live until the next day! Talking over with the other medical team members, we came up with a game plan.

We started him on antibiotic medications, and I began to sharp debride his foot, cutting away as much dead tissue as I could then packing it with advanced wound care dressings that I brought with me. No pain medications were necessary, for he felt no pain due to the disease process. Each day I would visit him, cut out as much dead tissue as I could, make him take his medicine, and then ask him to go to the hospital. Each day he said, "Thank you for coming, but I'm staying here." "Even if you die?" I asked. "Yes" was his only response. I even told the family to notify the local priest so that he could receive the sacrament of the sick before he succumbed to his illness.

On my Thursday visit, I informed the family that we would be packing up Friday and leaving, but I would stop by one last time Friday morning. His foot was so rotten that I was now debriding tissue down to his bone. After performing the procedure and packing it with advanced wound care dressings, I emphasized the importance of going to the hospital. Again, the man says no. I prayed with the family and said goodbye. I was still surprised that he was alive. Friday morning, I packed a lot of medical supplies to bring to his family. Walking to his home, I was going over in my mind the teaching methods I would use to train his family one last time in wound care procedures. Arriving at the home, I was met by his wife at the gate, and she informed me her husband had their sons bring him to the hospital in Guatemala City late last night. I was totally caught off guard. I was surprised but very happy that he went. At that moment when I turned and left his wife, a voice whispered in my head, "This is why I wanted you in Guatemala instead of Haiti." I finally understood. Going to Haiti was for my glory so that I could tell everyone back home I went to Haiti, but going to Guatemala was for the glory of God. Although I heard his call and at first resisted, I kept an open mind and went where God wanted me to serve Him best.

There are a few more incredible stories regarding God's calling that I will share with you. This true story involves two airmen from different nations that participated in an international episode that fabricated and sparked hatred and brutal atrocities against one another's country. Matsudo Fuchida was the lead Japanese pilot of 360 planes who led the surprising raid at Pearl Harbor on December 7, 1941. His shout of "Tora! Tora! Tora!" was the order commencing the attack on the sleeping American Fleet. In response to the surprise Japanese attack, Jake DeShazer was one of eighty Americans that volunteered for a very dangerous mission to fly over Tokyo, Japan, to bomb the city in a daylight raid using B-25 bombers. The American crew would eventually become known as the Doolittle Raiders. As the bombardier in plane 16, Jake, along with eight other aircrew members, were captured by the Japanese Army after being forced to bail out of their plane. For the next forty months, Jake would endure severe beatings, torture, and a starvation diet along with two years in solitary confinement at the hands of his brutal adversary. Around 1944, for three weeks, Jake was given a Bible for his review. Festering with rage at his captors, God spoke to Jake at a time when he needed a sign of God's existence. From his book *The First Heroes* by Craig Nelson, Jake studied for a second time *Romans 10:9*:

> *That if thou shalt confess with thy mouth the Lord Jesus and believe in thine heart that God hath raised him from the dead, thou shall be saved.* Jake prayed: "Lord though I am far from home and

though I am in prison, I must have forgiveness." As he prayed, he was overcome with a tremendous sensation. Oh, what a great joy it was to know that I was saved. My heart was filled with joy and I wouldn't have traded places with anyone at that time. Even death could hold no threat when I knew that God saved me.

Filled with the Holy Spirit, Jake was able to befriend his Japanese brutal guards who would go on to assist him with better food and physical treatment. On August 10, 1945, Jake awoke to the voice of the Holy Spirit around seven in the morning instructing him to

pray for peace without ceasing. I thought it seemed useless to pray for peace for God could stop the war at any time. At two o'clock in the afternoon, the Holy Spirit told me, "You don't need to pray anymore. The victory is won." That afternoon Jake learned that the Atomic bomb was dropped on Japan and the war was over.[57]

After the war, Jake returned to Japan, where he spent the next thirty years spreading the good words of Jesus Christ while converting thousands to Christianity. In 1948, Mitsuo Fuchida was at a railroad station in Tokyo when someone handed him a leaflet titled "I Was a Prisoner of Japan" by Jake DeShazer, a brave Doolittle Raider. Fuchida wept as he read *Luke 23:24* from the leaflet: "Father forgive them for they know not what they do."

Realizing the Jesus Christ had prayed and died for him too; Mituso submitted to the will of Jesus and accepted Him as his savior. In 1951 on Easter Sunday, Mituso Fuchida was baptized a Christian. Fuchida stated that it was like having the sun come up. Enemies a lifetime ago, Fuchida and Jake DeShazer would now spend many years together as brothers in Christ serving the call of God. In the spring of 1949 two men stepped forward to tell Jake they had also

---

[57] Craig Nelson, *The First Heroes* (New York City, NY: Viking Penguin, 2002), pp. 304, 305, 327, 328.

accepted Christ in their lives. They knew Jake already, since they'd guarded him in prison in Nanking.[58]

Immaculee Ilibagiza claims that being born and growing up in Rwanda was paradise. A tiny country in Central Africa, Immaculee believed that she could see God's hands in the breathtaking countryside that is filled with mountains, valleys of green, undulating hills, and lakes that twinkle and shine. Living in a loving family, the Ilibagizas were passionate and dedicated Catholics. Celebrating mass was obligatory on Sundays along with prayers in the evening with the family. Young Immaculee loved everything about God: going to church, praying, and believing in the golden rule. Watching from heaven was her second mother, the Virgin Mary.

All I knew of the world was the lovely landscape surrounding me, the kindness of my neighbors, and the deep love of my parents and brothers. In our home racism and prejudice were completely unknown.[59]

So secured in her faith, little Immaculee hiked seven miles with a friend to visit Father Clement to profess her faith and dedicate her life to God. As a young child, Immaculee could not foretell when God would be calling, but she did know that one day she would hear Him. That call would not come until she was twenty-four years old.

April 6, 1994, Immaculee was at home visiting her family for Easter break when Rwanda's president Habyarimana (a Hutu tribal leader) and Burundian president Cyprien Ntaryamira were killed when the Rwandan leader's plane was shot down as it was about to land at Kigali Airport. The next day, Hutu extremists began a three-month genocide murdering a million ethnic Tutsis—men, women, and children, including Immaculee's mother, father, and two brothers. Immaculee survived the slaughter by hiding in a Hutu minister's minuscule bathroom (six by four feet) with seven other women for the

---

[58] Ibid.
[59] Immaculee Ilibagiza, *Left to Tell* (New York City, New York: Hay House), p. 3.

next ninety-one petrifying days. Unable to move, eat, and speak to one another for fear of being murdered, it is here in this solitary confinement that God called Immaculee and put her faith to the test.

> *I heard the killers call my name. They were on the other side of the wall and less than an inch of plaster and wood separated us. Their voices were cold, hard, and determine. She is here…we know she is here somewhere…Find her—find Immaculee. I have killed 399 cockroaches said one of the killers. Immaculee will make 400. It's a good number to kill.*

If that was not enough to bear, the eight women were starving to death; Immaculee found herself becoming physically, emotionally, and spiritually weakened. Then, Satan finds her in a vulnerable state, and he puts on a fullcourt press. "Find them, find them, and kill them all!"

> *"Dear God, save us…" I whispered but could not remember the words to any of my prayers. A wave of despair washed over me and I was overwhelmed by fear. That's when the devil first whispered in my ear. "Why are you calling on God? Look at all of them out there…hundreds of them looking for you. They are legions, and you are one. You can't possibly survive—you won't survive! They are inside the house and they are moving throughout the rooms. They're close, almost here…they are going to find you, rape you, cut you, and kill you"! I grasped the red and white rosary my father has given me, and silently prayed with all my might: "God, in the Bible You said that you can do anything for anybody. Well I am one of those anybody's, and I need you to do something for me now. Please God, blind the killers when they reached the pastors' bedroom—don't let them find the bathroom door and don't let them see us! You saved Daniel in the lions' den, God you stopped the lion from ripping them apart…stop these killers from ripping us apart, God! Save us like you saved Daniel!"*[60]

---

[60] Ibid., p. 70.

As if Satan was sitting on her shoulder, he continued to taunt her.

"You're going to die, Immaculee!" The voice taunted. "You compare yourself to Daniel? How conceited you are...Daniel was pure of heart and loved by God—He was a prophet, a saint! What are you? You are nothing...you deserve suffering and pain...you deserve to die!" I clutched my rosary as though it was a life-line to God. I cried out to Him for help. "Yes, I am nothing, but you are forgiving. I am human and I am weak, but please God, give me your forgiveness. Forgive my trespasses... and please send these killers away before they find us!" The dark voice was in my head, filling it with fearful, unspeakable images. "Dead bodies are everywhere. Mothers have seen their babies chopped in half, their fetuses ripped from their wombs... and you think you should be spared? Mothers prayed to God and He ignored them—why should He save you when innocent babies are being murdered? You are selfish, and you have no shame. Listen, Immaculee...do you hear them? The killers are outside your door—they're here for you." My head was burning, but I did hear the killers in the hall screaming kill them all! "No! God is love," I told the voice. "He loves me and will not fill me with fear. He will not abandon me. He will not let me die cowering on a bathroom floor. He will not let me die in shame!"[61]

For the next ninety days the devil was relentless in his pursuit to taunt, harass, seduce, and try to remove Immaculee's focus from God. Staying pure to her faith, God provided an invisible miracle protecting her and the other ladies from the killers. So deep in her bond with God, Immaculee was filled with His presence, His love, and such an intense spiritual union with her Creator that "she was able to stare down a determined killer and watch in certainty as he dropped his weapon and became immobilized as his contempt was converted to kindness. And finally, as she abandoned all of her feelings of hatred and revenge toward the killers—and despite what once seemed an impossibility—she

---

[61] Ibid., pp. 78–79.

merged into Divine union with God by offering her tormentors not only compassion, but total forgiveness and unconditional love as well."[62] Today, Immaculee continues to share her story and the love of God in her many books: *Left to Tell*, *Led by Faith*, *Our Lady of Kibeho*, and *The Boy Who Met Jesus*. In addition to the books, she spreads the word of God as she travels across the globe as a lecturer and Christian speaker. Immaculee also established the Left to Tell Charitable Fund, which continues to financially support Rwandan orphans.

In 2007, Coach Tony Dungy became the first African American coach to win the Super Bowl as he led his team, the Indianapolis Colts, to victory over the Chicago Bears. In his memoir *Quiet Strength*, Coach Tony Dungy used his professional opportunity to showcase the world that he credits God for all his wins and losses on the football field.

> *Sure, I absolutely wanted to reach the Super Bowl, but I always tried to keep that goal in its proper place in my life. With the Lord beside me, I felt that goal in its proper place in my life. With the Lord beside me, I felt certain that whatever was supposed to happen was going to happen. He didn't call me to be successful in the world's eyes; He called me to be faithful.*[63]

"The Super Bowl is great, but it's not the greatest thing. My focus over the two weeks leading up to the Super Bowl was *Matthew 16:26*, in which Jesus asks: 'And what do you benefit if you gain the whole world, but you lose your own soul?'"

> *Our guys could gain all the accolades and success of this world; yet lose touch with the priorities, their principles, and the God who love them. I knew that if my faith was that central to me, giving me such hope and joy and peace, it would be irresponsible for me not to share it on possibly the biggest platform I would have in my life. I used every opportunity I could do just that in the two weeks*

---

[62] Ibid., p. xiv.
[63] Tony Dungy, *Quiet Strength* (Carol Stream, Illinois, 2007), p. 289.

leading up to the Super Bowl. I believe that was one of the reasons the Lord allowed me to be the head coach there that week.[64]

In front of a live televised audience of millions, Coach Dungy gave thanks to God for his success.

Although coaching professional football was the way Tony Dungy earned a living and supported his family, it was his highway to spreading the word of God. Coaching gave Tony the opportunity to speak to his players, coaches, fans, and the news media about his love of God. He established the All Pro Dad association in 1998 that assisted men with ways to be a better father and learn new ways to interrelate with their children. Along with his strong Christian wife, Lauren, the Dungys were known off the field as role models for God. Today Coach Dungy is retired from professional coaching but continues his ministry from his home in Tampa, Florida. He is still spreading the word of God with various organizations such as Fellowship of Christian Athletes, Family First, Basket of Hope, Abe Brown Ministries, and with his writings and lectures.

Then there is the most incredible story of a young preacher named Nicholas James Vujicic. In 1982, this Australian boy was born with tetraamelia syndrome (a very rare disorder that has the absence of all extremities). Where his left leg should have been, Nicholas only has a foot and two toes. When Nicholas was very young, he struggled with low selfesteem and extreme loneliness. If that wasn't enough, Nicholas was being bullied by fellow adolescents. By the time he reached age eight, Nicholas was so depressed that he thought about committing suicide. At age ten, he tried to drown himself, but the love he felt for his parents prevented him from completing that task. Nick did not embrace his disability until his mother showed him a picture of a man from a newspaper suffering from a severe disability. Speaking at prayer meetings, Nicholas stopped feeling sorry for himself, and he started a nonprofit organization called Life without Limbs to help bring awareness to those with disabilities. From that moment on, Nicholas

---

[64] Ibid.

changed his life around, and he began to master his struggles. He learned to write, use a computer, and type with his toes. In addition, he also learned to throw a tennis ball, putt a golf ball, swim, throw a tennis ball, drink from a glass, brush his teeth, shave, comb his hair, and answer the phone. When Nicholas turned twenty-one, he graduated from Griffith University with a double major. Today Nicholas J. Vujicic credits his faith in God for saving his life and helping him overcome his struggles. Nicholas has travelled around the world speaking to millions about his love for Jesus Christ. From his website, Nick is quoted saying,

> *If God can use a man without arms and legs to be His hands and feet, then He will certainly use any willing heart! I found the purpose of my existence, and also the purpose of my circumstance. There's a purpose for why you're in the fire.*[65]

Nicholas can be contacted at his website *Life without Limbs* for motivation speaking engagements. His dream is to encourage all struggling people and to bring them to Jesus through the Gospels.

> *Nick wholeheartedly believes that there is a purpose in each of the struggles we each encounter in our lives, and that our attitude towards those struggles, along with our faith and trust in the Lord can be the keys to overcoming the challenges we face.*

> *For more information about this incredible young man from God, go to YouTube and watch his amazing videos. Seeking to five thousand people is no more important than quietly teaching one. And as long as our hearts are right, God will honor both endeavors, accomplishing what He will in each setting.*[66]

Nick married Ratish Narodr on Valentine's Day 2012.

Segatashya of Kibeho is the incredible story of a young illiterate and pagan Rwanda boy. According to all who knew him, Segatashya

---

[65] lifewithoutlimbs.com.
[66] Ibid.

never saw a Bible, heard about God, visited a church, or was educated in any school. In her book *The Boy Who Met Jesus*, Immaculee Ilibagiza records in wonderful detail about a boy with an innocent heart who only knew a world of hardship and poverty. A boy always smiling, he has a life-changing experience once Jesus Himself offers him a chance to step into the shoes of all God's previous prophets proclaiming the news of God and how to reach heaven. Before thousands, this illiterate twelve-year-old boy now has the ability to speak the words, prayers, and teachings that Jesus Himself taught Segatashya.

July 2, 1982, while Segatashya was napping under a tree, he heard a voice, and it said,

> *"You there, my child!" I couldn't see anyone near me. My sense was that the voice was coming from the sky above me. I suppose I should have been afraid, but that voice was like music playing in my heart. I was overcome by a feeling of great peace and felt so happy that I wanted to sing. And then the voice addressed me again saying, "You there, child, if you are given a message to deliver to the world, will you deliver it?" Without a moment hesitation, I agreed to deliver any message he gave me. So I said yes. "But who are you? If people ask me who sent me, what am I going to tell them?" "I am Jesus Christ."* [67]

Jesus taught Segatashya many things including His prayers and the words of the Bible. He was instructed to spread His message to the village of his people and to the thousands of pilgrims witnessing the apparitions the Kibeho schoolgirls were having of the Virgin Mary. Eventually Segatashya accepted dangerous assignments by Jesus to spread His message to the neighboring countries of Burundi and the Congo.

> *Although he was often accused of being a charlatan and beaten as a result, Segatashya's innocent heart and powerful spiritual wisdom won over the most cynical of critics. Soon this teenage boy who never learned to read or write was discussing theology with scholars and*

---

[67] Immaculee Ilibagiza, *The Boy Who Met Jesus* (Carlsbad, CA, Hay House, Inc., 2011), pp. 77–78.

advising pastors, ambassadors, bishops and presidents. He became so famous in Rwanda that the Catholic Church investigated his story. The doctors and psychiatrists who examined Segatashya all agreed that they were witnessing a miracle. His words and simple truths converted thousands of hearts and souls wherever he went." For the next eight years, Segatashya traveled the countryside of Rwanda broadcasting the words of Jesus and converting thousands to God. Even knowing that his life on earth was going to be short, Segatashya embraced all that Jesus asked of him. After being showed what was past the open gates of Heaven by the Blessed Mother; Segatashya said "I saw the most beautiful place imaginable. I'm sorry I cannot describe it to you, because it is indescribable. All I know that with all my being to be there and everything I've had or known on Earth lost all meaning to me. Mary said that because I had glimpse of heaven, nothing in this world would ever please me again. She was right."[68]

In an interview in July 20, 1982, Segatashya was asked this question: "Did you—a pagan boy who never heard of God, never been to a church, never been baptized, never said a prayer, nor seen a Bible—ask Jesus why he chose you?" Segatashya replied,

I did ask him that, sir. He said that he chose me as a sign to show people who don't believe in Him—like pagans and any other nonbelievers— that he is not forgetting them. He sees them, he cares about them, he loves them, and he hopes that they invite him into their hearts. By choosing a pagan a pagan boy as his messenger, he let the world know that his love and salvation are available for everyone.[69]

During a conversation with Jesus, Segatashya said,

"Someone might kill me just to shut me up. And then all of these messages you gave me would be useless because I'd end up dying like you did."

---

[68] Ibid.
[69] Ibid., p. 120.

Jesus replied: "Are you willing to die for mankind?"

"I'm not saying it would be easy...I mean, no one wants to die for nothing."[70]

Segatashya did say he would die for Jesus. He was shot and killed by a death squad in the genocide of Rwanda—a martyr for the cause of glorifying God.

My last story is that of Akiane Kramarik, who was just four years old when she announced to her nonreligious family, "Today I met God!" According to her mother, "Akiane and her brothers had only a few acquaintances and had never formed deep relationships with anyone outside the family, they played mostly with one another. Our family never talked about religion, never prayed together, and never went to any church. I had been raised as an atheist in Lithuania, and Markus (my husband) had been raised in an environment not conductive to spiritual growth. The children did not watch television, had never been out of our sights and were homeschooled; therefore, we were certain that no one else could have influenced Akiane's sudden and detailed description of an invisible realm. We can't remember the exact month, but one morning when Akiane was four, she began sharing her visions of heaven with us."[71]

> *"Today I met God," Akiane whispered to me one morning. What is God? I was surprised to hear this. To me, God's name always sounded absurd and primitive. "God is light-warm and good. It knows everything and talks with me. It is my parent." About the same time as the vision began, Akiane suddenly began showing an intense interest in drawing. She began sketching hundreds of figures and portraits on whatever surfaces she found at hand including walls, windows, furniture, books and even her own legs and arms. Our four-year-old daughter was most inspired by faces and she*

---

[70] Ibid., pp. 112–113.
[71] Akiane Kramari Foreli Kramarik, *Akiane* (Nashville, TN: Thomas Nelson, 2006), p. 7.

would sit for hours drawing, erasing and shading their features. She was so dedicated to her work. Not a perfectionist in any other area of her life she would leave her room untidy or her hair uncombed, but her portraits always had to be perfect.[72]

By the time Akiane turned ten years old, words about her paintings, drawings, and poems were spreading, and museums were inviting her for showing. Thousands showed up and waited for many hours just to get her autograph. Among the crowds were handicap people in wheelchairs, doctors and lawyers, public officials, artists, journalists, art collectors, teenagers, parents, students, professionals, and the elderly. Everyone wanted to ask her questions. Here are some of the questions asked of her:

"What Church do you belong to?" "I belong to God," Akiane responded.

"I am a Buddhist. You called Jesus the 'Prince of Peace,' yet in His name so many people were massacred. How do you explain that?"

"Jesus is peace just like calm water. But anyone can drop a stone into water and make it muddy."

"Why did you choose Christianity instead of another religion?"

"I didn't choose Christianity; I chose Jesus Christ. I am painting and writing what God shows me. I don't know much about the religions, but I know this: God looks at love."

"Who taught you how to paint?"

"I'm self-taught. In other words, God is my teacher."

"What message do you want people to get from your art and poetry?"

"I want my art to draw people's attention to God, and I want my poetry to keep their attention on God."[73]

---

[72] Ibid., pp. 2–8.
[73] Ibid., pp. 37–38.

Today, Akiane is an internationally renowned artist and poet. At the age of eight, she sold her first painting for $10,000. Original paintings can command upward to $100,000. She speaks four languages and continues to use her God-given talent to spread the word of God and to raise money to help needy children all over the world.

We are all called to serve. I have a brother who participated in mission trips to Africa; and my nephew Steven and his wife, Brit, operated a medical mission in Belize for a year. I have a nurse friend that is always going to places like Jordan, Sudan, Vietnam, Russia, and Africa while others I know often traveled to Mexico and the Philippines. Mother Teresa and Pope John Paul have heard the call to serve as every other sister, clergy, minister, or priest. Many others hear the call, both local and abroad, by sending monetary donations, clothing, or cans of food to various charities around the world. It does not matter what the requirement of serving instills. It may be a visit to a homeless shelter; giving money to a street person at a stop sign; visiting a hospital, a jail; or just volunteering your time to spend with a neighbor. Just be open to God's call, and He will call.

Therefore, brethren, be all the more diligent to make certain about His calling and choosing you; for as long as you practice these things, you will never stumble.[74]

God calls everyone to serve and share in the endless joy of His kingdom. Sadly, not everyone heeds the call. Matthew 22:1–14 is a parable about a king's invitation to his son's wedding banquet, and those he invited did not attend:

He sent his servants to call those who had been invited, but they would not come. Next he sent more servants. Tell those who have been invited he said that I have my banquet all prepared, my oxen and fattened cattle have been slaughter, everything is ready. Come to the wedding. But they were not interested. Many did as

---

[74] 2 Peters 1:10, National Conferences of Bishops, the New American Bible (Wichita, KS: Devore & Sons, 1981), p. 1099.

they pleased and the others seized his servants, maltreated them and killed them. The king was furious and dispatched his troops and destroyed those murders and burnt their town. The king then said, the wedding is ready. Go into the town and invite all those unworthy they could find, bad and good alike, and the wedding hall was filled with guests.[75]

Others may hear the call and want to serve; however, the requirements of the cross are too much to bear, and they end up walking away. We find this example in *Mark 10:17–22*:

A man ran up, knelt down before Jesus and asked him, "Good teacher, what must I do to inherit eternal life?" "Know the commandments and follow them," Jesus tells the man. The man replies, "Teacher, all of these I have observed from my youth." Jesus looking at him loved him and said to him, "You are lacking in one thing. Go and sell what you have and give to the poor and you will have treasure in heaven. Then, come and follow me." At that statement his face fell, and he went away sad for he had many possessions.[76]

We are all called and invited to show witness to the kingdom of God—to encourage, defend, and promote human virtues and values while spreading and speaking the wonderful news of salvation and the love of Jesus Christ. We are called to live our lives on earth as saints and to bring as many people as we can into His heavenly kingdom, to defeat the works of the devil. At times the mission may appear to be hard, unreasonable, and daunting. We can find excuses for why we are not up to the task and wallow in self-pity. We are called to serve, but it is a freewill choice.

In the end, all that will matter is what we have done for Christ and our neighbor. We will not be asked how much money we made, how many awards we won, how famous we became, how many

---

[75] Ibid., Matthew 22:1–14, pp. 1046–1047.
[76] Ibid., Mark 10:17–22, p. 1079.

discoveries we made, how many achievements we accomplished, how much we enjoyed ourselves, or how many people are working under us. We will be asked one question: What did you do for me in your neighbor? Christ teaches us repeatedly in the Gospels by word and example that the secret to happiness in this life and the life to come is self-giving, selfforgetful love, serving the spiritual and material needs of our brothers and sisters, through Christ, with Christ, and in Christ. Only self-giving—the mark of authentic love—counteracts the epidemic of self-centeredness, self-indulgence and selfsufficiency that has scourged the human family ever since the fall.[77]

Go outside and stand on the mountain for the Lord will be passing by. A strong and heavy wind was rending the mountains and crushing rocks before the Lord—but the Lord was not in the wind. After the wind there was an earthquake—but the Lord was not in the earthquake. After the earthquake there was a fire—but the Lord was not in the fire. After the fire there was a tiny whispering sound. When he heard this, Elijah hid his face in his cloak and went and stood at the entrance of the cave.[78]

Be mindful of the whispering, it will most likely be the voice of God calling you.

"GOTTA SERVE SOMEBODY"
by Bob Dylan

You may be an ambassador to England or France
You may like to gamble, you might like to dance
You may be the heavyweight champion of the world
You may be a socialite with a long string of pearls.
But you're gonna have to serve somebody, yes indeed

---

[77] Fr. John Bartunek, *The Better Part* (Hamden, CT: Circle Press, 2007), p. 295.
[78] 1 Kings 11–13, National Conferences of Bishops, the New American Bible (Wichita, KS: Devore & Sons, 1981), p. 1099.

You're gonna have to serve somebody,
It may be the devil or it may be the Lord
But you're gonna have to serve somebody.
Might be a rock'n'roll addict prancing on the stage
Might have money and drugs at your commands, women in a cage
You may be a business man or some high degree thief
They may call you Doctor or they may call you Chief.[79]
But you're gonna have to serve somebody, yes indeed
You're gonna have to serve somebody,
Well, it may be the devil or it may be the Lord
But you're gonna have to serve somebody.

Things to ponder alone or with a group:

- What about this story that caught your attention, and why?
- How often does God call you?
- Have you ever heard God's calling?
- What is your expectation of God's call?
- Do you believe that God speaks to us today?
- Have you ever witnessed an experience you cannot explain?
- Is the call of God just for holy and saintly people?
- Do you believe that we are all called to live holy lives and strive to be saintly?
- Do you ever do things for your neighbors without expecting anything in return?
- Who is God speaking about when He talks about your neighbors?
- Is it the people living next door?
- Does richness hamper the call of God?
- When was the last time you just sat alone and listened for the whisper of God?

---

[79] Bob Dylan, "Gotta Serve Somebody," *Slow Train Coming* (1979).

CHAPTER 4

THE DARK SIDE

If anyone reading this does not believe there is a dark side, you should have seen my son's room when he was a teenager. And if that did not convince you, try waking up my daughter when she too was a teenager. I used to tell her all the time that someday I am going to write a book entitled *I'd Rather Slay a Dragon Than Wake Up My Daughter*. I know there are thousands of parents who are nodding their heads in agreement. I used to send my son in there to do my dirty work. I swear he would rather pee on himself than wake her up. He would plead with me, "You do it! Hell no!" "Child, you're talking to a man who's laughed in the face of death, sneered at doom, and chuckled at catastrophe…I was petrified."[80] Dominic replied, "All right, I'll go in there. Wicked Witch or no Wicked Witch, guards or no guards, I'll tear them apart. I may not come out alive, but I'm going in there. There's only one thing I want you fellows to do." "What's that?" "Talk me out of it."[81]

This is how my beautiful daughter Alissa would enter the kitchen before going off to class in high school. Her back is all hunched over, her hands are dragging on the floor, and snakes are hissing out of her hair. As she dismounts from her broomstick, the music from *Star Wars*

---

[80] *Wizard of Oz*, movie (MGM, 1939).
[81] Ibid.

movie introducing Darth Vader fills the air, and all the flying monkeys are dropping crap on the floor.

Father: Good morning, sweetness. Did my princess sleep well?

Daughter growls.

Father (nervous): Can I get you some breakfast?

Daughter: Did you say something?

Father: Ooh! What a smell of sulfur. Help! Help!

Daughter: It's no use screaming at a time like this. Nobody will hear you. You dare to come to me for a heart, do you? You clinking, clanking, and clattering collection of kaligenous junk! Who killed my sister? Who killed the Witch of the East? Was it you?

Father: No, no! It was an accident! I didn't mean to kill anybody!

Daughter: Well, my little pretty, I can cause accidents too!

Father: Dominic! Go away and save yourself! I've got a witch mad at me, and you might get into trouble!

Then she mounts her broomstick, and out of the house she goes with her flying monkeys (Hee hee hee hee hee hee!).
 I pee on myself. That was our daily morning routine for four long high school years. So, don't tell me that there is not a dark side of man!
 Speaking of Darth Vader, when *Star Wars* hit the big screen, I could not wait for the second movie. My fellow moviegoers and I were so excited about the heroic efforts of Luke defeating that big, bad, bully Darth Vader in the first episode. Goodness defeated evil; righteousness always triumphs. The hero rides off into the sunset, he gets the girl, and the bad guy is banished in the voided dark space of infinity. So, when the climactic scene of the *The Empire Strikes Back* is in my sight, I am on the edge of my seat waiting to find the out if the gossip really could be possible.

Darth Vader: If you only knew the power of the dark side. Obi-Wan never told you what happened to your father.

Luke: He told me enough! He told me that you killed him.

Darth Vader: No. I am your father.

Luke: No! That's not true! That's impossible!

Darth Vader: Search your feelings. You know it to be true.

Luke: Nooo![82]

George Lucas, how can you do this to me? Vader is pure evil! He represents everything that is so bad in the world. His music is dark, his clothes are dark, his face is distorted, and he has no emotion—no love, only cruelty. To top it all off, he has that scary James Earl Jones voice talking through a scuba regulator. Vader is bowing down to the evil emperor. How did he cross over? Who seduced him? We need answers, and we need them now! Who will save our Luke? The wonder boy dressed in white, our warrior archangel as a Jedi knight. But it is true. There is a dark side; this sinister force is so strong that if one loses focus of the "Force," anyone can be turned. Just ask any LSU football fan. After Nick Saban won the national championship at LSU, he crossed over to the evil empire—Alabama! Yuck!

When I Googled for a list of devil movies, my search resulted in 1–10 of 148 million, but when asked for God movies, it was 1–10 of 59 million. That is 89 million more for the devil than God. Why are we so preoccupied and fascinated with the devil but not so much with God? I asked my CCD student to name a few movies about God. They all replied *Bruce Almighty*. Any others? A few more retorts. But when I asked them the same question about devil movies, the answers kept coming and coming like the Energizer Bunny. My next question to them was this: "How many of you are afraid of God?" No raised hands. "How many of you are afraid of Satan?" All hands went up! Making his rounds, Father John Talamo just happened to walk into my class as

---

[82] George Lucas, *Star Wars*, movie (1977).

the students were putting their hands down. I told Father John about my impromptu survey. He looked at the students and said, "Why do you fear the devil? He is not the one that can cast you into hell. Only God has that power!"

I believe man gives Satan too much authority and acknowledgment and that we undervalue his role in this world. Satan's power in this world is only temporary, and his major goal is to tempt man to deny, violate, desecrate, rebuff, and reject God's love for us. It is the truth of God that scares Satan himself. Satan misguides man by luring him into believing a falsehood with destructive behaviors that seem fun, attractive, and entertaining. His lies will convince man that greed, lust, pride, and self-centeredness is enticing. By giving in to the forces of Satan, man will push God out of sight, all the while convincing himself that God has given man permission to fulfill his every need and desire while doing whatever he pleases. The dark side of Satan has no hope, love, compassion, and no truth as its foundation. The dark side of Satan's force is a rejection of God's sovereignty. Since the beginning of time, Satan has persistently sought to subvert man's attention away from God. He does this in many ways, not like the special effects in the movies; many times, it's just a whisper.

A good example to Satan's whisper is this extraordinarily interesting story. Back in 2008, I planned to attend a friend's opening art exhibit in Mobile, Alabama. The day before the event, I began to hear a whisper, a soft-spoken voice in my head telling me not to attend the event. All day long I kept hearing the influential voice instructing me not to attend the event. The last thing I heard before I fell asleep that night was this same soft whisper: "Do not drive to Mobile." When I awoke the next day, the whisper again began with the same message. I started to become very concerned. Would something happen to my kids? Would I get in a wreck? Was this a warning? I never, ever, received a message so strongly. When I asked the voice if this was God speaking to me, the reply was a whispered yes! But when I questioned the voice if it would bow down to the power of Jesus, I heard only silence. Something was telling me that this was not a whisper from God. That day I had several unexplained obstacles to overcome if I would be able to travel to Mobile.

The event started at 6:00 p.m., and it is a two-hour drive. Trusting in God, I decided to go to the event, and I began my journey to Mobile at 4:00 p.m. As I began to drive to Mobile, it started to rain. Again, the whisper entered my thoughts, *Turn around. Do not go to Mobile.* The light rain became a heavy thunderstorm, and the whisper repeated over and over in my thoughts. I began reciting the rosary, and a curious thing occurred—the whisper disappeared. I arrived safely in Mobile and met my friend at the art gallery. As expected, I viewed her incredible creation of several Latin-themed paintings. The Lord has definitely provided Susan with a gift—a gift to paint, draw, and create. As I walked around the gallery, I noticed Susan and some visitors viewing a very unique painting of the crucifixion of Jesus. I was unaware that Susan created the painting until I heard her story. That very day of the exhibit, Susan wanted to create a painting for the show to thank God for her talent and for giving her the opportunity to showcase her work. She informed us that she closed her eyes, applied her brush to the canvas, and began painting. The result was this exceptional masterpiece of the crucifixion of Jesus that I cannot begin to even elucidate in detail. The canvas is a mixture of colors running down in streaks as if someone poured water onto it. Susan described that her vision was exactly that. God was letting it rain down upon the crucifixion washing away man's sin. I was very moved by what I was witnessing.

Susan enlightened me with another interesting story regarding this representation. While she was painting, she decided that whoever acquired the piece, she would donate the earnings to a homeless person. Just then, as she was painting the picture, she received a weird phone call from a person that she did not know that bothered her. It was as if someone wanted to distract her away from completing the project. Later that evening while driving back home, I was thunderstruck with the fact that the whispering ended when I started praying. Then I understood everything about the whispering and Susan's painting. The devil was trying to distract Susan and me from the goodness of God's work. Had I not gone to the gallery that night, I might have never viewed Susan's amazing rendition of the crucifixion, listen to her story of her own distraction, and hear her profession of her faith in God. All this from

GOD AND FREE WILL

just a simple whisper! Remember, not everything that we perceive that is good or good for our sake comes from God. Satan will do anything to take your focus off from God, and many times he does it with a simple whisper.

Satan has no real power over man. Because of free will, man has to invite Satan in his heart and soul: "So submit yourselves to God. Resist the Devil and he will flee from you."[83]

Satan's time is futile. Jesus submitting to God's will by sacrificing himself as the new lamb of the cross broke Satan's back. In the end, God's will still triumphed. In *Revelation 12:10–12*, it speaks of God's victory and a defeated Satan:

> *Then I heard a loud voice in the heaven say: Now have salvation and power come and the kingdom of our God and the authority of His Anointed. For the accuser of our brothers is cast out, who accuses them before our God day and night? They conquered him by the blood of the Lamb and by the word of their testimony; love for life did not deter them from death. Therefore, rejoice, you heavens, and you who dwell in them. But woe to you, earth and sea, for the Devil has come down to you in great fury for he knows he has but a short time.*[84]

In a recent homily of Father John's, he reads a story about a man praying. It goes something like this: "Thank You, Lord, for this great and awesome morning. I am thankful for Your love and graces that You have bestowed upon me. Today I have not fornicated, told lies, stole, killed, and committed fraud or gluttony. I have not been prideful, jealous, or envious of my brothers. I have even followed the strict guidance of the Ten Commandments. But, Lord, please help me, for I have just woken up, and I am still in bed."

Sin and the dark side are tantamount; they signify everything awful, wicked, depraved, and immoral in the world. All things that are synonymous with sin are man-made because "God looked at everything

---

[83] James 4:7, National Conferences of Bishops, the New American Bible (Wichita, KS: Devore &Sons, 1981), p. 1099.

[84] Ibid., Revelation 12:10–12, p. 1384.

he had made, and He found it very good."⁸⁵ God cannot do anything unhealthy, for it is not in His divine nature like it is in man.

> *"In no single case are we obliged to sin. In we sin again and again because we are weak, ignorant, and easily misled." A sin committed always involves a free will decision. At the core of sin is a rejection of God and the refusal to accept His love. This is manifested in a disregard for His commandments. Sin is more than incorrect behavior; it is not just a psychological weakness. In the deepest sense every rejection or destruction of something good is the rejection of good in itself, the rejection of God. In its most profound and terrible dimension, sin is separation from God and, thus, separation from the source of life.*⁸⁶

As a result of man's nature, man made sin, and sin is the following: war, famine, murder, physical abuse, pornography, rape, slavery, abortion, greed, suffering, old age, molestation, pain, racism, disease, plagues, crimes, poverty, hunger, disaster, injustice, rage, atomic weapons, fornication, torture, anger, hate, pride, envy, gluttony, lust, sloth, and even death, etc. and are all woven back to the creation of man. Sin is self-destruction. Man's chosen path was not the self-destructive path that God wanted. Oftentimes, we as men will think about how things ought to be; but in reality, we do not live in peace within ourselves. It was man himself who upset God's original idea to reside in paradise—a life with eternal peace and love between God and man. "Because sin crept in, Adam and Eve had to leave paradise, in which they were in harmony with each other and God. The toil of work, suffering, mortality, and the temptation to sin are signs of this loss of paradise."⁸⁷

I personally have seen the dark side of sin. As a child, the dark side seduced me unwillingly by a family friend who was a sexual predator. Many years later I would wallow in the dark side, and then for a long time, I was drowning in it. I eventually lost my marriage because of

---

[85] Ibid., Genesis 1:31, p. 9.
[86] Rev. John Trigilio Jr., PhD, and Rev. Kenneth Brighenti, PhD, *Youth Catechism of the Catholic Church* (San Francisco, CA: Ignatius Press, 2010), pp. 49–52.
[87] Ibid., p. 48.

it. Just as the serpent tricked an innocent Eve, I too was innocent and tricked by "Roy," a family friend who began molesting me around the age of ten, thus beginning my descent into hell and "toxic shame" that I subdued into my unconsciousness for forty-plus years. Dr. John Bradshaw describes *toxic shame* in his book *Home Coming*:

> *Toxic shame says that nothing about you is okay. What you feel do and think are wrong. You are defective as a human being. You have a feeling of being flawed and diminished and never measuring up. Toxic shame feels much worse than guilt. With guilt, you've done something wrong; but you can repair that— you can do something about it. With toxic shame there is something wrong with you and there is nothing you can do about it; you are inadequate and defective. Toxic shame is the core of the wounded child. Once toxically shamed, a person loses contact with his authentic self. What follows is a chromic mourning of the lost child. Toxic shame binds all our emotions. It binds our feelings in shame so that whenever we feel anger, distress, fear or even joy we also feel shame. Once one's feelings are bound in shame, one numbs out. The spiritual wound inflicted by toxic shame is a rupture of the self with the self. One becomes painfully diminished on one's own eyes; he becomes an object of contempt to himself. When a person believes that he cannot be himself, he is no longer at-one with himself. Whenever a shamed-based person feels his real feelings, he feels ashamed. So, to avoid that pain he numbs out. Numbing out can be achieved by many different defenses: denial, repression, dissociation, conversion, projection, conversion and minimizing.*

Well, I did not know any of this wisdom until it was way too late— forty years too late! I was an innocent lamb brought to a slaughterhouse by a trusted family friend. Because of his actions, and as I grew into adulthood, I could tell something was not right with me. I felt on edge, jittery, and angry. I constantly felt that I was imperfect, and I had to be perfect and make all the right choices. Looking back in time, I had a chronic life of repeated bad choices, projection, repression, and denial.

THE DARK SIDE

Exposed to the dark side at such an early age placed me on a path of self-destruction that nobody in my family ever noticed the signs and symptoms until it almost killed me later in my adult life. All of my choices in life can be traced back to that moment in time when I froze in maturity. Since I was very young, I was always afraid of being alone, but I did not know why. As I grew older, this fear stayed with me in the back of my brain. When I began dating my ex-wife in nursing school, we had many horrible arguments that could have come to blow. I never hit her or anyone else, but I sure had the desire to do so. I always felt threatened, angry, and pissed off. In 1982 while I was a nursing student, I began seeing a therapist. And for the next twenty years, I would be in and out of a therapist's office seeking answers to unanswered burning questions. However, no one—not ever—asked me that one important question!

Hindsight is twenty-twenty, so they say. My descent with the dark side really began to awaken in 1994. That year I was fired from a job that I actually loved. Long story short, I was fired, and the physician that I admired and respected made me the scapegoat: the hospital threatened him with the possible loss of his ER contract if he defended me. I was deeply hurt, angry, embarrassed, but mostly humiliated and ashamed. What would my wife think of me? What would my family and friends say? Just as Vader is tempted to the dark side in *Star Wars*, I could feel the dark side stirring in me. I could hear the evil emperor say, "Good, I can feel your anger. I am defenseless. Take your weapon. Strike me down with all of your hatred, and your journey toward the dark side will be complete!" You know what? It actually made sense and felt good to have that evil emotion!

As time went on, I was soon offered two great employment opportunities: one with a national wound care company and the other—to be a partner in a home health company with two women I knew. I heard the Lord speaking to me, to choose the path that was best for me—the National Wound Care Corporation. But I wanted no part of it. My pride and arrogance told me that ownership and being my own boss was the route to go. My wife at the time was deep in her studies in nurse anesthesia school. She voiced her opinions, but I dismissed it. Wanda, a nurse whom I had known for some time, was tired of nursing;

and she wanted to spend more time developing her costume company, and she was selling her home health company. So, my two partners and I took over operations immediately. I was the acting administrator. Although I had no idea of how to operate a business, much less one that was supervised with federal Medicare laws and implications, I was now "Tony Soprano." The boss of all bosses.

October 31, 1997, I was reading the morning paper when I came across an article about a nurse being arrested for Medicare fraud. It was Wanda! She was running the cost of her costume company through Medicare and billing the federal government. Two days later on Monday morning, representatives from the IRS, Office of Inspector General, and the Department of Justice were waiting for me at my office. "I'm innocent!" I retorted. It matters not that you are innocent; you purchased her provider number, and that makes you responsible for her actions. "But what about Wanda?" I asked. They told me that Wanda would be facing serious charges, but now that I owned Wanda's provider number, they wanted the reimbursement that was owed back to the federal government under the Medicare regulations. My descent into hell began!

Shortly after that incident, the other sharks arrived. A friend of mine who owned a home health company for twenty years arrived in my office offering free advice and assistance. He spent several weeks helping me clean up my provider number. Then he attacked and took his first bite. "John, I want to help you! Transfer all of your patients to my company and sell your provider number. Then you can purchase a new provider number that has no deficiencies. After you get a clean state provider number, I will transfer all of your patients back to you!" Then another shark I knew in the industry arrived and began telling me ways to play the system. He told me how I could push the limit regarding medical homebound status all the while, billing Medicare as a swindler. I never participated! Many doctors even offered me free office space in their clinics if I would agree to designate my new space as a branch of my home health company. This way the physician(s) would not have any overhead, and I could expense all of their office operational cost through my company to Medicare. As if that was not enough, my pregnant business partner was calling pharmacies around town posing as different doctors' offices ordering the narcotic Stadol inhaler in her name. The other business partner was having an affair with our physical therapist who was also having an affair with my director of nursing. Meanwhile, my medical director was having an affair with both of my business partners and my accounting assistant. He was also supplying them with drugs. My physical therapist was giving my medical director kickbacks for referrals for his private PT clinic. This PT actually purchased this MD a $40,000 sailboat one year thanking the MD for all the business he received. I learned that this behavior was the norm of business practice in the medical community. I was able to get rid of the partner who was pregnant, but then I found out that my other partner (CFO) and my accounting assistant embezzled about $500,000 and failed to pay $25,000 in federal payroll taxes. My wife and I had to put up our property that we owned as collateral to the bank so that I could acquire a loan to pay the federal payroll taxes. Again, I was finally able to get rid of my CFO partner, and I fired my accounting assistant. The accounting assistant then filed a sexual harassment suit against me. The suit never made it to court because I found out that this girl had filed three previous sexual harassment suits against three previous business owners, and they were going to testify on my behalf. Later the following year, my two ex-partners and my exaccounting assistance formed their own health agency with my former medical director and physical therapist.

Sixteen years later, not much has changed. In 2010, when I opened a wound care clinic, I was still getting the same payment request for referral from many local and well-respected physicians. OMG! If people truly realized that medicine is a business first and health care second or third, they would be scared to death. After two years of frustration trying to keep my wound clinic open, I was forced to close the clinic.

In 1997, the federal government passed the Balanced Budget Act, which included a small statute eliminating all Medicare home health companies that did not have a twelve-month cost report beginning in 1994. The reason for this little clause, which the general public was probably completely unaware of, is that beginning in 1994, the home care industry exploded across the United States. Twenty percent of

Medicare/Medicaid dollars were spent on this industry. The hospital industry saw a decline in patient census and revenue dollars, and they in turn spent over $10 million lobbying Congress to get these patients back into their hospitals. The problem here is that the home health industry was very cost-effective; patients received better outcomes and quality of care. But the home care industry did not have the power or clout to fight against the National Hospital Association. Although it appeared that Congress was concerned with the plight of the home care industry, it was all just a dog and pony show. Heading the dog and pony show on behalf of Congress was my own senator, John Breaux from Louisiana. Congress already had a plan to slay the dragon from the home health care industry to shore up the hospital industry. I had to find a lifesaver, and my lifesaver led me to "Steve F," and I was seduced into his den with false hopes, and I joined his organization.

Steve was the CEO of Home Care Alliance of the South, an organization he founded to operate in a similar manner that hospitals do. Hospitals will join a GPO—group purchasing organizations—to be able to purchase products at a discount price. With thirty home care agencies in this organization, Steve was charging $1,000 a month to be a member. If you do the math, that comes out to $12,000 a year for an individual agency or $600,000 per year for all fifty home health care agencies. While the organization did send Steve to Washington to lobby and meet with our Louisiana congressional leaders, we received little for our investments. Why? Because Steve was scamming us too! With the industry collapsing all around us, Steve introduced the owners and members of Home Care Alliance of the South to Bill D. from Houston, Texas. Bill was CEO of a company called Comtec, and Comtec had deep pockets. His company was buying up financially troubled agencies, and Steve handed Bill a silver platter—thirty weary and troublesome honest working owners looking for some light. Unknown to us, Steve had a huge financial incentive investment into Bill's company. Oh yes, did I mention that Bill was an ordained minister? I sold my small company to this organization from Houston, Texas, that was gobbling up pre-1994 agencies that were desperate to part from their dying industry. It was a stock-for-stock transaction, and then the owners of the company were given jobs in this well-funded and organized conglomerate. In a nutshell, the scam was this: They were taking the acquired agencies Medicare receivables and leaving the former owners with all of the debt. A year after employment with this organization, I quit after I figured out it was a scam. But I did not know about my debt, a fact that would surface the following year.

At first the debt arrived slowly and in small amounts. The scam of this organization is that the ownership was never legally transferred. Once they had over five hundred home care agencies' receivables (worth millions), they shut the operation down and filed bankruptcy. Because it was an African American operation, the Texas attorney general did not want to implicate anyone. The godfather of one of the owners' children was a nationally known civil rights activist from Chicago, and no one wanted to touch this organization and be labeled a racist. Embarrassed, outraged, angry, irate, and livid! I was more afraid of what my wife was going to say to me. So, I had all of the bills sent to a post office box at a UPS store. I even went so far as to forge her name on some joint stock accounts to pay for the debts that were growing larger and more out of hand by the day. I even provided my wife with forged Legg Mason statements that I made so that she would not see my deceitful actions. I began to rob Peter to pay Paul. This went on for the next six years.

The longer the lie continued, the more I descended into hell. I convinced myself that lying to my wife was actually protecting her, but in reality, I was more afraid of confronting the truth and encountering her emotional outrage and disbeliefs. I have since learned over the years from therapy that sexually abused people often run to lying, for it is their comfort zone—a safe house behavior pattern to cope with the abuser's infliction. However, lying is a very dark place. For me, I was forever in a bad mood, tired, distant, confrontational, and angry. I let our relationship turn sour and tumble down. I was diseased and too weak to do anything about it. Deeper into depression I plunged. I prayed for a miracle, but God refused to bail me out. My wife kept asking me, "What was so bad that you could not tell me?" I pleaded to my godfather Father Charles Mallet for divine help. He kept telling me to tell my wife. No way! "She will divorce me." "Maybe, maybe not," he would say, "but she has to know the truth." My plan was to stall as long as I could: keep my marriage and family together until I could figure a way out of this hellhole I created. I continued to pray for an answer, and I would always hear the same reply from God: "Tell your wife." I also heard other answers from the seducer. They were not good answers: stop taking your heart medicine and let nature take its course; let the stress kill you; shoot yourself. Many times while driving, I heard a voice tell me to speed up and drive into the concrete culverts—Satan's whispers! This went on for six straight years.

Driving back from my godfather's house one day, I received a call from my wife on my cell phone. "John, is there something you want to tell me?" Does this sound familiar to anyone? "And the Lord called to man, where are you?"[88] Instantly I knew she found out my secret, and out of my mouth it came. Blah, blah, blah, blah, etc. I had eaten from the tree, and now that slimy snake was nowhere around. My wife went to a different bank to open a new account, and the teller asked her if she wanted to place it under our existing accounts. "I have no existing accounts," she replied. The teller turned the computer screen toward her, stood up, and walked away, leaving my wife alone to view all of my transactions. Needless to say, the gates of hell opened up on me. "If you lied about this, what else have you been lying about?" It was not a pretty sight. Her trust from me was gone. Eventually I moved out to my next-door neighbor's house to give my wife some room. He is a single dad with a large house, and I occupied the unused upstairs bedroom. It was then I began to have wicked and satanic dreams. Toxic shame was doing a good job on me.

During this time of living at my neighbor's home, my wife and I were trying to work things out. Back in therapy with a new therapist, she finally asked me that all-important question that nobody ever asked me. "John, were you ever sexually molested?" "No, I have never been sexually molested!" I replied. The rest of the session, this therapist kept probing with molestation questions, and I kept laughing at her and denying them

---

[88] Genesis 3:10, National Conferences of Bishops, the New American Bible (Wichita, KS: Devore &Sons, 1981), p. 1099.

all. That night alone in the kitchen with my wife, she inquired about the session, and I told her the therapist was a quack as all she wanted to talk about was sexual abuse. Like, where did that come from?

Strange how God works! Sometimes it is like a chess game. God will strategically place people in your life for reasons you cannot understand until God makes the next move. Unknown to me, the day of my new therapist's appointment, a woman name Venetia, who is the mother in law to my wife's brother, called Juanita (my mother in law) and told her that I was molested. The story that I do not recall goes like this: Nine years earlier, Venetia and I were sitting together on the porch during a family function, and I was watching my two-year-old son playing. Apparently, we were discussing sexual abuse in the Catholic Church when for some unknown reason, I told her you do not know what you are talking about! I then blurted out to her that I was molested. Just then my son falls off the porch injuring himself. Picking up my crying son I then went inside the house. End of discussion! Venetia never tells anyone about that conversation until nine years later when she is speaking to Juanita, Juanita then calls my wife and inform her of the story. Paula then calls my brother Robert who says "It all now makes sense." That night, my wife asked me, "John, were you ever molested?" Moving to sit on the floor and with my back to her, I can remember asking her to define *molested*. After a few silent minutes of listening to her questions, the tears began to fall, and I said…yes!

For a while I thought we were working things out. But…my wife did not want to seek marriage counseling. She was even unwilling to bear that "in good times and bad till death do us part" clause. She was overwhelmed and felt she could no longer trust me. My friend Pat told me it was much more than trust. He said that my wife told him it was all about the money. I showed her the money trail, but she refused to believe it. She divorced me for reasons that after fourteen years I can somehow now understand. In 2013, we had the chance to talk frankly to one another, and I asked her about Pat's statement if that was the reason she divorced me. She said, "Absolutely not! I became fearful of you. You exhibit a Jekyll and Hyde personality. I was frightened for myself and our kids. I could never trust you again." It was never my intention to lie or hurt her much less than to be divorced. But my actions were all mine—free will! The knowledge of my sexual abuse and the divorce plunged me deeper into despair. Finally, my abuser came into light. He had a bar business near my home that I could ride my bike to, and he paid me to clean up the place. Several of my older brothers worked for him as bartenders while working their way through college. "Roy" was often at my parents' house for Sunday dinner. The mind has a unique way of protecting the body when traumatic events occur by suppressing the event(s) in the subconscious mind. For me, I do not know what is worse: the suppression of the truth that causes symptomatic outbursts in the form of anger, yelling, punching walls, etc. or actually finding out the unfolding tragic truth itself.

Again, from John Bradshaw's book *Home Coming*, he can explain what I was feeling:

When a child trusts completely he is vulnerable to violation and abuse. Later in life when a child is abused and shamed, his openness and trust are deadened. The bond that allowed him to trust and move forward optimistically is severed. No longer able to rely on the safety of his caretaker, he becomes pessimistic. He loses his sense of hope and comes to believe that he must manipulate in order to get his needs met. The wounded child also contaminates adult life with a low-grade chronic depression experienced as emptiness. The depression is the result of the child having to adopt a false self, leaving the true self behind. When a person loses his authentic self, he has lost contact with his true feelings, needs, and desires. What he experiences instead are the true feelings required by the false self. This falseself leads to loneliness. Because we are never who we really are, we are never truly present. Adult children are self-absorbed. When one is in chronic pain, all one can think of is himself. The wounded child has no allies, no one to whom they can express their emotions. So they express them in the only way they know —by acting them out. The earlier the repression takes place, the more the destructive and repressed emotions are. Once these feelings are brought to light shock is the beginning of grief. After shock comes depression and the denial follow by anger, hurt, sadness, remorse then toxic shame and loneliness. Staying with this last layer of painful feelings is the hardest part of the grief process.

My continued tormented descent was compounded with nightmares, loneliness, alcohol, separation from my children, abandonment from friends choosing sides in the divorce, financial trouble, guilt, Hurricane Katrina, and the silence of my God. All this time I was still employed as the wound care rep for a national medical organization. My territory included covering all of Mississippi and Louisiana. Checking into hotels, I had to make sure my room was on the first floor. One night in Shreveport, I was on the eighteenth floor, and I had a long talk with myself all night long. It's ironic how Satan is never around when one is happy and feeling the presence of God. Satan made his presence known, and he encouraged me to jump. With his whispering and my alcohol intake, it sounded to me like the logical solution. Early that morning I requested a change in room below the third floor. Another time I was spending the night in Greenwood, Mississippi, to meet with a customer the next day. Around 5:00 p.m. I went for a run through the quaint town that had two long bridges crossing the river. The town was in the center of these two bridges. After crossing one of the bridges, a thought popped into my mind—jump! There was a nearby park on the riverbank, and I sat on a bench alone for several hours because my car was on the other side of that bridge. I was afraid that I would not have enough willpower, strength, and muscle to cross back over without jumping into the water below. I was only able to physically cross the bridge because I started praying the rosary from the bench all the way across the bridge and back to my hotel. For the next four years I was not prepared for the continued rage, anguish, and seething emotions I encountered while new memories of such unspeakable cruelty set in. The more I plunged into despair, the more I embraced the dark side. I used the power of the dark side to blame everyone for my failures, hurts, and pain.

Man's demise has changed little since Adam and Eve's fall from God's grace. We still hate one another's countries, races, neighborhoods, and religions. However, we try to shade it; the dark side is still evil. *De Malo* of Saint Thomas defined *evil* as "a defect in perfection that is insufferable to residue in God."

> *When the only intelligent creation on earth knowingly and deliberately refuses to obey God and his laws, evil (sin) is the privation man pays. Sin (evil) is a voluntary act opposite of God's rectitude. Whatever is not from faith is sin.*[89]

In his book *The Better Part*, John Bartunek speaks of sin in many chapters:

> *Sin is purposely choosing to do evil, to break the moral law that God built into humans as a natural guide to happiness and fulfillment. Sin is so damaging—because it separates the soul from God, its sustainer and goal—that any physical suffering, deformation or deprivation is infinitely preferable to even the slightest moral evil. Sin is a spiritual decision and it always from the heart. Sin has consequences. It mutilates the soul. It incapacitates the heart. Sin is self-destructive. Judas epitomizes the self-destructive nature of sin and the case of Judas is its tragic icon. Judas goes to the leaders of the Sanhedrin to repent. He returns with the traitor's prize and confess his sins. They brush him off; they couldn't care less. A soul in dire needs comes to them seeking redemption, and they give him a cold word of indifference instead. How different Jesus is. If only Judas had gone to Jesus and asked for forgiveness, he would have found new life.*

Ashamed and guilt-ridden, Judas chose death over life. Rather than approach Jesus and ask for forgiveness, Judas chose the coward way out and hanged himself. I too felt the pain of Judas. Maybe had I gone to my wife and told the truth, she would have forgiven me, and things would be far different from today. But I did not do that! My pride, arrogance, and embellished sense of "I can do it alone, I'm

---

[89] Ibid., Romans 14:23, p. 1225.

self-important" prevented humility. I was always taught that we are all invited to be saints in the kingdom of heaven. Growing up Catholic, I was aware of the lives of the many saints but never knew really what made them saintly. Again, John Bartunek clearly explains the definition of *saintly*: "The saints don't become saints because they are eloquent, bright, or athletic. They become saints because they discovered God's love and let it conquer their heart." I ponder God's love, but I could not reason with God conquering my heart; too much sin was pressing me down, keeping me confused, troubled, and guilt-ridden. That is Satan working his magic. If all one feels is guilt, there is no room for meekness. Jesus repeatedly offers mercy seventy times seventy. No sin so great that Jesus will not forgive the accuser. I could reason Jesus forgiving everyone else, but I could not reason Him forgiving me—that is Satan's whisper. That's pride!

Man endowed with free will and logic must accept responsibility for the outcome of the free individual act of his personal will. There are many accounts of sins throughout the Bible. Here are a few interpretations that you can look up: Genesis 2:16–17, 3:11, 3:14–19, 4:9–16; Tobit 12:10; Psalm 1:19; Romans 2:23, 5:12–20, 6:16–18; Hebrews 2:2, 10:26–31; John 12:43; 1 John 3:4–10.

Today's culture rarely—if ever—speaks of sin. It's not a popular culture topic. It's not hip or stylish. Sin is not mainstream media attention. Sin has been redefined and softened up so as not to make us feel bad about ourselves. "That's a sin" has been replaced with a more liberal expression: "It's not my fault." We are no longer accountable for our actions in this modern world. It is always someone else's fault. There are many sayings in this current world of ours that remits sins and personal behavior. Just ask any network television reporter, social advocacy group, or psychologists about sin; and the reply to you will be "What?" It's like the natural process has redefined morality. Is it any wonder we have so many confused and misguided people today? Commercialism is all about getting what you want now and as much as you can. Take no prisoners, and if you crush the little people in the process, well, that is just good business practice.

> *Now hold on to yourselves…There's one more thing. A terrible presence is in there with her. So much rage, so much betrayal, I've never sensed anything like it. I don't know what hovers over this house, but it was strong enough to punch a hole into this world and take your daughter away from you. It keeps Carol Anne very close to it and away from the spectral light. It LIES to her, it tells her things only a child could understand. It has been using her to restrain the others. To her, it simply is another child. To us, it is the BEAST. Now, let's go get your daughter.*[90]

Blaise Pascal is quoted as saying, "Man is neither angel nor beast, and anyone who tries to make an angel out of him makes him a beast." That can surely be applied to the many names that are synonymous with the beast: Jezebel, Qin Shi Huangdi, Crassus, Pedro the Cruel, Gilles de Rais, Sawney Beane, Hitler, Stalin, Josef Mengele, Charles Manson, Jeffrey Dahmer, Tomas de Torquemada of the Spanish Inquisition, Genghis Khan, Maximilien Robespierre, Idi Amin, Pol Pot, Leopold II of Belgium, Vlad Tepes, Ivan IV of Russia, Osama bin Laden, Mussolini, Tito, and Mao Zedong, Dr. Hawley Harvey Crippen, Talaat Pasha, Hideki Tojo, Lavrenti Beria, and Idi Amin, just to name a few. Dr. Michael noted in his book *The Evil 100* that Mao Zedong "is perhaps the bloodiest in all human history killer." He had an estimated 49 to 79 million people murdered between the years 1949 and 1969. Stalin is reported to have murdered 8 million Christians! According to the World War II museum, 60 million people died in that conflict.

The dark side has a very real and bona fide presence. I know, I felt it, wallowed in it, bathed in it, and was consumed and engulfed by its charisma. I was suck into its false lies and promises of a better outcome. All I ever received from the dark side was more separation from all that is good and a deeper fall into more darkness. I have witnessed the dark side's cruelty, brutality, vindictiveness, and malicious behavior. As a trauma nurse, I have seen my share of heads split open, gunshot wounds, stab wounds, rapes, assaults, battery, domestic violence, incest,

---

[90] *Poltergeist*, movie (1982).

child abuse, drug overdose, murder, and more murders than I care to remember! My first job out of nursing school was with Charity Hospital in New Orleans. I joined the nursing staff in the trauma emergency room department. In the 1980s, the military would send its physicians there to be trained in order to receive experience with trauma, but mostly it was for the knife and gunshot wound experiences. It's sad to think that New Orleans provided Charity Hospital with so many injuries from the knife and gun club. As a young and inexperienced new nurse, it was a very exciting time for me to have gained such clinical experience with trauma. However, I was also able to see for the first time in my young life how cruel man was and what men were capable of doing to one another. While I saw immeasurable atrocious incidents, two stories stand out.

The first begins with a man babysitting his girlfriend's two young children. As I recall, they were the age of about four and five. For a reason I do not recall, the man was angry with his girlfriend, and so to retaliate against her, he slit the children's throats and then placed them in the tub. He then proceeded to pour salt into their wounds and then turned on the hot water. At some point during this horrendous act of violence, the children died. The man was eventually convicted and sent to life in prison at Angola State Penitentiary. Charity's emergency room often treated Angola's inmates. One day I was attending to an Angola inmate, and we started discussing this crime. The inmate told me to my disbelief, "Even prisoners have a code of ethics among themselves. You do not hurt children or grandmothers. He will not survive long in prison. Someone will take him out." Several years later, I read in the paper that an unknown attacker using a knife killed the killer of those children.

The other story that has burned itself in my memory is one in which I again personally participated in. It occurred on a beautiful October Saturday morning. Around 11:00 a.m., a woman was taking her seven-year-old daughter to the public library. The library is located several blocks from the hospital heading toward the Mississippi River. After parking her car and helping her daughter out of the car, an unknown attacker walked up to the mother and calmly said, "Today you and your daughter are going to die." He then shot them both twice. An unknown witness saw the incident, ran to the car, and placed the victims in the front seat. The witness tried to start the car, but it would not start. He then ran until he found a public phone and called the police. The police called the emergency room, and the seven months pregnant head nurse and I raced to the location of the shooting. Arriving first at the scene, I found the mother was shot in the neck and the abdomen, but she was alive. She was slumped over her daughter. I found no pulse on the daughter, and her eyes were fixed and dilated. She was, medically speaking, dead. She had been shot in the arm and the chest. By the time Susan (the head nurse) arrived, a police car also arrived. Placing the mother in the front seat and her daughter in the back, we raced off to Charity. The officer was driving like a bat out of hell, while Susan and I were performing CPR on the girl.

Arriving at the ER, our incredible trauma team was waiting. The mother went into room 4 (the do-or-die room) while the daughter went into room 7 (close to be a do-or-die patient). After placing a chest tube in the right lung of the daughter, she awoke! The mother went from room 4 to surgery where she received 17,000 cc of blood. She would survive; however, she would remain paralyzed from the neck on down. About fifteen years later, I was reading the newspaper when I came across a letter to the editor from a woman thanking the city for saving her life. She left her name and a city in North Carolina. It was her! I tracked her down through the local TV station. When I spoke to her, she described her attacker to me in vivid detail and told me of the evil she felt. She also told me about her paralysis and confinement. I informed her of my guilt in saving her life because I knew that she was a quadriplegic. She thanked me for my service and said that if I had not saved her life, she would have never been able to watch her daughter grow up, graduate from high school and college with academic honors. She attended her daughter's wedding, and she was waiting on her first grandbaby's birth.

As a business owner, I have observed shakedowns, bribes, kickbacks, and greed. I have been exploited, broken, browbeaten, oppressed, and downtrodden. I wanted to lash out, strike back, and retaliate to all those who have inflicted harm to me and betrayed my trust and friendship. Lashing out and seeking harmful revenge means selling my soul to the dark side, and I feared that if I did that, then I would be lost forever. However, the person that truly betrayed me was my business partner in the wound clinic. The night before my auto accident trial in 2010, my business partner —my friend—called me and asked if I would speak to this certain man. She would not say what I had to speak to him about, just call him. The number she gave me indicated that the man lived in North Louisiana, about a sixhour drive from my home. I found that to be very odd that SQ would ask this of me. Nevertheless, she was my friend, so I obliged her. It turned out that the man I was calling was an attorney and—to my surprise—was SQ's fiancé, and he was representing her in an attempt to shake me down for money if the auto trial would be financial in my favor. Needless to say, I did not win the lawsuit. The jury agreed that the woman who hit me was in the wrong, that I have endured pain, and that the pain will be lifelong. They awarded me barely enough money to cover the medical expense I endured. SQ did not receive any money from me, and she ended a great friendship.

A few things finally reached my darkened soul and prevented me from retaliating: fear of submitting my soul to the dark side and the readings of Matthew 6:38–48. Mathew 6:38–42 concerning Jesus's teaching about retaliation:

> *You heard that it was said: An eye for an eye and a tooth for a tooth. But I say to you, offer no resistances to one who is evil. When someone strikes you on your right cheek, turn the other to him as well. If anyone wants to go to law with you over your tunic, hand him your clock as well. Should anyone press you into service for a mile, go with him two miles. Give to the one who asks of you and do not turn your back on one who wants to borrow.*[91]

Matthew 5:43–48 is *love of enemies*:

> *You have heard that it was said, you shall love your neighbor and hate your enemy. But I say to you, love your enemies and pray for*

---

[91] Matthew 6:19–21, National Conferences of Bishops, the New American Bible (Wichita, KS: Devore & Sons, 1981), p. 1018.

those who persecute you that you may be children of your heavenly Father, for He makes his sun rise on the bad and the good, and causes rain to fall on the just and the unjust. For if you love those who love you what recompense will you have? Do not the tax collectors do the same? And if you greet your brothers only, what is unusual about that? Do not pagans do the same? So be perfect just as your heavenly father is perfect.[92]

I am elated to say that only with the grace of God was I able to escape from the pull and seduction of the dark side. The dark side gave me rational lies and excuses to harbor hate and resentment. I longed for justice in an evil manner; I wanted hurtful revenge. When one walks with the dark side, it is virtually impossible to see the light. The light is truth, and the truth is Jesus Christ. Today I continue to witness the power of the dark side from afar. Little has changed in sixteen years when I began my journey with the dark side: I'm still approached for kickbacks and enticements, all the while being an eyewitness to backroom shady business transactions, and a spectator to hate, racism, greed, lies, violence, murders, wars, and genocides. But this time I am able to handle the enticements of the dark side by walking in the light of the Lord. When you surrender yourself to walk in the light of Jesus Christ, the brightness of His love will overcome any and all darkness.

The lamp of the body is the eye. If the eye is sound, your whole body will be filled with the light; but if your eye is bad, your whole body will be in darkness. And if the light in you is darkness, how great will the darkness be.[93]

Knowing that Jesus was in darkness was also a boost to my recovery. Saint Matthew describes His Agony in the Garden with great "sorrow to the point of death." Jesus's human nature was virtually opposed to succumbing to a violent and brutal end of life. It was human nature to resist rather than to accept all that the Father was asking of Him. How

---

[92] Ibid., Matthew 5:43–48, p. 1016.
[93] Ibid., Matthew 6:22–23, p. 1018.

bad was it for Jesus? Satan was pounding Him from every side while showing Him all of man's sins committed to that present time and all sins committed until the very end of time. And where was God? Silent! Letting Jesus work through the darkness alone in a darkened world. Jesus prevailed and sought strength and solace through prayers; three times He prayed then sought support from His disciples. At his darkest moment when He needed His friends the most, they were asleep. Near despair, exhibiting His free will with obedience and complete trust in God, He accepted the cup from which He will drink. Other quotes that helped me see the light are the following:

- *We have lost paradise, but we have received heaven and therefore the gain is greater than the loss.*[94]
- *O God, to turn away from you is to fall. To turn to you is to stand up. To remain in you is to have support.*[95]
- *Where sin increased, grace abounded all the more.*[96]
- *The worst thing is not to commit crimes but, rather, not to accomplish the good that one could have done. It is the sin of omission, which is nothing other than to be unloving, and no one accuses himself of it.*[97]
- *A moral approach to the world is possible and beneficial only when one takes himself the whole awful mess of life, one's share in the responsibility for death and sin, in short, original sins as a whole, and stops seeing guilt always in others.*[98]

Science has determined that all matter seeks the path of least resistance. It is the same with matters of the heart and soul. Jesus's teaching warns against seeking the path of least resistance and to be on guard. Accepting the seduction of the dark side, I too sought the path of least resistance.

---

[94] St. John Chrysostom.
[95] St. Augustine.
[96] Romans 5:21, National Conferences of Bishops, the New American Bible (Wichita, KS: Devore &Sons, 1981), p. 1216.
[97] Leon Bloy.
[98] Hermann Hesse.

GOD AND FREE WILL

Enter through the narrow gate; for the gate is wide and the road broad that leads to destruction and those who enter through it are many. How narrow the gate and constricted the road that leads to life. And those who find it are few.[99]

Walking in the light will lure away detractors of the dark side to try and sway you away from doing good and keeping to the narrow gate and the light of the world. It is in these trying times that I am reminded of a prayer from Mother Teresa of Calcutta:

People are often unreasonable, irrational, and self-centered. Forgive them anyway.

If you are kind, people may accuse you of selfish, ulterior motives. Be kind any way.

If you are successful, you will win some unfaithful friends and some genuine enemies. Succeed anyway.

If you are honest and sincere, people may deceive you. Be honest and sincere anyway.

What you spend years creating, others could destroy overnight. Create anyway.

If you find serenity and happiness, some may be jealous. Be happy anyway.

Give the best you have, and it will never be enough. Give the best anyway.

In the final analysis, it is between you and God. It was never between you and them anyway.[100]

---

[99] Matthew 7:13–14, National Conferences of Bishops, the New American Bible (Wichita, KS: Devore & Sons, 1981), p. 1019.
[100] Mother Teresa of Calcutta, www.life-changing-inspirational-quotes.com.

I was thinking about interviewing a very sinister character for this story, and I was going to interview a vampire; but Anne Rice beat me to that and published a book about it. So, I looked around to find another ominous and menacing creature. Too bad Satan was busy; he would have made a great evil subject. I really would have liked to know if he ate shrooms (mushrooms) with Eve. Next on my list was Dr. Evil, but he was somewhere in space with his beloved Mini-Me. But Satan did help me out. Through his PR company, *Dante's Inferno*, they gave me a name of a friend of Satan who he believed would give me about ten minutes for a phone interview. I was instructed that any questions regarding his big black cap, boots, helmet, and sexual orientation would be out of the question! It seemed I waited an eternity for this scary monster to call me. At first, I thought his voice sounded so much like the actor James Earl Jones. Once I heard his breath, I quickly got goose bumps, and a cold shiver ran down my spine. Speaking to me on the phone was the second most hideous, vile, repugnant, dreadful, and evil life-form that ever roamed the galaxy. "I'm frightened, Auntie Elm!"[101] I repeatedly said to myself. However, I have to say he did put me at ease (probably through his mind-control power), and I really found him to be a very nice guy. I did have to ask him to tone down that daunting and intimidating music that follows him wherever he goes. Without further delays, here is my short interview with my new friend—Darth (he said I could call him that).

INTERVIEW WITH DARTH VADER

(Not to be confused with *Interview with the Vampire*)

John: What do you think about man's ability to overcome sin and evil?
Vader: I find your lack of faith disturbing.

John: Man has Hillary Clinton to fear, why should I fear the dark side?

Vader: Don't be too proud of this technological terror you've constructed. The ability to destroy a planet is insignificant next to the power of the dark side.

---

[101] *Wizard of Oz*, movie (MGM Studio, 1939).

GOD AND FREE WILL

John: Do you know Jesus Christ?

Vader: Now, that's a name I've not heard in a long time—a long time.

John: Have you accepted Jesus Christ as your personal savior? Vader: I sense something, a presence I've not felt since… John: What do you think about Jesus's power?

Vader: The Force is strong with this one. The last time I felt it was in the presence of my old master.

John: What are your thoughts concerning Jesus's teachings of love and forgiveness?

Vader: I have a very bad feeling about this.

John: What about Jesus's teachings regarding love and forgiveness?

Vader: What is it? Some kind of local trouble?

John: If you met Jesus today, what do you think you would say to Him?

Vader: I've been waiting for you, Jesus Christ. We meet again, at last. The circle is now complete. When I left you, I was but the learner. Now *I* am the master.

John: What do you think Jesus would say to you?

Vader: Only a master of evil, Vader.

John: What is it that you want from the dark side?

Vader: Well, more wealth than you can imagine!

John: I understand you met God once? Where did that meeting take place?

Vader: A long time ago in a galaxy far, far away.[102]

---

[102] Darth Vader's answers are taken from *Star Wars* movie (1977).

Things to ponder alone or with a group:

- What about this story that caught your attention, and why?
- Is there really a dark side full of seduction and lies?
- Is the devil real or just made up to keep morality in balance?
- Is man basically intrinsic evil or good?
- How often do you feel getting in touch with your darkest feelings? How do you get out of the dark feelings?
- Did Jesus come into this world to shed a little light on a darkened world, or was that again made up to appeal to one's morality?
- Does goodness always conquer evil?
- What is your definition of *sin*? Does it follow authorized church doctrine?
- What makes you want to lash out at your fellow man? What pushes your buttons?
- How do you change all that pushes your buttons?
- In the Bible, God triumphs over Satan. Is this true, and why?
- Does Satan interfere with free will? Why? Why not?
- Does today's culture believe in the devil or ignores Satan as mind-altering tricks?

CHAPTER 5

LIZARD MAN AND ROCKY BALBOA

One day I was speaking with a very good friend of mine at his snowball stand Chilly, but I call it the Chilly Willie. I noticed that there were no angry, hostile, sad, distraught, or irritated people. Everyone at a snowball stand is happy! Standing in line in the hot sun and humidity of Louisiana, people are polite and friendly despite dripping wet with sweat while waiting patiently for their turn to purchase a snowball. Life should be like waiting in line at one giant snowball stand. I now believe that this is the answer for world peace. I wonder if there are any snowball stands in Israel, the Gaza Strip, Iran, Iraq, India, Pakistan, North Korea, Afghanistan, Sudan, and so many other hostile nations. Maybe my friend should open a new stand just outside the doors of the United Nations. For all you Miss American contestants, the next time a judge asks you how you would bring about world peace, just answer *snowball stands*.

My friend Hillary is the funniest man I know. He has to be; after all, can you imagine growing up male with a name like that? Anyway, if Al Bundy and Rodney Dangerfield would ever have a love child together, the end result would be my friend Hillary. We got to talking about life and things; remember, no one is upset at a snowball stand. He inquired as to how I was doing, and I told him of my new plans to reopen my wound clinic. He said, "John, you're like a lizard." "What?" "Every time your tail gets cut off, you keep moving forward and growing a new tail. You were fired once, laid off twice, lost your home health company, your wife divorced you, you have no friends, no girlfriend, you can't get a date, you are broke and bankrupt [I was eating a free snowball], you're Italian, and you closed your wound clinic as fast as you opened it. Hell, if you had a truck and your dog ran away, you could be a country song. But you are so persistent! In fact, from now on, I am going to call you the Lizard Man." Wow, Hillary! Thanks for the recap of my pathetic loser life. As I drove away, I began thinking about what he said and also about the last Rocky Balboa movie. Not the "Yo, Adrian, we did it… we did it" part, but the part when he is speaking to his dumb-ass son:

I'd hold you up to say to your mother, "This kid's gonna be the best kid in the world. This kid's gonna be somebody better than anybody I ever knew." And you grew up good and wonderful. It was great just watching you; every day was like a privilege. Then the time came for you to be your own man and take on the world, and you did. But somewhere along the line, you changed. You stopped being you. You let people stick a finger in your face and tell you you're no good. And when things got hard, you started looking for something to blame, like a big shadow. Let me tell you something you already know. The world ain't all sunshine and rainbows. It's a very mean and nasty place and I don't care how tough you are, it will beat you to your knees and keep you there permanently if you let it. You, me, or nobody is gonna hit as hard as life. But it ain't about how hard ya hit. It's about how hard you can get hit and keep moving forward. How much you can take and keep moving forward. That's how winning is done! Now if you know what you're worth then go out and get what you're worth. But ya gotta be willing to take the hits, and not pointing fingers saying you ain't where you wanna be because of him, or her, or anybody! Cowards do that and that ain't you! You're better than that! I'm always gonna love you no matter what. No matter what happens. You're my son and you're my blood. You're the best thing in my life. But until you start believing in yourself, ya ain't gonna have a life. Don't forget to visit your mother.[103]

I like that mother touch.

The same thing Rocky Balboa is saying can be found in *2 Corinthians 4:7–10*:

We ourselves are like fragile clay jars containing this great treasure. This makes it clear that our great power is from God, not from ourselves. We are pressed on ever side by troubles, but we are not crushed. We are perplexed, but not driven to despair.

We are hunted down, but ever abandoned by God. We get knocked down, but we are not destroyed. Through suffering…the life of Jesus may also be seen in our bodies.[104]

Life is hard: it's nasty, cruel, mean, malicious, spiteful, and tough. Sometimes life has moments filled with rainbows, but most of the time, it will beat you into the ground. There are no free rides. Like Jesus, we all have to pick up our crosses and carry a heavy burden. From Jerusalem to the top of Golgotha, where Jesus was crucified, the route is uphill and about a mile long. Bearing his cross after a day of brutal torture, Jesus struggles under the heavy weight as He makes his way among the jeering crowds who continue to taunt and throw things at Him, all the while being whipped by the Roman guards. Jesus was physically exhausted, but He was physically determined to achieve salvation. Father John Bartunek clarified this in his book *Inside the Passion*:

The weight of the cross is often symbolically equated with the weight of mankind's sins, the sins which Christ took upon Himself for the salvation of the human family. The thieves had to carry the burden of their own sins; Christ carried the much heavier burden

---

[103] Sylvester Stallone, *Rocky* (2006).
[104] 2 Corinthians 4:7–10, National Conferences of Bishops, the New American Bible (Wichita, KS:Devore & Sons, 1981), p. 1256.

of all mankind's sins. The Gospels of Matthew, Mark, and Luke all record Jesus summing up what it means to be His disciple the same way: "And He said to all, If any man would come after me, let him deny himself and take up his daily cross and follow me."[105]

The man Jesus was also the divine one. He too had free will. At any time, Jesus could have called the whole thing off. He could have summoned His "twelve legions of angels" to rescue Him during the Agony in the Garden, before the trial of Herod and Pilate, during the brutal scourging, falling to the ground under the crushing weight of the cross, stripped naked in front of his holy women, or while hanging from nails atop a tree that would take His life in a few hours. He could have mutinied against His Father's omnipotent plan. He could have, but He did not. He was obedient to God's call. The salvation of man was more important than the frailty of His legs failing to stand under the magnitude of man's sins. So, Christ falls over and over, carrying His cross. The falls are a representation of our spiritual falls: our sins, offense, wrongdoing, peccadilloes, weakness, lack of faith, and loveless hearts. Jesus had to die for both the salvation of man and the will of God. No amount of human atonement would be sufficient to rectify the transgression against God. Humanity needed a savior, and no mere man was capable of fulfilling redemption in God's plans. Humanity's sins could only be atoned by the ghastly torture and death of God incarnate. Jesus's death at Calvary was crucial to demonstrate God's colossal love for man. Jesus states in *John 15:13*, "No one has greater love than this, to lay down one's life for one's friends."[106]

Best-selling author Laurie Beth Jones writes in her book *Jesus, Life Coach* about a ten-day trip she took to the Holy Land:

Our guide, who was a Palestinian Christian, told us many tales we did not know prior to our visit. One of the most disturbing things

---

[105] Fr. John Bartunek, *Inside the Passion* (West Chester, PA: Ascension Press, 2005), p. 112.
[106] John 15:13, National Conferences of Bishops, the New American Bible (Wichita, KS: Devore &Sons, 1981), p. 1160.

he shared was that the Romans had a habit of crucifying people, especially Jews, every Friday. These weekly executions were meant to intimidate the Jews who were coming into Jerusalem because the people were hung outside the city gates for all passersby to see. What that meant to me, but was not voiced at the time, was that Jesus had to see those dying people every time He went into town. Imagine what it must have done to His spirit to have to watch people suffer and die; knowing that he had the capability to save them.

As I read that paragraph, I often wonder what this did to Jesus's spirit knowing that He too would soon suffer the same cruel fate. An illusion to life that we fail to comprehend is that "we cannot do it alone." In thousands of years, man has not learned that he cannot do anything without God's involvement. Dependence on God is written in *Matthew 6:25–34*:

Therefore I tell you, do not worry about your life, what you eat or drink, or about your body, what you wear. Is not life more than food and the body more than clothing? Look at the birds in the sky; they do not sow or reap, they gather nothing in barns, yet your heavenly Father feeds them. Are not you more important than they? Can any of you by worrying add a single moment to your life span? Why are you anxious about clothes?

Learn from the way the wildflowers grow. They do not work or spin. But I tell you that not even Solomon in his entire splendor was clothed like one of them. If God so clothed the grass of the field, which grows today and is thrown into the oven tomorrow, will he not much more provide for you? O you of little faith? So, do not worry and say what are we to eat? Or what are we to drink? Or what are we to wear? Your heavenly Father knows that you need them all. But seek first the kingdom of God and his righteousness and all these things will be given you besides. Do not worry about tomorrow; tomorrow will take care of itself. Sufficient for a day is its own evil.[107]

---

[107] Ibid., Matthew 6:25–34, p. 1018.

Even Jesus needed help.

> *They pressed into service a passer-by, Simon, a Cyrenian, who was coming in from the country, the father of Alexander and Rufus, to carry His cross.*[108]

Jesus was so near death that unless Simon did not alleviate His struggle, Jesus could have died right there on the street. Jesus could have been prevented from reaching His goal—to die on the cross—had it not been for the act of Simon's bravery. So, stay focused and persistent. Do not let pride stand before you and God; ask for help. How awesome it must have been for Simon to have the privilege to assist Jesus in His time of need? He stepped up to the plate, even though he was scared and afraid of what people might think of him for helping a condemned man. Another act of courage that I often think about is when Seraphia (Veronica) defies the chaos and threatening soldiers and wipes the face of Jesus. Again from *Inside the Passion*, Father John Bartunek records that astounding moment:

> *She kneels in front of Him to offer Him drink. Somehow, in the midst of Jesus' unbearable pain, those eyes tell you that He is thinking more of her, of her courage and her love, of her generosity, than of Himself. Christ's Passion makes Himself weak on purpose, so that He would have to depend on others, calling forth in them the courage of love and faith, just as He did for Veronica and Simon.*[109]

My friend Hillary says I'm persistence, and so here are two of my favorite "persistence" stories from the Bible: *Luke 8:40–48* and *Mark 2:1–12*. In *Luke*:

> *A woman afflicted with hemorrhages for twelve years, she had spent her whole livelihood on doctors and was unable to be cured*

---

[108] Ibid., Mark 15:21, p. 1087.
[109] Fr. John Bartunek, *Inside the Passion* (West Chester, PA: Ascension Press, 2005), p. 121.

by anyone came up through the large crowds and touched the tassel on His cloak. Immediately her bleeding stopped. Jesus then asked, "Who touched me?" Peter said, "The crowds are pushing and pressing in upon you." But Jesus said, "Someone has touched me for I know that power has gone out from me." When the woman realized that she had not escaped notice felled before His feet trembling and explained in front of all why she had touched Him and how she had been healed immediately. He said to her, "Daughter your faith has saved you, go in peace."[110]

The story from *Mark* goes like this:

Jesus returned from Capernaum and was at home. So many gathered that there was no longer room for them, not even around the door and He preached the word to them. They came bringing to him a paralytic carried by four men. Unable to get near Jesus because of the crowd, they opened up the roof above Him. After they broke through, they let down the mat on which the paralytic was lying. When Jesus saw their faith, he said to the paralytic, Child your sins are forgiven. He then said rise, pick up your mat and walk. He rose, picked up his mat at once, and went away in the sight of everyone.[111]

To bounce back from the brink of death with the dark side, I asked for help from my six brothers: Anthony, Carl, Chris, Paul, Francis, and Robert. I asked for shelter, guidance, money, reassurance, love, and support. I found the most spiritual soul to heal me of my past and my tortured demons in the soothing voice of several therapists: Carmen Falgout, Tim Crowley, and Cindy Ashkins. At times I even leaned on my sister-in-law Elise and, of course, my friends Charlie and Julie, Bart and Gina, Mark and Bonnie,

---

[110] Luke 8:40–48, National Conferences of Bishops, the New American Bible (Wichita, KS: Devore & Sons, 1981), p. 1108.

[111] Ibid., Mark 2:1–12, p. 1067.

Joseph, Hillary, Rick, and Cheryl. And yes, many times I even called...my ex-wife, Paula! If you missed the lesson here, it is to stay focused, be persistent, humble yourself, and ask for help. Never succumb—never give up! So, if I'm to be the Lizard Man, then the Lizard Man I will be!

Mona Lisa Vito: So what's your problem?

Vinny Gambini: My problem is, I wanted to win my first case without any help from anybody.

Mona Lisa Vito: Well, I guess that plan's moot.

Vinny Gambini: Yeah.

Mona Lisa Vito: You know, this could be a sign of things to come. You win all your cases, but with somebody else's help, right? You win case after case, and then afterward, you have to go up to somebody, and you have to say thank-you.[112]

Things to ponder alone or with a group:

- What about this story caught your attention, and why?
- Is there a Lizard Man inside of you?
- What is the lesson of the snowball stand?
- Why do people wait patiently in the blistering sun and heat for a snowball?
- How can you apply a snowball stand to your life?
- What does Rocky teach us about life? Is it hard or easy? Why was Jesus so moved by the people cutting a hole in the roof?
- Why is persistence a very good thing in the eyes of the Lord?
- What is far easier to do from Jesus's standpoint—heal the illness or forgive sins?
- Who is Simon for you?
- Who are you a Simon for?

---

[112] Dale Launer, *My Cousin Vinny*, movie (1998).

CHAPTER 6

WOUND CARE

In 1978, I was the recipient of the Rotary Award at my high school graduation. It's no great honor; the award was given to the senior with the best paper entitled "What I Want to Be and Why?" I wrote that I wanted to be a physical therapist and work in the field of sports medicine. After graduating from high school, I attended Louisiana State University, where I worked for the football team as a student trainer. What a glorious time that was. I had all of the same privileges the players had except I had no curfew, and I did not get my head banged in. I ate in the same cafeteria and slept in the same dorm as the players. I had a guarantee class card (meaning I got the classes I wanted), received all the same freebies, and traveled with the team. I had a girlfriend on the Lady Tigers Golf team, and two married older brothers were also attending LSU. Life was sweet!

The wonderful thing about working with athletes is that they are so motivated, so focused, so healthy. If an athlete is injured, he will do everything you say to get fit so he can play again. An athlete will eat the right kind of food, spend hours in the gym exercising, and follow the therapeutic rehab program to get back in the game. No questions asked. Trainers have so much influence. They can clear a player for the game, or they can ground him/her until the trainer feels certain that the player is ready for action. However, from time to time, some athletes will try and defy your better judgment.

As the semester was winding down and the football season was over, I found myself one day standing in the wrong line—by *line* I mean life's line. Physical therapy school required a GPA of 3.0 or higher, and the line for nursing school at Charity Hospital in New Orleans was a 2.0. My GPA was a 2.1. So one day before a football game, I was speaking with the exassisted head trainer of the LSU football department, Dell Flair (currently a student at Charity School of Nursing), and he suggested to me, "Why don't you go to nursing school and become a registered nurse? Once you do that, then you can then take your athletic training certification and then combine the two and have a much better understanding of sports medicine." I liked what I heard in that conversation that day. After much pondering, it sounded like a plan. Taking Dell's advice, I applied to nursing school and graduated three years later.

It's funny what you may think God's will is for you. Unless you talk it over with God, you may miss the line that you are supposed to be standing in. Well, I did not talk it over with God, and I found myself in the wrong line, or so I thought. I told God, "I'm in the wrong line." God replied, "No, you are not. You are in the line that I have been planning for you since I knew and formed you in the womb." "I am supposed to be in the sports medicine line!" I shouted back. "That line is closed," God quietly answered. "Well then, what line did you put me in?" I asked. "You are in the line to become a registered nurse who will one day specialize in wound care." "Nooo! I hate wounds. They stink, they smell, they drip, and they are nasty, nasty, nasty, nasty! They are usually associated with old and sick people like in the nursing home, not the beautiful healthy athletes, the gods and goddesses of Aphrodite, Artemis, Hermes, and Zeus! Gee, Grandpa, what the heck! Like the little girl in that broccoli commercial said, 'I don't think I like broccoli!' I know I don't like wounds either!"

OMG! Why oh why did God place me in that line? For the three years I was in nursing school, I could not wait to get out of that program. While I like learning about medicine and the physiology of the body, I did not like working with the ill, the very sick, and the dying. Coming from an environment of superathletes and God-given healthy and muscular bodies, I had difficulties coping with the frailties of humanness. So…why did I stay in nursing? Well…there was this beautiful nurse God introduced me to, and the rest is history. I never went back to finish that athletic training certification. That is until you read the last chapter.

The first time I took care of a wound, I was working as a student nurse at Charity Hospital in New Orleans. This is where we did our clinical training during nursing school. The patient was a "warrior" (a slang reference to a street gang member) that was paralyzed from a gunshot wound. He had the most horrendous, foul-smelling, brownish, copiously draining bedsore (now called pressure ulcers) on his sacrum and his hips. I thought I was going to puke when I took that dressing off! Several days later I could still smell that putrid stench in my nose. To me, taking care of that man's wounds was incredulous. As disgusting as it was, along with my incompetence as a student nurse, I felt immense sympathy for that man, and I did my best to convey that feeling toward him. He thanked me over and over for the poor care I was providing him. I felt lower than a slimeball. After that rotation, I knew I did not have what it took to be that kind of nurse, and I hoped and prayed that I never wound see another wound till my dying day.

Wow! How wrong I was! Remember, God is playing chess. Where He put you yesterday may seem inconsequential, but based on past lessons learned, His move for you tomorrow is where you may shine. In man's time, it may seem like a lifetime, while in God's time, His next move is just a few seconds. Regardless of the line you are standing in, if you have an open heart and mind, you may realize that is the line that God wants you to be in. God will steer you in the direction that He can use you for His greatest glory. But the heart and mind must remain open to His call.

Well, after nursing school graduation and several years working as a trauma nurse, God steered me to Dr. Keith VanMeter's hyperbaric wound care medical team. After working for Dr. VanMeter for five years, I realized that waiting to get into physical therapy school would have been a waste of time. Being with the golden athletes is not where God wanted me to be. God needed for me to learn humility, and there is no better way than being placed with patients that have a stigma as old as the Bible—nonhealing chronic wounds. God placed me where He wanted me to shine for His glory, and I was open to the call. Once Dr. VanMeter started teaching me how to heal a wound, I became hooked. For the next thirty-three years I worked in the field of wound care either as a clinical wound care nurse specialist or as a wound care medical sales rep. Over the last thirty-three years, wound care was my passion and obsession. It was my zeal in life and why I get up in the morning and get excited to go to work! Working with wounds is not glamorous and exciting as it is working in the ER, ICU, the operating room, or sports medicine. Little has changed today regarding the stigma associated with wounds as it was in antiquity. People still recoil at the thought of it, smelling it, and helping someone with a chronic nonhealing wound in the same way that people were aghast when Jesus helped the lepers. Today, individuals suffering with chronic wounds are still sort of shunned. Due to the heavy, foul-smelling odor and wound drainage, even physicians who are not wound care doctors really do not like these ill people mixing with their ordinary patients in their waiting rooms. Most medical caretakers do not have any idea as to how to care for a chronic wound, nor do they want to. Amazingly, physicians today have little training with wound care in their residency. Many are still using outdated techniques that still go back many, many years. Only recently in the past ten years wound care became a specialized department of medicine. Wounds are very time-consuming and extremely expensive. The reimbursement for taking care of a wound is nothing compared to what a cardiologist, radiologist, surgeon, and anesthesiologist make.

So why do it? For me it's the sheer satisfaction of helping a suffering patient that no one wants to deal with. The patient suffering with the longest chronic wounds in my care had ankle ulcers for twenty-five years. He walked in front of a cobalt oil field radiation machine while the machine was on and operating at the highest capacity, and he suffered radiation burns to both his legs and ankles. When Dr. VanMeter and my team finally healed that man and discharged him, he cooked a great big lunch for us. That was a fun day!

Three of the four authors of the Gospels tell stories regarding Jesus curing wounds: *Matthew 8:1–4, Mark 1:40–45,* and in *Luke 5:12–16:*

There was a man full of leprosy in one of the towns where he was; and when he saw Jesus, he fell prostate, pleaded with him, and said, "Lord if you wish, you can make me clean." Jesus stretched out his hand, touched him, and said, "I do will it, be clean" and the leprosy left the leper immediately.[113]

In the Bible, the meaning of *leprosy* is written sixty-eight times: fiftyfive times in the Old Testament and thirteen times in the New Testament. The Hebrew word *Tzara'ath* indicates a smiting—a punishment from God for certain behaviors. The Hebrews believed that misfortunes such as receiving an illness in life or being born with disfigurement were a retribution from God for sins of the parents. "As he passed by he saw a blind man from birth. His disciples asked him, Rabbi, who sinned, this manor his parents, that he was born blind? Jesus answered, neither he nor his parents sinned."[114]

Contacting leprosy was a death sentence. One could expect a lifetime of disfigurement, suffering, wounds, and banishment. Lepers were so feared that they were banished to far-off distant places like the hills and caves on the outskirts of towns. The leper would carry a clapper and/or a bell to warn of his approach, and they would shout, "Unclean! Unclean!" Lepers were often isolated, abandoned, and left to fend for themselves until they died. Jesus was moved to compassion and felt not only the physical but also the emotional pain of this ostracized group of people. In biblical times as it is today, sometimes the emotional and social taboo is far worse than the disease itself.

For thirty-three years I provided loving care to chronic wound patients. I am fervent and passionate about wounds, and to pat myself on my back, I am good at what I do. I believe it was a gift from God. As a student I was appalled by the order of wounds, but nowadays, I

---

[113] Luke 5:12–16, National Conferences of Bishops, the New American Bible (Wichita, KS: Devore& Sons, 1981), p. 1101.

[114] Ibid., John 9:1–3, p. 1203.

do not even mind the odors of a wound because now I understand that odors are a sign, a clue, and a road map to healing. Wounds are nondiscriminatory; they affect males and females, young and old, black and white, poor and the rich. But the wounds I deal with usually affect the elderly population. Their wounds are usually on the lower extremities and are typically nonhealing ulcers such as venous, pressure, arterial, and diabetic ischemia wounds. At other times I do have to provide care to decubitus ulcers (pressure-related bedsores), traumatic injuries, burns, failed flap and grafts, and surgical infections.

Caring for wounds is a privilege. I often think how magnificent, how humbling it would have been to clean and bandage the wounds of Jesus Christ. Wound care is a great lesson in life. I always keep in mind the simple teaching of Jesus in *Matthew 25:35*.

> *For I was hungry and you gave me food, I was thirsty and you gave me drink, a stranger and you welcomed me, naked you clothed me, ill you cared for me, in prison you visited me. When did I do this Lord? And the King will say to them in reply Amen I say to you, whatever you did for one of these least brothers of mine, you did for me.*[115]

When a person suffers from chronic wounds, everything else in life becomes more important while the wound becomes secondary. These patients have been shunted from one doctor to another, and often with poor healing outcomes. And if the patient is large or obese, society frowns upon them even more, and many medical clinicians do not want to deal with them. If they developed lymphedema (elephant-type swelling of the lower extremities secondary to a failed lymph system), the embarrassment and shame from the stares of people can be heartbreaking. Many times, suffering from a chronic wound(s), patients become very noncooperative and are angry as a result of dealing with many years of frustrations, hopelessness, desperation, and isolations. But wound healing takes time, sometimes a very long time. Every wound is different, just as every person is different. One simple wound

---

[115] Ibid., Matthew 25:35, p. 1054.

site may take over an hour of my time or more, and often patients have more than one wound. Sometimes wounds have mixed etiologies—several different medical disorders contributing to the wound factors. Regardless of the wound(s), I treat every wound the same way—with respect, tenderness, compassion, and with prayers. I often find myself praying to God to guide me while I am cleaning and dressing a wound. There is no better medicine I can apply to a person's wounds than the medicine of prayers. I am only an instrument used by God to exhibit my wound care knowledge to give relief to a suffering soul.

To begin the healing process, there are many aspects of wound care.

Step 1: After removing the bandage, I first inspect the wound—looking at the color of the wound, evaluating if it is dry or moist, how much drainage is being produced, and if there is an odor. Certain bacteria have distinct odors, and we can determine how to kill the bacteria keeping the wound from healing. During this initial phase, this is the time that the untrained person may believe the wound is the very worst they have ever seen. At first glance, the wound may appear very unhealthy and may be infected and hopeless. But this is not true. Applying a simple cleaning solution will remove bacteria, odor, exudate (draining), and any debris lingering inside the wound. Only then after removing all of the debris can I have a clear inspection of the next step.

Step 2 is determining if the wound bed is viable or nonviable. In layman's terms, this simply means if the wound is a dead wound or a living wound? If the wound has dead tissue, I must remove all the dead tissue before healing can begin. Nothing will heal a wound as long as dead and/or necrotic tissue is present. If the dead tissue is not removed, the wound will continue to necrosis and can easily spread to other sites. After removing the nonviable necrotic tissue, I can then go on to the next step. If the wound is healthy and pink, then I continue to support the therapy that is working. This is how I explain healthy versus nonhealthy tissue to all my patients. Healthy tissue is the bright red steak you see in the market while unhealthy tissue is that pale to brown steak. In fact I will document healthy beefy red granulation in the wound bed. If the wound has unhealthy or dead tissue, I may use shape debridement to cut out the dead tissue, or I may place a product inside the wound that will autolytic (dissolve) debride the dead tissue for removal.

Step 3 involves determination of wound exudate (draining). Is the wound dry or wet? Too much moisture, and the healing process can slow down. Too dry, and the healing can stop. It must have just the right amount of moisture to heal. If the wound is wet, I must place a dressing to absorb the exudate; and if the wound is dry, I must apply a product to keep the wound moist. Wound characteristics can change day to day. One day it's dry, the next day it's wet, and so on. After those steps are completed, I must take into consideration the bioburden of the wound bed. This is a fancy word for *bacteria*.

This would be *step 4*. Bioburden or bacteria count must be addressed. If the wound has a high bacteria count, it can generate an infection. The infection kills healthy cells, producing dead tissue, resulting in impeding healing, where the nonhealing cycle repeats itself over and over again. If the bacteria cannot be contained or eliminated, the wound can become larger and more unmanageable. I may then consider placing a product inside the wound that kills bacteria but protects the healthy viable cells. The doctor will most likely start the patient on oral or IV antibiotics.

The last step, *step 5*, is to cover the wound with a bandage: a Band-Aid to protect the delicate tissue. Wound dressings may be changed daily or several times a day, once a week, twice a week, or three times a week. If wounds are left untreated, they can lead to gangrene and even the flesheating disease—necrotizing fasciitis. At times, the wound care team's only option to save a limb or a life is to have a surgeon amputate the affected area.

Wound healing must not be rushed. I treat all wounds as if it is an egg—very delicate. I must also address the issue of pain. Pain is a very motivating response. If the patient feels pain, he/she will be very cooperative. If he/she feels no pain, I may have an uncooperative patient, and that patient may not show up for his scheduled treatment. For example, you have a bad headache, and you open the medicine cabinet in your home looking for Tylenol, and there are none. You will then get in your car and drive to the very first store that sells the product—even if it is 3:00 a.m., raining, and ice-cold outside. It is the same in wound care. Painful wounds result in patients showing up. It is not uncommon to see a wound that is in such a serious state of existence, and when I ask the patient, "How long has this been like this?" I may get a response like "Five weeks or longer." "Why did you wait so long to see me?" "It did not hurt." If pain is absent, life goes on, and the wound is secondary.

Many patients have other coexisting medical factors that need to be addressed such as the following: blood perfusion (circulation), medications, disease etiologies (cause), smoking, financial status, support at home, transportation, etc. To heal a wound, the entire picture of the person must be evaluated. If I look simply at just the wound itself, I can be remiss in my ability to produce a positive healing outcome. The patient must continue to visit his primary care physician in addition to all the secondary physicians providing medical care: heart, vascular, internist, and orthopedic doctors, just to mention a few. The patient in treatment may also be required to have orthotics and physical therapy. The patient must take his antibiotics, insulin, daily prescribed medications, adhere to his strict diet, elevate the lower extremities, stop smoking, go to therapy, no weight-bearing, have his blood evaluated, and monitor his sugar. Needless to say, there are a lot of other people involved in the decision-making process to help heal the wound.

One must always remember that the wound may become worse before it becomes better. At times I may have to physically remove layer after layer of dead and necrotic tissue before healthy granulating epithelialization cells begin filling the void of the once nonviable ulcer. But with a lot of tender loving care, over time this wound will become healthy and viable and will completely close. When I speak of time to heal a wound, it can vary from weeks to many, many, many months! I guess I like wound care so much because the person afflicted with the disorder(s) is arriving at my door with a last ray of hope. They may have had so much failure that when I begin to explain the process, they are nonbelievers. God has blessed me with the training and knowledge of taking something that is so nasty, nauseating, and sickening and making it whole and healthy again. That is so cool. God can do the same with emotional wounds as well.

The stigma of a wounded heart can be just as difficult to heal as that of a physical wound. Take me for example; it has taken almost forty years to heal the insult of my sexual molestation. In fact, the emotional scar may last a lifetime and may never heal.

> *Insult has broken my heart and I am weak. I look for compassion but there was none, for comforters but found none.*[116]

Like a physical wound, people with emotional wounds and a broken heart may not recognize the symptoms at first, for it may take time for the pain, hurt, ache, sting, grief, agony, anguish, and sorrow, embarrassment, and shame of the loss to be fully acknowledged. Other symptoms may surface as the depth of the wound becomes more apparent: loneliness, despair, depression, hopelessness, apathy, nostalgia, anxiety, and suicidal thoughts. Emotional wounds may occur from the sting of a sharp tongue, the death of a loved one, divorce or rejection in any form, trauma, etc. Sometimes, the sting of a sharp tongue can be the deadliest form of inflicting emotional scarring. The mouth of Judas betrayed Jesus. Like Judas, how many times did we betray our fellow brothers with words of angry, deadly gossip, insults, lies, and rash judgments? How many times with this same tongue did we receive the body and blood of our Lord and Savior? *Psalm 52* gives warnings concerning a deceitful tongue:

> *All day long you plot destruction; your tongue is like a sharpened razor, your love evil rather good, lies rather than honest speech. You love any word that destroys, your deceitful tongue.*[117]

---

[116] Ibid., Psalm 69:21, p. 586.
[117] Ibid., Psalm 52, p. 577.

Often the embattled person may have feelings that nothing will make them happy again, so they resort to drugs, alcohol, sex, gambling, shopping, eating, exercising, dieting, or any other type of addiction. There is even a syndrome that affects teenage girls more than boys called "cutting." This is where the tormented person mutilates his/herself on purpose with multiple scratching or cuttings of the skin until bleeding begins. However, the escape from any form of pain and the reality of a wounded heart is often temporary; masking these hurtful feelings will only build up and prolong the grief and sadness.

Previously I wrote about my own struggles with my childhood molestation. In addition to sex abuse, I also had emotional feelings of abandonment from a mother who, no fault to her own, struggled with her own demons as a manic-depressive. However, the sting and rejection associated with my wife's decision to divorce me was by far the worst pain I have ever experienced in my life. I do not wish that pain on anyone. It felt like a hot iron rod pierced my heart and exited through my back. I too felt loneliness, despair, depression, hopelessness, apathy, nostalgia, and anxiety. I even had suicidal thoughts. I tried to ease the pain with alcohol, work, and intensive exercise workouts at the gym. My recovery back to a healthy life could not have happened without the recognition that I had to ask others for help. I needed redemption and salvation! I turned to many people and God in my time of need. Take my advice: if you know someone going through a difficult time, please do not wait to have that person ask for help. A person besieged with emotional trauma may not even know what to ask for.

To heal a broken heart is similar to healing a physical wound. The steps are the same. To repair a broken heart, we must first clean the heart of all debris. I find that tears are the perfect solution to remove the excess baggage and necrotic emotions attached to a wounded or dying heart. This stage must not be rushed. It may take months; it may take years. Once the fragile heart is on the mend, it must be protected from additional harm. The heart must be kept from all things toxic and infectious. A strong bandage must be applied. The Band-Aid is called support; and that support can come from loved ones, friends, support groups, church communities, and above all else, the medicine of Jesus

Christ. Pray, pray, pray, and pray some more! Although Jesus is the Son of God, He too needed to go off and pray. During the Agony in the Garden, Jesus's heart was wounded, heavy, and crushed. He turned to prayers of strength and comfort. Prayers are so powerful they can defeat and conquer immorality, evil, wickedness, depression, and illness.

At times in my own struggles I felt that just breathing was difficult enough. The actor Tom Cruise did not help the emotional malady when he announced on a talk show that Brooke Shields was wrong when she used the drug Paxil to fight postnatal depression after the birth of her daughter. On *Access Hollywood*, he blurted out, "She should have used vitamins to help her feelings of despair." Had it not been for antidepressants, I, along with Brooke Shields, my mother, and millions of others may have given in to those thoughts of suicide. The Bible has story after story of Jesus Christ healing despair. He ate and spent time with the outcast, the prostitutes, the sick, the mentally ill, the poor, the homeless, the maimed, the lonely, the thieves, the diseased, the possessed, and the sinners. He gave them hope and comfort. He gave them love; He gave Himself. Besides the story of the good Samaritan (Luke 10:25–37), two of my other favorite stories in the Bible are about Jesus interacting with outcast women.

In *John 4:2–42*, Jesus meets a Samaritan woman at the well during the high noon of the sun. She is alone because she is an outcast of the village and must draw water at the hottest part of the day instead of in the early morning coolness with the other women. Jesus is thirsty, and He asks the woman for a drink:

> *"How can you, a Jew, ask me, a Samaritan woman for a drink?" "If you knew the gift of God and who is saying to you, 'Give me a drink,' you would have asked him instead and he would have given you living water. Everyone who drinks my water will never thirst." The woman said to Him, "Sir, give me this water so that I may not be thirsty or have to keep coming here to draw water." Jesus said to her, "Go call your husband and come back." The woman answered, "I have no husband." Jesus answered her, "You are right in saying I do not have a husband. For you have had five*

husbands and the one you are with now is not your husband." As the conversation continues the woman then says to Jesus, "I know the messiah is coming, the one called the Anointed; when he comes, he will tell us everything." Jesus said to her, "I am He, the one who is speaking to you."[118]

In *John 8:4–10*, the scribes and Pharisees bring before Jesus a woman caught in the act of adultery, and they made her stand before the Teacher.

The law of the day was from Moses that commanded a woman convicted of adultery was to be stoned:

They said to Him, "Teacher, this woman was caught in the very act of committing adultery. Now in the law, Moses commanded us to stone such women. So, what do you say?" They said this to test him so that could have charges brought against him. Jesus bent down and began to write in the ground with his finger. When he straightened up, he said, "Let the one among you who is without sin be the first to throw a stone at her." In response they went away one by one. Then Jesus said, "Woman, where are they? Has no one condemned you?" "No one," she answered. Then Jesus replied, "Neither do I condemn you. Go and from now on do not sin anymore."[119]

In the movie *The Passion*, one of my favorite parts of the film is when the adulterous woman is brought before Christ. The camera zooms in on the woman as she makes her way to the feet of Jesus. This episode is in slow motion. Sensing goodness or just protection, the adulterous woman crawls on her hands and knees with her head hung low. She is humiliated, embarrassed, frightened, and humbled. She reaches out just so she can touch His foot. She knows that if she can just touch His foot, she is in His care, His protection. He does not condemn her, nor does He exploit or judge her. He simply forgives her, embraces her, and loves her. His heart is so filled with love. She is forgiven!

---

[118] Ibid., John 4–42, p. 1142–1143.
[119] Ibid., John 8:4–10, p. 1149.

Throughout my ordeal, there were times I could not feel man's kindness, much less God's. But I swear I could hear angels encouraging me, "Hang on," "Help is on the way," "Call your brothers," "Call your therapist," "Visit a friend," "Work out," "Go to the chapel," "Eat, sleep, pray," "Say the rosary," etc. I was reminded time and time again about Jesus trying to reach the place of the Skull—Calvary. Beaten near to death, with no food, water, or rest, how did He make it to His Cross? Mel Gibson's movie *The Passion* is based on the book by Saint Anne Catherine Emmerich, a nineteenth-century German stigmatic and visionary. An illiterate nun, she had her visions, her ecstasy of the Passion of Jesus, dictated by her to a scribe. In her visions she constantly made referrals to the angels interacting on Christ's behalf. Many times in her writings she implies that had it not been for the angels' constant attention to Jesus, He would have died before reaching the cross. She had visions of the angels administering to Him with drink and picking His limbs up. God's angels are there for you and me. Call on them in time of need. Thank them daily for their love and interactions. Remember, we all have guardian angles to assist us. That's what they are there for. I was told as a young child, "If you pray to your guardian angel, he/she will tell you his/her name." My guardian angel told me his name. Luke.

There are many readings regarding Jesus's healing of the sick that you may consult. I provide just a few for your review: Matthew 8:13 (the centurion's servant); Luke 8:43–48 (the woman who bled); John 9:1–7 (a blind man); Matthew 8:14–15, Mark 1:29–31, Luke 4:38–39 (Peter's mother-in-law); Matthew 8:1–4, Mark 1:40–45, Luke 5:12–19 (the leper); John 5:1–15 (the cure at Bethsaida); Matthew 12:9–13, Mark 3:1–6, Luke 6:6–11 (a withered hand); Mark 7:31–37 (a deaf-mute); Luke 17:11–19 (ten lepers); Luke 22:49–51 (the servant's ear healed); Mark 1:23–28, Luke 4:33–37 (the cure of the demoniac); Luke 22:49–51 (the servant ear's healed); John 1:1–38 (the man born blind).

So, call on God and let the wound healing begin. Take the "mask off" and be patient with yourself, your spouse, family, friends, and God. Be gentle, kind, and most of all, forgive yourself. The old saying regarding time is true: time heals all wounds. But all things are made new with Jesus.

"DREAMING WITH A BROKEN HEART"
by John Mayer

When you're dreaming with a broken heart the waking up is the hardest part

You roll outta bed and down on your knees and for the moment you can hardly breathe

Wondering was she really here? Is she standing in my room?

No she's not, 'cause she's gone, gone, gone, gone, gone…

When you're dreaming with a broken heart

The giving up is the hardest part

She takes you in with your crying eyes

Then all at once you have to say goodbye

Wondering could you stay my love? Will you wake up by my side?

No she can't, 'cause she's gone, gone, gone, gone, gone…

Now do I have to fall asleep with roses in my hand? Do I have to fall asleep with roses in my hand? Do I have to fall asleep with roses in my hand? Baby won't you get them if I did?

No you won't, 'cause you're gone, gone, gone, gone, gone…

When you're dreaming with a broken heart. The waking up is the hardest part.[120]

---

[120] John Mayer, "Dreaming with a Broken Heart" (2010).

Things to ponder alone or with a group:

- What about this story caught your attention, and why?
- What wounds to you are more devastating—physical or those from the tongue?
- How often do you speak harsh words to your family, friends, and neighbors?
- Have you ever offered to clean the broken heart of another with your tears? How did you feel, and was it reciprocated?
- How long have you been weighed down by carrying a grudge against someone?
- How often do you walk past the lepers of today (street people, homeless) and continue to ignore their plight?
- Have you felt like a leper any time in your life? What did you do about it?
- When wounded, was Jesus called to heal your wounds? If not, why not?
- Do you believe in the power of angels, or do you think that angels are nothing but fairy tales and Hollywood?

CHAPTER 7

HURRICANE KATRINA

When the Lord saw how great man's wickedness on earth is and how every desire that his heart conceived was ever anything but evil, He regretted that He made man on the earth, and His heart was grieved. So, the Lord said,

> *I will wipe out from the earth the men I have created, and not only the men, but also the beasts and the creeping things and the birds of the air, for I am sorry that I made them. But Noah found favor with the Lord for Noah was a good man and blameless in that age, for he walked with the God. In the eyes of God, the earth was corrupt and full of lawlessness. When God saw how corrupt the earth had become, since all mortals led depraved lives on earth, he said to Noah: I have decided to put an end to all mortals on earth; the earth is full of lawlessness because of them. So, I will destroy them and all life on earth. Make yourself an ark and put into it your family and every living creature one male and one female with you so that I may keep you alive for I on my part am about to bring the flood (waters) on the earth to destroy everywhere all creatures in which there is the breath of life. But with you I will establish my covenant; you and your sons, your wife and your son's wives, shall*

go into the ark. This Noah did; he carried out all the commands that God gave him.[121]

Sounds like someone needs a little bit of anger management!

As a kid in the 1960s, I used to listen to Bill Cosby (way before he was convicted of sexual assault) albums all of the time. To this day, one of my favorite stories that he did was Noah and the ark. I will attempt to paraphrase it from memory, but I will update it a little.

Noah is minding his own business when God calls out to him.

God: Noah.

Noah: Who's there?

God: It is I, the Lord your God.

Noah: What's upppppppppp?

God: What is it you're doing?

Noah: Chilling.

God: I hear that.

Noah: What's cooking?

God: I'm going to destroy the earth and all that inhabits it. But you, Noah, I have found favor and will spare you and your family's lives.

Noah: Cool.

God: To survive, you must build an ark with specific dimensions. The blueprints are in cubits format!

Noah: Wait, what the hell is an ark and a cubit? I only know the metric system.

God: Google it!

---

[121] Genesis 6:5–20, National Conferences of Bishops, the New American Bible (Wichita, KS: Devore& Sons, 1981), pp. 62–63.

GOD AND FREE WILL

Noah: Okay, okay. You don't have to shout! Let me turn on my PC. Okay, let me see here. Oh, an ark…it's a boat! You want me to build a boat?

God: Yes.

Noah: Why?

God: I can't tell you.

Noah: Look, Lord, I do not know if You noticed, but my GPS indicates where I stand right now: I am at an elevation of six thousand feet above seawater. The nearest body of water is over one thousand miles away. Can you give me a hint?

God: You want a hint?

Noah: Yes, please.

God: Noah.

Norah: Yes, Lord.

God: How long can you tread water?

Building that monstrous boat has now caught the attention of the media. CNN, MSNBC, NBC, ABC, BBC, CBS, Fox, and Al Jazeera news are all there covering this wild, new, and exhilarating story. Even the paparazzi record Noah's comings and goings, constructing the ark, and collecting the animals. "Lions and tigers and bears! Oh my!"[122] Regis and Kelly tape a live show with the neighborhood association, who were complaining about all the noise and traffic. Animal rights groups were protesting on behalf of the rabbits because Noah kept saying, "Only two, only two." On Larry King's talk show, Frasier Crane (world-renowned radio psychiatrist) was attributing Noah's erratic behavior to someone who is taking hallucinogenic drugs, possibly shrooms. The ACLU filed injunctions on behalf of the same-sex animal partners that wanted to board the boat. "Name's Barf. I'm a Mog, half man, half dog.

---

[122] *Wizard of Oz*, movie quote (MGM Studio, 1939).

I'm my own best friend."[123] YouTube has videos of his neighbors saying stuff like "I always thought he was a crackhead." Finally, on a crystal clear day, Noah enters the ark, and the "hot American newscaster" Megan Kelly yells out to him, "Can you please tell us why you are doing this?" "I can't tell you," replies Noah. "For our live viewing audience, can you give us a hint?" "Sure, how long can y'all tread water?"

Growing up in Southwest Louisiana, I have experienced my fair share of hurricanes. Those that were very mild, I tend not to remember; but those that hit us with a punch like Hurricane Betsy and Hilda, I never forget. I was ten years old when Camille hit Mississippi in 1969, and I still can recall the devastation it produced. In 1992, Andrew brought destruction to South Florida then skimmed the Louisiana coast. "Ivan the Terrible" made an impact on the Gulf Coast in 2004. After hitting Cuba with 150 mph winds (a category 5), Ivan was going to hit somewhere between New Orleans and Panama City, Florida. The entire Gulf Coast bugged out! At the last minute, Ivan turned just a few degrees east, and the storm hit Pensacola instead of New Orleans. Talk about a bunch of upset New Orleans residents forced by the authorities to evacuate. Many vowed never to leave again. The traffic congestion, lack of hotels, fuel, and food and so on was worse than that damn storm. This experience would have dire consequences to New Orleans when Katrina invades the coast in 2005.

If I have to choose a natural disaster to deal with, I choose hurricanes. Tornadoes, earthquakes, and tsunamis all hit without warning while hurricanes may take several weeks to finally strike land. So, there is a warning system, thus giving you enough time to formulate your game plan and evacuate. Every year between June 1 and November 30, the residents of the Caribbean Islands and the Gulf Coast keep a watchful eye on what the weather is doing off the coast of Africa. Once a storm enters the Caribbean waters, all eyes start to become glued to the Weather Channel. When the hurricane enters the Gulf of Mexico, that is when the praying begins.

---

[123] Mel Brooks, *Spaceballs* movie quote (1987).

Louisiana residents are praying that the hurricane makes landfall in Mississippi, Texas, Florida, Alabama, or Mexico; while the residents of those states are praying that it hits any other state but their own. It's not that we wish harm on Mexico or our neighboring states, we just don't want the harm to come to our state.

In 1981, I moved from my small hometown of Abbeville to New Orleans to attend nursing school. After graduating, I remained in the Nawlins area for the next twenty-one years. Unlike New Orleans, my hometown is not surrounded by water, and the sea level is higher than the −8 feet below sea level in New Orleans. During my first hurricane season in New Orleans, I began to read and watch on TV the stories about the prediction of the "big storm" hitting New Orleans and the destruction that could occur. For the next twenty-one years, it was always the same story, just with better graphics, videos, pictures, and statistics. One could find the same warning from all the local newspapers, TV stations, and even from the Discovery Channel and the Weather Channel. The great trepidation was that if a slowmoving category 3 hurricane (winds of 111–130 mph) hits the mouth of the Mississippi River, it would produce a storm tidal surge of nine to twelve feet. The levees surrounding New Orleans were only designed to protect the city from a category 3 storm, which meant that a storm surge of nine to twelve feet would overtop the levees and cost the city its life by fabricating a "punch bowl" effect. Water would enter the city, but the levees would prevent drainage out of the city. It was extensively reported that the city could be stranded in water of forty feet or more for weeks. Even with all of these statistics and predictions about the "big storm," the reality of the devastation that would occur was unimaginable. However, it was this overwhelming realization that one day something catastrophic would occur that led me to move out of the city to the North Shore and the city of Mandeville in 1988. Just twenty-four miles across Lake Pontchartrain, Mandeville's elevation is twenty-six feet above sea level, and there is no need for levees.

So, the point to all of this is that New Orleans had predictions and warnings and warnings and warnings and warnings year after year. But they were ignored. Dodging the bullet of "Ivan the Terrible" in 2004 contributed to the aftereffect of Katrina the following year. New Orleans' worst fear was about to become a reality. On August 28, 2005, this colossal storm entered the Gulf of Mexico as a category 5 with sustained winds at 175 mph. Its course was directly pointed to the mouth of the Mississippi River. With biblical enormity, those residents that could flee did. However, because of the previous year's evacuation difficulties of Ivan, many chose to stay and ride out the storm. The residents of New Orleans were once again relying on their prayers that the storm would veer elsewhere. A small prayer was answered. On August 29 at 7:10 a.m., Katrina made landfall south of New Orleans in Plaquemine Parish, just south of Buras, as a category 3 with maximum winds near 125 mph. The Mississippi Gulf Coast would receive the brunt of the wind's vicious power. So, for a very slight time, New Orleans could breathe a sigh of relief. Again, it looked as if they dodged another bullet. But then, the levees broke!

According to the US National Hurricane Center, "Hurricane Katrina was the sixth strongest hurricane ever recorded and the third strongest ever recorded to make landfall in the United States."[124] The storm surge that battered New Orleans was twenty feet high. It was estimated that 80 percent of New Orleans was under water, and in some places, it was twenty feet deep. Years later it was determined that the failure of the levees was due to a combination of design flaws by the Army Corps of Engineers along with a lack of adequate maintenance and devotion to the entire levee system. But that would be of little comfort to the countless people who were stranded in the rising water. What I cannot comprehend is that everyone knew this was going to happen someday. Once it did happen, there was no backup plan. Mayor Ray C. Nagin did finally admit that he once saw the hurricane evacuation playbook for the city, but he never read it.

Hurricane Katrina brought the worst and the best out of man at the very same time, and I was a firsthand witness to some of the accounts. At the time of the storm, I was working as a wound care product nurse specialist for a national medical supplies and manufacture corporation.

---

[124] National Oceanic and Atmospheric Administration (NOAA) website.

GOD AND FREE WILL

I was living in an apartment on Saint Charles Avenue in New Orleans that my sister-in-law owned. My wife and I had been separated just six months when the storm hit. Once the storm passed, and I knew my kids and wife were safe, I began to assist my hospital customers in any way that I could. During the first few days of the aftermath, the news media was having a field day covering the rising water, people stranded on rooftops, the pillaging and raiding, the burning businesses, and the shootings. The stranded residents were interviewed hysterically crying, begging for water, food, and any help. It was wildly reported that gangs were ransacking gun stores, pawnshops, banks, and pharmacies. Several times on TV, the news showed individuals on the streets firing guns at the above circling helicopters. Several murders and rapes were erroneously reported to have occurred at the Superdome and the New Orleans Convention Center. I heard tales from many nurses working in the hospitals about gangs attempting to assault the hospitals in search of drugs. It was pandemonium at its worst! Every form of hope or terror was infectious. Local, state, and federal authorities were stunned and too paralyzed to response initially. Later, reports surfaced detailing the fights going on between our president, the governor of Louisiana, and the mayor of New Orleans. Memos would emerge about our governor having concerns of looking weak politically if she bowed to the pressure of the president.

Even some New Orleans Police Department officers did not uphold their sworn duty to protect and serve as some of them looted a local Wal-Mart and an auto dealership, where they hauled off Corvettes and Cadillac. By the time the military arrived, New Orleans was in chaos, and people were dying or had already died. They died in the water, on rooftops, in attics, in swept-away homes, beneath mud and rubble, in a wheelchair at the convention center, on the airport tarmac, in a nursing home, and even in some hospitals. One distinguished veteran police officer was so overwhelmed that he died by his own hands with his own gun. The power of the water showed no mercy. It made no difference if you were rich or poor, male or female, black or white; the water destroyed everything. It smashed homes, schools, universities, churches, playgrounds, cars, buses, trolleys, businesses, museums, military installations, roads, highways, bridges, amusement parks, airports, cemeteries, hospitals, police stations, golf courses, country clubs, parks, animals, plants, and trees. It destroyed New Orleans; it destroyed lives! It affected even the evacuees watching the live broadcasts of their dying city. It was like watching your child die, and you were powerless to do anything about it. It broke the heart and soul of the city. Man—at its worst!

Several weeks after the flood receded and the city was empty of most life, I crossed a military checkpoint on River Road at the Metairie-New Orleans parish line. Dressed in my scrubs, the MP (military police) asked me where I thought I was going. I told him I needed to get to my apartment on Saint Charles Avenue. I had some medical supplies in it that Ochsner Hospital needed. He warned me that if I entered, I was on my own and they were not responsible for my safety. I said I understood and started driving. Making my way down the avenue, I was appalled by the stench in the air. It was repulsive! Driving toward my apartment, I was stunned to see thousands and thousands of freezers and refrigerators lining the streets. As I drove throughout the city, they were everywhere. Shoulder to shoulder and on both sides of the street. Some wrapped with duct tape, rope, and bungee cords. Many had signs posted on them: "Warning! Do not open! Toxic waste! Not for consumption!" The stench was the perishable food and meat that was rotting in the sweltering heat in the homes, restaurants, and so on. Several days earlier, the residents, who were returning for a few hours to evaluate their own personal items, placed those dripping appliances on the streets. Entering my darkened apartment, I was on the verge of vomiting as the aroma of my ten rotting stuffed chickens greeted me. The rest of the four-story complex had similar odors.

After retrieving the medical supplies, curiosity got a hold of me. I got in my car and went on a sightseeing tour. I saw neither man, bird, dog, nor any other sign of life. I found myself moving through slow motion as I made my way to the French Quarter. Standing in front of Jackson Square, I had a strange childhood flashback. The city reminded me of the movie *Omega Man* with Charlton Heston. The updated version is *I Am Legend* with Will Smith. With the sun going down and the movie in my vision, I began to feel creepy and scared. The stench of the rotting food, the smell of

GOD AND FREE WILL

the mud, the feeling of death from the city was all I could handle. I turned my car toward Canal Street for my drive back to the hospital.

Seeing all of this reminded me of *Matthew 24:15–28*:

> *When you see the desolating abomination spoken through Daniel let the reader understand; a person on the housetop must not go down to get things out of his house, a person in the field must not return to get his cloak; pray that your flight not in winter or the Sabbath, for all that time there will be great tribulation, such as not been since the beginning of the world until now, nor ever will be. Wherever the corpse is, there the vultures will gather.*[125]

The worst of man was not just limited to the period during the storm but continued well after, even during the recovery phase. Insurance companies refused to pay for damages; scammers were posing as first aid volunteers, construction workers, government authorities, etc. Local authorities blamed the state authorities while the state blamed the federal government. The federal government blamed the local and the state authorities, and everyone blamed FEMA and the Army Corps of Engineers. Many residents rebuilding continue to deal with fraud, scams, red tape, frustration, and theft. Often residents found their materials stolen while some were robbed at gunpoint and murdered. The water itself robbed thousands of people of irreplaceable valuables, pictures, and memories.

> *Do not store up your treasure on earth where moth and decay destroy, and thieves break in and steal. But store you treasure in heaven where neither moth nor decays, nor thieves break in and steal. For where your treasure is, there also will your heart be.*[126]

My faith teaches me that man is good and will come to the aid of those in need in desperate times. Before the final blessing at the end of

---

[125] Matthew 24: 15–28, National Conferences of Bishops, the New American Bible (Wichita, KS: Devore & Sons, 1981), pp. 1051–1052.

[126] Ibid., Matthew 6:19–21, p. 1018.

mass at the church Our Lady of the Lake, Father Joe would always say, "Show a little random act of kindness and goodness to someone this week." "Do to others whatever you would have them do to you."[127] The nation must have heard Father Joe's request for the nation, and the world responded with multiple acts of kindness. Men with boats from all over Louisiana began to descend on the city to assist in the rescue operations.

The owners of the company I worked for hired a private helicopter rescue team from the Chicago area and had them land at Tulane Medical Center to evacuate stranded patients and staff. Theirs was the very first helicopter in the city after the storm. An out-of-town sixteen-year-old boy stole (*borrowed* he said) a bus and made a daring rescue to get evacuees out of harm's way. A former Marine prevented thugs from entering his waterfilled apartment complex. He rescued two hundred residents. A private medical MASH (mobile army medical hospital) unit from North Carolina set up operations in Bay Saint Louis, Mississippi. The NASCAR industry flew teams of volunteer doctors, nurses, and technicians on a weekly rotation to aid in the recovery. Thousands of volunteers set up centers in Houma, Baton Rouge, Lafayette, Monroe, and other parts of the state. LSU students showed up at the Pete MAC (basketball arena) to lend a hand. Other students descended on area shelters to distribute cots, blankets, food, clothing, and so on. High school and college students along with church groups spent their summers and spring break time cleaning the city, building homes, and removing debris, while celebrities like Brad Pitt, Harry Connick Jr., and Ellen DeGeneres used their star power and influence to keep the drive alive.

The military arrived with cargo planes, helicopters, trucks, medical teams, food, water, ice, ice, and more ice. Our neighboring states took in the Gulf Coast evacuees and housed them in centers, hotels, and campgrounds and even in their homes. Neighboring states also took in the medically needy; the babies and the sick were accepted into their medical systems. Like New York City four years earlier in the wake of 9/11, this nation stepped up to the plate and united once again.

---

[127] Ibid., 7–12, p. 1018.

It matters not to this nation that you were young, old, male, female, white, black, rich, or poor. What mattered most were safety, shelter, asylum, sanctuary, safe haven, compassion, kindness, sympathy, and a smiling face. Schools across this vast country made available space, provided uniforms, waived tuition, and found books. Over seventy foreign countries pledged assistance or monetary donations including Kuwait, which pledged close to $500 million. Large donations were even made by Bangladesh, Qatar, China, India, and Pakistan.

There are so many countless untold stories of heroes. Close to my heart are the many doctors, nurses, and emergency personnel that remained in the hospitals caring for their patients too sick to evacuate. Horrible stories emerged such as the temperature rising past the 100-degree-plus mark, no ventilation, no lights, no toilets, no showers, no fresh water, and little food. Nurses and doctors would start intravenous fluids on themselves while giving the patients their food. When the military arrived and told several hospitals' medical staff they had room for just them and not the patients, many refused to leave and remained faithful to their duty—caring for those unmovable patients. While mankind made such atrocious, ghastly, and sinful decisions during this wearisome period, there were others whose actions I'm sure pleased the heart of the Almighty.

> *Do to others as you would have them do to you. For if you love those who love you, what credit is that to you? Even sinners do the same. But, rather love your enemies and do good to them and expect nothing back, then your just reward will be great. Be merciful as your Father is merciful.*[128]

"Where I come from, there are men who do nothing but good deeds all day long. They are called…uh…good-deed doers!"[129]

In *James 2:17–18*, he writes about performing good deeds:

---

[128] Luke 6:27–36, National Conferences of Bishops, the New American Bible (Wichita, KS: Devore & Sons, 1981), p. 1103.
[129] *Wizard of Oz*, movie quote (MGM Studio, 1939).

Faith by itself isn't enough. Unless it produces good deeds, it is dead and useless. Now someone may argue, "Some people have faith; others have good deeds." But I say, "How can you show me your faith if you don't have good deeds? I will show you my faith by my good deeds."[130]

While this is a wonderful story, what does it have to do with free will? In the Old Testament, God provided man with angels and prophets time and time again forewarning man about his upcoming demise unless man changed his heart. Man has free will to make his own choices—to believe or not to believe, listen or not listen, make right or wrong choices, to choose the grapes or the Oreos. Because man chose to ignore God's warnings, man suffered the consequences. There are countless stories in the Old Testament where man suffered for not heeding God's warning. Besides the story of Noah, another good example is Genesis's destruction of Sodom and Gomorrah.

Then the angels said to Lot: "We are about to destroy this place, for the outcry reaching the Lord against those in the city is so great that he has sent us to destroy it."[131]

So, I made the same comparison to New Orleans and the many years of hurricane warnings by the expert authorities. Despite many years of warning, many residents chose to ignore the public warnings to the possible cataclysmic catastrophe. Free will—to stay or evacuate. In addition, I wanted to showcase man's reaction to his affliction and hardship in this terrible tragedy. Many chose to only look after their own self-interest with the continuation of malicious behavior such as looting, murdering, scamming, raping, and robbing and so on. Then there were those individuals that rose to the call to serve their brothers and sisters rather than taking from them. Hurricane Katrina is a great illustration of what to do and what not to do.

---

[130] James 2:17–18, National Conferences of Bishops, the New American Bible (Wichita, KS: Devore & Sons, 1981), p. 1344.
[131] Ibid., Genesis 19:12, p. 24.

Another lesson that can be learned from this story is to always be prepared at a moment's notice and that *time* is a deception. The people of New Orleans and the surrounding area always believed there would always be plenty of time—time to prepare, time to evacuate, time to return. Unlike tornadoes and earthquake that strike with little warnings, hurricanes may take several weeks to reach landfall. When I think about Hurricane Katrina, I am reminded of *Matthew 24:36–44* and a fable from Aesop—"The Ant and the Grasshopper":

> In a field one summer's day a grasshopper was hopping about, chirping and singing to its heart's content. An ant passed by bearing along with great toil an ear of corn he was taking to the nest. "Why not come and chat with me," said the grasshopper, "instead of toiling and moiling in that way?" "I am helping to lay up food for the winter," said the ant, "and recommend you do the same." "Why bother about winter?" said the grasshopper. "We have got plenty of food at present." But the ant went on its way and continued its toil. When the winter came the grasshopper had no food and found itself dying of hunger, while it saw the ants distributing everyday corn and grain from the stores they had collected in the summer. Then the grasshopper knew: It is best to prepare for the days of necessity.

In *Matthew 24:36–44*, Jesus is explaining to the apostles to always be prepared and heed His warnings, for no one knows when the day and hour will come.

> *But of that day and hour no one knows, neither the angels of heaven, nor the Son, but the Father alone. For as it was in the days of Noah, so it will be at the coming of the Son of Man. In those days before the flood, they were eating and drinking, marrying and giving in marriage, up to the day that Noah entered the Ark. They did not know until the flood came and carried them all away. So, it will be (also) at the coming of the Son of Man. Two men will be out in the field; one will be taken, and one will be left. Two women*

will be grinding at the mill; one will be taken, and one will be left. Therefore, stay awake! For you do not know which day your Lord will come. Be sure of this; if the master of the house had known the hour of night when the thief was coming, he would have stayed awake and not let his house be broken into. So too, you also must be prepared, for at an hour notice you do not expect, the Son of Man will come.[132]

While I was preparing to evacuate from New Orleans, my sister-in-law Tricia was going about her business preparing to attend a wedding in a few hours that very night. She said not to worry, that the storm was going to miss us at the very last minute like it always does. I'm glad to say she finally fled the city as well. So, heed thy warnings, be prepared, and remember time will deceive you. Not too long after the storm Katrina, I came upon a destroyed car with a bumper sticker that summed up New Orleans' demise. The sticker simply stated, "The Titanic was built by professionals, but Noah's Ark was built by amateurs." At that very moment I wished I had a camera so that I could have sent a picture of that car to the New Orleans Levee District and the Army Corp of Engineers with a note asking, "Learn anything?"

Often, we read of God becoming angry and punishing His people, Israel, when they sinned, rejected His will, and went their own way. He was incensed with jealously when they chose to worship other gods. When they made the golden calf in the wilderness at the time, he was revealing His law to guide them, God, in anger, decided to wipe them off the face of the earth, until Moses intervened. God is absolutely holy, and it would be a violation of his nature to allow sin in His presence. His sovereignty demands absolute, unequivocal submission and obedience. For our affections and devotions to be given to anything else is considered adulterous and worthy of God's wrath.

In demonstrating His power and majesty, a response of praise and worship is required. He is to be feared by all the kings of the earth,

---

[132] Ibid., Matthew 24:36–44, pp. 1052–1053.

GOD AND FREE WILL

for His wrath will be poured out to all those who fail to humble themselves before Him and bring gifts of devotion to Him. Our fear of the Lord should be due to the awe and respect we have for Him, as we comprehend his greatness. But it also should be due to our awareness of His wrath and the punishment that is inevitable for those who fail to live in a way that acknowledges his lordship and rule.[133]

When I think of what happened to New Orleans from Hurricane Katrina, it is hard not to think about God's anger at His people during Noah's time. There are many connecting similarities between the two stories. PostKatrina, many people affected by the floods were actually saying God was angered by the decadent behavior of the New Orleans citizens, and that is why God allowed the flooding. They do have a point! I can attest to attending many decadent events encouraged and sponsored by the city. Perhaps what saved New Orleans from total destruction is that all mortals of New Orleans do not live depraved lives. Just maybe, God had more compassion than He did during Noah's time. Nevertheless, the breaking of the levees and the flooding of the city did get the people's attention that God was looking for. Sad to say, the warning was heeded for only a very short while. Six years later, the city is back to its old self. According to a recent survey, New Orleans is back to be the highest murder city in the US. Just as in the post-Noah flooding, generations later, man is back on the path to destruction and rejecting God's warnings. But this time, after all the heavy downpours and tropical depressions that last for days or hurricanes with destructive power as Katrina, God always placed His rainbow in the sky as His reminder that He will never again ask man, "How long can you tread water?"

---

[133] Jerry Rankin, *In the Secret Place* (Nashville, TN: B&H Books, 2009), pp. 162–163.

WHEN THE LEVEE BREAKS

If it keeps on rainin', levee's goin' to break,
When The Levee Breaks I'll have no place to stay.
Mean old levee taught me to weep and moan,
Got what it takes to make a mountain man leave his home,
Oh, well, oh, well, oh, well.
Don't it make you feel bad
When you're tryin' to find your way home,
You don't know which way to go?
If you're goin' down South
They go no work to do,
If you don't know about Chicago.
Cryin' won't help you, prayin' won't do you no good,
Now, cryin' won't help you, prayin' won't do you no good,
When the levee breaks, mama, you got to move.[134]

Things to contemplate alone or with a group:

- What about this story caught your attention, and why?
- Are there storms brewing in your life?
- Are you yielding to the warnings signs or going about life like tomorrow is another day?
- In times of spiritual storms, what side of you is showing more: the best of man or the worst of man?
- Is your life running like the ant or the grasshopper? Why? In a local or worldwide crisis, do you respond to the cry for help or just walk away?
- What made Noah a good and righteous man?
- Do you think that the present-day headline crises (Japan's tsunami, Haiti's earthquake, world's financial trouble) are God made or man-made?
- Can you identify three things that are toxins in your life that must be removed?
- How long can you tread water?

---

[134] Led Zeppelin, "When the Levee Breaks," *Led Zeppelin IV* album (1971).

CHAPTER 8

MIRACLES

Indigo Montoya: That's a miracle pill?

Miracle Max: You rush a miracle man, you get rotten miracles.

Valerie: The chocolate coating makes it go down easier. But you have to wait fifteen minutes for full potency. And you shouldn't go swimming after, for at least, what? An hour."[135]

W*ebster*'s dictionary defines *miracles* as "an extraordinary event manifesting divine intervention in human affairs; an extremely outstanding, amazing or wonderful occurrence, thing, or accomplishments." In the English language, *miracle* comes from the Latin word *miraculum*, meaning "to marvel" or "something wondered." When I skimmed through the Gospels, I found thirty-six miracles performed by Jesus (one cannot count the same miracle recorded in the other Gospels). When I logged onto my computer and I Googled "miracles by Jesus," I got search results ranging from eight to one hundred. So how many miracles did Jesus actually perform? The Gospel writer John has the answer:

---

[135] *Princess Bride* movie quote, directed by Rob Reiner (1987).

MIRACLES

It is this disciple who testifies to these things and has written them, and we know that his testimony is true. There are also many other things that Jesus did, but if these were to be described individually, I do not think the whole world would contain the books that would be written.[136]

Regardless of an accurate number of miracles recorded in the Bible, Jesus performed them; they were witnessed and recorded. In *Matthew 11:4–5*, Jesus is instructing His disciples to inform John the Baptist of the miracles they have witnessed.

Go and tell John what you hear and see. The blind regain their sight, the lame walk, lepers are cleansed, the deaf hear, the dead are raised and the poor have the good news proclaimed to them.[137]

I would say that Jesus walking on the water and calming the wind and sea (Matthew 14:22–33), changing water into wine (John 2:1–11), feeding five thousand with two fish and five loaves (Matthew 14:13–21), feeding four thousand with seven loaves (Mark 8:1–9), healing ten lepers (Luke 17:11–19), and raising the dead Lazarus (John 11:1–44) are some pretty powerful miracles.

Why did Jesus need to perform miracles? After all, one can believe in God without seeing a miracle. Jesus performed miracles to attest to His divinity. Weak-minded as man is, "seeing is believing," and Jesus adapted to man's thought processes.

Jesus' miracles were not self-aggrandizing of magic. He was filled with the power of God's healing love. Through His miracles he showed that He is the Messiah and the kingdom of God begins in Him. Thus it became possible to experience the dawn of the new world: He freed people from hunger (john 6:5– 15), injustice (Luke 19:18), sickness and death (Matthew 11:5). By driving out demons,

---

[136] John 21:24, National Conferences of Bishops, the New American Bible (Wichita, KS: Devore & Sons, 1981), p. 1168.
[137] Ibid., Matthew 11:4–5, p. 1025.

He began his victorious advance against the "ruler of this world" (Satan). Nevertheless, Jesus did not remove all misfortune and evil from this world. He directed his attention principally to free man form the slavery of sin. His central concern was faith, which he also elicited through miracles.[138]

Bishop Sheen alludes,

Our Lord worked many miracles as signs to convince men of the fact he who came to work these miracles was the One who was promised. He never worked a miracle to satisfy His hunger or thirst. He refused to convert the stones of the wilderness into bread to satisfy His own hunger or to cause water to gush out of a rock to slake His thirst; instead, He asked a woman to let down her bucket to give Him a drink. He never received money for the things which He accomplished. He never worked a miracle to obtain a living. The vast majority of the miracles never took place in the secret places of people's lives but in what might be called the physical world where they could be verified scientifically. Our Lord never performed a miracle unless there were witnesses present. Jesus never went up into a mountain to perform some miracle alone with no person being present, and then come out saying He had done it. His works were accomplished before the eyes of multitudes of people, and that is why none of the miracles of our blessed Lord were ever actually denied, not even His Resurrection. His miracles are inseparable from His person. They differed from prophets and others since theirs were an answer to a prayer granted by a higher power. If you expel miracles from the life of Christ you destroy the identity of Christ and the gospels. How many miracles did He work? The specific number mentioned in the gospel is thirty-five. Three tell of raising the dead: a child, a young man, and an adult; nine relate to nature and twenty-three to healing.[139]

---

[138] Rev. John Trigilio Jr., PhD, and Rev. Kenneth Brighenti, PhD, *Youth Catechism of the Catholic Church* (San Francisco, CA: Ignatius Press, 2010), p. 66.

[139] Bishop Fulton L. Sheen, *Your Life Is Worth Living* (Schnecksville, PA: St. Andrew's Press, 2014), pp. 41–44.

MIRACLES

One day in my CCD class, we were discussing miracles when one of my students asked me if miracles occur today like they did in the Old Testament. He meant the *big* ones like the parting of the sea (Exodus 14:10– 22) and the promulgation of the Passover (Exodus 12:21–30). He even said, "Like large miracles for all to see." The next week I brought to class the *USA Today* issue with US Airway's Flight 1549 in the Hudson River after Captain Chesley B. "Sully" Sullenberger and his crew made an emergency landing and emerged with all 155 passengers alive. "You mean like this!" I said.

Jesus's miracles were indeed an extraordinary facet of His ministry. His authority over nature, disease, evil, and death served to authenticate His divine revelation as the Son of God and to fulfill the Old Testament prophecies. Many times Jesus refused to perform a miracle because He encouraged the petitioner to show faith rather than look for a magic show.

> *Then some of the scribes and Pharisees said to him, "Teacher, we wish to see a sign from you." He said to them in reply, "An evil and unfaithful generation seeks a sign, but no sign will be given it."*[140]

Even today, why must a miracle be so grand to be believed? Why can't we believe in the simple, smaller ones that take place daily before our eyes?

Miracles occur every day, but we dismiss them as coincidence. Just because we woke up today does not mean we will be putting our heads on the pillow tonight. There is no guarantee that we will see another sunrise. "That day and hour no one knows, neither the angels of heaven, nor the Son, but the Father alone or sun set."[141] It continues for several more verses warning about the day death knocks on our door.

---

[140] Matthew 13:38–39, National Conferences of Bishops, the New American Bible (Wichita, KS: Devore & Sons, 1981), p. 1028.

[141] Ibid., Mark 14:32–34, p. 1084.

> *Therefore, stay awake! For you do not know on which day your Lord will come. So too, you also must be prepared, for at an hour you do not expect the Son of Man will come.*[142]

Life is so precious, and yet we rarely think of how fragile our bodies are. Are we so desensitized that we cannot even recognize a small miracle before our eyes? Maybe we are desensitized to the miracle of life. We do not even respect life anymore. Life is taken for granted, and we do not realize the wonder of it. We kill unmercifully through murder, abortions, and in our thoughts and hearts. One early morning, I was working out in the weight room of a local gym when an elderly man fell to the ground in front of all the active people walking and running on the treadmills. I heard a plea for help over the intercom, so I rushed over to see a crowd gathered around an unresponsive man who was a shade of deep purple. I shouted for someone to call 9-1-1, and I began CPR. When the medics arrived, they proceeded to revive him with multiple cardio shocks while I searched in vain to start an IV but to no avail. Father Rene happened to be playing tennis at the gym and responded to the call. He asked me if he could do anything. I said, "You can give him the last rites, I believe he is dead." The paramedics left with the deceased man, and when I stood up and faced the immeasurable activity on the treadmills, I was shaken! In all that time we tried to save that man's life, not one of those men and women stopped what they were doing. Just five feet in front of them, a team of medics and I tried in vain to save a life. We worked on that man in vain for about for about thirty minutes. While we were trying to save this man's life, all those people working out on the treadmills continued to drink their Starbucks lattés, talk to one another, watch TV, and listen to their iPods without a care in the world. They acted as if we were not in the room as this man's life was slipping away. I turned to Father Rene and said, "Did I miss something?" Father Rene, too stunned to say anything, just walked away with his head down. The reactions of those people that day gave me the impression that our fallen world is of out of touch with the

---

[142] Ibid., 35–37, p. 1084.

teaching of God. Instead of serving, my impression that day was "Do what you have to as long as I'm not inconvenient!"

Besides the miracle of life, there is the miracle of love, a kiss, a hug, touch of a hand, growing old, marriage, laughter, the birth of a baby, joy, a tear, breathing, recovering from surgery or an illness, watching a flower open, surviving a traumatic event, near miss of an accident or a storm, music, being young, good news, getting to your destination, coming home from war, surviving cancer and other diseases, feeling a heartbeat, falling in love, getting married, adopting a child, recovering from divorce, illness, addiction, bankruptcy, getting a job, participating on a mission trip, feeling the sun's warmth, snow, wind, the earth's rotation, gravity, space, the cosmos, stars, returning from space, walking on the moon, four seasons, tidal flow, migration, a butterfly, a hummingbird, waking up, human conception, and fetal development. Have you ever wondered how the cellular structure of building a baby occurs? Everything in life is a miracle.

In *Matthew 10:1*, Jesus gives His disciples the power to perform miracles:

Then he summoned his twelve disciples and gave them authority over unclean spirits to drive them out and to cure every disease and illnesses.[143]

After Jesus's ascension into heaven, there were many recorded miracles in the early church. One can read the many lives of the saints and the miracles they performed in life as well as in death. My favorite Saint is Francesco Forgione, widely known as Saint Padre Pio of Pietrelcina. Volumes of books are written about his life and the many gifts Jesus granted him. Padre Pio was granted the stigmata (the wounds of Christ) for fifty years. In addition, he had the ability of bilocation and read the souls of those confessing to him. During World War II, the American fliers in Italy called him the Flying Monk, for many airmen testified to their witnessing him walking in the clouds guiding them. I

---

[143] Ibid., Matthew 10:1, p. 1023.

had a great-aunt that was one of his caretakers, and my godfather had a miracle from him after meeting him in his early days as a young priest. Also close to my heart is Blessed Anne Catherine Emmerich, a German nun who also was a stigmatist. She too has many miracles attributing to her. She is best known for witnessing the passion with Jesus. It is her oral descriptions during her ecstasy vision of Christ's passion that led to the publication of the book *The Dolorous Passion of Our Lord Jesus Christ* and to Mel Gibson's movie *The Passion*. It is important to note at this time that the Catholic Church is extremely skeptical and incredulous of any miracle claim and supernatural events. All claims are reviewed and investigated with tremendous diligence. Investigations always include skeptical or suspicious scientists and professionals before the church approves the claims. This work may require the church to take many years to render a decision. With that said, let me tell you about some miracles I witnessed.

In 1988, I was married to my former wife, who was three months pregnant with our first child; and the doctor discovered a fast heartbeat that was unusual for a fetus in that stage of development. Monitoring the fetus for several weeks, our doctor noticed it was not getting better. In fact, it was getting dangerous. The fetus was developing ascites (abnormal accumulation of serous fluid in the spaces between tissues and organs in the cavity of the abdomen). Complication of this can lead to blood clots, stroke, paralysis, and death. To treat the fetus, they had to make my wife toxic with the medications. So now I had a very sick wife and an even sicker baby. Nothing was working. So, they increased the dosage. For a time, my wife had to be hospitalized because the toxicity of her medication was presenting symptoms of a heart attack and trying to induce labor. One day I told my wife, "It is time to go and see Charlene." "Who is Charlene?" she asked.

Charlene Richard was a very young, devout Catholic girl that died of leukemia at the age of twelve in 1959. Her burial site is only about thirty miles from my hometown, and I grew up hearing about her miracle intercession stories. Many miracles have been attributed to her.

> *An example of such saintly love is found in the life of a young girl from Acadian who died decades ago, but who leaves behind a legacy of love that all of us can emulate. Charlene Richard is an example to all of us living our life in Christ. She accepted everything that came to her, the bad as well as the good, as coming from the hands of a good and loving God. She knew that God was good and would not treat her badly, and so she had confidence in his continuing goodness to her, even in the light of illness and pain.*[144]

My wife had a doctor's visit the day after we visited her grave and asked for intercession on behalf of our sick unborn baby. Before the visit to the grave, my wife and I had evidence from many ultrasounds that nothing was working. The day after the visit to Charlene's grave, my wife's ultrasound revealed a healthy baby girl! No sign of sickness or illness! A miracle? Yes! Charlene's middle name is *Maria*, and that is also the name of my wife's favorite grandmother. So, the middle name of our daughter became *Maria*.

My father died just three months before my daughter was born. The day my wife called me at the hospital where I was working and said they were going to do an emergency C-section, I was so nervous. By the time I reached the hospital and entered the OR, my wife was already prepped, and the doctor was about to begin the C-section when all of a sudden, I smelled the scent of my father! I told my wife, "My dad is here!" I could smell him; it was overpowering! I knew then everything was going to be all right. Another miracle!

So, miracles do occur every day in front of your eyes. They might be extremely small, or they may be large like the heroic flight of US Airways flight 1549, but they do take place. Just look for them!

The Pharisees and scribes wanted signs (miracles). How many signs and miracles did these so-called educated men of the Hebrew God need? They studied the words of the prophets, so they knew exactly when the Savior would be born and where He would be born. They knew that time of His arrival. These educated men of God are dazzled

---

[144] www.CharleneRichard.com (2013).

GOD AND FREE WILL

and in awe of Jesus when they first met Him teaching in the temple at the age of twelve.

> *After three days they found Jesus in the temple, sitting in the midst of the teachers, listening to them and asking them questions, and all who heard him were astounded at his understanding and his answers.*[145]

It's amazing to me that these same men of the temple who were astounded of a twelve-year-old Jesus were the same men who were asking for His death twenty-one years later!

Now the Pharisees and scribes were inundated with multiple stories of miracles that defy the laws of nature. They saw with their own eyes the results of the sick, cripple, and cursed individuals cured by Jesus. They even spent time following and questioning Him. And still, they could not believe that He was actually the Savior in their mist—the Savior they had spent a lifetime studying and preparing for His coming, the Savior predicted and foretold in the sacred scriptures. They still needed more signs and miracles that would leave them with no doubt!

As I have come to believe just by reading the miracles of Jesus, it is hard to fathom what part of "miracles" they did not understand. Jesus performed some powerful phenomena, wonders, and miracles. I can assure you, the first time I saw someone walk on water, feed five thousand people with a few fish and bread, and bring back a dead man that resided in his grave for three days, I would be on my knees like Wayne and Garth from the movie *Wayne's World* saying, "We're not worthy, we're not worthy, we're not worthy!"

In our own life, how often do we bargain with God and ask for a sign or a miracle? God does not bargain! If you do not believe in the prophets, the historical record of the Bible, or the resurrection of Jesus from the dead, what is it going to take to make you a believer? In other words, we have all that we need. God wants all of us to walk in faith and believe despite the "absence" of signs and miracles. Faith creates trust, and trust shapes and forms a belief. How many times are we just

---
[145] Luke 3: 46–47, National Conferences of Bishops, the New American Bible (Wichita, KS: Devore & Sons, 1981), p. 1097.

as guilty as these scribes and Pharisees still asking for signs when the truth is just before our own eyes?

> *When God does will it, it makes us uncomfortable, we often sidestep it by asking for clearer signs. It's not that we don't know what God wants of us, it's just that we don't trust him enough to want it with him.*[146]

With all our advanced science technology and movie special effects, we have become a world of disbelief. Is it any wonder man still has trouble finding God? To me it seems that miracle skeptics will place their faith in the proof of science rather than their faith. Like the doubting Thomas disciple, we still demand positive evidence before we convert as believers.

Hence, God still has His disciples performing miracles today just as they did since the days of Jesus. Padre Pio, who died in 1968, has thousands of miracles attributed to him. Padre Pio died in 1968, and forty years later, in 2008, his body was exhumed and found to be incorrupt? Perfectly preserved without the slightest hint of decay. Now that's a miracle! After the death of Pope John Paul II, a Roman Catholic nun was proclaimed cured after praying to the deceased pope for intervention. Miracles have been ongoing in Medugorje since June 24, 1981, after the Blessed Mother appeared to children in that communist country. Let's not forget about the countless miracles at Lourdes, Fatima, and Kibeho!

Baton Rouge, Louisiana, is home to Sister Dulce Maria, a Mercedarian Sister of the Blessed Sacrament. Accordingly to her website, Sister Dulce, as she is known, "serves as a catalyst for those wanting and seeking to further their spiritual life as well as interceding with God to heal those suffering with terminal and debilitating illnesses." Since 2005, I have sent hundreds of people that I cared for suffering with cancer to seek Sister's help and intercession. I have witnessed many physical healing and miracles from those patients after visiting Sister. I can spend hours talking about her. I give her contact number and

---

[146] Fr. John Bartunek, *The Better Part* (Hamden, CT: Circle Press, 2007), p. 74.

her information sheet to cancer patients I come in contact with. I am writing about the miracle worker Sister Dulce Maria. This is her story that I copied from an article written by Michaela York:

Georgette, her little pug dog, covered with welts. "Georgie" had eaten poisonous fish and was suffering from a severe reaction. Sister held Georgie and prayed: "Papa, please don't take my dog. I know she has no glory to give you, but please."

Baton Rouge was blessed several years ago with the arrival of Sister Dulce Maria, a nun of the Mercedarian sisters of the Blessed Sacrament. A religious for nearly 50 years, all Sister Dulce ever really wanted in life was to live in community, pray and teach; but papa, as Sister affectionately refers to God, had other plans. Some years ago, after a particularly difficult day ministering to the needs of the immigrant families in her area of California, Sister prayed before the Blessed Sacrament. She said, I was in humungous pain and Papa asked me, what's wrong? "I said, Papa I am in pain." He said, "Show me your hands." I put out my hands, but it was not my hands. My hands were like a crystal, like a glass and inside my hands were His own, wounds and all. He said, "Put your hands where they hurt" and when I did, I woke up. Sister considered the experience a wonderful dream from God.

After a particularly excruciating next day of helping people find apartments, get jobs and receive medical care, Sister returned to her home to find Catherine Alexander sister felt as though another hand was upon her own, and as she stroked her dog which was covered in welts; the welts vanished. Papa had answered her prayers and healed her pug.

Time passed and Sister was called to the home of a lady dying form pancreatic cancer. As was common, Sister had Communion to administer, but the woman was in too much anguish to receive it. Again, sister felt a hand, a force upon her own, that was placed near the woman's pancreas. As sister prayed, searing pain surged through her hands, but she could not physically remove them from the sick woman's body. When the pain subsided, the lady slept, and Sister's swollen hand were released by the invisible power that held it. Papa was calling, and Sister understood. God would heal His suffering people through her touch! *Sister kept silent about her gift, but word spread, and she was sought out for prayers and healing. As she lays hands on the suffering, Sister prays the words given to her by God: "In you name Lord and through your power, heal your servant of (name the problem). I receive and accept (name) into my hands and I give it to you."*

As Sister Dulce Maria continued to pray and worry about the people to whom she ministered, Papa gave her 10 promises. But Sister questioned whether these promises were God given or a result of her own anguish for those who suffered. To alleviate Sister's concern, God would give her "the sign of the dancing fish." She would receive a dolphin, but no one would give it to her and she would not purchase it. Not long afterward, as Sister left a breakfast meeting, something flashed in her face, and when she stooped to pick-up the object, it was a bracelet with 10 dancing dolphins. Some years later, God gave Sister another sign of the dolphin. She was working as a school principal in the Mojave Desert, but Papa said he was sending her East. This time Sister asked for a sign of the white dolphin. One day, sister's precocious 8th graders gave her a present: a white, antique dolphin. Sister understood. "Every time there's going to be a miracle, I get a dolphin." So, she waited for the priest God promised who would move her East.

Today, dolphins surround Sister at the Cypress Springs Mercedarian Prayer Center, built in 2009 through the efforts of "The Sister Dulce Foundation." Through the portals of Baton Rouge, Sister lays hands on God's suffering people: those with cancer, families of the terminally ill, people needing spiritual guidance and lost souls searching healing grace throughout the country and around

GOD AND FREE WILL

the world. Humbly, Sisters says that her job is simply to pray and listen; Papa does the work, she's merely an instrument in His hands.

While suffering is a fact of life, all suffering can lead to greater communion with God. "We have forgotten this is not the only life there is," Sister says. "We are walking toward our eternity; we will be eternal some day; and what a joy to be eternal with the Lord."

I can attest to the many miracles of the patients and friends who contacted me after meeting Sister Dulce. I have several friends cured of breast cancer, a buddy of mine from nursing school cured from liver cancer, and many other patients who were cured or in remission from a number of cancers. A great story that I can personally attest to is about a thirty-yearold female patient that I took care of. She was undergoing her third cervical biopsy for cancer. She was also thirteen weeks pregnant. Her results came back positive for cancer, and her doctor was planning a D&C surgical procedure to remove the cancer. However, the D&C was also going to abort the fetus. So, I spoke with the girl at her bedside in the recovery room and then again with her husband in her hospital room. They were so excited to hear what I had to say about God working miracles through Sister Dulce. I contacted Sister's staff in Baton Rouge that afternoon and asked to have Sister call the girl in her hospital room that night. Well, to my surprise, the next day when I checked the surgery schedule, this girl was not on the surgery list. I then went up to her room, and she was not there. She checked out from the hospital. About two years later, she showed up at the hospital looking for me to show me her beautiful baby girl. Not only did she have the darling baby, but she also had three negative cervical biopsies. All of this occurred after visiting God's modern-day miracle worker.

This is my favorite story about Sister Dulce. In the summer of 2018, I was working at Our Lady of Lourdes Medical Center in Lafayette, Louisiana, as an emergency room staff nurse. One Tuesday morning, the dean of University of Louisiana Nursing School brought her sister to the ER after her sister's doctor called and said she needed to be in the ER now! A CAT scan that morning confirmed the doctor's suspicion that her sister was full of cancer. I informed the patient and her sister that she will be in the ER for quite a while as the hospital was full. There were no rooms at the inn. Throughout the day as I cared for the ill sister, we had several conversations about her cancer, and her outcome was looking bleak. Well, I started taking about Sister Dulce, and by 5:00 p.m. that day, the dean of Nursing said, "We have an appointment with Sister this coming Thursday!" I was shocked! That never happens! It usually takes several weeks to a few months to get an appointment. Later that night I brought the patient to her room and said I would keep her in my prayers. Early the next day while I was again working in the ER, I received word that this patient and her sister wanted to speak to me. It was late afternoon when I finally got upstairs to her room. The patient's sister, the dean, said, "Sister called last night and prayed with my sister and said she will see what she can do. This morning they repeated the CAT scan— !"

In 1982, thousands of people cried out to Segatashya requesting a miracle. They wanted proof that the apparitions they were witnessing before their eyes were really from Jesus and Mary.

"Show us a miracle…Make us believe!" Thousands of pleading voices poured out of the crackly speaker of the tape recorder belonging to our priest, Father Apollinaire Rwagema.

"We want a miracle!" the voices called again and again.

What you're hearing is the sound of 15,000 people some from this very village, pressed together in front of a wooden podium and calling out a young man to make his appearance. They have been waiting for hours to hear the boy, but they weren't really interested in what he was going to say—because they'd come to listen to Jesus. Then a young man began to speak in a gentle, reverent voice. "Yes, Lord, I have told them many times," he said. "No, Lord, they don't listen…they always tell me they want a miracle. They won't believe that you are talking to me, Jesus… not without seeing a miracle or a sign." He paused, as though waiting for a response, then added, "Yes, I will tell them what you say."

Before the young man could finish his sentence, an enormous thunderclap erupted. It was a clear blue, day but the thunder dropped from heaven like a hammer. These many thousands wanted proof, and when God gave it to them, they were terrified. Many of them ran away, some fainted, and others failed to the ground and covered their ears or dropped to their knees crossing themselves. It was a miracle!

"Yes, Lord, I'll tell them as you say...Jesus is telling me that he gave you thunder so you'd listen to his message and not ask for miracles that have no meaning. Our Lord says to stop asking for miracles because your lives are miracles. A true miracle is a child in the womb; a mother's love is a miracle; a forgiving heart is a miracle. Your lives are filled with miracles, but you're distracted by material things to see them. Jesus tells you to open your ears to hear his message and open your hearts to receive his love. Too many people have lost their way and walk the easy road that leads away from God. Jesus says to pray to his mother, and the Blessed Virgin Mary will lead you to God Almighty. The Lord has come to you with message of love and the promise of eternal happiness, yet you ask for miracles instead. Stop looking to the sky for miracles. Open your heart to God; true miracles occur in the heart."[147]

One last miracle story about a little boy as told by Father John on Christmas Day at Our Lady of the Lake Catholic Church. He told us, "As a recently new priest, I was assigned pastor of a very poor church. The parish raised some funds to buy a beautiful Christmas manger scene. Getting ready for the first Christmas Day mass, I noticed that the statue of baby Jesus was missing from His manger. When I asked the few people already in the church about the missing Jesus, they all

---

[147] Immaculee Ilibagiza, *Our Lady of Kibeho* (New York City: Hay House Inc., 2008), pp. xiii–xvi.

said a little boy just came in and removed baby Jesus and ran out the front door. So, I ran out of the church and found the little boy with baby Jesus in a new and bright shiny wagon. When I asked the little boy why he removed baby Jesus from the manger, the little boy replied, 'I promised baby Jesus if I got a wagon for Christmas, I was going to take Him for a ride!' Giving baby Jesus a ride—now that's a miracle!"

It has been said that every conversion to God is a miracle. If you thought that your conversion to God was your own doing, you are very wrong. God's intervention into your heart is why you converted. The miracle of all the miracles is the resurrection. It is written in *Acts 3:40–41* that after hearing Peter's testimony about Jesus Christ's death and resurrection, around three thousand people were baptized that day! What a glorious and miraculous day that was.

Some biblical miracles of Jesus:

- John 2:1–11, simple water turned into wine at the wedding at Cana
- John 4:49–54, healing of a royal official's son from death
- Luke 4:31–37, the cure of a demoniac
- Luke 4:32–39, the cure of Simon's mother-in-law
- Luke 5:1–7, a fishing net full of fish
- Luke 5:12–16, the cleansing of a leper
- Matthew 8:1–4, cleansing of a leper
- Matthew 8:5–13, the healing of a centurion
- Matthew 8:22–27, the calming of the seas
- Matthew 8:28–34, healing of the Gadarene demoniacs
- Mark 2:1–12, healing of a paralytic
- John 5:1–18, cure on a Sabbath
- John 6:1–15, multiplication of the loaves (feeding five thousand)
- John 6:16–21, walking on water
- Mark 3:1–6, healing a withered hand
- Luke 7:1–10, healing of a centurion slave
- Luke 7:11–17, raising of the widow's son

- Mark 5:21–43, healing of Jairus's daughter and the hemorrhage woman
- Matthew 9:27–31, healing of two blind men
- Matthew 9:32–34, healing of a mute person
- Mark 8:1–9, feeding of four thousand
- Luke 9:37–43, healing of a boy with demons
- John 11:1–44, raising Lazarus from the dead
- Luke 17:11–19, healing of ten lepers
- Luke 22:49–51, healing of a servant's ear
- Matthew 21:18–22, the cursing of a fig tree
- Matthew 17:1–8, the transfiguration
- Matthew 28:1–9, the resurrection

Parting your soup is not a miracle, Bruce, it's a magic trick. A single mom who's working two jobs and still finds time to take her son to soccer practice, that's a miracle. A teenager who says no to drugs and yes to an education, that's a miracle. People want Me to do everything for them. What they don't realize is *they* have the power. You want to see a miracle, son? Be the miracle.[148]

Things to ponder alone or with a group:

- What about this story caught your attention, and why?
- Did miracles really occur in the Bible like they are written?
- Are miracles fabricated stories to make us feel good?
- Have you ever experienced a miracle in your life?
- Are miracles truly miracles or just coincidence?
- Do you really need a miracle to believe in Jesus?
- Is Jesus sufficient for this day in your life?
- How many miracles can you attest to be a part of?
- How many times did you behave just like the scribes and Pharisees asking for more signs?

---

[148] *Bruce Almighty* movie quote, written by Steve Koran, Mark O'Keefe, and Steve Oedekerk (2003).

CHAPTER 9

SO MUCH LOVE, SO MUCH SUFFERING

One might ask, how can there be so much love, but yet so much suffering? To understand the question, one must be a fan of the New Orleans Saints football team. After a forty-two-year losing streak, the Saints have finally brought home a Super Bowl trophy in 2010. The fans of the Black and Gold have so much love for the team that they sell out season tickets year after year. However, before becoming Super Bowl champs, many years were wrought with embarrassment and suffering. When I attended nursing school in the 1980s, the Saints were so bad that fans would put paper bags over their heads. Can you imagine going to a professional sporting event with a paper bag over your head? And yet thousands of Saints fans did that! So much love for the team, and yet so much suffering that they hid behind bags. I hope you now understand "so much love, so much suffering."

> *We know that all things work for good for those who love God, who are called according to His purpose.*[149]

---

[149] Romans 8:28, National Conferences of Bishops, the New American Bible (Wichita, KS: Devore &Sons, 1981), p. 1219.

This is usually a very difficult thing to believe and understand when God does not show up to help us the way we believe He should help us in our time of suffering. I know I have asked that question a thousand times. I'm pretty sure Lazarus was wondering the same as his illness worsened. After all, Lazarus was a very good and intimate friend of Jesus. When news of his illness reached Jesus, He remained in Bethany for two more days. Jesus remarked,

> *This illness is not to end in death, but is for the glory of God, that the Son of God may be glorified through it.*[150]

Bethany is about a two-mile hike from where Lazarus lay suffering. Jesus could have quickly walked to his friend's house and relieved him of his illness that was consuming his life. Even if Jesus did not have the ability to leave Bethany, it is apparent that Jesus could have healed Lazarus just through His thoughts, but He did not. Four days later, Jesus is greeted by Martha, the sister of Lazarus, and informs Him that Lazarus is dead.

> *When Jesus saw her weeping and the Jews who had come with her weeping, he became perturbed and deeply troubled.*[151]

In times of great anxieties and trouble, God is testing us to determine our faith just as Jesus tested Martha and her faith. Like Martha, will we endure our faith or give in to the disillusionment of doubt? So strong in her faith,
Martha tells Jesus,

> *I know that whatever you ask of God, God will give you. Jesus replied, I am the resurrection and the life; whoever believes in me, even if he dies, will live and everyone who lives and believes in me will never die. Do you believe this? She said to him, yes Lord. I*

---

[150] Ibid., John 11:4, p. 1153.
[151] Ibid., John 11:33, p. 1154.

have come to believe that you are the Messiah, the Son of God, the one who is coming into the world.[152]

Nothing is beyond Jesus's ability to end suffering. Many had witnessed his love and compassion through His miraculous healing of the blind, lame, deaf, mute, and chronic wounds from leprosy. So, why do we suffer? Where is love in suffering? Why did Jesus pick and choose who suffered and who died and who was cured? After all, even his stepfather, Joseph, succumbed to death. Why did He not use His power to cure this man, of all men, who submitted to God's will to take Mary as his wife and to raise Jesus as his own? To many, including me at times, such questions can haunt us for a lifetime to prayers that were silent from God or answers that took what seemed a million years to answer.

Isaiah 53:1–12 prophesied the suffering Jesus would endure. The prediction describes that Jesus would be hated, rejected, and His life filled with sadness, grief, sorrow, and suffering. But in the end, He is redeemed as King of kings!

> *There was in him no stately bearing to make us look at him, nor appearance that would attract us to him. He was spurned and avoided by men, a man of suffering, accustomed to infirmity, one of those from whom men hide their faces, spurned, and we held him in no esteem. Yet it was our infirmities that He bore and our sufferings that He endured. While we believed Him as stricken, as one infatuated by God and afflicted. He was pierced for our offenses and crushed for our sins. Upon Him was the punishment that makes us whole, and His wounds healed us. We had all gone astray like sheep, each following his own way. But the Lord laid upon Him the guilt of us all. Though He was harshly treated, He submitted and opened not His mouth; like a lamb led to the slaughter or a sheep before the shearers; He was silent and opened not His mouth. Oppressed and condemned He was taken away, and who would*

---

[152] Ibid., 11:22–27, p. 1154.

have thought any more of His destiny? When He was cut off from the land of the living, and stricken for the sins of the people, a grave was assigned Him among the wicked and a burial place with evildoers. Though He had done no wrong nor spoken any falsehood. But the Lord was pleased to crush His infirmity. If He gives His life as an offering of sin, He shall see his descendants in a long life and the will of the Lord shall be accomplished through Him. Because of his affliction He shall see the light in fullness of days. Through His suffering, my servant shall justify many, and their guilt He shall bear. Therefore I will give him his portion among the great and he shall divide the spoils with the mighty, because He surrendered himself to death and was counted among the wicked; and he shall take away the sins of many and win pardon for their offenses.[153]

I often contemplated how bad Jesus's suffering really was. In the garden, several Gospel writers concur that Jesus was "sorrowful unto death."[154] So atrocious was His suffering that "His sweat became as drops of blood trickling down upon the ground."[155] However, the Gospel writers do not go into graphic details of His actual flogging and crucifixion. Was it really grotesque as portrayed in the movie *The Passion*? Yes, according to Dr. Alexander Metherell (board-certified MD, researcher, PhD in engineering, and author of multipublications).

Jesus was suffering from what is called hematidrosis. It's not very common but it is associated with a high degree of psychological stress. Severe anxiety release chemicals that breakdown the capillaries in the sweet glands producing bleeding. This sweat mixed with blood set up the skin to be extremely fragile when flogged by the Roman soldiers. Roman flogging was intentionally brutalized to extract maximum suffering. They usually consisted of thirty-nine lashes but frequently were a lot more. The back would be so shredded that part

---

[153] Isaiah 53:1–12, National Conferences of Bishops, the New American Bible (Wichita, KS: Devore& Sons, 1981), p. 792.
[154] Ibid., Matthew 26:38, p. 1056.
[155] Ibid., Luke 22:44, p. 1130.

of the spine were sometimes exposed. The whipping would have gone all the way from the shoulder down to the back, the buttocks and the back of the legs. One physician who has studied Roman beatings said "the lacerations would tear into the underlying skeletal muscle and the veins were laid bare, and the very muscles, sinews and bowels of the victim were open to exposure." At the crucifixion, "the pain was absolutely unbearable." In fact, it was literally beyond words to describe; they had to invent a new word excruciating; *literally, excruciating means "out of the cross."*[156]

Suffering on the cross and struggling to stay alive, Jesus willfully accomplished the task and surrendered to God's love: "'It is finished,' and bowing His head, He handed over his spirit."[157] Why did Jesus suffer? Jesus suffered to pave the way, to remind the world that He did it first. Pure and simple, to save us! As member of the Trinity, He loves us unconditionally!

God could not show His love more forcibly than by allowing Himself in the presence of the Son to be nailed to the Cross for us. Crucifixion was the most shameful and most horrible method of execution in antiquity. It was forbidden to crucify Roman citizens, whatever crimes they were guilty of. Therefore God entered into the most abysmal suffering of mankind. Since then, no one can say "God does not know what I'm suffering."[158]

Remember it was never God's intention for man to suffer. The sin of Adam and Eve is why we suffer. I have seen my share of suffering as a nurse in the hospitals and as a wound care specialist visiting the nursing homes. I even wrote in previous chapters my own experience of suffering. While no one wants to suffer, suffering can result in

---

[156] Lee Strobel, *The Case for Christ* (Grand Rapids, MI: Zondervan, 1998), pp. 209, 210, 212.
[157] Ibid., John 19:30, p. 1165.
[158] Rev. John Trigilio Jr., PhD, and Rev. Kenneth Brighenti, PhD, *Youth Catechism of the Catholic Church* (San Francisco, CA: Ignatius Press, 2010), p. 67.

a positive outcome. Suffering can bring a person to his/her knees. Suffering produces weakness, and when we are weak and afflicted, it humbles us to ask for help. God wants us to be totally dependent upon Him for all our needs. Please refer back to *Matthew 6:25–33*: "Dependence on God."

Toward the end of his life, Pope John Paul II was so frail and weak that he required help to carry out his final teaching. Many critics expressed remorse seeing the holy pontiff leaning on his staff shaking and confused. Some were hollering to have him step down and resign from his role as the Good Shepherd. But he refused. Pope John Paul was still trying to show the world that with his suffering, one could see God's greatness compared to the smallness of life's problems; that even in dying, there is greatness and dignity.

> *The surest test of love consists in suffering for the loved one, and if God suffered so much for love, the pain we suffer for Him becomes as lovable as love itself. In the troubles which the Lord bestows on you, be patient and conform yourself gladly to the divine heart in the knowledge that all is a continual game on the part of your Lover: Jesus Christ.*[159]

When St. Paul was struggling from a thorn in his flesh placed by an angel of Satan who also beat him, Paul asked God,

> *Three times I begged the Lord about this that it might leave me, but he said to me, "My grace is sufficient for you, for power is made perfect in weakness."*[160]

In simplicity, when the tough gets going, the tough must turn to Christ. When you are undergoing the trial, when you are at your weakest point physically, emotionally, spiritually, this is the prime time to dig into your faith and witness firsthand the power of God working

---

[159] Saint Pio of Pietrelcina.
[160] 2 Corinthians 12: 9, National Conferences of Bishops, the New American Bible (Wichita, KS:Devore & Sons, 1981), p. 1256.

within you. It is this time to produce your great strength and let it shine forth. "The Lord stood by me and gave me strength, so that through me the proclamation might be completed, and all the Gentiles might hear it."[161] God will throw at us many challenges, but the greatest challenge will be death. Our souls are held in the hands of God. So, let not the fear of death cause us to lose our courage, strength, and faith.

Growing up in a small town, my father was the proud papa of seven musically and athletically talented boys. It was not uncommon to read about one of his sons in the paper regarding a great game or a good performance in the school play. My father was a sports fanatic; he loved to play sports with us in the neighborhood, and he coached us in baseball as the Jets. Because my father loved us so much, he sacrificed his ability to watch us play high school sports in favor of watching other parents' children play. It was the wish of my parents that we have a religious education. So, to make that dream come true, my father took a job teaching high school band at the public school so that he could earn the money to send us to the local private Catholic school. Every Friday night, my father was with his band watching the kids of the Wild Cats play, while my mother was watching her sons play for the Screaming Eagles. Can you even fathom the sadness and loneliness my father must have felt not watching his sons exceed in sports or that of my mother's unhappiness in not sharing her joy with her husband? But they did it out of love. My older brother was selected as an all-state player and would receive a scholarship to Tulane. The rest of us excelled as local "all districts" players. My father had to settle for the stories he read in the paper and the firsthand accounts of our play-by-play commentaries. As the seventh brother, by the time I reached high school, the situation was no different. But many afternoons while I was at football practice, I would see my father sitting in the stands watching me.

In 1988, just three months before my daughter was born, my father died of a sudden heart attack while playing golf with some of his friends. The following is a tribute to my father, written by his old elementary school band teacher, Brad Daigle, and published in the local Abbeville

---

[161] Ibid., 2 Timothy 4:17, p. 1317.

paper. For a man who gave so much to others, he received much back in death.

> It was Oliver Wendell Homes Sr. who said "If your name is to live at all, it is so much more to have it live in people's hearts rather than only in their brains! I don't know that one's eyes fill with tears when he thinks of the famous inventor of logarithms." Surely Oliver Wendell Holmes Sr. knew someone like Tony Fontana to be inspired to make such a statement.
>
> I have known Tony Fontana for most of his life, having taught him in elementary school in Donaldsonville, Louisiana in the early 40's. I have seen him through the years at LMEA, LBA and other professional meetings and it was always a delight to be in his company. Never did I realize who Tony Fontana really was in Abbeville, Louisiana.
>
> Tony passed away Wednesday, September 28. The local newspaper said, "It was a sad day in Abbeville Wednesday, September 28, as word of the death of Anthony Jerome Fontana Sr. spread among family, friends and acquaintances who admire his many years of dedication to the church, school, and community." I stopped at a local service station to gas up and ask for directions to the funeral home. The attendant, when I mentioned that I taught Tony said, "He taught us all." It was as evident as I talked to people young and old that Tony had not only been a band director, but he had given of himself to help all in the community.
>
> If a measurement of a man's life is his funeral in death, Tony had to be a giant in the community. To see so many people fill the funeral home and the church to pay their last respects to Tony was an inspiring sight. Rev. Fred Reynolds of Grand Coteau said, "He was an exemplary husband and father and a humble man." To Tony's wife, Evelyn, and their seven sons and their families, we of LMEA who knew him know that although he has left this earth,

his spirit, and his dedication to goodness, his strong love of family, church, friends and country will always live on.[162]

After forty years of teaching, my father informed his sons that he was retiring. Speaking to my father, I expressed dismay. "Why do you want to do this? You love music. You love those kids. It's your life, it's your passion!" His reply to me threw me for a loop. "No, it's not. Jesus and your mother are my life and my passion. And I fear that with her suffering, her depression, I may come home one day to find her dead." My parents were joined as one. When one felt joy and happiness, so did the other; when one suffered, so did the other. Despite the hardships they faced as a couple, as parents, they never wavered in their love for God, their seven sons, or for each other. I honored my father as my best man when I married. I then honored him again with my tears and breaking heart when I gave his eulogy at his funeral.

If you then, who are wicked, know how to give good gifts to your children, how much more with the Father in heaven give.[163]

My mother passed away January 16, 2008, from a long battle with emphysema, but she really died from a broken heart twenty years earlier when my father died. Going through her things, my brother Francis found a letter titled "The Parable of the Popcorn Ball" written by my mother during a time when she was struggling and suffering with her bipolar disorder. Her illness caused her desolation and tested her faith. At this particular moment, she found consolation from God and the purpose to live with hope for another day in making popcorn balls for one of her sons. Sometimes God will use the most ordinary moments of our tormented lives to remind us that we are His children and can trust God with our lives even when the darkness of depression rears its ugly and vicious head. This is her story.

---

[162] Letter to the Editor, *Abbeville Meridional* newspaper (September 1988).
[163] Luke 11:13, National Conferences of Bishops, the New American Bible (Wichita, KS: Devore &Sons, 1981), p. 1113.

At a time in my life when I was struggling to understand, and feel the Father's love for me, many people told me that being able to think of their earthly father's love had helped them. My own father died when I was an infant, so this advice didn't help me at all. At that time, my son Francis was attending college, meeting his expenses by working as a youth director at a nearby Catholic Church. Halloween was approaching, and he called me on a Monday morning to ask if I'd make popcorn balls for a Halloween party for his youth group was having the Friday of the same week. I said I would make the popcorn balls and after finding out how many he wanted and when he would come to pick them up, he said, "Thanks mom," and hung up.

Popcorn balls at Halloween were sort of a tradition in our family when our sons were growing up. Our town has a syrup mill directly across the street from the Catholic Church and we boast it makes the best cane syrup in the world. It's called Steen's Syrup. Their operation of grinding the cane and cooking the syrup always seems to coincide with Halloween, and to leave mass and smell the syrup cooking automatically brings popcorn balls to mind. Since my sons were past the age for "trick or treating" and were no longer even living at home, I was glad to have the opportunity to have someone to make the popcorn balls for.

Friday morning, I assembled the necessary ingredients, got out the gumbo pot and started cooking syrup. As I was stirring the syrup, I sensed a voice saying to me "You see Evelyn, I love you the same way you love Francis, and I want you to trust me the same way he trusts you. When you received his request, you asked how many he needed and the time he would pick them up, and now you are doing exactly what needs doing at exactly the right time it needs to be done.

"Francis knows you love him and because you do, he trusts you. He made the request on Monday, and knew then that when he comes today, the popcorn balls will be ready. He did not call Tuesday to ask if you bought the popcorn, he did not call on Wednesday to find

out if you had enough syrup. He did not call Thursday to tell you what size pot to use; he did not call today to remind you this was the day! He'll be here this afternoon, knowing that the popcorn balls he requested, in just the right number, will be ready.

"I love you in exactly the same way you love Francis, and I want to fill your needs once you tell me what they are. I want you to trust me as Francis trusts you to do exactly what needs to be done at exactly the right time. I won't disappoint you. I am trustworthy, you can count on me."

This next story of love and suffering is from my daughter who was assigned this task by her college professor. She had to write a paper in her mass comm class, and her teacher asked her to write about her recently deceased grandfather—her mother's father—and his sudden death from multiple myeloma:

Alissa Fontana
Professor Anderson
Mass Comm 2010

21 March 2009

In 2008, the Multiple Myeloma Research Foundation expected 19,920 new cases of the blood cancer to be diagnosed in the United States. Most people never imagine he or she will become part of a cancer statistic, but each year five to seven new cases per 100,000 persons of multiple myeloma are diagnosed. Today, there are 46,000 people living in the United States with multiple myeloma, said Michelle Anthony, a nurse practitioner at Ochsner Hospital. Anthony works for Dr. Bizzett, a hematologist-oncologist, a blood cancer doctor. Multiple myeloma is cancer of the blood, which is made in the bone marrow. Usually, it is a very chemotherapy responsive cancer. In most cases, a person receives chemo and the cancer disappears. Then, about three to five years later, the cancer usually comes back and no longer responds to chemo, said Anthony.

Regina Blanz was diagnosed with multiple myeloma at age 47. "I started the chemo. Amazingly, after one round, I achieved complete remission," said Blanz. Three years later, Blanz still remains in remission. However, not every case has a happy ending. Multiple myeloma is more frequent in men than in women. The average age diagnosis is 62 for men and 61 for women. Ninety-six percent of cases are diagnosed in people over 45, and more than 75 percent occur over the age of 70, said Anthony.

Robert Gilberti was a healthy man. He worked out every day and took care of his body. He never imagined at age 74 he would be diagnosed with multiple myeloma and left with only a few weeks to live. Gilberti devoted his entire life to his family. The final days before the multiple myeloma took his life, Gilberti looked around his bedroom at his adoring family and repeatedly told them, "so much love, so much love." Gilberti was born into an Italian family on September 29, 1934 in Summit Hill, PA. While growing up, Gilberti's family lived in many different places such as Long Island, NY. Eventually, his family moved south and settled in New Orleans. When Gilberti was 18, Juanita Matherne moved in the house next door with her family. She quickly captured Gilberti's heart completely. "The first time I saw him, I was in the park and a group of teenage boys was chasing another boy. Bob was the leader of the group. I remember him yelling to his friends 'off with his pants,'" laughed Juanita. "My mom wouldn't let me go to the park after that. Then, we moved into the house next door to his and the rest is history," said Juanita.

Gilberti and Matherne were married on October 11, 1958 and had four children together, three beautiful daughters and one son. For the next 50 years, Gilberti would begin and end everyday with the person he loved the most, his wife Juanita. Two days after their fiftieth wedding anniversary in 2008, Gilberti went into Ochsner Hospital for routine blood work. The primary care physician told Gilberti his blood work showed abnormal kidney function and sent Gilberti to a nephrologist, or a kidney doctor. The nephrologist ran a kidney function test and told Gilberti only 20 percent of his kidneys were functioning.

The reason Gilberti's kidneys were failing was an effect of the multiple myeloma. Multiple myeloma quietly kills the body by pumping misshaped plasma proteins into the body. The kidney's job is to filter out these proteins, but because of the cancer, the misshaped proteins are not filtered out. "As a result, the kidneys are destroyed because the proteins tear up the kidneys," said Paula Fontana, Gilberti's daughter. The nephrologist then sent Gilberti to a hematologist-oncologist who administered a bone marrow aspiration. "My blood ran cold, because oncology is cancer," shivered Juanita. A bone marrow aspiration uses a needle to suck out the liquid bone marrow, which produces elements of blood. "The sample of bone marrow is used to diagnose a number of cancers such as leukemia and multiple Myeloma," said Dr. LeBlanc, Gilberti's oldest grandchild. "I was pretty certain he had multiple myeloma before the diagnosis was actually made," said Dr. LeBlanc. He was right.

Christmas Eve at 2 a.m. Gilberti experienced pain so severe he screamed to his wife for help. He was taken to the emergency room at Ochsner Hospital. "Bob continued to say he did not want to hurt anymore, and the doctor told him he was going to hurt anyway," said Juanita. "He told us Bob had multiple myeloma. He said it was right there in Bob's records," sighed Juanita. A common effect of multiple myeloma is bone pain. "Tumors develop in the bones because of the cancer, causing pain," said Dr. LeBlanc. Gilberti was allowed to go home for Christmas day. The next day he went back to Ochsner for his first chemotherapy treatment. While at Ochsner for chemo, Gilberti began to feel short of breath, and then he could not breathe. He was admitted into Ochsner Hospital that night. "He was on chemo, radiation and dialysis. He was like a pincushion. The nurses were in and out of him with all different kinds of medicines. Being in the hospital was a roller coaster ride. In the morning, everything was good and by the evening everything was wrong," said Juanita.

Then, the worst news came. The doctor told Gilberti the myeloma was in the worst stage, stage 3, and that his prognosis was poor. Gilberti always told his family, if he were ever diagnosed with cancer, he would not take treatment. "He watched too many family members and friends go through awful months of treatment and still pass away. Bob tried the treatment for his family, but it was just too much. It was too late," said Juanita. As a result, "Gilberti decided it was time to go home and let nature take its course," said Juanita. Gilberti went back home Monday January 5, 2009. Gilberti's daughter, Paula Fontana, is a nurse anesthetist, which is a registered nurse who is able to administer drugs. The family hired a hospice nurse to go over the pain medicines with Fontana. "The hospice nurse went over the drugs with me, and I assumed the hospice role. I knew I'd be staying with him until the end. Before the nurse left, she made sure I knew I was his daughter first, and his hospice nurse second," said Fontana. Over the next week, Gilberti's wife, four children and seven grandchildren stayed close by his side." We made sure, as a family, that he knew how much we loved him. We did not want him to have any doubts about the incredible man that he was. He was our family's rock, our heart and soul," said Rebecca Ruppert, Gilberti's youngest child.

The first four days home Gilberti felt good. He was awake, hungry and not in any pain, said Fontana. "The nurses told us he wouldn't make it past the weekend, but he looked so good those first four days back at home. He was joking around, acting like his normal self. I kept thinking there was no way the nurses were right," said Ruppert. Gilberti told his family, "I'm not afraid to die; I just do not want to leave you." However, "Friday night Gilberti became much sicker. He lost his appetite, he could no longer urinate, and he had trouble breathing," said Fontana. "It's difficult to sedate someone into oblivion and be that person's daughter. My heart did not want to let him go, but I knew he was miserable," whispered Fontana. "As a result of Gilberti's kidney failure, a buildup of toxic products eventually put Gilberti into a uremic coma," said Dr. LeBlanc. "We had four beautiful days together as a family. Then, on Saturday a little after 5 p.m., he died in my arms," said Juanita as her tears began to fall.

Gilberti lived 74 years of life to the fullest. He made taking care of his family the priority in his life and was able to watch each person grow into the person they are today. "It turned out to be a blessing. Within the last year of his life, he got to see the birth of his last grandchild. He got to see his oldest grandchild become a doctor and get married. He got to celebrate our fiftieth wedding anniversary with our whole family there. He got to do and see all of these wonderful things without knowing he had a killer disease," said Juanita.

"Multiple myeloma represents two percent of all cancer deaths. The five-year survival rate for multiple myeloma is only 32 percent," said Dr. LeBlanc. "The MMRF is the largest nonprofit foundation dedicated to the search for a cure of multiple myeloma and is considered the number one funder of research in multiple myeloma. The MMRF has raised over $110 million to fund more than 130 research grants at more than 100 research institutions around the world," said Anthony. "Today there are new things coming out all the time. People with myeloma have a better chance than people a few years ago, and it keeps getting better and better. Listen to your doctor and read everything you can. Keep up with all new treatments and trial drugs and procedures. The most important tool I had was information, and I used it to fight this cancer," said Gary Rucato, a multiple myeloma survivor. Along with the 46,000 other people in the United States with multiple myeloma, Gilberti was *never alone in his fight against multiple myeloma. He left his life on Earth, the same way he came in. He was constantly surrounded by "so much love, so much love."*

In my line of work, I hear the same question over and over again from patients: why do we suffer? Why does God allow people to suffer? My real answers to those questions are ones that I keep to myself and do not tell the patients. It is not an answer they want to hear. God did not allow suffering, sin did! In other words, man did! God's plan was altered by sin. As a result, man feels every aspect of sin, and suffering is included. Suffering happens, and it is integrated into our daily life. Suffering does not discriminate, and no one can escape from it. Suffering affects the rich to the poor, from sinners to saints. God will stay by our side and help see us through the trying time. If we embrace suffering and know God is by our side, maybe we can endure it better. Maybe suffering is a way God gets a person to move closer to Him through discipline.

In difficult times, God presence often evades us. But He is there all the same—in fact, He is the one who sends or permits those difficulties. It's his way of driving self-centeredness, arrogance, sensuality and superficiality out of His disciples' hearts, just as He drives these vendors out of the Temple. Jesus sees the true beauty and purpose of our lives more clearly than we do. We have become used to things—habits of the heart and mind, unhealthy attachments, subtly self-seeking desires and false justification—that in fact hinder our growth in holiness.[164] Perhaps suffering is a purging of the soul. In any case, when a person has had enough suffering, they ask for help; no one wants to suffer alone. "Christians should not seek suffering, but when they are confronted with unavoidable suffering, it can become meaningful for them if they unite their suffering with the suffering of Christ."[165]

---

[164] John Bartunek, *The Better Part* (Hamden, CT: Circle Press, 2007), p. 247.
[165] Rev. John Trigilio Jr., PhD, and Rev. Kenneth Brighenti, PhD, *Youth Catechism of the Catholic Church* (San Francisco, CA: Ignatius Press, 2010), p. 67.

SO MUCH LOVE, SO MUCH SUFFERING

Christ suffered for you, leaving you an example that you should follow in his footsteps.[166]

If anyone can understand suffering, it is Job. Have you ever read his story? If you have not, please read it. For you just might be able to rationalize and draw strength from his suffering. In short, here are the CliffsNotes: "Job, an oriental chieftain, pious and upright, richly endowed in his own person and in domestic prosperity, suffers a sudden and complete reversal of fortune. He loses his property and his children; a loathsome disease afflicts his body; and sorrow oppresses his soul. Nevertheless, Job does not complain against God." The CliffsNotes are nothing compared to the entire story of Job. Job does endure unmerciful suffering. He does have very difficult times, and his faith is shaken. But he remains to his keeping in not cursing God, and he preserves. In the end, Job is rewarded many times over. Even as I write this, I can relate to Job; trust me! I lost my wife, lost many friends, lost jobs, lost my car accident lawsuit, lost my house and had to file bankruptcy. To make matters worse, God seemed to be nowhere around. Did I feel frustrated and alone? Yeah! Did I suffer financial hardship? Hell yeah! Sometimes I was so broke I had to scrounge up loose change to put gas into my car. So, what keeps me going you may ask? It is my faith in God.

Suffering was in store for Jesus. It was foretold very early on in the Old Testament (remember reading *Isaiah 53:1–12* prophesy). Jesus cannot escape it; it is His destiny. As a newborn baby, suffering surrounds Jesus as King Herod begins his killing rampage of innocent children.

Behold, the angel of the Lord appears to Joseph in a dream and said; rise, take the child and his mother, flee to Egypt and stay there until I tell. Herod is had been deceived by the Magi he became furious. He ordered the massacre of all the boys in Bethlehem and its vicinity two years and under.[167]

---

[166] 1 Peter 2:21, National Conferences of Bishops, the New American Bible (Wichita, KS: Devore &Sons, 1981), p. 1350.
[167] Ibid., Matthew 2:16, p. 1011.

In the Gospel of *Luke 2:34*, Simeon, who was blessed by God to live to see the Savior, gives the mother of the child Jesus a warning of her suffering to come:

Simeon blessed them and say to his mother Mary, "Behold, this child is destined for the fall and rise of many in Israel, and to be a sign that will be contradicted and you yourself a sword will pierce so that the thoughts of many hearts may be revealed."[168]

What a way to enter the world!

In his ministry, Jesus warns the chosen twelve that they too will have a life of hardship and suffering for following the Savior and heeding to His teaching. Jesus explicitly wanted the apostles to know ahead of time what is required of them if they dip their bread into the cup: "They will hand you over to be tortured and put to death and you will be hated by all the nations on account of my name."[169] How would you like to start off a friendship with someone who gives you a warning like that? Painful execution awaits both Jesus and the Twelve. Jesus suffered to show love and obedience to God for the salvation of man.

Suffering with the love of Christ can build character. I once told my friend Bart, "Embrace your suffering. Don't look at suffering as your cross to bear, rather look at suffering as a gift." We all have our painful crossroads in life. I tell my kids and my CCD students all of the time, "Jesus and the cross are a pair. You will not find one without the other. If you accept Jesus in your heart, the cross will be yours to uphold, and if you uphold the cross, Jesus is there to carry it with you." Jesus suffered to show the world that He is human, and humans depend on one another for help in trying times. Remember the story I wrote in an earlier chapter about Simon of Cyrene coming in from the field as an exhausted and dying Jesus is falling under the heavy burden of the cross and of sin? Simon helps Jesus to Calvary, the site of man's salvation. All in all, suffering is from sin. In the beginning, Adam and Eve were in communion with God. Their freewill act of rebelling, sinning against

---

[168] Ibid., Luke 2:34, p. 1096.
[169] Ibid., Matthew 24:9, p. 1051.

God stained the soul of all generations to come. Jesus came into being so that He may eradicate the stain of original sin. If you are suffering now, remember that Jesus suffered first. He suffered for you, and He suffered for me. Embrace your suffering and call on Jesus to help carry the cross. It will be much easier if you ask for Jesus's help. After all, He is familiar with the route; He traveled that road once before.

> *Now I rejoice in my sufferings for your sake, and in my flesh, I am filling up what is lacking in the afflictions of Christ on behalf of his body, which is the Church.*[170]

There is no Easter Sunday unless we work through Good Friday. In simple words, Jesus suffered immensely and beyond our comprehension on Good Friday, but He received new and everlasting life through the resurrection on Easter. Saint Bridget of Sweden, who died in 1373, wanted to know the numbers of inflictions the Lord received during His passion:

"*I received 5480 blows on my body.*"[171]

Segatashya of Kibeho stated,

> *Jesus said there were 15 other tortures He suffered that people don't know much about. Of course, I wanted to know every pain that the Lord endured for us because He did it for our salvation, so I asked Him to tell me what they were. In retrospect, that was a big mistake on my part. But it seemed like a good idea at the time. Jesus asked, "Do you really want to know what I endure during those 15 sufferings? Very well my child, wait here just a moment." I was really excited and happy because I thought I'd learn secrets, that hidden things would be revealed to me. I thought I was about to embark on a mystical journey of revelation, which I was. I just didn't know it would also be a mystical journey of pain.*

---

[170] Ibid., Colossians 1:24, p. 1294.
[171] *The Piera Prayer Book* (Hickory Corners, MI, 1972), p. 5.

I fell to the ground and felt like someone was smashing my body with clubs and iron rods. There was darkness all around me; I was traveling through a landscape of pure suffering. I tried to stand up—but a great, crushing weight kept knocking me back to the ground, as though boulders were being dropped on me form a great height. I cried out in fear and agony. There was no reply just more blows cracking my bones and breaking my skin. It seemed the battering would never end but after smashing my face against the floor for the 15th time, whatever power had me in its grip released me. I was sure my rib case had been crushed and my lungs ripped open. I was quite certain I would never be able to open my eyes or walk on my own again. After what seemed like an eternity the Virgin Mary returned to me and said, "Now you know some of the suffering my son endured to take the sins of the world away."[172]

To Saint Mary Magdalen of the Sancta Clara Order, Franciscan, Jesus revealed the fifteen secret tortures He suffered:

1. They fastened My feet with a rope and dragged Me over the stepping stones of the staircase, down into a filthy, nauseating cellar.
2. They took off My clothing and stung My body with iron joints.
3. They attached a rope around My body and pulled Me along the ground, from end to end.
4. They hanged Me on a wooden piece with a slipknot until I slipped out and fell down. Overwhelmed by this torture, I wept bloody tears.
5. They tied Me to a post and pierced My body with various arms.
6. They struck Me with stones and burnt Me with blazing embers and torches.
7. They pierced Me with awls; sharp spears tore My skin, flesh, and arteries out of My body.

---

[172] Lee Strobel, *The Case for Christ* (Grand Rapids, MI: Zondervan, 1998), pp. 152, 153, 154.

8. They tied Me to a post and made Me stand, barefoot, on an incandescent metal sheet.
9. They crowned Me with an iron crown and wrapped My eyes with the dirtiest possible rags.
10. They made Me sit on a chair covered with sharp pointed nails, causing deep wounds in My body.
11. They poured on My wounds liquid lead and resin, and after this torture, they pressed Me on the nailed chair, so the nails went deeper and deeper into My flesh.
12. For shame and affliction, they drove needles into the holes of My uprooted beard. Then they tied My hands behind My back and led Me walking out of prison with strikes and blows.
13. They threw Me upon a cross and attached Me so tightly that I could hardly breathe anymore.
14. They threw at My head as I lay on the earth, and they stepped on Me, hurting my breast.
15. They poured into My mouth the most immodest excretions, as they uttered the most infamous expressions about Me.[173]

In *Matthew 5:45*, Jesus is proclaiming that God treats the just and unjust equally and fairly, for the rain falls on both: "for he makes his sun rise on the bad and the good, and causes rain to fall on the just and unjust."[174] This explains the suffering befalling man in natural disasters rather than the judgment of the merits of man.

Death tolls:
    Communicable diseases (AD 165–present day): *650 million*
    Wars (755–present day): *465 million*
    Famine (1800–present day): *65 million*
    Genocides (1492–present day) *56 million*
    Floods (1287–present day): *7 million*
    Earthquakes (AD 526–present day): *5 million*
    Cyclones and hurricanes (1737–present day): *2 million*

---

[173] *Crusaders at Our Lady of Fatima* (Lancaster, CA).
[174] Matthew 5:45, the New American Bible, p. 1016.

Tsunamis (AD 400–present day): *700,000*
Volcanic (79 BC–present day): *300,000*
Atomic bombs (1945): *225,000*[175]

Jerry Rankin sums up suffering in his book *In the Secret Place*:

No one is exempt from suffering. The problem is our thinking of safety in worldly terms of comfort and the absence of suffering rather in terms of our spiritual security in Christ. God will protect us and deliver us, but it may not mean the absence of pain and affliction in this life. He is not only our shield but a bulwark that fortifies our security; however, that security is spiritual.

The Medjugorje visionary Vicka has this to say about suffering in the book *Medjugorje: What's Happening?* by James Mulligan:

For sure suffering cannot be explained. Suffering can only be lived in one's own heart. When the Lord gives us suffering, a cross, pain…this is really a great gift the God gives. We understandably think: How can sickness be a gift? But it's a great gift! Only God knows why He gives this gift and only he knows the reason why and the time when he takes it back. It is up to us how we accept this gift. The Madonna told us that many times, when this gift comes to us, we always ask a thousand questions—she says stop asking questions. It is enough to say, I thank you God for this gift. God has something he wants to give me. I am ready to receive it. I ask only strength and courage so that I may carry on. And also, the Madonna has told us; you don't know how great the value of suffering in the eyes of God is. I am telling you what I am able to through my own suffering… my suffering is a gift…. The Madonna may say to me, Vicka, do this, do that. I await (the suffering) with all my heart, with open arms. Because I want to respond to all the good that the Madonna has given to me, and with the little that my suffering is,

---

[175] "List of Wars and Anthropogenic Disasters by Estimates," "Death Toll," Wikipedia (2013).

I can respond to her love. And so I say to you, dear listeners, about suffering: today there are different kinds of suffering—there is the suffering that God gives, and there is the suffering that we make for ourselves and these are two different things, they don't have the same value. We must try to accept that which the Lord gives, and we must give thanks and when one gives thanks for this great gift, then graces and blessing and everything come sooner. And then we shouldn't say, I'm suffering, I'm in pain. God knows this: accept it, don't talk about it.... Suffering is to be lived in our souls and in our hearts.

I would think that if you saw the Blessed Mother daily for many years, you would have a pass from suffering. However, that is not the case. Vicka knows a great deal about suffering. Although she had many encounters with the Blessed Mother of God, Vicka has suffered with an inoperative brain tumor.

Christians have the task of alleviating suffering in the world. Nevertheless, there will be suffering. In faith we can accept our own suffering and share the suffering of others. In this way human suffering becomes united with the redeeming love of Christ and thus part of the divine power that changes the world for the better.[176]

"IF I HAD WINGS"
by Darius Rucker

Why do we hate, why do we suffer
Why do we make our mistakes and constantly blame one another
Why is there war and why is there killing
Have we forgotten some secret we knew back when we were just children
If I had wings, I'd fly up to heaven
I'd look down from the clouds on everything

---

[176] Rev. John Trigilio Jr., PhD, and Rev. Kenneth Brighenti, PhD, *Youth Catechism of the Catholic Church* (San Francisco, CA: Ignatius Press, 2010), p. 67.

Then I could find all the things we've been missing
I would have all the answers, if I had wings
Like why am I aching and where did I come from
And where will I go when my time here on this earth is done
And what will I leave that will go one forever, oh no
And what can I do while I'm here to make someones life better
If I had wings, I'd fly up to heaven
I'd look down from the clouds on everything
Then I could find all the things we've been missing
I would have all the answers, if I had wings
Ohoho now, If I had wings, I'd would fly up to heaven
I would have all the answers, if I had wings[177]
(http://www.lyricsmode.com/lyrics/d/darius_rucker/if_i_had_wings.html])

Things to contemplate alone or with a group:

- What about this story caught your attention, and why?
- Why do we suffer?
- In times of suffering, why do we think the worst about God? Is suffering part of the requirement to enter the kingdom of heaven?
- Did all the apostles encounter a life of suffering and painful death?
- Can suffering bring salvation?
- Is suffering an end result of sin?
- What is the most suffering you have ever experienced?
- Was Jesus invited into your suffering, or did you think the worst about Him?
- Was God picking on Job? Did he deserve all that suffering?
- Have you ever taken your suffering pain out on your loved ones? The world?

---

[177] Darius Rucker, "If I Had Wings," *Learn to Live* CD (2008).

CHAPTER 10

FAILURE IS NOT AN OPTION

I grew up in the era of the Apollo space program making its debut, and I can remember my parents waking my brothers and I up to watch Neil Armstrong and Buzz Aldrin walk on the moon. I was starstruck, fascinated, and enthralled. I knew right then and there I wanted to be Buck Rogers and become an astronaut. I would play with my next-door neighbor Byron Hebert (pronounced "A-bear") in a very tall tree in his yard, and we would pretend it was our Saturn V rocket. At times that tree became our space capsule and the lunar lander. Byron and I would even take space walks using the garden hose as our umbilical cord attached to our spacecraft. We would even talk in that ultracool way when after the astronaut finished speaking, you would hear the microphone go *beep*: "Roger Byron, I see you descending down the ladder. Beep." (We actually had a ladder against the tree so we could descend from the "lunar tree.") "Okay, John, you are go for lunar landing. Beep." We would actually say the word *beep*. To this day I believe that going into space would be the à la mode of my life. If I had $20 million to blow, you bet I would be calling the Russians and telling them to sign me up. But I would have just a few small problems with space. Fear of bouncing off the atmosphere is a biggie, but throwing up is the other issue. I throw up just going on a kiddie ride. The closest I came to space travel is when I rode on the Mission Space ride at Disney World. But, again, I threw up!

When Gene Kranz, flight director of Apollo 13, pronounced those now famous words, "Failure is not an option," I am sure he never knew the impact that those words would have on our everyday life. That quote and the one by Jim Lovell, "Houston, we have a problem," have been said often to accentuate the significance of any crisis situation. I know that I have used both phrases a thousand times when talking to my children, speaking to my nursing coworkers, and goofing off with my friends. I can guarantee you I have heard those phrases often as a motivating factor to sell more products and to keep my medical sales job.

"Failure is not an option" is true in so many different circumstances that we can apply this expression to our everyday life as we try to eradicate hunger, poverty, illiteracy, homelessness, diseases, racism, war, hate, crime, drug abuse, abortion, devaluing of life, litter, and world recessions. "Failure is not an option" surely was applied to World War II when Germany and Japan inflicted world havoc. Failure was not an option during the Cuban Missile Crisis of 1962. Had President John Kennedy and Soviet Premier Nikita Khrushchev failed in a peaceful resolution, the world might have exploded in its first nuclear war. Failing was definitely not an option for Jesus Christ. Had He failed His mission to the cross, resurrection and salvation for man would never have transpired. Please take a look in your own little world that surrounds you and see how you can apply "Failure is not an option."

Take it from me, no one likes to fail, nor do they want to fail. Failing implies not achieving the goal and earning that esteem that is attached to the accomplishment. In today's culture, failure has a stigma associated with it —defeat, loser, or incompetent; and no one likes to hang out with losers! But most of all, failure is unaccepted. Have you ever read the great Coach Vince Lombardi speech about being number one? I have heard this speech in high school football, as a trainer at LSU, from the head coach to his team during halftime and from the CEO of a billion-dollar-plus medical sales company. This speech is definitely applicable in today's culture about the importance of being number one. Being number 2 is unacceptable in today's culture.

WHAT IT TAKES TO BE NUMBER ONE

Winning is not a sometime thing; it's an all the time thing. You don't win once in a while; you don't do things right once in a while; you do them right all of the time. Winning is a habit. Unfortunately, so is losing. There is no room for second place. There is only one place in my game, and that's first place. I have finished second twice in my time at Green Bay, and I don't ever want to finish second again. There is a second place bowl game, but it is a game for losers played by losers. It is and always has been an American zeal to be first in anything we do, and to win, and to win, and to win. Every time a football player goes to ply his trade he's got to play from the ground up—from the soles of his feet right up to his head. Every inch of him has to play. Some guys play with their heads. That's O.K. You've got to be smart to be number one in any business. But more importantly, you've got to play with your heart, with every fiber of your body. If you're lucky enough to find a guy with a lot of head and a lot of heart, he's never going to come off the field second.

Running a football team is no different than running any other kind of organization—an army, a political party or a business. The principles are the same. The object is to win—to beat the other guy. Maybe that sounds hard or cruel. I don't think it is. It is a reality of life that men are competitive and the most competitive games draw the most competitive men. That's why they are there—to compete. The object is to win fairly, squarely, by the rules—but to win. And in truth, I've never known a man worth his salt who in the long run, deep down in his heart, didn't appreciate the grind, the discipline. There is something in good men that really yearns for discipline and the harsh reality of head to head combat.

I don't say these things because I believe in the "brute" nature of men or that men must be brutalized to be combative. I believe in God, and I believe in human decency. But I firmly believe that any man's finest hour—his greatest fulfillment to all he holds dear—is that moment when he has worked his heart out in a good cause and lies exhausted on the field of battle— victorious. (Coach Vincent T. Lombardi)

In many ways Coach Lombardi and our culture agree on this issue. As a sales rep, if I don't make quota, I will be placed on probation. Make quota, and I keep my job; miss quota two years in a row, and I'm looking for a new job. Everyone knows Neil Armstrong. He is the first man to walk on the moon. But what is the second man on the moon's name? His name is Buzz Aldrin. What's the name of the astronaut flying around the moon? His name is Michael Collins! How about the other ten men that walked on the moon, does anyone remember their names? The winning teams of all our sport championships are invited to visit the president at the White House. Have any of the second-place teams ever received a White House invitation? It does not matter that the second-place team won their division and might have an unbeaten record; they still came in second place. Have you ever attended a kid's ball game? From time to time I watch my friends' young children playing sports, and I am flabbergasted at the reactions of the parents in the bleachers. They are yelling at their kids like it was Super Bowl Sunday. Today's society is intent on not letting children fail; for example, no scores are kept, no wins/loss recorded, and every kid receives a trophy. Some high schools have policies that every child must make the team. I am no child psychologist, but I believe that if we go back to letting kids fail, then maybe they will learn a valuable lesson in life. As they grow into adults, they then can respond appropriately to letdowns and disappointments. Just maybe there would be less addiction and self-esteem disorders. We as a nation place so much emphasis on being number one that when the expectation is unattainable, we become astounded as we see a rise in social ailments, addictions, suicides, and violence.

If someone would ask me, "John, what are you good at?" My reply to that person would be "Failing!" In fact, I am an expert in this area. I have failed so much in my life that LSU should award me an honorary doctorate degree in failing. In fact, if you really examined my life, I actually failed at everything I have tried the first time. I failed first grade because I could not hear as a result of multiple ear surgeries and not being able to understand vowels and phonics. I failed to read, speak, and spell properly (I still have this problem). I failed the very first round of every spelling bee competition my elementary classes held for nine straight years (why nine years when elementary is eight years? I was held back). I struggled all throughout elementary and high school failing many classes. My summers were held in a classroom, not outside playing. I scored a whopping high 13 on my ACT; whereupon entering LSU, I had to take remedial classes my first semester. All of these classes were pass-fail only; no grades were attached. My first year at LSU, I had a GPA of 1.2, and I was placed on academic probation and had to sit out for a semester. I failed my first attempt at taking my nursing boards, my first and second attempts as a business owner, and I failed in my first marriage. I even failed trying to write a book about wound care in 1992. In 2012, I filed personal bankruptcy because my wound care center failed to make a profit. I have sent this manuscript to well over one hundred publishing companies, and I have been rejected well over one hundred times. I also know that each day, I fail in some small or big way with God and Jesus, as I am a struggling sinner. Do I like failing? Hell no!

Are there any times that failing can manufacture a positive outcome? Yes! In fact, the Irish playwright George Bernard Shaw once said, "A life spent making mistakes is not more honorable, but more useful than a life spent doing nothing." Academy Award director James Cameron concurs when he is quoted saying, "Failure is an option, but fear is not." Thomas Edison spoke about his failed attempts creating the light bulb, saying, "We now know a thousand ways not to build a light bulb" and "I haven't failed, I've found 10,000 ways that don't work" and "The most certain way to succeed is always to try just one more time." Robert Kennedy said, "Only those who dare to fail can achieve greatly."[178]

---

[178] All quotes and information taken from the website http://www.des.emory.edu/mfp/OnFailing.html.

His quote reminds me of a bumper sticker I once read that has always stayed in my mind: "Dream big, dare to fail." Those quotes should be embedded in every man, woman, and child in today's world. Then maybe we would have less divorce, addictions, broken hearts and dreams, crimes, etc. Parents, please tell your children that it is okay to succeed, and it's okay to fail. Remember, even Jesus fell to the ground; but He got up, picked that cross up, and continued His journey to Calvary and conquered death. Failing teaches discipline, wisdom, and patience. Life without failure would be monotonous at best. Without failing, how would the success be meaningful? In simple words, failing will eventually lead us to something greater. Here is a good example of one of my failures. When my brother turned forty, we joined him in Oregon to climb Mount Adam. The summit is around 12,276 feet. After a two-day climb, we failed to reach the summit due to inclement weather. We reached approximately eleven thousand feet. Even though I did not reach the top, I still experienced the incredible beauty of the mountain and the bonding and joy I had with my brothers. Spending the night on the mountain, I was able to experience the vast beauty of the stars above me while a thunderstorm rumbled below me. Although I would have liked to say I reached the top, I did not need that to validate the top with my attempt to reach it.

Let's take a look at my failed marriage. My ex-wife and I have failed at our inability to communicate, heal wounds, and stay together, but we have two beautiful and vivacious children. Also, my failed marriage had positive outcomes for me in other ways. I have done things I would probably not be able to do had I been married: buried my demons, opened a wound clinic, participated on foreign medical mission trips, climbed an active volcano, become a religion teacher, and writing this book, to name a few of a lot of things. While I am the "king of failing," it is important to learn from the act of failing. Each time I failed, I regrouped, reexamined what went wrong, adapted, and tried to find new solutions to overcome the obstacles and moved on. I learned from my mistakes. I just didn't give up. I'm persistent. After all, I am the Lizard Man. Here are some of my favorite stories of famous people's failures—people who eventually went on to achieve great things:

- *Apollo 13* failed to reach the moon, which resulted in NASA's finest hour by returning the men safely back to earth.
- *Abraham Lincoln* went to war and came back as a captain and returned a private. He failed in business, as a lawyer, in his first attempt in the legislature, his first attempt to be elected to Congress, for Commission of the General Land Office, in his senatorial election of 1858, and for the vice president position of 1856.
- *Winston Churchill* failed sixth grade and every attempt at public office until his election as prime minister at the age of sixty-two. *Sigmund Freud* was booed from the podium when he first presented his ideas to the scientific community of Europe.
- *Charles Darwin* gave up medical school and was considered by his father and teachers to be that of an "ordinary boy, rather below the common standard of intellect."
- *Albert Einstein* did not speak until he was four years old and did not read until he was seven. He was expelled from school and was refused admittance to the Zurich Polytechnic School. *Thomas Edison's* teachers thought him "too stupid to learn anything." He was fired from his first two employers and failed one thousand times at inventing the light bulb.
- *Louis Pasteur* ranked fifteenth out of twenty-two students in chemistry.
- *Henry Ford* went broke five times.
- *Michael Jordan* was cut from his high school basketball team.
- *Babe Ruth* struck out 1,330 times.
- *Walt Disney* was fired by a newspaper editor because "he lacked imagination and had no good ideas." And the city of Anaheim rejected his proposal for Disneyland "on the grounds that his
- attraction would only attract riffraff."
- *Charles Schultz* had every cartoon he submitted rejected by his high school yearbook staff. Walt Disney wouldn't hire him. *Lucille Ball* was told by her acting instructor to try another profession.

- *Jerry Seinfeld* froze on stage during his first gig and "forgot the English language." He was jeered offstage.
- *Decca Records* and *Columbia Records* turned down signing the Beatles because they "didn't like their sound."
- *Elvis Presley* was fired by Jimmy Denny, manager of the Grand Ole Opry. After only one performance, Elvis was encouraged "to go back to driving a truck."
- *Van Gogh* sold only one painting in his lifetime for $50; he painted over eight hundred.
- *Dr. Seuss*'s first book was rejected twenty-seven times.
- *John Creasey* received 753 rejection slips before publishing 564 books.
- *Orville and Wilbur Wright* were once mischievous students who never graduated from high school.
- *Alvin Charles "Al" Copeland* dropped out of high school at sixteen years old. Net worth when he died estimated at $319 million after creating Popeyes Chicken & Biscuits and several restaurant chains and hotels.
- *Jesus* failed to convert the Jewish nation and many other nonbelievers that He is the Messiah.[179]

Joanne Rowling, a.k.a. J. K. Rowling, is the author of the famous children's book series Harry Potter. If you read her biography, she was divorced after a brief marriage and was trying to raise a baby girl while struggling through a period of poverty and depression when she began writing the Harry Potter series. Today the book series has been printed in over sixty languages with more than 300 million books sold worldwide. In 2004, *Forbes* magazine estimated that J. K. Rowling was worth an estimated $1 billion, making her the first writer to become a billionaire. Another of one of my favorite authors is Laura Hillenbrand. Despite suffering from chronic fatigue syndrome and vertigo, she wrote *Seabiscuit*, which landed her book on the *New York Times* #1 Best Seller

---

[179] All quotes and information taken from the website: http://www.des.emory.edu/mfp/OnFailing.html.

list. She also served as a consultant for Universal Studios when they were making the movie based on her book. She went on to write *Unbroken*, another bestselling book and soon to be a movie.

I was not sure where to place this next story. Although it is a story of "God is calling you," it is also a story concerning "Failure is not an option." Then again, it is a success story in the reverse. The man in this story heard the call of God only after he underwent a metamorphosis as the result of a private crisis. This is the true story of a poor man becoming so wealthy with material items that he finally realized he failed at the most important thing —he was spiritually insolvent, and his marriage was over. Only after he failed did Millard Fuller realize he received a gift from God. Growing up poor in a small Southern town, Millard Fuller learned at an early age that a man's worth was measured by the size of his personal holdings, bank account, and his assets. By the time Millard finished law school in the early sixties, he was earning $50,000 a year. In 1964, Millard Fuller employed over 150 people, and sales exceeded more than $3 million. Not even thirty years of age, Millard had aspiration of sales now exceeding $10 million. This was a huge amount of money for the sixties! However, successful in business, Millard was becoming a failure in his marriage and with his health. The pressure was so great that at times Millard felt he could not breathe, and he had trouble getting himself out of his chair. Stressed wounds were developing on one of his legs. Successful in his business, Millard neglected his wife, and she left him in 1965. At that point, Millard had an examination with himself—a "come to Jesus" moment. He envisioned himself standing before God trying to explain his life's accountability. "Lord, I sold a hell of a lot of cookbooks. In the presence of God, that sounded so ridiculous that I could only cringe."[180] Finally, understanding that his love for God and his wife was his biggest failure, Millard Fuller bared his soul to both God and his wife. To save his soul, Millard sold his business and all his multimillion-dollar financial interests and gave away all the proceeds. Millard Fuller failing at his

---

[180] Sarah Ban Breathnach, *A Man's Journey to Simple Abundance* (Press Book, 2000), p. 277.

marriage made him humble, and he was able to save it. Renewed in faith and love, Millard and his wife would go on to establish Habitat for Humanity International. "Twenty-five years later Habitat for Humanity International has built 85,000 homes for nearly half a million-indigent people."[181]

Steven Paul Jobs, CEO of Apple Inc. Computers, died from pancreatic cancer on October 5, 2011. At the time of his death, Apple Inc. has an estimated net worth of $8.3 billion dollars. It is widely known that Steve dropped out of college and started Apple computers from his garage in the early 1970s. After much financial success, the same company he founded fired Steve in 1985. In 1996, Apple rehired Steve as CEO, a position he would hold until the day he died. In a commencement speech to Stanford University in 2005, Steve Jobs admitted that being fired was the best thing that could had ever happened to him. He too felt devastation and failure, but he did not give up. To truly understand his story, here is a transcript of his commencement speech.

> *I'm honored to be with you today for your commencement from one of the finest universities in the world. Truth be told, I never graduated from college and this is the closest I've ever gotten to a college graduation. Today I want to tell you three stories from my life. That's it. No big deal. Just three stories. The first story is about connecting the dots.*
>
> *I dropped out of Reed College after the first six months but then stayed around as a drop-in for another eighteen months or so before I really quiet. So why did I drop out? It started before I was born. My biological mother was a young, unwed graduate student, and she decided to put me up for adoption. She felt very strongly that I should be adopted by college graduates, so everything was all set for me to be adopted at birth by a lawyer and his wife, except that when I popped out, they decided at the last minute that they really wanted a girl. So my parents, who were on a waiting list, got a call in the*

---

[181] Ibid.

middle of the night asking, "We've got an unexpected baby boy. Do you want him?" They said, "Of course." My biological mother found out later that my mother had never graduated from college and that my father had never graduated from high school. She refused to sign the final adoption papers. She only relented a few months later when my parents promised that I would go to college.

This was the start in my life. And seventeen years later, I did go to college, but I naïvely chose a college that was almost as expensive as Stanford, and all of my working-class parents' savings were being spent on my college tuition. After six months, I couldn't see the value in it. I had no idea what I wanted to do with my life, and no idea of how college was going to help me figure it out, and here I was, spending all the money my parents had saved their entire life. So I decided to drop out and trust that it would all work out OK. It was pretty scary at the time, but looking back, it was one of the best decisions I ever made. The minute I dropped out, I could stop taking the required classes that didn't interest me and begin dropping in on the ones that looked far more interesting. It wasn't all romantic. I didn't have a dorm room, so I slept on the floor in friends' rooms. I returned Coke bottles for the five-cent deposits to buy food with, and I would walk the seven miles across town every Sunday night to get one good meal a week at the Hare Krishna temple. I loved it. And much of what I stumbled into by following my curiosity and intuition turned out to be priceless later on. Let me give you one example.

Reed College at that time offered perhaps the best calligraphy instruction in the country. Throughout the campus every poster, every label on every drawer was beautifully handcalligraphed. Because I had dropped out and didn't have to take the normal classes, I decided to take a calligraphy class to learn how to do this. I learned about serif and sans-serif typefaces, about varying the amount of space between different letter combinations, about what *makes great typography great. It was beautiful, historical, artistically subtle in a way that science can't capture, and I found it fascinating.*

None of this had even a hope of any practical application in my life. But ten years later when we were designing the first Macintosh computer, it all came back to me, and we designed it all into the Mac. It was the first computer with beautiful typography. If I had never dropped in on that single course in college, the Mac would have never had multiple typefaces or proportionally spaced fonts, and since Windows just copied the Mac, it's likely that no personal computer would have them. If I had never dropped out, I would have never dropped in on that calligraphy class and personals computers might not have the wonderful typography that they do. Of course it was impossible to connect the dots looking forward when I was in college, but it was very, very clear looking backwards 10 years later. Again, you can't connect the dots looking forward. You can only connect them looking backwards, so you have to trust that the dots will somehow connect in your future. You have to trust in something—your gut, destiny, life, karma, whatever—because believing that the dots will connect down the road will give you the confidence to follow your heart, even when it leads you off the well-worn path, and that will make all the difference.

My second story is about love and loss. I was lucky. I found what I loved to do early in life. Woz and I started Apple in my parents' garage when I was twenty. We worked hard and in ten years, Apple had grown from just the two of us in a garage into a $2 billion company with over 4,000 employees. We'd just released our finest creation, the Macintosh, a year earlier, and I'd just turned thirty, and then I got fired. How can you get fired from a company you started? Well, as Apple grew, we hired someone who I thought was very talented to run the company with me, and for the first year or so, things went well. But then our visions of the future began to diverge, and eventually we had a falling out. When we did, our board of directors sided with him, and so at thirty, I was out, and *very publicly out. What had been the focus of my entire adult life was gone, and it was devastating. I really didn't know what to do for a few months. I felt that I had let the previous generation of entrepreneurs down, that I had dropped the baton as it was being passed to me. I met with David Packard and Bob Noyce and tried to apologize for screwing up so badly. I was a very public failure and I even thought about running away from the Valley. But something slowly began to dawn on me. I still loved what I did. The turn of events at Apple had not changed that one bit. I'd been rejected but I was still in love. And so I decided to start over.*

I didn't see it then, but it turned out that getting fired from Apple was the best thing that could have ever happened to me. The heaviness of being successful was replaced by the lightness of being a beginner again, less sure about everything. It freed me to enter one of the most creative periods in my life. During the next five years I started a company named NeXT, another company named Pixar and fell in love with an amazing woman who would become my wife. Pixar went on to create the world's first computer-animated feature film, "Toy Story," and is now the most successful animation studio in the world. In a remarkable turn of events, Apple bought NeXT and I returned to Apple and the technology we developed at NeXT is at the heart of Apple's current renaissance, and Lorene and I have a wonderful family together.

I'm pretty sure none of this would have happened if I hadn't been fired from Apple. It was awful-tasting medicine but I guess the patient needed it. Sometimes life's going to hit you in the head with a brick. Don't lose faith. I'm convinced that the only thing that kept me going was that I loved what I did. You've got to find what you love, and that is as true for work as it is for your lovers. Your work is going to fill a large part of your life, and the only way to be truly satisfied is to do what you believe is great work, and the only way to do great work is to love what you do. If you haven't found it yet, keep looking, and don't settle. As with all matters of the heart, you'll know when you find it, and like any great relationship it just gets better and better as the years roll on. So keep looking. Don't settle.

My third story is about death. When I was 17 I read a quote that went something like "If you live each day as if it was your last, someday you'll most certainly be right." It made an impression on me, and since then, for the past 33 years, I have looked in the mirror every morning and asked myself, "If today were the last day of my life, would I want to do what I am about to do today?" And whenever the answer has been "no" for too many days in a row, I know I need to change something. Remembering that I'll be dead soon is the most important thing I've ever encountered to help me make the big choices in life, because almost everything—all external expectations, all pride, all fear of embarrassment or failure—these things just fall away in the face of death, leaving only what is truly important. Remembering that you are going to die is the best way I know to avoid the trap of thinking you have something to lose. You are already naked. There is no reason not to follow your heart.

About a year ago, I was diagnosed with cancer. I had a scan at 7:30 in the morning and it clearly showed a tumor on my pancreas. I didn't even know what a pancreas was. The doctors told me this was almost certainly a type of cancer that is incurable, and that I should expect to live no longer than three to six months. My doctor advised me to go home and get my affairs in order, which is doctors' code for "prepare to die." It means to try and tell your kids everything you thought you'd have the next ten years to tell them, in just a few months. It means to make sure that everything is buttoned up so that it will be as easy as possible for your family. It means to say your goodbyes. I lived with that diagnosis all day. Later that evening I had a biopsy where they stuck an endoscope down my throat, through my stomach into my intestines, put a needle into my pancreas and got a few cells from the tumor. I was sedated but my wife, who was there, told me that when they viewed the cells under a microscope, the doctor started crying, because it turned out to be a very rare form of pancreatic cancer that is curable with surgery. I had the surgery and, thankfully, I am fine now.

This was the closest I've been to facing death, and I hope it's the closest I get for a few more decades. Having lived through it, I can now say this to you with a bit more certainty than when death was a useful but purely intellectual concept. No one wants to die, even people who want to go to Heaven don't want to die to get there, and yet, death is the destination we all share. No one has ever escaped it. And that is as it should be, because death is very likely the single best invention of life. It's life's change agent; it clears out the old to make way for the new. Right now, the new is you. But someday, not too long from now, you will gradually become the old and be cleared away. Sorry to be so dramatic, but it's quite true. Your time is limited; so don't waste it living someone else's life. Don't be trapped by dogma, which is living with the results of other people's thinking. Don't let the noise of others' opinions drown out your own inner voice, heart and intuition. They somehow already know what you truly want to become. Everything else is secondary.

When I was young, there was an amazing publication called The Whole Earth Catalogue, which was one of the bibles of my generation. It was created by a fellow named Stuart Brand not far from here in Menlo Park, and he brought it to life with his poetic touch. This was in the late Sixties, before personal computers and desktop publishing, so it was all made with typewriters, scissors, and Polaroid cameras. It was sort of like Google in paperback form thirty-five years before Google came along. I was idealistic, overflowing with neat tools and great notions. Stuart and his team put out several issues of the The Whole Earth Catalogue, and then when it had run its course, they put out a final issue. It was the mid-Seventies and I was your age. On the back cover of their final issue was a photograph of an early morning country road, the kind you might find yourself hitchhiking on if you were so adventurous. Beneath were the words, "Stay hungry, and stay foolish." It was their farewell message as they signed off. "Stay hungry, stay foolish." And I have always wished that for myself, and now, as you graduate to begin anew, I wish that for you. Stay hungry, stay foolish.[182]

Even Saint Peter failed when he denied Jesus three times and when he had a lack of faith while walking on the water, but that did not stop him from becoming Christ's first bishop and the head of His church. The rest of the apostles failed to recognize the divinity of Jesus, and they were nowhere to be found at the crucifixion. After all the miracles and wonders they witnessed Jesus performing, they still failed to see that He was indeed the Son of God. "Who do people say that the Son of man is? They replied: some say John the Baptist, others Elijah, still others Jeremiah or one of the other prophets."[183] In the garden, Jesus asked the apostles to stay "awake and keep watch with me because my soul is sorrowful even to death."[184] But they fell asleep. Such a crucial time to help the Son of God and the future leaders of Jesus's church could not stay awake. Again, at the crucifixion, where are our future church bishops? Only John was at the cross with the holy women; the rest of the apostles were running for the hills. Eventually, all these men who failed Christ in life would become martyrs in death for Him. Do you now get the point that failure can actually be a good thing?

So, what is the moral of this story you may ask? Make opportunity for failures! If you never failed, then maybe you are not doing anything productive. Failing actually indicates that you are putting your fears aside and stepping outside of your comfort zone. Jesus never said it would be easy to be His disciple nor did He promise any earthly reward or a troublefree life just because one declares oneself to be a Christian—on the contrary! So, when things are rough, Jesus is always there for you. In times of failures, embrace the difficulties and remind yourself of the poem "Footprints in the Sand" by Mary Stevenson:

---

[182] Commencement Address 2013, www.huffingtonpost.com/steve-jobs-standford.
[183] Matthew 16:13–14, National Conferences of Bishops, the New American Bible (Wichita, KS:Devore & Sons, 1981), pp. 1034–1035.
[184] Matthew 26:38, the New American Bible, p. 1056.

> *One night I had a dream—I dreamed I was walking along the beach with the Lord and across the sky flashed scenes from my life. For each scene I noticed two sets of footprints, one belonged to me and the other to the Lord. When the last scene of my life flashed before me, I looked back at the footprints in the sand. I noticed that many times along the path of my life, there was only one set of footprints. I also noticed that it happened at the very lowest and saddest times in my life. This really bothered me and I questioned the Lord about it. "Lord, you said that once I decided to follow you, you would walk with me all the way, but I have noticed that during the most troublesome times in my life there is only one set of footprints. I don't understand why in times when I needed you most, you should leave me." The Lord replied, "My precious, precious child, I love you and I would never, never leave you during your times of trial and suffering. When you saw only one set of footprints, it was then that I carried you."*[185]

Regarding this "Footprints in the Sand" poem, there is a cartoon outside of the chaplain's office at Touro Infirmary in New Orleans that goes like this: In frame 1, Jesus is explaining to the man why there are only one set of footprints in the sand. In frame 2, the man asks Jesus, "What is that long wide mark in the sand?" Jesus replies, "Oh, that's when I am dragging you kicking and screaming!"

I don't know what Jesus would say about failing in the eyes of the world, but I believe He would agree with Father John Bartunek's statement: "Christ's Lordship is real, but it differs from what we tend to expect. For Christ, and thus for the Christian, success means fulfilling God's will, even if that requires suffering, humiliation, rejection, and total failure in the eyes of the world."[186] Therefore, never give up, remain persistent in faith, and be strong. God will always accept us regardless of our success and failures. But when it comes to the salvation of your soul, failure is not an option with God.

---

[185] www.footprint-inthesand.com.
[186] Father John Bartunek, *The Better Part* (Hamden, CT: Circle Press, 2007), p. 628.

Things to contemplate alone or with a group:

- What about this story caught your attention, and why?
- How often do we fail at our daily task?
- Why is it that we fail?
- Is God in the center of our lives, or does He revolve around us? Do you invite God in the discussion before accepting the task at hand?
- Is persistence a good thing? What can you learn from it?
- To save a soul, your soul, what are you willing to fail or not to fail?
- What is the key to success that kept the Apollo mission from failing? How can you discern that mission into your daily mission?
- Did Jesus needed help to reach Calvary? Did he accept it willingly or with a grudge?
- What are you willing to do to reach Calvary?
- Dream big—dare to fail. What are your aspirations in life?

CHAPTER 11

TITLES

In September 1997, two women living oceans apart died within six days of each other, and their funerals were televised and watched by billions worldwide. Agnes Gonxha Bojaxhiu, age eighty-seven, died of heart failure while Diana Frances Spencer, age thirty-six, was killed in an auto accident. Diana Frances Spencer had the world at her beck and call while Agnes Gonxha Bojaxhiu gave herself to the world. Diana was bestowed titles after titles while Agnes shunned them except for the one called Mother. If you are my age, then you probably figured out that I am writing about Princess Diana and Mother Teresa. Diana's fairy-tale life began with her marriage to Prince Charles. In her honor, she beheld the titles Princess of Wales, Duchess of Cornwell, Duchess of Rothesay, and Countess of Chester. Princess Diana was known for her beauty, her charity work for AIDS awareness, and leprosy research fundraising. She was also passionate about removing land mines from impoverished and war-torn countries. She appeared in magazines worldwide, and the public and the press focused on her fashion image. She traveled internationally by private planes and royal yachts, dined in the world's finest restaurants, lived in a palace and on private islands, and was protected by military bodyguards. Her public devotion swelled after the birth of her two boys, one of which is destined to become the future king of England. Princess Diana became Lady Diana after divorcing Prince Charles. Shortly after her divorce, the press and public opinions turned against her; and in 1992, Andrew Morton published his unflattering biography of Lady Diana titled *Diana: Her True Story*. Morton fueled the public dismays with his revelations regarding Diana's suicide attempts and many scandalous love affairs. She died alongside her boyfriend in a car crash while fleeing from the paparazzi. The father of the dead boyfriend claimed that the royal family had Diana killed because she was pregnant with his son's baby. This rumor has never been confirmed.

Meanwhile, Agnes Gonxha Bojaxhiu chose the name *Teresa* as her namesake after becoming a Roman Catholic nun. From 1931 to 1948, Sister Teresa taught at St. Mary's high School in Calcutta, India. Moved by the sorrows of her witness, Sister Teresa founded the Missionaries of Charity. This mission was devoted to the sick, poor, orphaned, and dying in the slums of Calcutta. At some point in time, the children of the slums began referring to Sister Teresa as Mother Teresa, an honor that lasted well past her death. "At the time of her death, Mother Teresa's Missionaries of Charity had over 4,000 sisters, and an associated brotherhood of 300 members, operating 610 missions in 123 countries. These included hospices and homes for people with HIV/AIDS, leprosy and tuberculosis, soup kitchens, children's and family counseling programs, personal helpers, orphanages, and schools. The Missionaries of Charity were also aided by co-workers, who numbered over 1 million by the 1990s."[187] Her work for the poor brought her numerous acclaims worldwide, and in 1971, she became the recipient of the Nobel Peace Prize. Other awards included the Nehru Prize, the Balzan Prize, the Templeton Prize, and Magsaysay Award. In death she was beatified by Pope John Paul and honored with *the Saint Teresa of Calcutta*. Of the two popular and powerful women, which one in your opinion held the most humbling titles?

Pasquale Fontana was one of my father's older siblings, and by far he was my favorite uncle from both sides of my parents' relatives. An uneducated man who served in the army during WWII, he went on to become a successful realtor, bar and grocery store owner, reserved

---

[187] www.motherteresa.org.

police officer, sheriff deputy, state police officer, and chief of the fire department. His nickname to all his friends was *Rocky*, but my brothers and I called him Uncle Pas. Uncle Pas was the original Rocky Balboa. Short in stature, he was a powerful strong man with an infectious laugh who took great pride in his physical shape by exercising through boxing, karate, and weight training in his converted garage gym. When I was a tiny tot, he was larger than life when he lifted me off the ground as I hung on his bulging arm muscles. He always encouraged me to exercise, and I enjoyed working out with him in his gym. In the gym I learned many valuable lessons about life and weight training; however, I could never master punching the small hanging boxing bag. I admired and love this man so much that I wanted to honor him by naming my son after him. That did not go over very well, and my daughter and her mother quickly vetoed me. Anyway, *Dominic* is a much more appropriate name for the twenty-first century than *Pasquale*.

Uncle Pas lived his entire life as a bachelor with his bachelor brother Peter and their two unmarried sisters, Annie and Bee. The four siblings lived their final days in the house in which they grew up. The two men shared the back bedroom while my aunts shared the front bedroom. While this may seem very odd in today's culture, my uncles and aunts were extremely devoted to one another as they continued to operate the grocery store that was started by their parents many years earlier. Never blessed with children, my six older brothers and I grew up in their eyes as if we were their own children. Uncle Pas dropped out of high school in the ninth grade to help run the store after his father died. Because his formal education was so limited, my brothers and I became his focus—to see that we received a proper education. Every time we saw him, Uncle Pas was always stressing to us the importance of receiving a formal education. Did I say *stress*? More like shoved down our throats! In my uncle's mind, graduating from college was the only option and key to a successful life and a way of being respected. Being the sons of public school teachers, my Uncle Pas helped many of his seven nephews with financial aid to complete our dreams; I should say his dream— seeing us graduate with a college degree. He was a man impressed with titles! As each one of my brothers graduated from college, our first name somehow become lost in translation as Uncle Pas omitted it when he introduced us to his friends. Rather than saying our names, he would announce the occupation or field of study we were in. For example, my older brother Anthony would be introduced as "his nephew the lawyer" and so on and on! So, in order from oldest to youngest, we were introduced with our *titles*, and we then became "his nephew the lawyer"; Carl was "the actor"; Chris was "the geologist"; Paul was "the doctor" (Paul is actually an occupational therapist, but in Uncle Pas's eyes, he was a doctor); Francis was "the financier"; Robert was "the priest" (he was not a priest; he was studying to be a priest. Later he became a father to six children); and John was…well, I was still in high school, so I was still just "the nephew"—no new title.

Throughout my high school years, my Uncle Pas was always searching for a title for me, and he gave me many suggestions. "Would you like to go to the fire academy at LSU?" "Nope, not for me!" "Maybe you could enter the military academy?" "Don't think so!" "How about a coach or a teacher?" "Does not sound good to me!" Hmm…a title? What would it be? I only had one dream, and that was to play college football. With my poor school performance in the academic arena and my low self-esteem, I actually believed that the only thing I was good in life was sports. Like Rocky Balboa, I believed I was too stupid to earn a college degree, so I focused my attention to developing my body for a future in sports. I excelled in football receiving many "all district and all parish" honors for four straight years. The only title I ever thought of perusing was to become a defensive end for the LSU Tigers and the Dallas Cowboys. I was deeply distressed when no football scholarships were offered. I was invited to USL as a "recruited walk-on" but declined the offer because of my ego and stupid pride. "Are you kidding me? A walk-on? I am way better than that!" Perhaps if I was opened to the Lord's plan and accepted the walk-on position, I could have earned the title of Hall of Famer. Ha ha—not! Pride kept me from trying.

Titles, titles, titles, titles, titles? Why are people so impressed with a title? Why must I have a title? Can't I just be a kid for a while? My mindset was fixed as a failure at such an early age that I never ever thought I would amount to anything. This onset of failure was set in motion when I was held back in first grade for my very poor school performance. The next eight years of elementary was a prison sentence as I struggled to survive taunts, ridicules, and laughter from my fellow classmates regarding my troubles reading, speaking, and failing every weekly spelling bee competition in the first round. Summers were no picnic either. I was always in one summer school program or another, but the end result was always the same—I hated the stigma associated with summer school. With all this working against me, I can still remember to this very day the feeling of doom; and this was during elementary school. High school was no different as I began my freshman year in remedial classes. The only saving grace to me during this first year of academic misery was the fact that I started varsity football and was selected to the all-district team as a freshman. The next three years of high school were filled with more academic horror as I skimped by barely enough to have the GPA (grade point average) for sports eligibility. I was shocked to say the least when my parents forced me to take advanced math (calculus) my senior year. What were they thinking? I could barely pass general math, how would I pass advanced math? How in the world was I going to get into a college if I can't spell, read, write, or pass math? A 36 is a perfect ACT college entrance score. My highest score was a staggering and pathetic 13, and that was after two tries. My exciting ACT score of 13 landed me in the dumb squad my first year of college. All my classes were remedial courses with no grades, just a *passed* or *failed* indication. I felt enormous pressure to select a suitable title to satisfy my Uncle Pas. I felt enormous pressure to excel as my brothers had. This false pressure was something I created in my mind and did not come from my brothers.

My first semester at LSU, I had finished with a whopping 1.9 GPA. My second semester was not much better: 1.2! I was placed on academic probation and sent home. While my brothers and my life passed me by, I was still being introduced as "the nephew." Sitting out of school for a semester was humiliating. I found employment as a truck driver, offshore roustabout, and a bartender. Living at home I often joined my father for his evening walks with our dog Glory. It was during one of these walks that my father enlightened me that his only expectation for me was to develop a righteous relationship with God, to marry, become a husband and a father. His words of wisdom fell on deaf ears as it took almost forty years to comprehend and to penetrate my low self-esteem and title-less world.

Removed from academic probation, I returned to LSU with an epiphany. Prior to first grade, I had multiple ear infections and ear surgeries. The damage to my ears that produced my hearing troubles caused me to hear vowels and phonics wrong. This disorder was the reason that I struggled with reading, spelling, speaking, and comprehending complex problems. Equipped with this knowledge, I now had a better understanding that my poor hearing had a lot to do with my poor academic performance. Empowered with this knowledge, I developed better study skills that improved my grades and school performance. To gain some sports medicine experience, I joined the LSU football team as a student trainer to assist me in reaching my high school goal of becoming a physical therapist and work in the sports medical industry. My Uncle Pas was so proud of me that he was introducing me to his friends as his "nephew the trainer" for the fighting Tigers.

My "trainer" title only lasted for two semesters. After that, I hit a new roadblock. I did not have the GPA for physical therapy school. However, it was high enough to enter nursing school. Dell Flair, a good friend of mine and the head trainer of the LSU football program, left LSU the previous semester for Charity Hospital School of Nursing, and he talked me into following him. While I was not too keen on nursing school, I decided to try nursing school. Once again I struggled in nursing school. I could not pronounce all the medical words much less spell them. However, I remained focus to complete the nursing program, then take the trainer certification exam, and then enter back into the sports medical arena as a nurse-trainer. Well, that never transpired. I fell in love with a classmate during nursing school, eventually married her, and had two children with her. I have remained employed in the nursing community ever since. Since graduating from nursing school in 1983, I have held many titles: husband, father, brother, son, friend, registered nurse, first lieutenant in the Army, business owner, territory manager, diving medic instructor, and clinical wound care specialist.

TITLES

The saddest of all my titles was bestowed on me in 2006; I would become the ex-husband. I am glad that my father and my Uncle Pas never lived to see me earn that title. It was humiliating to share that title with my children, mother, and brothers.

Many years later during one of my therapeutic sessions with my counselor Tim Crowley, Tim quietly gasped and scolded me after I expressed to him, I thought I received my self-worth from the "title" of work I performed. In simpler words, my identity of myself merged into the validation of my work (occupation) performance. Six years later after making that statement to Tim, I now have a much clearer head to understand how shallow and insignificant that comment was. However, over the years, I have often scrutinized and struggled with this notion; what is it about the word *title* that many others like myself seek out to validate self-worth?

The definition of *title* from Wikipedia is "a prefix or suffix added to someone's name to signify either veneration, an official position or academic qualification." In other words, titles denote recognition, honor, prestige, accomplishment, triumph, and success. That's it! Respect and success equal identity! That's why I have been chasing titles all of these years. As a kid struggling with low self-esteem and failing school performance, I was conflicted with the success of my six older brothers and the constant barrage of trying to find myself in a title-less world. In other words, I never had my own identity. My identity was attached to my brothers via the false perceptions of my educators and parents' friends. In other words, I was expected to excel and perform just like my older brothers had. Up until my senior year in high school, I followed in my brothers' footsteps, and I excelled and performed just as a Fontana boy would have. However, the first week of my senior year, I tried to step out from under my brothers' shadows, and I got clobbered. The music teacher at school was a very close friend of our family, and he had taught all my brothers. Because I was so strongly encouraged to take calculus, I quit chorus so that I could have a study hall for calculus. Well, this did not go over well with our music teacher friend, and he actually shunned me. He did not speak to me again until my father's funeral, twelve years later! His behavior toward me had a rippling effect! Other family teachers expressed dismay at my behavior and complained to my parents, who were also furious at me from dropping out of choir. Once I dropped out, once the "Fontana son" dropped out, all the other boys in choir also dropped the class. The rippling effect impacted several very close friends of mine as well; they gave me the cold shoulder as well. Needlessly, I suffered in silence.

Consequently, I grew up believing the false notion that triumph, success, and recognition from a title would fill the void inside my hopeless, empty, lonely, and no-self-esteem soul. Many people just like me, experiencing the same lack of emotions I have felt, may seek out drugs, sex, alcohol, violence, rage, and many other addictions to fulfill that void; I guess I sought out titles. In our culture today, our society emphasizes "the bigger the title, the greater the esteem, respect, and status the general public bestows." But why does our society and culture confuse success with monetary gain and recognizable appellation? Many times, success in life has little or nothing to do with monetary gains. Just like my Uncle Pas addressing his "nephew titles" rather than our names, society today tends to address a certain set of individuals by their recognizable professional occupation status rather than the birth name. The social protocol is to acknowledge their professional work title first, then their name second. Here are many examples:

- Medical: *Doctor so and so*
- Religious: *Father, Cardinal, Reverend, Rabbi, Pastor*
- Royalty: *King, Queen, Prince, Princess, Duke, Earl*
- Judicial: *Attorney General, Supreme Justice, Judge, Police Chief, Sheriff*
- Athletics: *Coach*
- Political: *President, Senator, Congressman/woman, Governor, Mayor*
- Military: *General, Colonel, Major, Captain, Ensign, Sergeant, Specialist, Private*
- Sport: *Hall of Famer*
- Entertainment: *Academy Award Winner*
- Educational: *PhD Doctoral*

Here is another way to look at the above list when I add names to the tittles—now it sounds so much more impressive: President Ronald Reagan; Queen Elizabeth, Prince William, Senator John Glenn, Congresswoman Michele Bachmann; Governor Sarah Palin, Mayor Mark Piazza, Judge Roy Bean, General Colin Powell, Dr. Oz, Dr. Jill Bidden (PhD in education), Academy Award winner Steven Spielberg, Coach Bear Bryant and Coach O., and basketball Hall of Famer Michael Jordan. I may not have had the success as these people have, but I have had some success and personal accomplishments. So, am I not allowed the same courtesy and respect as those previously mentioned names receive? How come I am not introduced as "Louisiana Great 100 Nurse John Fontana" (I received that designation in 1996), Diving and Hyperbaric Instructor John Fontana, Wound Care Certified Specialist Fontana, and Religious Author John Fontana? Thousands of people today are successfully living their ordinary lives working as Jane Doe or Mr. Smith as teachers, plumbers, housekeepers, cooks, construction workers, truck drivers, postal workers, flight attendants, accountants, reporters, engineers, zookeepers, mechanics, nurses, florists, and so on. Are these individuals less important or unsuccessful and deserving of a lesser amount of respect and honor than those who are in the political, military, governmental, and entertainment world? I think not! Does making more money than your neighbor earns or having a bigger title make it any more righteous to behave in a manner unbefitting as if they are better than you? In the old days we all tried to keep up with the Joneses. Today we try to keep up with the Kardashians! Maybe it's time to stop the identity crisis and just be the person we are.

We will now examine some very recognizable famous names that we as a society admired. The next five examples are very small demonstrations of individuals that we as a civilization perceived them to have achieved the highest level of respect, honor, success, fame, notoriety, power, and wealth that an individual can acquire. Many of these individuals appeared to reach the pinnacle of life with all they had achieved, and they were envied by immeasurable amounts of populace throughout this nation and abroad. Despite their broad persona, influential and authoritative titles, this very small random sample of folks you are about to become familiar with may or may not have had what we hoped they had and what we envied and perceived they acquired. Regardless of the titles held by these individuals, for most of them, the outcome of their lives was not so honorable. I obtained this information through Wikipedia research:

Political scandals:
- President Bill Clinton: impeached for perjury; lying about a sexual relationship with a young intern
- President Richard Nixon: resigned in disgrace after covering up Watergate
- Senator Gary Hart, Ted Kennedy, and David Vitter: caught in sex scandal
- Rep. Gary Condit, Bob Packwood, Barney Frank, Anthony Weiner: caught in sex scandals
- Rep. Charles Rangel: guilty of eleven charges by the House Ethic Committee
- Senator Tom Delay: convicted of money laundering
- Rep. Bill Jefferson: convicted of eleven counts of bribery
- Governor Edwin Edward: convicted of racketeering and extortion
- Governor George Ryan: convicted of federal corruption charges
- Governor John Rowland: convicted of mail and tax fraud
- Governor Rod Blagojevich: convicted of eleven charges including trying to sell or trade President Obama's old Senate seat
- Governor Arnold Schwarzenegger: engaged in an adulterous affair and fathered a son with an employee of his
- Senator John Edward: caught in adulterous affair during his failed presidential run; fathered a child with his mistress
- General David Petraeus: resigned as head of the CIA in November of 2012 after admitting to a sexual affair with Paula Broadwell, his biographer

Celebrities' deaths:
- John Belushi (actor): speedball of cocaine and heroin
- John Bonham (Led Zeppelin drummer): choked on vomit after forty shots of vodka
- Chris Bowman (professional ice-skater): cocaine, Valium, pot, and alcohol
- Kurt Cobain (musician, Nirvana): self-inflicted shotgun wound to head
- Chris Farley (actor): cocaine and morphine
- Althea Flynt (copublisher of *Hustler* magazine): heroin
- Judy Garland (actress): secobarbital overdose
- Margaux Hemingway (model/actress): phenobarbital overdose
- Jimi Hendrix (musician): barbiturate overdose
- Abbie Hoffman (political activist): phenobarbital overdose
- Philip Seymour Hoffman (actor): heroin overdose
- Michael Jackson (pop singer): lethal dose of propofol, lorazepam, diazepam, and midazolam
- Janis Joplin (musician): heroin overdose
- Heath Ledger (actor): oxycodone, hydrocodone, diazepam overdose
- Mike "Crash Holly" Lockwood (wrestler): alcohol intoxication
- Vickie Lynn, a.k.a. Anna Nicole Smith (*Playboy* playmate): chloral hydrate and benzodiazepines overdose
- Marilyn Monroe (actress): acute *barbiturate* poisoning
- Jim Morrison (musician, The Doors): heroin overdose
- Brittany Murphy (actress): multiple drug intoxication
- Alice Ormsby-Gore (socialite): heroin overdose
- River Phoenix (actor): heroin and cocaine overdose
- Elvis Presley (singer/actor): multiple drug intoxication
- Freddie Prinze (actor): self-inflicted gunshot wound
- Pat Screen (American football): unspecified drug overdose
- Rod Scurry (Major League Baseball pitcher): cocaine-induced heart attack
- Don Simpson (film producer): cocaine-induced heart attack
- Amy Winehouse (singer): alcohol poisoning

- Whitney Houston (singer/actress): accidental drowning related to cardiac arrest by long history of drug abuse
- Paul Walker (actor): car accident
- Robin Williams (comic/actor): suicide by hanging

Financial misconduct:
- Bernard Madoff: $19 billion Ponzi scheme conviction; sentenced to 150 years in jail
- Timothy Durham (CEO of National Lampoon): arrested for $200 million Ponzi scheme
- Allen Stanford (Stanford International Bank): arrested for massive $8 billion fraud
- Nevin Shapiro: $800 million Ponzi scheme; connected with violating NCAA rules with University of Miami football program
- Ken Lay (CEO, Enron): died before being sentenced to twenty to thirty years in jail for $101 billion corruption scandal

Accused of murder:
- Phil Spector (music producer for the Beatles, Ramones, Teddy Bears, John Lennon, Ike & Tina Turner, and the Righteous Brothers; inducted into the Rock and Roll Hall of Fame): convicted of second-degree murder in 2003 for shooting to death actress Lana Clarkson; serving nineteen years to life
- O. J. Simpson (NFL Hall of Famer/actor): convicted of kidnapping, assault, robbery, and criminal conspiracy; sentenced to thirty-three years; acquitted of murdering his wife Nicole Simpson and Ron Goldman
- Robert Blake (actor): tried and acquitted for the 2001 murder of his wife, but on November 18, 2005, Blake was found liable in a California civil court for her wrongful death
- Vince Marinello (sports radio broadcaster): life in prison for murdering his wife
- C-Murder (Louisiana rapper also known as Corey Miller): sentenced in August 2009, life in prison for the 2002 beating and shooting to death of a sixteen-year-old fan.

- Joseph Lyle Menendez and Erik Galen Menendez: brothers who are known for their conviction in a highly publicized trial for the shotgun murders in 1989 of their wealthy parents—entertainment executive Jose Menendez and his wife Mary; under the terms of the sentences for their multiple crimes, the brothers are expected to spend the remainder of their lives in prison
- Dr. Conrad Murray: guilty for criminal manslaughter in the death of pop singer Michael Jackson; sentenced to four years in prison

Sports celebrities' sex scandals:
- Coach Jerry Sandusky (assistant head coach to Hall of Famer Penn State coach Joe Paterno, former coach for Penn State University): arrested for multiple child molestations in November 2011; sentenced to life imprisonment; convicted in 2012 on forty-five counts of sexual abuse of ten young boys; he faces four hundred years in prison; he most likely will spend the rest of his life in prison; the sex scandal of Penn State forced legendary Head Coach Joe Paterno into retirement and sanctions against the entire football program; NCAA sanctions against Penn State include a $60 million fine and vacated of all wins dating back to 1998
- Coach Dana "Pokey" Chatman (LSU woman basketball coach): resigned in 2007 after having inappropriate conduct and relationship with members of her team
- Tiger Woods (number 1 male golfer in the world): entered a medical clinic for sex addiction after being caught with numerous extramarital affairs, including porn stars and prostitution (2010)
- Rick Pation (head coach for Louisville men basketball): had an extramarital affair involving the estranged wife of his equipment manager; she became pregnant and had an abortion; she demanded $10 million dollars in hush money
- Koby Bryant (professional basketball player for the Los Angeles Lakers): arrested in 2003 for sexual assault of a nineteen-year-old

female; charges were later dropped after the victim refused to testify against him
- Marv Albert (popular sports broadcaster): accused in 1997 for sexual assault; he pleaded guilty to misdemeanor assault and battery
- Jackie Gallagher (LPGA): participated in an extramarital affair with her caddie, resulting in a pregnancy
- Danna Chatman: Head Coach LSU girl basketball. Resigned in 2006 after having sexual relationship with players
- Fritz Peterson and Mike KeKich (Major League Baseball players for the New York Yankees in 1973): made national news when they were caught wife swapping
- Mike Tyson (world champion boxer): convicted in 1992 for rape; sentenced to prison for six years
- Players of the Minnesota Viking professional football team: in 2005, seventeen members of the football team were charged with lewd or lascivious behavior after participating in an all-day sex party at Lake Minnetonka, Minnesota, where prostitutes were brought in from Atlanta and Florida
- Coach Jerry Sandusky: Former Coach for Penn State University was convicted in 2012 on 45 counts of sexual abuse of 10 young boys. He faces 400 years in prison. He most likely will spend the rest of his life in prison. The sex scandal of Penn State forced legendary Head Coach Joe Paterno into force retirement and sanctions against the entire football program. NCAA sanctions against Penn State include a $60 million fine and vacated of all wins dating back to 1998.
- Jimmy Savile: the 2012 ongoing investigation into the deceased knighted BBC television personality has reviled over three hundred people believed to be victims of molestation by Mr. Savile
- Arnold Schwarzenegger (actor/governor/professional bodybuilder): fathered a child outside his marriage
- Matt Laurer: fired from NBC "Today" show November 2017 for multiple inappropriate sexual conduct at work

- Bill O Reilly: Fired from Fox. April 19, 2007 for inappropriate sexual conduct at work
- Chris Matthew: forced to resign from MSNBC for alleged sexual harassment at work
- Harvey Weinstein: CEO, Miramax, movie produced. Found guilty of criminal sex act and rape and sentenced to 23 years in prison

Christian evangelists' and Catholic priests' scandals:
- Jimmy Swaggart (Pentecostal pastor and televangelist seen nationwide and abroad on seventy-eight channels in 104 countries): admitted to soliciting prostitutes
- Jim Baker (televangelist and host of the PTL Club): a sex scandal led to his resignation from the ministry; subsequent revelations of accounting fraud brought about his imprisonment and divorce, which effectively ended his time in the larger public eye
- Robert Tilton: American televangelist who achieved notoriety in the 1980s and early 1990s through his infomercial-styled religious television program Success-N-Life, which at its peak in 1991 aired in all 235 American TV markets (daily in the majority of them), brought in nearly $80 million per year, and was described as "the fastest-growing television ministry in America. However, within two years after ABC's Primetime Live aired an expose into Tilton's fundraising practices, which started a series of investigations into the ministry, Tilton's program was no longer being broadcast
- Kent Hovind (American Baptist minister): had been charged with falsely declaring bankruptcy, making threats against federal officials, filing false complaints, failing to get necessary building permits, and various tax-related charges; he was convicted of fifty-eight federal tax offenses and related charges, for which he is currently serving a ten-year sentence
- Ted Haggard (pastor of the New Life Church in Colorado Springs and was the president of the National Association of Evangelicals [NAE]: it was alleged that Haggard had been

regularly visiting a male prostitute who also provided him with methamphetamines; Haggard admitted to a second homosexual relationship with a male church member
- Cardinal Bernard Law (American cardinal of the Roman Catholic Church): he resigned as archbishop of Boston after documents were revealed that suggested he had covered up thousands of sexual abuses committed by priests in his communities
- Father Gilbert Gauthe (from my hometown church parish): admitted under oath to sexually molesting thirty-seven youngsters; he served jail time
- Bishop Robert Finn: convicted of failing to report suspected child abuse in Kansas City, Missouri, 2012
- Rev. Marcial Maciel Degollado (founder of the Catholic group Regnum Christi): charged of sexual misconduct, including fathering a daughter
- Catholic Church worldwide sex scandal: the Catholic sex abuse cases are a series of convictions, trials, and ongoing investigations into allegations of sex crimes committed by Catholic priests and members of religious orders; these cases began receiving public attention beginning in the mid-1980s; there have been criminal prosecutions of the abusers and civil lawsuits against the church's dioceses and parishes; sexual abuse of minors by priests receives significant media attention in Canada, Ireland, the United States, the United Kingdom, Mexico, Belgium, France, Germany, and many other countries throughout the world.

When all is said and done, does it really matter what titles you have? Although titles do distinguish between the rich and the poor, the famous and the nonfamous, as human beings we all still perform a certain number of tasks the same way despite the title(s) we have or not have. We all put our jeans on one leg at a time, we will all individually die (no one can die for us), and contrary to what women believe and say they don't do, we all fart and poop. Imagine that! Your hottest Victoria's Secret model, president of the United States, Queen of England, etc.—all poop! I guess that's why a toilet is called a throne.

By now I hope that you are beginning to comprehend that titles really do not matter when we put it in perspective to our relationship with God. The only title that we should be seeking to fulfill is the one that designates "through faith you are all children of God in Christ Jesus"[188] and "as proof that you are children, God sent the spirit of his Son into our heart, crying out, Abba, Father"! So, you are no longer a slave but a child, and if a child, then also an heir through God."[189]

Jesus is so unmoved with titles. Just look at the way He reacts to the scribes and the Pharisees.

> Some *scribes, who were Pharisees, saw that he was eating with sinners and tax collectors and said to his disciples "why does he eat with sinners and tax collectors"? Jesus heard this and said to them (that) those who are well do not need a physician, but the sick do. I did not come to call the righteous but sinners.*[190]

In antiquity, dining with someone was a show of mutual respect and a symbolic gesture of friendship and community. Jesus is sharing a meal among sinners, and that is something the righteous Pharisees and scribes would never do lest they become defiled. The religious leaders who held the biggest title of all during the time of Jesus were the "scribes and the Pharisees." In the days of Jesus, these religious but separate groups of priests had immense authority and power over political and religious affairs. In Aramaic, *Pharisees* means "separated ones," and they advocated Jewish religious passion and purity. Caiaphas, the high priest, led the Sadducees, who were members from a dynasty of family-ruling priests. Both these groups of clerics, with strict and obedient training and dedication to the scriptures from the Mosaic laws, set themselves apart from the Gentiles and pagan Romans. By following the strict laws of Moses, these so-called religious leaders blindly thought they would gain moral and spiritual superiority over the rest of the common people.

---

[188] Galatians 3:26, National Conferences of Bishops, the New American Bible (Wichita, KS: Devore& Sons, 1981), p. 1273.
[189] Ibid., 4:6, p. 1273.
[190] Mark 2:16–17, p. 1067.

> *The Pharisees believed in meticulous obedience to Hebrew law which brought every detail of daily life within the province of religion, but they took account of the changing circumstances and oral traditions of interpreting the law, which made them more flexible than that other main group the Sadducees. The Sadducees were violently opposed to the Pharisees and rejected any attempt to adapt the written law to new situations, but their oppositions were intensified by their political stance and their religion privileges.*[191]

Though many scribes and Pharisees may have actually been faithful to the law, most of the religious order devotion was superficial, and their pride was apparent to Jesus, who was not intimidated with their narcissism, insincerity, snobbery, and arrogance. With their immense title as scribes and Pharisees,

> *Jesus understands them perfectly and tirelessly tries to get them to see their own error so that they will be free to see him as their Savior. They are perhaps the most pitiful sinners of all those Jesus came to save, because they failed to recognize their own sin—a persistent phenomenon in the history of salvation.*[192]

By simply dining with sinners, Jesus becomes a threat to the wicked and corrupt temple faction's prominence and temple position. Their only interest is to undermine Jesus with clever condemnation and circulate doubt and to get rid of Him by whatever means. Time and time again, Jesus demonstrates that He can be trusted and that He is the one, the Messiah, that they have been waiting for. What moves Jesus is the character of the heart —those that are open to change and redemption. Because of this openness, it's the sinners, not the Pharisees, who realize that they are in the presence of God.

---

[191] Dr. Ian Barnes, *The Historical Atlas of the Bible* (New York City, NY, Chartwell Books, 2006), p. 257–258.
[192] Fr. John Bartunek, *The Better Part* (Hamden, CT: Circle Press, 2007), p. 361.

I say to you, tax collectors and prostitutes are entering the kingdom of God before you. When John came to you in the way of righteousness, you did not believe him. Yet even when you saw that you did not later change your minds and believe him.[193]

In 1737, Alexander Cruden published *Cruden's Concordance*, where he records 198 different names and titles for Jesus from the King James Bible. In the first chapter of Luke's Gospel, the angel Gabriel addresses Mary with the news she is to bear God's son, and she shall name Him *Jesus*—Hebrew for "God saves."

Behold you shall conceive in your womb and bear a son and he shall be called Jesus. He will be great and will be called Son of the Most High and the Lord God will give him the throne of David.[194]

She was and still is worthy of such a title.

While many people attach the word *Christ* behind *Jesus*, I want to put emphasis that Jesus's last name was not *Christ*. The word *Christ* appears over four hundred times in the New Testament, and *Christ* is another title given to Jesus. *Christ* is the Greek conversion of the Hebrew word meaning *messiah* or *anointed one*. Jesus is assessed many titles from his disciples and the locals who heard his sermons, witnessed his miracles and forgiving of sins. He is often called teacher, lord, rabbi, ribbon, master, and prophet, Lamb of God, the Nazorean, Son of Man, and the Son of God. Pilate even had a plaque placed above his crucified head saying, "King of the Jews." In *John 6:35*, Jesus refers to himself as "I am the bread of Life."[195]

Some in the crowd who heard these words said this is truly the Prophet. But others said the Messiah will not come from Galilee, will he? Does not scripture say that the Messiah will be of David's

---

[193] Matthew 21:31–32, National Conferences of Bishops, the New American Bible (Wichita, KS:Devore & Sons, 1981), p. 1045.
[194] Luke 1:31, the New American Bible, p. 1093.
[195] John 6:35, the New American Bible, p. 1146.

GOD AND FREE WILL

family and come from Bethlehem, the village where David lived? So, a division occurred in the crowd because of him.[196]

With his disciples in the region of Caesarea Philippi, Jesus asked His disciples,

"Who do people say the Son of Man is?" They replied, "Some say you are John the Baptist, others Elijah, still others Jeremiah or one of the prophets." He said to them, "But who do you say that I am?" Simon Peter said in reply, "You are the Messiah, the Son of the living God!"[197]

Now who can top a title like that? No one, except God! My favorite title that God bestows upon Jesus is recorded in *Matthew 3:17*, "And a voice came from the heavens, saying, 'This is my beloved Son, with whom I am well pleased.'"[198]

Why do you presuming have so low an opinion of yourself, when you are so precious to God? Why do you so dishonor yourself when you are so honored by God?[199]

I have often thought of this quotation throughout my life but never could ascribe to it. Consequently, throughout most of my life I can assert that I acted more like the scribes and Pharisees. I was caught up with the false notion believing a title (name, heading, and label) would earn me the respect from my brothers, uncles, parents, friends, and peers. I was too blind to comprehend that my title, my identity that I've been searching for most of my life, is tied to God and only to God. It's that simple! All of my ridiculous fears consumed worthless time going after the wrong values in my life.

---

[196] John 7:40–43, the New American Bible, pp. 1148–1149.
[197] Matthew 16:13–16, the New American Bible, pp. 1034–1035.
[198] Matthew 3:17, the New American Bible, p. 1013.
[199] Saint Peter Chrysologus.

While I often associated myself with the blind scribes and Pharisees, I should have aspired myself to the story of Bartimaeus. Bartimaeus is a blind beggar sitting along the side of the road when he hears that Jesus of Nazareth is approaching. He may be physically impaired from sight, but he is not impaired of the heart. He knows that Jesus can cure him. As Bartimaeus shouts for Jesus's attention, he is scolded and rebuked to remain quiet. Remaining steadfast in his faith, Bartimaeus shouts even louder,

> *"Son of David, have pity on me." Jesus stopped and said, "Call him here." So, they called the blind man saying to him, "Take courage; get up, he is calling you." He threw aside his cloak, sprang up, and came to Jesus. Jesus said to him in reply, "What do you want me to do for you?" The blind man replied to him, "Master, I want to see." Jesus told him, "Go your way; your faith has saved you." Immediately he received his sight and followed him on the way.*[200]

This story of Bartimaeus teaches us many things. First of all, though he is blind, Bartimaeus can see the power and glory of Jesus because he has a heart full of faith. Walking in faith toward God will open the eyes of any and all believers, just as Bartimaeus was allowed to see Jesus as he truly is —the Son of David. Bartimaeus's faith is so strong that he is unmoved by those rebuking him. He will not let this opportunity pass him by. He knows Jesus is full of goodness and compassion, and he will not be stopped in getting what he wants. So, he remains persistent shouting out to Jesus as loud as he can. Being persistent will get you Jesus's attention. So, remain steadfast in your prayers, shout and be persistent! Do not let the moment pass you by when Jesus comes near to you. Did you notice that Jesus did not force Himself upon Bartimaeus? He simply asked, "What do you want Me to do for you?" Jesus is asking us that same question each and every day. He wants us to be totally dependent upon Him. So, tell Jesus each day what you would like from Him. The best part of this story, in my humble opinion, is often

---

[200] Mark 10:46–52, National Conferences of Bishops, the New American Bible (Wichita, KS: Devore& Sons, 1981), p. 1080.

overlooked: "He threw aside his cloak." In the days of Jesus, a person's cloak was more than a coat; it was a valuable item for survival against the harsh elements. A cloak had special compartments (pockets) to hold bread, oil, brush, money, water, and other items to survive. A staff could be placed in the middle of the cloak in order to shield the individual from the sun or protect him from the night's air. So, this phrase, "He threw aside his cloak," represents Bartimaeus abandoning all that he has for the sake of Jesus. In other words, Bartimaeus threw away his material things. We too should be so strong in our faith to abandon all that we have for the sake of Jesus.

May 17, 2019, I received a new title that I am extremely proud of—*husband* and *bonus dad*! I think I will keep this one. I hope and pray that I am able to convey to you that titles do not matter. Being a child of God is the grandest title that we as Christians can have. What other recognition is there?

Jerry: So what about the "maestro" stuff? Did he make you call him *Maestro*?

Elaine: Yeah, I called him *Maestro*.

Jerry: You didn't mind?

Elaine: Well, I did at first, but actually I kind of got used to it.

Jerry: Okay, from now on, I want you to call me "Jerry the Great."

Elaine: I am not calling you "Jerry the Great."

Jerry: Why not? You call him *Maestro*! Elaine: He is a maestro.

Jerry: Well, I'm great.[201]

---

[201] *Seinfeld* TV show, season 7, the "maestro" script.

Things to contemplate alone or with a group:

- What about this story caught your attention, and why?
- What title do you have?
- Does your title make you feel more powerful and entitled than others?
- Does your title exceed that of God's?
- Can you act like Bartimaeus and throw aside your cloak? Why?
- Why not?
- How can you humble yourself?

CHAPTER 12

TEN COMMANDMENTS

Moses: "The Lord, the Lord Jehovah, has given unto you these fifteen—" *Crash!* One of the tablets drops. "Oy...*ten*! Ten Commandments for all to obey!"[202]

I really fail to understand why God gave us Ten Commandments. After all, being the Alpha and the Omega, He knows full well that Adam and Eve were not going to obey their only one directive. For that reason alone, if our maternal great-great-great—(and a whole lot of other "greats") grandparents can't even get one commandment right, what was God thinking when He issued ten more commandments for their inbred descendants to obey? By the way, why did God give Adam and Eve only one commandment (thy shall not eat of the tree...) and then give Moses ten to be handed down for the generations to come?

Do not think that I have come to abolish the law or the prophets. I have not come to abolish but to fulfill. Therefore, whoever break one of these commandments and teach other to do so will be called least in the kingdom of heaven. But whoever obeys and teaches these commandments will be called the greatest in the kingdom of heaven.[203]

---

[202] *History of the World Part I* movie quote, Mel Brooks (1981).
[203] Matthew 5:17–19, National Conferences of Bishops, the New American Bible (Wichita, KS: Devore & Sons, 1981), p. 1015.

TEN COMMANDMENTS

In my Catholic Bible, the Ten Commandments are found in *Exodus 20:1–17*. Silly me, I thought Dave Letterman started the top ten lists! Remember the key word here is *commandments*! It means "divine rule." Notice God did not say these are ten suggestions, ideas, and insinuations. Ten simple commands. Yeah, right! It's not so easy once I break it down. So let's begin.

1: I am the Lord your God. You shall not have other gods besides me. You shall not carve idols for yourself in the sky above or the on the earth below or in the water beneath the earth, you shall not bow down before them or worship them for I the Lord your God, am a jealous God.

Sorry, Rosie Huntington-Whiteley (Victoria's Secret model), Sofia Vergara (actress), Danica Patrick (race car driver), Michelle Pfeiffer (actress), Natascha McElhone (actress), Carla Gugino (actress), Charlize Theron (actress), Paulina Porizkova (model), Paige Spiranac (pro golfer), Margot Robbie (actress), Andrea Canning (*Dateline* anchor), and the Dallas Cowboys Cheerleaders, I can no longer worship you! Because as our Creator, it is only right that we give all of our love, adoration, and attention to God alone. Strange gods before Him is anything worshipped, valued, honored, or held to be more important than God: money, power, fame, materialism, internet, lust, sex, food, new age practices, magic, fortunetellers, esoteric, spiritualism, occult, superstition, divination, simony, etc.

"I am the Lord thy God" also implies to do away with placing *me* first and God second. God is a jealous God—not in the sense when a man becomes jealous, but God must be first. Otherwise, placing God in any other positions means you lost God overall.

"The reality is that we live in a nation that has more idolatry than any other nation on the face of the planet. In the United States and worldwide, idolatry is rampant. We admire songwriters and singers. We idolize sports figures, movie celebrities, preachers, speakers and anyone in high-level positions. We teach our kids idolatry and we do not even realize it. We idolize anyone who looks like they are better than us. We hold them up in the highest of esteem. But that position of esteem belongs only to God."[204] Honoring God also implies that we must pray and give worship to God. Saint Augustine writes, "Idolatry is worshipping anything that ought to be used, or using anything that is meant to be worshipped."[205] The biggest idolatry I find among my tenth-grade CCD students is the *cell phone*! At the beginning of class, I make my students put their cell phones on my desk. I swear they rather lose a limb than part with that cell phone. I am currently attending Southeastern Louisiana University while working toward a master's degree in athletic training. While working across campus, my fellow students do not make eye contact with me or say hello. Why? Because they are looking down at their cell phones! I am amazed they can even walk without bumping into something.

In a recent interview with teenagers, they were asked, "What things do people idolize and put at the center of their lives instead of God?" The most common answers were money, video games, sports, celebrities, and television. One teen said, "You can't live without money, and people find more comfort in something tangible than they find in God, who is intangible." Another teen said, "Our society is very materialistic. The media consistently portray that having money and things bring happiness. God is almost never mentioned as the source of happiness." Regarding video games, another teen said, "All the action in video games is very exciting and makes you feel like you are doing something more interesting than normal life."[206] Idolatry comes in many forms.

Colossians 3:5 reads, "Greed is idolatry and idolatry will lead to greed."[207]

---

[204] Dani Johnson, *Spirit-Driven Success* (Worldwide Distribution, 2009), pp. 71 and 72.
[205] Brian Singer-Towns, *Christian Morality* (Winona, MN: Saint Mary Press, 2012), p. 85.
[206] Brian Singer-Towns, *Christian Morality* (Winona, MN: Saint Mary Press, 2012), p. 81.
[207] Colossians 3:5, the New American Bible, p. 1296.

TEN COMMANDMENTS

2: You shall not take the name of the Lord your God in vain. For the Lord will not leave unpunished him those who takes His name in vain.

Smite me, O Mighty Smiter. Now, I'm not big on blasphemy, but that last one made me laugh.[208]

Then the high priest tore his robes and said he has blasphemed.[209]

The definition of *blasphemy* from Wikipedia is "the act or offense of speaking sacrilegiously about God." In the time of Jesus, blasphemy was such a serious offense against God that you would be put to death. Throughout the Bible, the Jews feared (respected) the Lord so much that it was offensive to even mention or evoke the name of God.

You shall not take the name of the Lord, your God, in vain, for the Lord will not leave him unpunished who takes His name in vain.[210]

Recently there has been a drive to eradicate the use of the N-word because it is so offensive to our African American brothers and sisters. This word is racist, provocative, hurtful, spiteful, and not at all respectful. It is the same way with God. Using *God* as an expletive or any word wishing our Creator to the damnation of hell is taking His name in vain. The commandment about taking the Lord's name in vain has been so demoralized that saying/damning God (*Goddamn*) is an everyday occurrence. It's said so matter-of-fact; most people say it simply without even thinking about it. Be careful using any causal catchphrases, mottos, or slogans that have the intention for the name of God to be used as a curse. Each one of us has a given name we like to be called by, and that is the same with God. God's name is sacred. Using the name of God in any other manner shows a lack of respect.

---

[208] Steven Koren, Mark O'Keefe, Steve Oedekerk, *Bruce Almighty* movie quote (2003).
[209] Matthew 26:65, National Conferences of Bishops, the New American Bible (Wichita, KS: Devore& Sons, 1981), p. 1057.
[210] Deuteronomy 6:11, the New American Bible, p. 167.

Using the name of God in any purposely offensive manner is blasphemy. The name of God is your sincerity and beliefs concerning God. Your conception of God will determine your life and relationship. God created us, so just like the song Aretha Franklin sings, show Him some r-e-s-p-e-c-t! Stop cursing God with that word. Love for God is piety.

"To tell someone your name is a sign of trust. Since God has told us His name, He makes Himself recognizable and grants us access to Him through this name. One must not pronounce the name of God irreverently. For we know Him only because he has entrusted Himself to us. The holy name, after all, is the key to the heart of the Almighty. Therefore, it is a terrible offense to blaspheme God, to curse using God's name, or to make false promises in his name."[211] Respecting God's name is showing reverence. If one is not showing reverence, that is called profanity, and profanity is meaningless, and God is not meaningless!

3: Remember to keep holy the Lord's Day.

God is very clear-cut here. He gave us six days to do as we please, and He is asking us to come and visit Him on the seventh day to give Him thanks and praise. After all, He is our Creator:

Six days you may labor and do work, but the seventh day is the Sabbath of the Lord, your God.[212]

God is asking the very minimum from us. Most church services are around an hour long, so, four services a month for fifty-two weeks is a total of 208 hours of worshiping a year. Can you not give the bare minimum, one hour, out of your week to your Creator? Let's look at it another way. Your employer demands that you give him/her a minimum of forty hours a week.

---

[211] Rev. John Trigilio Jr., PhD, and Rev. Kenneth Brighenti, PhD, *Youth Catechism of the Catholic Church* (San Francisco, CA: Ignatius Press, 2010), pp. 198–199.

[212] Exodus 20:12, National Conferences of Bishops, the New American Bible (Wichita, KS: Devore& Sons, 1981), p. 75.

That is a minimal of 2,080 hours a year of work. In return, your employer gives you a paycheck and maybe some benefits. God gives you eternal life, and for that, we show up just one measly hour a week. If you are praying every day and realize that God is active in every aspect of your daily life, you will conclude that every day of the week is the Sabbath day, for each and every day will be sacred to you. Keeping the Lord's Day is also meant to celebrate together as a community rather than in the privacy of your home.

> *We worship God because He exists and because worship are the appropriate response to His revelation and presence. Worshipping God, however, is also beneficial to men, for it frees them form servitude to the powers of this world. When God is no longer worshipped and when He is no longer thought to be Lord over life and death, others assume that position and put human dignity at risk.*[213]

Around AD 150, Saint Justin Martyr wrote the following:

> *On the day called Sunday, all who live in cities or in the country gather together in one place, and the memoirs of the apostles or the writings of the prophets are read, as long as time permits. When the reader has ceased, the president verbally instructs, and exhorts to the imitation of these good things. Then we all rise and pray, and…when our prayer is ended, bread and wine and water are brought, and the president, in like manner offers prayers and thanksgiving, according to his ability, and the people assent, saying Amen. There is a distribution of the Eucharistic to each person… and to those who are absent a portion is sent by the deacons. And they who are well to do and willing, give what each think fit; and what is collected is used to aid orphans and widows and those who, through sickness or and other cause, are in want. Sunday is the day on which we hold our common assembly, because it is the first day on which God, having worked a change in the darkness and*

---

[213] Rev. John Trigilio Jr., PhD, and Rev. Kenneth Brighenti, PhD, *Youth Catechism of the Catholic Church* (San Francisco, CA: Ignatius Press, 2010), pp. 198–199.

matter, made the world; and Jesus Christ our Savior on the same day rose from the dead.[214]

The lack of respect in which we present ourselves to God at Sunday services is not keeping the Lord's Day respectful and sacred. I'm talking about our lack of proper dress code. When did going to church become causal Friday? Did I miss that memo? I bet you there's a dress code of some sort at your place of work. I know the hospitals where I have worked all have a very strict uniform policy that even includes how you should keep your fingernails, as well as what type of jewelry and shoes you are allowed to wear. Most people attend weddings in a very nice dress or in a coat with a tie. Even going on a date, most people are dressed to the nines. But who changed the rule regarding the dress code for Sunday services? Come on, do you really have to wear flip-flops, T-shirts, short pants, halter-tops, gogo boots, stripper clothes, etc.? I can recall that your Sunday best actually meant just that—the best clothes you have in your closet. Did you know that there was a time when people put on their Sunday best to receive their paycheck from his/her employer? Try going to church to worship God as if you are dressed for a wedding, a date, or work. Give that to God. Beachwear is for the beach, stripper clothes are for…well, strip joints, and Sunday best is for church.

I am often asked, "Why should I go to church? I can pray at home or find God in nature." Yes, that is true, but you cannot receive the incredible gift that Jesus has reserved for you, his body and blood while celebrating with community. "We should not stay away from assembly, as is the custom of some, but encourage one another" (Hebrews 10:25). Responding to this same question poised to me, Saint John Chrysostom replied,

You cannot pray at home as at church, where there is a great multitude, where exclamation are cried out to God as from one great heart, and where there is something more: the union of minds, the accord of souls, the bond of charity, the prayers of the priests.[215]

---

[214] Brian Singer-Towns, *Christian Morality* (Winona, MN: Saint Mary Press, 2012), p. 110.
[215] Ibid., p. 111.

TEN COMMANDMENTS

Out of all the Ten Commandments, the first three pertain to God: worship only Him, respect His name, and make a visit to Him once a week.

4: Honor thy Mother and Father.

Disrespecting your parents is not honoring God!

Honor your father and mother so that you may have a long life in the Land which the Lord, your God, is giving you. Whoever curses his father and mother shall be put to death.[216]

This one commandment is designed to give respect (love) to the two people that gave you life—your parents. This is way different than Father's Day and Mother's Day. God wants us to honor and respect our parents as if every day were Mother's and Father's Days. "The Lord declares for I will honor those who honor me but those who spun me shall be accursed."[217] In simplicity, God is saying, "I will bestow honor to those who honor Me." And honoring your parents is honoring God. Honoring your parents also means giving your parents gratitude, respect, obedience, and assistance in their old age. In the old days, parents became grandparents and then were brought to the children's homes and given a place of honor and respect. They were cared for until the day they died. Honoring your mother and father does not mean putting them in a nursing home to rot to death if you have the means to care for them. If placing your parents in a nursing home is the only option that you have, then so be it; but do not forget about them. Make regular daily visits and take them out to lunch, church, dinner, shopping, etc.; in other words, make sure they are cared for and still considered a valued member of the family. Putting them away because it inconveniences you is not honoring your parents.

---

[216] Deuteronomy 6:16, National Conferences of Bishops, the New American Bible (Wichita, KS:Devore & Sons, 1981), p. 167.

[217] 1 Samuel 2:30, the New American Bible, p. 245.

Are we the only society that has so little love and honor for mom and dad? When my former wife and I built our dream home, we included a fifth bedroom with a full bath, for we knew that someday a member of our elderly family would be coming to live with us. When my mother was in her final years of life, my brothers and I were fortunate enough to provide care for her in her own home with round-the-clock sitters. Please do not abandon your parents. After all, they were up in the middle of the night wiping your butt, changing your diaper, comforting you when you were sick, and so on.

Now, on the flip side, just because you are a sperm or ovary donor does not entitle you to receive the fourth commandment. Abusing and neglecting one's child in any manner is not in keeping with the format of this directive. From the Letters to the Ephesians: "Children obey your parents in everything, for this is pleasing to the Lord. Fathers do not provoke your children, so they may not become discouraged…whatever you do, do from the heart, as for the Lord and not for others."[218] Other references to "honor thy parents": *Proverbs 19:26*, "He who mistreats his father or drives away his mother is a worthless and disgraceful son. *Proverbs 30:17*, "The eye that mocks a father or scorns an aged mother will be plucked out by the ravens in the valley; the young eagles will devour it." And finally, *Psalm 27:10*, "Even if my father and mother forsake me, the Lord will take me in."

5: You shall not kill.

Burt Johnson [*smiling broadly*]: When I was eleven years old, I *killed* a man.

Arthur: Well, when you're eleven, you probably didn't even know there's a law against that. Is Susan here?

Burt Johnson: I knew what I was doing. We were poor. He came into our house to steal our food.

---

[218] Brian Singer-Towns, *Christian Morality* (Winona, MN: Saint Mary Press, 2012), p. 123.

TEN COMMANDMENTS

Arthur: Well, he was asking for it.

Burt Johnson: I took a knife, and I killed him in the kitchen.

Arthur: You, uh…probably ate out that night, what with that man lying in your kitchen.[219]

Killing is not honoring God. There's nothing difficult to understand about this law (unless you happen to live in New Orleans, where killing has become a pastime daily activity). This law actually means you cannot kill. Man is created in the image of God's likeness. When we kill our neighbor, we are also killing the image of our Creator. Man seems to think otherwise. Man has been killing each other since *Genesis 4:1–16*. The story of the "first murder" is on page 5 of the 1,488 pages in my Bible. Page 5! The story of man is just beginning, and suddenly killing makes a very early entrance in history with the story of Cain and Abel. So early in the Bible, and man is already "resentful and crestfallen."[220] Cain seems to think that his only option is killing his brother. The Bible does talk about justified killing, but abortion and euthanasia is not justified killing no matter how much the spin doctors rephrase the word *killing*. As a nurse for thirty-six years, I watched thousands of patients suffer. I used to believe how man can come to think he is easing the burden of the infirmed by offering euthanasia, but Pope John Paul's slow and public death taught me that there is grace and dignity in suffering and dying. Only God has the right to take a life. Killing is offensive to the Creator—God!

> *When men have a fight and hurt a pregnant woman, so that she suffers a miscarriage the guilty one shall be fined as much as the husband demands of him and he shall pay in the presence of the judges. If injury ensures give life for life, hand for hand, foot for foot, burn for burn, wound for wound, stripe for stripe.*[221]

---

[219] Steve Gordon, *Arthur* movie quote (1981).
[220] Genesis 4:5, National Conferences of Bishops, the New American Bible (Wichita, KS: Devore &Sons, 1981), p. 11.
[221] Exodus 21:22, the New American Bible, p. 76.

In the US, some states have laws stipulating, "If harming a mother who is pregnant results in the fetus dying, that person can be charged with feticide. But if a doctor aborts a baby for the sake of the mother's convenience, then it is called justified." Some of these same states have laws prohibiting a condemned man to die by lethal injection, but it is reasonable to kill a fetus with a similar injection. The absurdity of man is spending billions of dollars to find a single germ or bacteria cell on Mars to excitedly declare *life*—but ignoring and killing the cells of life in a woman's womb. In 1973, the USA passed the Endangered Species Act, protecting the killing of certain animals that can result in hefty fines and even prison. For example, killing a bald eagle can result in $100,000 to $500,000 fine and/or imprisonment for one year or both. But killing unborn babies is legal in all fifty US states!

> According to US 2019 abortion statistics, there were 61,905,193 abortions; of this amount, 18,571,558 were black babies. In my state of Louisiana there were 8097 abortions in 2018; 2019 states are not yet compiled. World-wide since 1980, there are 1,521,271,010 abortions. In the first 12 days of the new year, 2020, the US reported 29,663 abortions.

As for murders in the US, Statista.com reports 16,214 murders in the year 2018. Looking at Matt Wright's "Worldwide Statistics of Casualties," he reports there were between 167 million–175 million people killed in wars during the twentieth and twenty-first century. The *Death Penalty Information Center* website reports twenty-two death row executions for the year 2019. In God's view, killing is killing.

"You shall not kill" also means you shall not kill with words and thoughts. In the book *Around the Year with Emmet Fox*, Emmet elaborates on this meaning:

> *Nothing ever dies from the outside. No one can kill your character. No one can kill your peace of mind. No one can kill your business, or your reputation, or anything that is yours. You can, but nobody else can. As soon as you know that nobody can hurt you, then you*

are free to overtake any mistakes, and to be and do the things you want.[222]

First Corinthians 6:19 implies that your body does not belong to you; therefore, you are not allowed to destroy it by any means:

Do you not know that your body is a temple of the Holy Spirit within you, whom you have from God, and that you are not your own? For you have been purchased at a price. Therefore, glorify God in your body.[223]

In other words, your body does not belong to you, it belongs to God. Till death do you part, you are charged as the caretaker of your body. You are not allowed to kill your body with any self-destructive behavior such as eating disorders, drugs, alcohol, euthanasia, suicides, etc. Our bodies and souls do not belong to us, it is the property of God. Our bodies were nothing until God blew life into our souls, and it is for this reason only God can take life back from us.

The fifth commandment is more than just murder. It's also about respecting life. This includes preventing harm in any manner—from rape, torture, assaults of any kind, hazing, euthanasia, suicide, war, and selfindulgences (addictions such as food, alcohol, sex, drugs).

Count Rugen: Are you coming down into the pit? Wesley's got his strength back. I'm starting him on the machine tonight.

Prince Humperdinck: Tyrone, you know how much I love watching you work, but I've got my country's five hundredth anniversary to plan, my wedding to arrange, my wife to murder, and Guilder to frame for it—I'm swamped.[224]

---

[222] Emmet Fox, *Around the Year*.
[223] 1 Corinthians 6:19, National Conferences of Bishops, the New American Bible (Wichita, KS: Devore & Sons, 1981), p. 1236.
[224] Rob Reiner, *Princess Bride* movie quote (1987).

6: You shall not commit adultery.

Rose: Why do men chase women?

Johnny: Well, there's a Bible story…God…God took a rib from Adam and made Eve. Now maybe men chase women to get the rib back. When God took the rib, he left a big hole there, where there used to be something. And the women have that. Now maybe, just maybe, a man isn't complete as a man without a woman.

Rose[*frustrated*]: But why would a man need more than one woman?

Johnny: I don't know. maybe because he fears death. [*Rose looks up, eyes wide, suspicions confirmed*] <u>Rose</u>: That's it! That's the reason!

Johnny: I don't know…

Rose: No! That's it! Thank you! Thank you for answering my question![225]

Committing adultery is not honoring God! I found thirty-four references to "Thou shall not do this deed" in the Bible (beginning with *Genesis* and ending with *Revelation 2:21–23*). The Bible takes an equal position in the Old and New Testament. In both books, "Thou shall not commit adultery" is mentioned seventeen times in one form or another. So, I guess this is a pretty big issue with God.

This standard of conduct is for the sanctity of family. In *Mark 10:11–12*, Jesus says, "Whoever divorces his wife and marries another commits adultery against her and if she divorces her husband and marries another commits adultery against him."[226] The importance of marriage is implied as far back as *Genesis 1:-28* and *2:23–24*.[227] He cannot have Adam and Eve cavorting together in non-matrimony blissful sin as our first maternal parents, now can He? Aha, proof that even our first parents were married! My guess is that God performed

---

[225] John Patrick Shanley, *Moonstruck* movie quote (1987).
[226] Mark 10:11–12, National Conferences of Bishops, the New American Bible (Wichita, KS: Devore & Sons, 1981), p. 1079.
[227] Ibid., pp. 3, 4.

the ceremony. And in *Matthew 19:6*, Jesus validates the Old Testament importance of marriage with his quote: "They are no longer two but one flesh."[228] Jesus validates marriage as He performs His first miracle at a wedding feast.

Archangel Michael: You know, I invented marriage.

Pansy Milbank: Oh really?

Archangel Michael: Yep. All these people were milling around, trying to get together, everything was in chaos, so I told 'em, have a ceremony.[229]

According to the Catholic Church, a valid Catholic marriage is a perpetual bond between a man and a woman that can only be dissolved by death. Upon death of a spouse, the living spouse is allowed to remarry. A valid Catholic marriage is a bond blessed by God with His grace and is expected to last forever. But what happens if a couple divorce? Does the church recognize divorce? Yes, it does. However, in the eyes of the Catholic Church, a divorcee is not permitted to remarry unless the church declares that the marriage was not a valid sacramental act. This is done by way of an annulment. A misconception of an annulment is the dissolution of the marriage per the civil bond. That is not true. The civil bond of the marriage remains, but the sacramental implication is governed to be null. If the annulment is approved, the divorced Catholic is permitted to remarry in the Catholic Church. If the outcome of the marriage is determined to be a valid sacramental deed, then the divorced Catholic is prohibited to remarry. Even the apostle Paul agreed that it is okay to remarry, provided that the marriage is null and void by death.

> *A wife is bound to her husband as long as he lives. But if her husband dies, she is free to be married to whomever she wishes, provided it be in the Lord.*[230]

---

[228] Ibid., p. 1092.
[229] *Michael* movie quote (1996).
[230] 1 Corinthians 7:39, the New American Bible, p. 1238.

Paul also writes,

> *To the married I give this instruction (not I but the Lord): a wife should not separate from her husband—and if she does separate she must either remain single or become reconciled to her husband. It is the same for a husband.*[231]

I need to add a little caveat at this point. If a married couple separates and either of the pair begins a relationship with another, this is considered adultery. Just because one is separated and not divorced still means you are still married!

If you think this is unfair, read *Leviticus 20:10*.

> *If there is a man who commits adultery with another man's wife, one who commits adultery with his friend's wife, the adulterer and the adulteress shall surely be put to death.*[232]

Now that is a dangerous law. Today, some countries in the Middle East have sharia law enforcing this archaic rule.

Proverbs 6:12–14 states that just thinking about an affair of the heart is grounds for adultery:

> *A worthless person, a wicked man, is the one who walks with a perverse mouth, who winks with his eyes, who signals with his feet, Who points with his fingers; who with perversity in his heart continually devises evil.*[233]

Jesus reiterates this aphorism in Matthew 18:8–9.

> *If your hand or foot causes you to sin cut it off and throw it away. It is better for you to enter life maimed or crippled than with two*

---

[231] Ibid., 7:10–11, p. 1236.
[232] Leviticus 20:10, the New American Bible, p. 113.
[233] Proverbs 6:12–14, the New American Bible, p. 639.

hands or two feet to be thrown in eternal fire. And if your eyes cause you to sin, tear it out and throw it away.[234]

Other references to matrimony, divorce, and remarriage are as follows: Mark 10:7–12, "What God joined together let no man separate";[235] Ephesians 5:22–23, "Union of man and wife is the imagine of Christ and his Church";[236] Hebrews 13:4, "Let marriage be honored among all";[237] Malachi 2:14–16, "For I hate divorce says the Lord";[238] 1 Corinthians 7:10–11, "If wife separates, stay single or reconcile."[239]

I am often asked, why does the Catholic Church take such a hard stance on this issue? God created humans to express sexuality; however, expressing sexuality is more than just physical contact, for it involves our emotions, our thoughts, and our spirit. God has every intention for man to be sexual. It was and still is a precious gift given to us by Him. However, God's gift of sexuality is for the purpose of expressing a communion love for one another, creating life, and to provide joy and pleasure. All three purpose of sexuality must not be separated from one another, for they are integrated just as one needs to understand we need our emotions, mind, and spirituality to show our love and commitment to our spouse. Marriage is a sacred covenant, and sexual expression is a sign of that covenant. Today's society would have you think otherwise about marriage and sex. The sacredness of marriage and sexuality has taken a perverse and buzzard approach in today's society. One only has to read any pop culture magazines, watch movies and television shows and commercials to understand that sex is a powerful selling point. For example. I recently read a book called *A Billion Wicked Thoughts* by Ogi Ogas and Sai Gaddam. This book examined Dr. Alfred Kinsey's sexual interview of eighteen thousand people along with the investigation of a billion sex websites that included, but not limited to, erotic stories and

---

[234] Matthew 18:8–9, the New American Bible, p. 1038.
[235] Mark 10:9, the New American Bible, p. 1078.
[236] Ephesians 5:22–23, p. 1283.
[237] Hebrews 13:4, the New American Bible, p. 1339.
[238] Malachi 2:14–16, the New American Bible, p. 993.
[239] 1 Corinthians 7:10–11, the New American Bible, p. 1237.

videos, personal ads, porn sites, and many other sex searches data. The conclusion of the book was mixed with many different opinions. After reading this book, I concluded that mankind is obsessed and consumed with sex in any form and fashion. No wonder we as a race have so much sexual disorders. The sacredness of the body is thrown out the window. It's as if Nike's advertising slogan, "Just do it," was created for sex rather than sportswear! We might as well just "do it in the road" like the Beatles's song implies. And some do! If sexuality were just about pleasing ourselves, then God would have created us just like the animals.

> *The more a person loves another, the more he resembles God. Sexuality must not be separated from love; they go together. The sexual encounter requires the framework of a true dependable love. When sexuality is separated from love and is sought only for the sake of satisfaction, one destroys the meaning of the sexual union of man and woman. Sexual union is the most beautiful bodily, sensual expression of love. People who look for sex without love are lying, because the closeness of their bodies does not correspond to the closeness of their hearts. Someone who does not take his own body language at its word does lasting damage to body and soul. Sex then becomes inhuman; it is degraded to a means of obtaining pleasure and degenerates into a commodity. Only committed, enduring love in a marriage creates a space for sexuality that is experienced in a human way and brings lasting happiness.*[240]

Just so we are all on the same page, the sixth commandment prohibits any desecration of the dignity in marriage. This includes polygamy and cohabitation as well as "friends with benefits"! In addition, falling into this category, the Catholic Church declares fornication, prostitution, masturbation, homosexuality, contraception, in vitro fertilization, artificial insemination, and surrogate mother—all to be immoral and goes against the sixth commandment. Do I agree with all of this? I do not. Nonetheless, this is what my church declares.

---

[240] Rev. John Trigilio Jr., PhD, and Rev. Kenneth Brighenti, PhD, *Youth Catechism of the Catholic Church* (San Francisco, CA: Ignatius Press, 2010), pp. 198–199.

Let me clear up any misconception regarding homosexuality and the Catholic Church. Regardless of the words *gay* or *homosexual*, both are welcome into the Catholic Church. "Same sex attraction is not always freely chosen. In today world, there is generally a greater social acceptance of people with a homosexual orientation, this has not always been true; homosexual men and women have been ridiculed, ostracized, and even attacked and killed. The Catholic Church affirms that people with a homosexual orientation are children of God and must be treated with respect, compassion, and sensitivity. It is a grave moral offense to discriminate, act violently toward, make jokes about or look down on them."[241] With that said, it's the next part of the church's decree that gets everyone confused and in an uproar. "Homosexual men and women, as part of the Body of Christ, homosexual acts are against natural law because they do not allow for the possibility of life."[242] In simple terms, the church is saying that same-sex people engaging in sexual relationship is sinful because same-sex couples cannot produce children in the same traditional manner as man and a woman who are *married* can. Creating a baby is where the term "making love" comes from. While this is the church's stance, I happen to disagree. But that's another topic for a later book. Anyway, if you would like to look up biblical references to this topic, here are a few: Genesis 1:27, Genesis 2:21–24, Genesis 19, Leviticus 18:22, Leviticus 20:13, Romans 1:27, 1 Corinthians 6:9, 1 Timothy 1:9–10. More about this in commandment number 9. So, moving on.

7: You shall not steal.

This one should be a no-brainer, but that is not always the case. Stealing is not honoring God. If you did not purchase, inherit, or receive it as a gift, then it is not yours; don't take it. Oh, just a small footnote: all of those little items that we take from our employer, like paperclips, pens, paper, WiteOut, toilet paper, folders, etc., things that the employer

---

[241] Brian Singer-Towns, *Christian Morality* (Winona, MN: Saint Mary Press, 2012), p. 217.
[242] Ibid., p. 217.

would never miss, that is also considered stealing. Plagiarism, lying on taxes, embezzlement, vandalism, fraud, corporate espionage, idleness at work, school cheating, dishonest business practice, destroying others' property, lust for wealth and materialism, and misleading people in any manner is also stealing. Calling in sick for work when you are not really sick is also stealing. Don't forget about downloading illegal movies and music that were not purchased honestly. One last thing: all those magazines taken from business offices (doctors, attorneys, dentists, etc.) is also stealing. The list can go on and on. Respect other people's property. Read Exodus 22:1–13; it is all about the law of stealing.

8: You shall not bear false witness against your neighbor.

Moral courage is the most valuable and usually the most absent characteristic in men.[243]

Bearing false witness is not honoring God! The Bible has twenty-one references that you can look up regarding this commandment: fourteen in the Old Testament and seven in the New Testament. This commandment pertains to the words we always hear in court: "I swear to tell the truth, the whole truth, and nothing but the truth, G." Be careful with that last part", G"! When you say these words, you are asking God to be a witness. Adam tried that when he threw Eve under the bus and said, "She did it!"

Anyway, just to prove the point, here are a few passages from the Bible regarding this commandment. Proverbs 14:5, "A truthful witness does not lie but a false witness utter lies."[244] Proverbs 19:9, "The false witness will not go unpunished and he who utters lies will perish."[245] Malachi 3:5, "I will draw near to you for judgment, and I will be swift to bear witness against the sorcerers, adulterers and perjurers, those who defraud a hired man of his wages, against those who defraud widows

---

[243] General George Patton quotes.
[244] Proverbs 15:5, National Conferences of Bishops, the New American Bible (Wichita, KS: Devore & Sons, 1981), p. 646.
[245] Proverbs 19:9, the New American Bible, p. 651.

and orphans, those who turn aside the strangers and those who do not fear me says the Lord of host."[246] And in Matthew 7:1–2, "Do not tell lies against other people. Judge not that ye be judged for against with what measure ye judge, ye shall be judged: and with what measure ye mete, it shall be measured to you again"![247]

Jesus tells us in John 14:6 that "I am the way and the truth and the life."[248] True fullness is a virtue. We are actually obligated to tell the truth. Anything else besides telling the truth will have dire consequences. Each time we fail to be honest, we tend to decrease our own morality.

9: You shall not covet your neighbor's wife.

To covet your neighbor's wife is not honoring God! And why would you want to do that? Have you seen her lately? She really isn't that hot after gaining forty pounds. And as for that man, have you seen his beer potbelly and that shinny bald head? I hear he is also a big farter! Well, we are back to the sex thing again. Much of the evil in this world has to do with wanting something that is not yours. Coveting something that you do not merit separates you from God, and it undermines and eventually putrefies your soul. Commandments number 6 and this one are interrelated. God considers His gift of human sexuality as an imperative, and He warns man not to abuse or exploit it. There are two commandments guarding the rule that only *married* people have the privilege to participate in sexual intercourse, just in case you missed, overlooked, or misunderstood commandment number 6. God knows that sexual relations are not intrinsically wicked given that it's intended to be an act of love. After all, he gave us that gift and deemed it good. God also sanctified sex as a sacramental expression of marriage. It's plain and simple really: anything not between a man and wife is insulting God's gift.

The erotic attraction between a man and a woman was created by God and is therefore good; it is part of a person's sexual nature and

---

[246] Malachi 3:5, the New American Bible, p. 993.
[247] Matthew 7:1–2, the New American Bible, p. 1018.
[248] John 14:6, the New American Bible, p. 1158.

biological constitution. It ensures that man and woman can unite with one another and descendants can spring from their love. The 9th Commandment is meant to protect this union. The shelter of marriage and family must not be endangered through playing with fire, in other words, through reckless indulgence in the erotic energy that crackles between man and woman.[249]

God is trying to drive the point through our thick skulls: all sex outside of marriage is wrong. Yes, even premarital sex, same-sex (homosexual) intercourse, and masturbation is off-limits. Oh yeah, I almost forgot, don't do the "hokeypokey" with animals either, and leave the children alone! This commandment primarily speaks out against lust.

Proverbs 6:25–29 broadcast a warning against adultery:

Lust not in your heart after her beauty, let her not captivate you with her glance! For the price of a loose woman may be scarcely a loaf of bread. But if she is married, she is a trap for your precious life. Can a man take fire to his bosom and his garments not burned? Or can a man walk on live coals and his feet not be scorched? So, with him who goes into his neighbor's wife—none who touches her shall go unpunished.[250]

If you are not totally discouraged at this point because you cannot do whatever you want to whomever you want whenever and however you want, Matthew 5:27 is just going to make you cry:[251] "But I say to you, everyone that looks at a woman with lust has already committed adultery with her in his heart."

Nooooo! Please say it isn't true! I only go to Rick's cabaret for the free lunch—honestly! Oh, that girl on Facebook, we are just friends, I have known her since high school. I read *Playboy* for the articles. Can't

---

[249] Rev. John Trigilio Jr., PhD, and Rev. Kenneth Brighenti, PhD, *Youth Catechism of the Catholic Church* (San Francisco, CA: Ignatius Press, 2010), p. 251.

[250] Proverb 6:25–29, National Conferences of Bishops, the New American Bible (Wichita, KS: Devore & Sons, 1981), p. 639.

[251] Matthew 5:27, the New American Bible, p. 1016.

I just keep my fantasy hot tub girls? Hey, girls! Everyone, out of the tub and out of my head. It was great and fun while it lasted. Girls, I am sorry, but it's not me, I have orders from the big man upstairs. God closed that "in your heart" loophole. I must bid a sorrowful farewell to all of you. Believe me, it hurts me more than you can ever know. Goodbye, Rachel Weisz, Alessandra Ambrosio, Claudia Schiffer, Kathy Ireland, Paulina Porizkova, Halle Berry, Marisa Miller (2020 *SI Swimsuit* cover girl), and the all of the Dallas Cowboys Cheerleaders! I'll miss you. Please write!

Now think about the implication this commandment has. No more watching HBO's *Bunny Ranch* and *Katie Morgan: A Porn Star Revealed* with her witty humor; no more HBO *Real Sex* (I think they are in their one thousandth series), *Californication*, *Girls Gone Wild*, and *9½ Weeks*. Say goodbye to *Playboy*, *Penthouse*, *Hustler*, *Sports Illustrated Swimsuit Special* (I swear I read them just for the articles), *Playgirl*, *Men Only*, and *Cosmopolitan*. Oh, can't forget Victoria's Secret and the National Geographic. When I searched Wikipedia for adult pornographic magazines, I counted 215 magazines. God only knows how many Internet porn sites there are. When I googled *porn sites*, I received over *100 million* sites! If you need more information on this, read *A Billion Wicked Thoughts*.

It's simple really: every sexual thought, wish, idea, expression, reflection, contemplation, desire, craving, fornication, and yearning with anyone but your married spouse is adultery. All those strip bar hotties, and Chippendales lap dancers are a no-no! Hey, New Orleans, y'all are going to have stop yelling, "Show us your t——! [rhymes with *it*! Oh yeah, another word for *breasts*]" at Mardi Gras, and no more Southern Decadence in the fall!

In contrast to what I just wrote, the California legislators in 2020 have "proposed a bill that would dictate what pastors preach from the pulpit. Specifically 'Assembly Concurrent Resolution 99 calls on counselors, pastors, religious workers, educators and institutions with great moral influence to stop perpetuating the idea that something is wrong with LGBT identities or sexual acts.'"[252] In simplicity, this bill

---

[252] Prophencynewswatch.com.

is to stop any religious leader discussing sexuality from the pulpit! So, what's y'all thoughts regarding this?

In her book *Our Lady of Kibeho*, author Immaculee Ilibagiza tells the story of Jesus giving a message to Agnes, a twenty-one-year-old visionary in Kibeho. The message to Agnes from Jesus regards sexuality:

> *Young people must stop treating their bodies as plaything and instruments of pleasure. So many of the youth are using any means they can to find love and to be loved by others—they have forgotten that true love comes only from God and God alone. Instead of serving Him, they live at the service of money. Young women must make their bodies instruments that will glorify Him, not serve as objects of pleasure for the lust of men. Young men must seek to satisfy the hunger of their spirit, not feed the desire of the flesh. Tell them all to pray to my Mother to intercede on their behalf. Tell the youth not to ruin their lives; the wrong way of living can weigh heavily on their future.*[253]

I think this message has fallen on deaf ears. Just look at all the posting of nude selfies and sex tapes on Snapchat, Instagram, cell phones, intranet, and many other social media outlets.

Jeff Dunham: What?

Melvin the Superhero Guy: Grown men wearing a rubber suit…hanging around with a young boy! I don't need to have X-ray vision to see what the hell is going on there!

Jeff Dunham: Yeah, I've always wondered about superheroes and their young men sidekicks.

Melvin the Superhero Guy[*stares at Jeff*]: You have five men in a suitcase, and one of them is on a stick! Who's sliding down the proverbial back pole now? If you had a theme song, it would be, "La lala laaaaaa!"

---

[253] Immaculee Ilibagiza, *Our Lady of Kibeho* (Carlsbad, CA: Hay House, Inc., 2008), p. 118.

Jeff Dunham: You know I have a wife and three kids.

Melvin the Superhero Guy: So does Tom Cruise!

Jeff Dunham: Do you have a weakness?

Melvin the Superhero Guy: Cupcakes…and porn.

[*Audience laughs*]

Melvin the Superhero Guy: Not at the same time! I need a free hand.[254]
   10: You shall not covet you neighbor's goods.

Coveting is not honoring God! This one supports commandment number 7 in a little more detail, in case you missed it. It implies that you shall not covet your neighbor's house, his male or female slave, his ox or ass, or anything else that belongs to him. Again, if it is not yours, leave it alone. Also included in this category is envy and greed. "Latin from Invidia, 'envy is an emotion which occurs when a person perceives they lack another's superior quality, achievement, or possession and either desire it or wishes that other lacked it.' Aristotle defined envy as pain at the sight of another's good fortune, stirred by those who have what we ought to have. Bertrand Russell said that envy was one of the most potent causes of unhappiness and he/she may wish to inflict misfortune on others."[255] The cousin of envy is greed. "When under the power of greed there is no limit to our desire for something: money, stocks, gold, fame, etc. The greedy heart has a thirst that is never quenched. Like envy, greed leaves us feeling dissatisfied no matter how much we have of the things we desire, there is always an empty place in us that wants more."[256] If left unchecked and unbalanced, greed and envy can cause serious damage and make you lose focus from what really matters to the heart.

"The point is ladies and gentleman, for a lack of better word, is good. Greed is right. Greed works. Greed clarifies, cuts through and captures

---

[254] Jeff Dunham, *Melvin the Superhero*, YouTube (2013).
[255] Wikipedia, *envy* definition.
[256] Brian Singer-Towns, *Christian Morality* (Winona, MN: Saint Mary Press, 2012), pp. 173, 174.

the essence of the evolutionary spirit. Greed, in all of its forms-greed for life, for money, knowledge has marked upward. Surge of mankind, and greed, mark my words, will not only save Teldar Paper but that other malfunctioning corporation call the USA. The main thing about money, Bud, is that it makes you do things you don't want to do."[257]

There is a very old saying "He who dies with the most toys wins." This is so wrong in so many ways. Greed is dangerous because it makes one believe in material possession and money acquisition rather than trusting in God. Hey, Kardashians, are you hearing me? In antiquity, wealth was considered a blessing from God. Then Jesus comes along and says the opposite.

> *Do not store up for yourself treasures on earth where moth and decay destroy and thieves break in and steal. But store up treasures in heaven, where neither moth nor decay destroys, nor thieves break in and steal. For where your treasure is, there also will be your heart.*[258]

And then He said,

> *No one can serve two masters. He will either hate one and love the other, or be devoted to one and despise the other. You cannot serve God and mammon.*[259]

Like Bugs Bunny used to say, "That's all, folks!"

Ten Commandments! So simple, but oh so complicated. I believe that many people reject Christianity because its morality emphasis is too essential, not because its theology is too complicated to comprehend. So, there they are, the Ten Commandments. Here's a simple recap:

There are three laws pertaining to God
One law is about your parents

---

[257] *Wall Street* movie quotes, written by Oliver Stone.
[258] Matthew 6:19–21.
[259] Ibid., 6:24.

One law is about killing (Hey, New Orleans! Get the hint yet!)
Two laws are warning about sexual perversity
One law is to tell the truth
Two laws are regarding personal property

BUT THE GREATEST COMMANDMENTS

The Pharisees came to Jesus and said,

"Teacher, which commandment in the law is the greatest?" He said to him, "You shall love the Lord your God with all your heart, with all your soul and with your entire mind." This is the greatest and the first commandment. The second is like it: "You shall love your neighbor as yourself." The whole law and the prophets depend on these two commandments.[260]

"Never lie, steal, cheat or drink. But if you must lie, lie in the arms of the one you love. If you must steal, steal away from bad company. If you must cheat, cheat death. And if you must drink, drink in the moments that take your breath away."

The Ten Commandments given to Moses by God are still practical for today's use. Again, we find them in the Old Testament. If you think they are hard to digest, wait until we get to the New Testament, where Jesus gives us the Beatitudes! This is where Jesus tells us to be blessed and happy in ways that are contradictory to what the Ten Commandments say. Now that's tough love. Again, that's for another book.

Things to contemplate alone or with a group:

- What about this story caught your attention, and why?
- Which commandment do you have difficulty obeying, and why?
- Which is the greatest commandment?
- Are the Beatitudes guidelines or added commandments?

---

[260] Matthew 22:34–40, the New American Bible, p. 1047.

- What about gay marriages? Is this okay in God's eyes?
- Does the Bible have anything to say about homosexual relations?
- In your church, to remarry, must you seek an annulment?
- Is an annulment an easy pass to remarry?
- What can you do when you hear someone take the Lord's name in vain?
- Is abortion really killing?
- What should you do if you lied or deceived another?
- What should you do when someone tells you he/she is having an affair?
- Is trashing the environment breaking a commandment?
- Why is it so hard to follow ten simple rules?
- Is skipping church service really that bad? Is leaving after communion bad? Is everyday streetclothes bad for church, or should one dress in his/her Sunday best?
- Is it better to show up late to church services than to never show up at all?

CHAPTER 13

CHANGE THE WORLD

One of my students challenged me to prove to him how one person alone can change the world. Was it possible, and how could that be? I answered that one person could and has changed the world for both bad and for good. History has witnessed copious endeavors by ordinary folks and by some non-ordinary folks who were explorers, scientists, kings, queens, inventors, mathematicians, teachers, clergy, philosophers, and inventors. All of whom were challenged to think outside of the box, thus making an everlasting mark on the world. Unfortunately, not everyone attempting to change the world makes an everlasting positive mark in history. As dictator of Germany, Hitler believed that Europe could be conquered for the German people. The problem was that he wanted to create a utopia for all Germans by eliminating the undesirable Jews, gypsies, Slavs, and anyone else standing in his way of creating his perfect race. Hitler definitely changed the world in his time; and even now, seventy-four years later, his impact still affects those concentration camp survivors.

Not everyone who rises to the call of change will make a global impression, but they just might make a colossal change in his/her local world: the home, the neighborhood, a community, school, church, children, a workplace, and in his/her heart and soul. All the great movers and shakers were not usually thrust upon the world scene immediately. The voice of change typically begins locally, on a small scale. As words of expression gather steam, listeners become followers, followers become activists, activists become apostles, and then all three groups unify and rally to support the rising cause. To initiate change, the individual expresses their own ideas, opinions, and visions of what they envision the change should be like. While the call for change is open for all to hear, there will always be an opposite force trying to derail your beliefs and ideas. It may be exceedingly complicated for anyone to revolutionize the world forever, but some thoughts, dreams, beliefs, ideas, attitudes, opinions, and philosophies may be more generally accepted than one can ever envision, thus enabling the action(s) or change to reign maybe for a thousand years or more.

The following short stories are about people of vision who were thinking outside of the box and those who forced change. It might have been a great discovery, or it may have turned out disastrous. Such as it may, change occurred.

Jesus Christ: The man who claimed to be the Son of God, who was born into a world of poverty. Like His father Joseph, Jesus became a carpenter. Luke 3:1 implies that "Jesus was baptized in the 15th year of the reign of Tiberius."[261] Luke 3:23 suggests Jesus "was about 30 years old"[262] at the start of his ministry. Jesus's philosophy was based on peace, love, and forgiveness. One of the original twelve apostles witnessed His death, and five hundred disciples witnessed His ascension to heaven, after which they continued His teachings by institutionalizing His religion. While His ministry lasted only three years, His church has survived over two thousand years. Christianity has a worldwide membership of 2.1 billion followers.

The Prophet Muhammad: Born around AD 570 in the city of Mecca (modern-day Saudi Arabia). His name means "highly praised." Muhammad's full name was Abu al-Qasim Muhammad Ibn Abd Allah Ibn Abd al-Muttalib Ibn Hashim. The religion of Islam claims that around AD 610, Muhammad received his first revelation from the

---

[261] Luke 3:23, National Conferences of Bishops, the New American Bible (Wichita, KS: Devore &Sons, 1981), p. 1097.
[262] Ibid., p. 1098.

Archangel Gabriel while on a retreat to Mount Hira. The Archangel Gabriel visited Muhammad over twenty-three years, instructing Muhammad in the verses. Muhammad then instructed his scribes to record them. All the revealed verses are compiled in the Qur'an. The Prophet Muhammad's sayings are recorded separately in collections known as the Hadith. Today's Muslims believe that Muhammad was a messenger of Allah (Arabic for "the One and Only God") and last of the prophets sent by Allah to guide man to the right path. Islam has a following of 1.5 billion.

Martin Luther: Upset at the Catholic Church for its lack of leadership, clergy discipline, response to scandals, selling of indulgences, and papal authority in state affairs, he led a campaign to reform the church. In 1517, he nailed his *Ninety-Five Theses* to the door of a church in Wittenberg, Germany, thus beginning the Reformation. Luther refused to recant, and he was excommunicated. Luther then established a Bible-based church called Lutheran.

Galileo Galilei: An Italian astronomer, physicist, and mathematician, he built a telescope and made astronomical discoveries looking into the heavenly night skies. In 1610, he published *The Starry Messenger* supporting the heliocentric view of Copernicus, which was the idea that the sun was at the center of the solar system. He felt the wrath of the Catholic Church, and he was forced to retract his findings before the church's tribunal in 1633. However, his beliefs and discoveries opened the door to a new scientific era.

John Locke: A natural philosopher born in England in the seventeenth century. He is noted for his publications on religious, scientific, and educational freedom. The Founding Fathers of the United States adapted and incorporated Locke's ideas concerning political freedom into a little document we call the Constitution. "People have certain rights, including life, liberty and property and their consent is the only legitimate basis of governing along with legislative representation and free speech."[263]

---

[263] www.johnlocke.biography.com.

William Shakespeare: Born and raised in Stratford-upon-Avon, a small town south of Warwickshire, England. He became a poet and playwright and was considered to have mastered the use of language as he explored emotional romantic comedies and tragedies. He wrote thirty-eight plays and 154 sonnets that still captivate audiences over 424 years later.

Vasco da Gama: Employed by the king of Portugal to demolish the profitable trade route between Europe and Asia that was controlled by the Genoese, Venetians, and Muslims. On his first voyage south, he exceeded his mission in 1497 when he rounded Africa's Cape of Good Hope to sail to India. This route made it possible to travel from Europe to Asia in open water.

Joan of Arc: A young peasant girl who was born in 1412 in Domremy, France. The legend in France says that she was born with an auspicious secret language with God. At the age of twelve, she began to have mystical visions in which God commanded her to revive the French nation. It has been written of her that she was greatly devoted to the services of Mary, the Blessed Mother of Jesus. In 1429 she led an army to defeat the English at Orleans that paved the way for King Charles's coronation. While trying to free Paris, she was captured, tried for heresy, and condemned to death by burning at the stake. Legend reports that over ten thousand people witnessed the execution and that her ashes were thrown into the Seine River. She was canonized in 1920.

Fredrick Douglass: Son of a slave woman, he disguised himself as a sailor to escape to the North. A self-made intellectual, he crisscrossed the Union testifying about the bigotry, brutality, and ignorance of the slave industry. Often physically attacked after his rousing speeches, his autobiography *North Star* became an overnight triumph.

Genghis Khans: At the age of thirteen, young Genghis became chief of a small tribe of Mongol herdsmen in 1175. Unifying other tribes, he formulated an army so strong, powerful, and swift that no resistance could stop the attacking Mongol invaders. Riding on horseback in hordes, Genghis Khan began his conquest of China in 1211. Reviewing a presentday map, Genghis Khan controlled all of Persia, the Middle

East, Russia, Korea, Vietnam, and Burma. Genghis Khan accumulated more land and territory than anyone in history.

Leo Tolstoy: Born at his family's estate Yasnaya Polyana on August 28, 1828, in Russia's Tula Province. Leo became a Russian writer and has been hailed as one of the greatest European novelists. He rejected the divinity of Jesus, renounced violence, and condemned ownership of private property. The Russian Orthodox Church excommunicated him, but his novel *War and Peace* captivated worldwide audiences, including Mohandas Gandhi.

Lech Wałęsa: In 1943, Lech was born to a poor peasant family in Popowo, Poland. Employed as an electrician in the shipyard, Lech was appalled by the workers' conditions, and he joined the occupation strikers at the age of thirty-seven. Soon Lech, a devout Catholic, was leading the striking workers union. When Polish communists agreed to free trade unions, the new union was labeled Solidarnosc (solidarity). As a Communist state, Poland declared martial law in 1981 and jailed Welch for eleven months. In 1983, Lech was awarded the Nobel Peace Prize; and then in 1990, he was elected as Poland's first non-Communist president, a post he held until 1995.

Oskar Schindler: In 1939, Hitler's army invaded Poland, and several weeks later, Director Schindler also arrived, enthusiastically looking to find a way to profit from the invasion. Oskar purchased a bankrupt kitchenware factory and relied on his panache, flamboyance, and his willingness to bribe highly placed German officials to secure numerous army contracts for his pots and pans factory. Exploiting Jewish slave prisoners obtained from the slums and ghettos, Director Schindler used the Jews for his own advantage. However, after rescuing some of his workers destined for death at the Auschwitz concentration camp, Oskar devised a list containing roughly 1,200 Jewish prisoners. Risking imprisonment and even death, Oskar used all profits earned from his factory to save the lives of his workers. Today, survivors and generations of family members are a living testament to Schindler's courageous act.

Nelson Mandela: Originally an advocate of nonviolence systems, Nelson founded a military party of the African National Congress to rebel against South Africa's racial totalitarianism called Apartheid. He was arrested and convicted on charges of sabotage and languished in prison for twenty-seven years before being released in 1990. Mandela was awarded the Nobel Peace Prize in 1993, and then he was elected president by a multiracial democracy in South Africa from 1994 until 1999.

William Franklin Graham: The world knows him as Billy Graham. An evangelical Christian, he made a personal commitment to accept Jesus Christ at the age of sixteen when a traveling evangelist stopped in his hometown. He took to heart the passage of Mark 16:15, "Go ye into all the world and preach the Gospel to every creature." He has visited 185 countries spreading his invitation to Christianity.

Martin Luther King: A nonviolence Southern Baptist preacher and Nobel Peace Prize recipient was one of America's most influential civil rights activists. Together with his Baptist faith and that of Gandhi's philosophy, Dr. King raised awareness to the racial dissimilarity in America, leading to significant political change.

Adolf Hitler: World War I brought defeat and turmoil for the German people. With the help of his own private militia and the powerful Nazi party, Hitler was elected chancellor. Declaring him supreme leader, Hitler ended any reform of democracy. Soon after, Hitler began a systematic program to harass the Jewish people along with any other race that did not fit into Hitler's view of the Aryan ideal. After invading Poland, France and Great Britain declared war on Germany. By the end of 1945, Germany was involved in a world war, and Hitler was responsible for the murder of over 6 million Jews.

Osama bin Mohammed bin Awad bin Laden: Born into the prominent and wealthy Saudi bin Laden family, Osama is the mastermind of the September 11, 2001 attack on the United States with commercial airplanes crashing into the World Trade Towers, or Twin Towers, in New York City, killing 2,974 people. Commercial aircrafts were also responsible for crashing into the Pentagon, killing many, and the failed attempt of Flight 93 that crashed into a field in Pennsylvania. Osma bin Laden is also associated with Al-Qaeda, a worldwide terrorism organization.

William Henry Gates: Founder of Microsoft, Bill Gates is worth an estimated 56 billion dollars. Microsoft's Windows computer system is a worldwide operation. Recently retired, Bill Gates is head of the Bill and Melinda Gates Foundation that has focus on global issues ignored by the government; he also expressed an interest in improving the standards of public school education in the US.

Confucius: A wise intellectual and philosopher, Confucius wanted to teach his fellow populace on the ancient knowledge, perception, and wisdom of honorable, honest, and just teaching and guidelines. He was born around 551 BC into what China is now. Confucius does not declare that he was responsible for any miracles nor was he of any God or divinity. His power lay in his teachings, support, and power of education as well as reverence of the past, righteous demeanor and conduct, and a reform of all dishonest customs, traditions, and practices.

Daibatsu Buddha: Born as a prince around 400 BC, Buddha left his place in search of the meaning of life. Wandering his kingdom, Buddha came face-to-face with old age, illness, suffering, and death. To him this was "transitory nature of life." Seeking enlightenment with meditation, Buddha sat under a tree until he was successful to enter a harmonious consciousness of nirvana for many days. Returning to normal consciousness, as he knew it, Buddha decided that the rest of his life would be dedicated to teaching all earthly people how to evade and avoid all the intrinsic and natural affliction of life. For most of his life, Buddha traveled around India and Nepal teaching his beliefs of consciousness liberation and enlightenment.

Alāad-Dīn Yūsuf ibn Ayyūb: Known to the Western world as Saladin. Ruler of Syria, Egypt, and most of Mesopotamia. In 1187, his massive army recaptured Jerusalem from the Christians. After the battle, the Christians would remember Saladin for his mercy and kindness in sheer disparity to the Crusaders.

Florence Nightingale: Born into a wealthy family in 1820, Florence felt smothered by the narcissism, vanities, and social snobbery of her upbringing. In a garden, she felt the calling of God that His will was for her to serve others. Courted by many, she refused all offers of marriage. When the Crimean War broke out in 1853, Florence traveled to the battlefield where she put her training as a nurse into practice. Her care for the wounded made news in the British press. By the end of the war, Florence received numerous awards. Queen Victoria also decorated Florence, and she became a national heroine. She established a nursing school and continued to work for the improvement of hospital conditions. Her writings helped established hygiene standards of care in hospitals worldwide.

Marie Curie: Marie's studies and discovery in radioactivity accelerated a new standard of excellence for all female academics in the scientific world that was dominated by men. In 1903, Marie along with her husband, Pierre, were awarded the Davy Medal (Britain) and the Nobel Prize for physics in 1903. Then in 1911, Marie Curie was awarded a second Nobel Prize in Chemistry for the discovery of actinium and further studies on radium and polonium. During World War I, Marie's X-ray machine was used in diagnostic evaluations for shrapnel to over 1 million soldiers.

Pope John Paul II: In 1978, Cardinal Karol Wojtyla was elected pope after the death of Pope Paul VI. Selecting the name *Paul the Second*, Pope Paul II became the youngest pope to serve as bishop of the Catholic Church. Pope John Paul quickly established his papacy, and he visited over 120 countries. Pope John Paul II's teaching, writings, and doctrines affected millions worldwide. He had a hand in everything including the fall of communism, the Berlin Wall, and the Soviet Union. On behalf of the Catholic Church, John Paul made over one hundred public apologies for various transgressions. In 1981, he survived a public assassination attempt on his life. After recovering from his wounds, he met his assassin, Mehmet Ali Agca, in prison to verbally offer his forgiveness.

Mother Teresa: In 1910, Agnesë Gonxhe Bojaxhiu was born in Akopje, Kosovo, in what is now the Republic of Macedonia. As a young girl she always felt the call of God to serve the poor. At the age of eighteen, she became a Catholic nun and traveled to India to serve the poorest of the poor. In 1950 she established the Missionaries of Charity in Kolkata (Calcutta) India. For the next forty-five years, Mother Teresa served the poor of the slums and ministered to the sick, orphaned, and dying. By 1979 she was awarded the Nobel Peace Prize for her work, writings, and teachings. At the time of her death, her charity organization was operating 610 missions in 123 countries. The Vatican has declared Mother Teresa formally beatified in October 2003 by Pope John Paul II, and she is now known as Blessed Teresa of Calcutta. This is the second step for canonization and sainthood.

Ts'ai Lun: Very little is known of him. In the official Chinese Han Dynasty records, Ts'ai Lun is credited with the invention of paper.

Henrietta Lacks: Obscure to the world, Henrietta died of cervical cancer in 1951 as a poor black tobacco farmer. However, it is because of her death that the world in science has changed forever. At the time of her death, human cells were difficult to culture and reproduce. When samples of Henrietta's cancer cells were cultured, they exploded with such growth that today, in 2011, they are still growing. Because of her living cells, scientists are able to replicate them constantly, and everything in modern medicine that we know today used the "HeLa cells" to conduct experiments. Her cells were used so much that I can only mention just a few advancements made in the field of science because of those cells: gene mapping, vaccines (measles, polio, mumps, herpes, fowl pox, etc.), cancer mapping, cloning, chemotherapy, stem cell research, and radiation and antibiotic therapy. Her cells have even been sent to outer space to study the effects of space travel and radiation. Author Rebecca Skloot states in her book *The Immortal Life of Henrietta Lacks*, "If you could place all HeLa cells ever grown onto a scale, they'd weigh more than 50 million metric tons. Another scientist calculated that if you lay all the HeLa cells ever grown end to end, they'd wrap around the earth at least three times." Henrietta Lacks died in October 4, 1951, as a very young woman, yet her cells have continued thriving to this very day, changing science for the betterment of mankind.

The individuals I selected to present to you were taken from a list I made of around four hundred people whom I found extraordinary in their contribution to world change. With the exception of Jesus Christ, I made my selection based on no reasons except that I found these people very appealing to me. If I had the capacity, I would have liked to include many more individuals such as the following: Ronald Reagan, Ho Chi

Minh, Indira Gandhi, Dalai Lama, Karl Marx, Plato, Aristotle, Homer, Winston Churchill, Vladimir Lenin, Catherine the Great, Peter the Great, Michelangelo, Ibn Sina, Dante, Christopher Columbus, Johann Gutenberg, Ferdinand Magellan, Gandhi, Napoleon, Robert E. Lee, Saint Peter, Mary Magdalene, Satan, Bernie Madoff, Leonardo Da Vinci, Jacques Cousteau, Judas, Pilate, Raphael, Attila the Hun, Isaac Newton, Einstein, Steven Hawkins, Homer, Moses, Saint Paul, Orville and Wilbur Wright, Ludwig van Beethoven, Johann Sebastian Bach, Mozart, Cyrus the Great, Abraham Lincoln, Archimedes, William the Conqueror, Voltaire, Sitting Bull, Tamerlane, Neil Armstrong, Steve Job, Suleiman the Magnificent, Saint Francis of Assisi, Teresa of Avila, Maximillian Kolbe, Herod the Great, and all the Apostles.

Then there is Charles Mulli. He is not so famous, but what he did made him famous in my eyes.

Charles Mulli was born in grinding poverty in Kenya to an alcoholic and abusive father. By the age of six, Charles awoke one morning to find he was alone, abandoned by his family. Charles was forced to live in the streets begging from neighbors while vultures circled above, and disease ran rampart throughout Africa. Charles lived and begged in the streets until he was eighteen years old when Cirion D'Souza hired him to work as a porter in his home. Recognizing that Charles was a hard and loyal worker, D'Souza employed Charles as a field clerk in Kakuzi Fibreland, where he was employed as an executive. It was not long before Charles was again promoted to supervisor then manager. Charles Mulli saved all of his money, and then in 1976, he took his life savings and purchased a public bus for transportation. By the end of 1976, Charles had four buses operating in the streets of Eldoret. Although Charles continued to work for the Fibre Corporation, it was not long before he added a maintenance shop and a garage for his buses. In addition, Charles added a store for the tire distribution, insurance brokerage, and workers' compensation, property management agency, a land development operation, and a vineyard and orchards to the Mullaways Agencies. Eventually Charles married, and he and Ester had several children.

Charles was never far away from his memories growing up in the street, and one day Charles had an encounter with the Lord when he asked some street kids to watch and protect his vehicles. Slowly but surely Charles came to realize that God was calling him to take care of the street kids. Charles and Ester sold all their possessions to take in street kids for refuge. He even assisted his father and family members with resurrection from their poverty. Using all of his wealth, Charles and Ester Mulli assisted over six thousand children in their orphanage and adopted 2,500 children. The Mullis are so blessed by God that they are able to support the orphanage with money earned from their following businesses: bean exportation to Europe, vineyards, tree and fish farms. Charles and his wife, Ester, also developed two lower-education schools and a high school. They are presently building a university. To learn more about this amazing man that changed the world, please read his story *Father to the Fatherless: The Charles Mulli Story*.

So, to all who are reading this, one person can affect the lives of others; one person's purpose, goal, drive, and vision may and can lead to marvels, miracles, and wonders far greater than anyone could ever imagine. These individuals I listed did not have the perfect plan, they just acted. If you truly want to make a difference in people's lives in this world, then get started today. Please do not worry about perfection. Like the Nike commercials say, "Just do it!" One person can change the world.

Things to contemplate alone or with a group:

- What about this story caught your attention, and why?
- Who is the person that you believe changed the world for good or bad?
- How can you change the world for someone?
- How can you change your own world?

"CHANGE THE WORLD"
by Eric Clapton

If I could reach the stars
Pull one down for you
Shine it on my heart
So you could see the truth
That this love I have inside
Is everything it seems
But for now I find
It's only in my dreams.

Chorus:
That I can
Change the world
I would be the sunlight in your universe
You would think my love was really something good
Baby, if I could change the world
If I could be king, even for a day
I'd take you as my queen
I'd have it no other way
And our love would rule this kingdom we have made
Till' then I'll be a fool
Wishing for the day[264]

---

[264] Eric Clapton, "Change the World" (1999).

CHAPTER 14

MIGHTY MOUSE

While still in high school, my two older brothers and I joined my father and his friend Bubba Stansbury for a day of fishing in the Atchafalaya Basin in Louisiana. My oldest brother Anthony brought his old beat-up flatboat, and Bubba had his super deluxe shiny red bass boat with all the bells and whistles. Nice! Looking at the two boats, my other brother Carl Jude made his choice and hopped in Bubba's boat while laughing and cracking jokes about Anthony's flat. Too my surprise, my meek and humble father also joined Carl in the fancy boat. After a few minutes thinking about it, I deduced that my father had good reasons to get into Bubba's boat. He did not know how to swim! If any boat had the slightest chance of sinking, it was Anthony's boat.

The trip started out with humiliation for Anthony as Bubba's boat started right up, and Anthony worked on his engine for an eternity before it sputtered to life complete with smoke and the smell of pungent oil filling the air. Off we went with Bubba, Carl, and my father in the cool-looking Goliath while I sat in the front of Anthony's flat listening to the sputtering sounds of that old Evinrude engine. All day long we stopped at potential fishing spots. Bubba would move silently around with his trolling motor while Anthony and I moved clumsily along with paddles making so much noise we probably scared all the fish away.

If the fish were not hitting, we would pull anchor and go to another spot. Bubba's engine roared to life immediately like Mario Andretti's Indy 500 racing car, and Anthony…well, he cursed, and Carl laughed because that damn engine would not start. When it did finally start, smoke would billow out like Patton's Third Army laying a smoke screen. I do not recall what was worse for Anthony that day: the mortification of his meek pathetic boat against Bubba's Goliath, or the constant taunts from his brother Carl. Now this story would be incomplete if I did not mention Bubba's smirks and sly underhand comments to Anthony. Bubba was proud of his hip-hop, sleek, and lustrous $30,000-plus bass skeeter (this was in the '70s). Every time Carl made a comment regarding Anthony's, he was just adding another notch in Bubba's belt.

The fish stopped biting, the sun was setting, and the mosquitoes were beginning their combat air assaults. It was time to pack it in and head home. Bubba cranked his engine. He cranked again then again and again and again —nothing! Using his trolling motor all day long drained the energy from his battery. Bubba's boat was lifeless and dead in the water, and we were deep in the swamp. Then God smiled down upon Anthony and filled his heart with courage and strength. He pulled the cord on his Evinrude, and it sputtered, and sputtered, and sputtered to life. David hit Goliath right there and dropped him. Securing a line between the two boats, Anthony slowly towed a wounded and prideless Bubba and Carl all the way back to the dock. If I remember correctly, Anthony didn't say too much; he did not have to because his broad smile was powerful enough for the defeated magnificent skeeter. However, that did not keep me from throwing jabs at Carl. It was awesome to see Bubba and Carl sulking. The meek mouse became mightier than the skeeter! Twenty years later, when Carl gets the best of me, I bounce back with the taunts of that crushing day. I love to see him squirm and put him in his place.

Throughout history, God has used some very meek individuals who turned out mighty to showcase His glorification. He used Abraham, a nomad; Moses, a murderer; David, a young boy; Mary, a poor peasant girl; Joseph, a poor carpenter; Peter, a fisherman; Thomas, an unbeliever; Paul, a persecutor; Noah, a peasant; Nebuchadnezzar, a king; Billy Graham, a country evangelist; Mother Teresa, a petite, soft-speaking nun; Martin Luther King Jr., a fiery Southern Baptist minister; Karol Wojtyla (Pope John Paul II), a Polish priest; Harold Kushner, an American rabbi; Desmond Tutu, a South African archbishop; Rick Warren, a pastor and author; Scott Hahn, an apologist and professor; Padre Pio—a Capuchin monk, stigmatic, and saint; and thousands of other everyday sinners. He is even using me, John Fontana—a father of two, a brother to six, and a nurse to thousands.

Those who know me know that I am not a preacher, an evangelist, or a member of the clergy, a stigmatic, or a writer—especially a writer! My grammar is so bad I am useless trying to help my kids with their English homework. My spelling is atrocious. I have already written about my difficulties to read, write, and speak correctly. When my ex-wife first met me, she could hardly understand what I was saying. My dialect was a mixture of a Cajun accent combined with a language of my own formed from my reading and hearing disorders. My friend Mark Koepp would laugh at me in nursing school because what most students expressed in their one paragraph care plan took me several pages. Mark would read my care plan, shake his head, and then say, "Give me the eraser." He would then erase my five hours of hard work and then ask me, "What is it that you're trying to say?" Mark would then put down my thoughts into a simple oneparagraph statement. "How in the hell do you do that?" I would exclaim. In the late 1980s, when I was married, my wife purchased a word processor for me. I thought I was going to write a book on wound care. The irony at that time was that I did not even know how to type, much less operate a word processor. So, at the age of thirty-three, I took a typing class at a local community college. My attempt to write my wound care book eventually failed, and I moved on to my next adventure. In 1979 while attending LSU, my friend Charlie LeMair asked me to take a computer class with him. "Why do I need to learn how to use a computer?" I remember asking. Fastforwarding to the nineties, I was constantly calling my friend Charlie asking him how to do something on the computer.

The first book that I can tell you that I actually read was *The Right Stuff* by Tom Wolfe. It was agonizing to read due to my reading impediment. But over time I began to read more and more, and then I noticed that my speech and reading ability improved. However, my spelling still sucked! One day when my daughter was about nine years old and she was doing her homework and she said, "Hey, Dad, how do you spell…never mind, you don't know how to spell. Mom! How do you spell…?" Little witch! The point to all of this is to inform you, the readers, regardless of my inability to read, spell, write, and speak correctly and use proper English, I am being used for God's glory. Trust me! It takes me several hours to sometimes a few days just to write a single page. Whoever invented spellchecker, I want to have a beer with you! And I don't drink beer.

I never understood the meaning "the writings were guided by the hand of the Holy Spirit" until right now. God's hand has been guiding me throughout this ordeal. Trust me! I am no biblical scholar, and I have already told you that I am no writer. The best quotation that truly sums up this writing experience is from Proverbs 3:5.

> *Trust in the Lord with all your heart; on your own intelligence rely not; in all of your ways be mindful of Him and He will make straight your paths.*[265]

However, writing this book—whew! If I get stuck, I say, "God?" And He sends me a passage, a thought, a paragraph. I am often amazed with my thoughts, and I often say, "Where did that come from? Well, I know it came from God.

God has directed my thoughts, contemplations, reflections, feelings and has even chosen the topics for me to write about. I had other ideas, and every time I try to put them to paper, my thoughts vanished— vetoed by God. Please believe me. I am not a witty person nor am I a historian or storyteller. My only explanation is that the Holy Spirit has been steering me. I have trouble remembering my work schedule, much less a biblical passage. The only thing I can truly say that I always wanted to do in life was to be a good father and to spread the good

---

[265] Proverbs 3:5, National Conferences of Bishops, the New American Bible (Wichita, KS: Devore &Sons, 1981), p. 636.

words and deeds of Jesus Christ. I believe participating in the medical mission trips and teaching CCD classes was my way of hearing God's call. Never in my wildest dreams did I imagine writing a book, much less a book about God. I have been working on this project for nine years now. I write, save, reread, edit, ponder, read, read, read, and read some more. I have taken long breaks away from this project thinking I am finished with this book, but slowly God places a passage, word, or thought in my head, and then it is back to the book. So, onward I ponder, contemplate, read, and write.

While I am working diligently in my writing and research, I often think and worry about all my earthly obligations: my children, my work, paying the rent, paying bills, etc. At times I have to admit, all my suffering, worries, and anxieties make me feel like Martha:

> *As they continued their journey, he entered a village where a woman whose name was Martha welcomed him. She had a sister named Mary who sat beside the Lord at his feet listening to him speak. Martha, burdened with much serving came to him and said, "Lord, do you not care that my sister has left me by myself to do the serving? Tell her to help me." The Lord said to her in reply, "Martha, Martha, you are anxious and worried by many things. Mary has chosen the better part and it will not be taken from her."*[266]

Ten years after my divorce, I am just beginning to feel some peace and closure in my life for the first time. It is all due to writing this book, humbling myself and feeling very meek about the call of God. I now understand the meaning of Matthew 5:3–10, the Beatitudes. In Guatemala I witnessed a peaceful and happy community in the poor mountain village, and I could not understand why. But Jesus's explanation in the Beatitudes explains it so beautifully. When one is so poor that he has nothing, then all he has is hope and faith in the Lord. There is nothing to distract him from honoring, worshiping, and giving God His glory despite his surroundings and collapsing life. Like

---

[266] Luke 10:38–41, the New American Bible, p. 1112.

the sign at Liz's Diner in Mandeville, Louisiana: "Peace is solicitude in the middle of chaos."

In his book *My Utmost for His Highest*, Oswald Chambers writes,

Paul was determined that nothing would stop him from doing exactly what God wanted. But before we choose to follow God's will, a crisis must develop in our lives. This happens because we tend to be unresponsive to God's gentler nudges. He brings us to the place where He asks us to be our utmost for Him and we begin to debate. He then produces a crisis where we have to decide—for or against. That moment becomes a great crossroads in our lives. If a crisis comes to you on any front, surrender your will to Jesus absolutely and irrevocably.[267]

Crossroads and crises can make you strong or make you bitter. I have been at many crossroads and crises in life. The reason for all that chaos was because of me. I did not yield to the will of God. God was not in control of my life; pride and ego controlled me. Although I still have trials and chaos in my life, I am not as troubled or faithless. Now I invite God to walk with me every day. I am very determined to seek God's daily grace and blessings. After all, my crossroad and crises are for His purpose—His glory.

Speaking of Glory, exactly what is the glory of God? Well, Moses had asked that same question. In Exodus 33:18–19, Moses saw the power of God's glory.

Then Moses said, "Do let me see your glory." He Answered, "I will make all my beauty pass before you and your presence I will pronounce my name, "Lord; I will show favors to whom I will, I who grant mercy to whom I will. But my face you cannot see, for no man sees me and stills lives." Here, continues the Lord, "is a place near me where you shall station yourself on the rock. When my glory

---

[267] Oswald Chamber, *My Utmost for His Highest* (Grand Rapids, MI: Discovery House, 1922), p. 1.

passes, I will set you in the hollow of the rock and will cover you with my hand until I have passed by. Then I will remove my hand, so that you may see my back; but may face is not to be seen."[268]

Praus is the Greek word for the meaning of *meek*; it implies gentle strength and freedom from pride, narcissism, arrogance, egotism, and vanity. A meek person is humble; a humble person is open and obedient to God's will. Meekness is not a weakness but rather a strength. The strength of Jesus is His loving heart, His love for the Father, and His love for man. No one is refused His kindness and compassion. As a man, Jesus is powerless; He knows that everything about Him comes from the Father. For Jesus to perform miracles, the power from Jesus comes from God. In other words, Jesus humbled Himself, acknowledged His Father's greatness, and then asked permission to show His Father's glory.

And Jesus raised his eyes and said, Father I thank you for hearing me. I know you always hear me; but because of the crowd here I have said this, that they may believe that you have sent me. And when he said this, he cried out in a loud voice; Lazarus come out.[269]

Jesus's greatest act of strength surged through Him when He accepted the cup of which His Father asked of Him. Obedience to God's will, Jesus is meek but mighty as He suffers through the agony in the garden, His arrest, and His scourging; stumbles under the heavy cross; listens to the insults and vile remarks from the crowd while abandoned by his disciples. Exhausted, week, and near death, it takes all of the strength He has left to lie on the cross and succumb to the nails. Finally, with His mission completed and meek to the very end, Jesus suffers a humiliating death as a criminal and dies on the cross. Throughout this entire ordeal, Jesus could have summoned twelve legions of angels to protect Him from even the slightest splinter of harm. But He does not. Staying firm and focused on God's will, Jesus

---

[268] Exodus 33:18–19, National Conferences of Bishops, the New American Bible (Wichita, KS: Devore & Sons, 1981), p. 88.

[269] John 11:41–42, the New American Bible, p. 1154.

accepts all that the Father asks so that communion between man and God is reestablished. *Praus*, all because of a gentle giant's unselfish act of obedience and love.

Things to ponder alone or with a group:

- What about this story caught your attention, and why?
- What can you do to show *Praus*?
- Have you ever been in a position to be a mighty mouse but chicken out? Why do you think you could not perform the task?
- Has there ever been a time in your life that you felt like David taking on the giant Goliath? Did you ask God to be with you when you did? If not, why did you not ask God for help? Who do you recognize as being a gentle giant, and why?

CHAPTER 15

AS YOU WISH

Grandson: A book?

Grandpa: That's right. When I was your age, television was called books. And this is a special book. It was the book my father used to read to me when I was sick, and I used to read it to your father. And today I'm gonna read it to you.

Grandson: Has it got any sports in it?

Grandpa: Are you kidding? Fencing, fighting, torture, revenge, giants, monsters, chases, escapes, true love, miracles...

Grandson: Doesn't sound too bad. I'll try to stay awake.

Grandpa: Oh, well, thank you very much, very nice of you. Your vote of confidence is overwhelming.

Grandpa: Nothing gave Buttercup as much pleasure as ordering Westley around.

Buttercup: Farm boy, polish my horse's saddle. I want to see my face shining in it by morning.

Westley: As you wish.

Grandpa: "As you wish" was all he ever said to her.

Buttercup: Farm boy, fill these with water, please.

GOD AND FREE WILL

Westley: As you wish.

Grandpa: That day, she was amazed to discover that when he was saying "As you wish," what he meant was "I love you." And even more amazing was the day she realized she truly loved him back.

Buttercup: Farm boy, fetch me that pitcher.

[*It's right over her head, so he has to stand next to her.*]

Westley: As you wish. [*Cut to them kissing*]

Grandson[*interrupting*]: Hold it, hold it. What is this? Are you trying to trick me? Where's the sports? [*suspicious*] Is this a kissing book?

Grandpa: Wait, just wait.

Grandson: Well, when does it get good?

Grandpa: Keep your shirt on and let me read.[270]

Sometimes whenever I am in a large gathering such as a Mardi Gras parade, the New Orleans Jazz Fest, or an LSU game in Tiger Stadium, I am always struck with a very morbid thought. Everyone in this large crowd will at some point die.

Rose Castorini: I just want you to know no matter what you do, you're gonna die, just like everybody else. Cosmo Castorini: Thank you, Rose.[271]

And while I am thinking this morbid and somber thought, I am witnessing so much life, excitement, yelling, dancing, friendship, camaraderie, happiness, joy, and love. I mean, when I am with my wife, children, friends, and brothers at an LSU or Saints game, my blood runs high with passion, delight, enthusiasm, and fervor. I cannot even begin to fathom the wonders that heaven has in store for us. What is the kingdom of God really like? Matthew 13:24–49 gives us some hints in the parable used by Jesus regarding God's kingdom:

---

[270] Rob Reiner, *The Princess Bride* movie quote (1987).
[271] John Patrick Stanley, *Moonstruck* movie quote (1987).

The kingdom of heaven is like a merchant searching for fine pearls. When he finds a pearl of great price, he goes and sells all that he has and buys it.[272]

I can only feebly try and imagine what the kingdom of God looks like. I envision heaven as a beautiful rainbow or sunset both filled with implausible colors and pastels, flickering with golden sparkles, and dancing lavender clouds. I look at the fantastic sun rising over Lake Pontchartrain and feel the warmth of the energy engulfing me. I watch with awe as the moon's refection bounces off the emerald-green waters of Destin, Florida, as I unwind in the cool tropic breeze. I gaze in admiration and astonishment from a mountaintop with a billion fireflies flickering overhead as the light of the stars and faraway galaxies let me know that they too are a part of the heavens. For several moments we can experience heaven on earth. The moments are there, but you have to have open eyes and minds and rejoice in the moments and praise the Lord for its glory. Heaven on earth is where your true heart lies: anticipation of that first kiss, date, dance; a first embrace; falling in love; marrying her and losing your virginity to that special loved one; hearing the pitter-patter of small feet running down the hall; children climbing into your bed; embracing your lover; walking your daughter down the aisle for marriage; your daughter returning from her first overseas trip safe and sound; your mother's cooking; your grandmother's cookies; your grandparents' love; fishing with your father; receiving an armada of goods after a national disaster; a bag of ice in the blistering heat after Hurricane Katrina; a loved one recovering from chemotherapy; surviving breast cancer; watching fireworks; opening presents around the tree on Christmas morning; watching the birth of your children; sitting by a fire; dinner with family and friends; serving the poor; your backyard; beating Oklahoma, Ohio State, and Clemson for the college football national championship; welcoming Nick Saban back to the SEC with a rousing defeat on the Crimson Tide's turf; snow

---

[272] Matthew 13:45–46, National Conferences of Bishops, the New American Bible (Wichita, KS:Devore & Sons, 1981), p. 1031.

in Louisiana; singing "Happy Birthday"; celebrating any wedding anniversary; a sleeping child; catching that perfect redfish or speckled trout; Easter Sunday and Christmas midnight mass; saying "I love you"; and celebrating the Eucharist with your community in church. Oh, and we cannot forget about the Saints winning the Super Bowl!

I also wonder that if Jesus Christ appeared today, would we recognize Him, as He truly is? Would we treat Him like a royal dignitary honoring Him at the White House and the United Nations, or would we ignore Him at the stop sign begging for food with a cardboard box sign? Would we place Him in King Rex's chair leading the Mardi Gras flotilla, or would He die on the street in a hail of bullets? Would we greet his motor parade with shouts of glee and flags waving with children held high, or would we riot in the streets destroying property and lives? Would we clean His wounds in a nursing home, or would we let Him die alone in prison? I wonder...what would we do?

I suppose if Jesus arrived in our world today, He would be proud of our achievements in science; the developing of our intellects to wipe out diseases, improve health care, curb starvation, enhance communication, expand travel, and space exploration. However, I think He would cry and hold a heavy heart over our endless killings, racial barriers, broken marriages, child abuse, abortion, sex trafficking, rising crime and prison populations, unrelenting wars, international conflicts, perpetual racisms, pornography and vanity obsession, drug tribulations, desensitizing to the homeless, worldwide greed, self-indulgence, quest for fame, wealth, and every kind of materialism. "We need possessions and material things of all kinds in order to live, and it's certainly no sin to enjoy them, but if we strive after them to the exclusion or neglect of our relationship with God, the Church and our neighbors, we will come to a tragic end."[273]

I believe that Jesus would be perplexed with our unvarying obsession with the downfall of celebrities and celebrity wannabes. The relentless magazines, Internet, and television (paparazzi) media covering of celebrities' tragedies and heart-wrenching stories are not in keeping

---

[273] Father John Bartunek, *The Better Part* (Hamden, CT: Circle Press, 2007), p. 659.

with the teachings of Jesus to forgive. Where is the empathy, sympathy, compassion, kindness, and forgiveness? I fail to understand why people are so drawn to reality shows that depict men and women as backstabbing liars, callous, pitiless, cruel, insensitive, and ruthless individuals. Is this the reality of today's society? Is this really a depiction of everyday life? For if these shows really represent the human heart in today's world, then we are indeed a sad, troubled, gloomy, and depressing species. Why is it that our nations thrive on people that become famous that should not become famous? It's pitiful that the deeper these individuals fall into miserable and tragic existence, the more money these people make, and the more we as a society admire and like them.

Today's society is so easily entertained, that we are so fascinated and mesmerized by celebrities that we cater one's dignity to earn a dollar and get those fifteen minutes of fame by any means available to us. It is heartwrenching to see common people air out their dirty laundry for television ratings and to make the cover of a magazine, talk show and reality show. The twenty-first century moves at such a fast pace that we have become wired for instant gratification. Steven K. Scott in his book *The Richest Man Who Ever Lived* simply states,

> *We want as much as we can get, as fast as we can get it with as little effort as possible and we do not care if we hurt people along the way to get it!*[274]

In his book *Rediscover the Saints*, Matthew Kelly writes, "We live in a time when people are gorging on entertainment of every type and yet we live in an age of boredom. Hundred of millions of people of all ages are board, They may say they are bored at Mass, but the underlying reality is that they are bored with their own lives. What are the poisons of our age? Lies and confusion, greed and selfishness, violence and hopelessness, indifference and meaninglessness, relativism and godlessness, self-loathing and lovelessness—these are just some of the poisons that have infected our hearts, minds, souls and society at this time."

---

[274] Steven K. Scott, *The Richest Man Who Ever Lived* (Doubleday, 2006), p. 10.

GOD AND FREE WILL

Somehow we forgot that Jesus came into this world "to shed a little light on a darken world." Where are the Simons (help carry Jesus's cross) of this world to help carry the cross for River Phoenix, Anna Nicole Smith, Michael Jackson, John Belushi, Chris Farley, Amy Winehouse, Elvis Presley, Whitney Houston, and a billion of others who are not famous people like you and me? Perhaps their lives would not have turned out so tragic if the vultures and parasites hanging on truly cared for the person rather than their power and wealth. Why are we so happy to build our brothers and sisters up in their success but show contempt for their actions in their demise? This is neither forgiveness nor love; this is only caustic, morbid curiosity and voyeuristic behavior. When did we as a nation become so narcissistic and vain? I wonder, does this make us feel better about ourselves to have such a macabre mindset toward the grief, anguish, and disgrace of others? Again, this is not keeping in the teaching of Jesus's peace, forgiveness, love, and truth.

Why is it that we as a race can achieve such technological wonders but spend such little effort to apprehend peace, forgiveness, love, and trust? It takes a lifetime to build a reputation, and only five minutes to destroy it. Saint Teresa (formerly Mother Teresa) "drew million into a new relationship with humanity. She effortless highlighted how cruel and judgmental we can be to each other as human beings, but in a way that was not judgmental itself, in a way that inspired men, women and children to love each other more deeply."[275]

I am reminded of a song by Don Henley and wonder if this song sums up today's thought process.

> I make my living off the Evening News.
> Just give me something—something I can use.
> People love it when you lose.
> Kick 'em when they're up.
> Kick 'em when they're down.
> Kick 'em all around.

---

[275] Matthew Kelly, *Rediscover the Saints* (North Palm Beach, FL: Blue Sparrow, 2019), p. 92.

They love dirty laundry.
We got the bubble-headed bleach-blonde who comes on at five.
She can tell you 'bout the plane crash with a gleam in her eye.
It's interesting when people die, give us dirty laundry.[276]

It must be true; otherwise, why do we have hundreds of gossip magazines and twenty-four-hour television programs geared to this mess? February 2012, Whitney Houston died of a drug overdose while in the bathtub. Her body was not yet cold, and the gossip crews were in full swing. The *National Enquirer* was able to obtain a picture of Whitney in her coffin. No doubt this was intended to sell their magazine at the price of a life. Where were these vultures when she was in trouble and her life was spinning out of control?

Additionally, I suppose that today, Jesus would be disheartened and perturbed with His church and the meaning of Christianity. In John 11:33, it states, "He became perturbed and deeply troubled."[277] I am sure Jesus shed many tears at His church for all the sex abuse going on. Since Martin Luther's excommunication from the church in 1521, the church that Christ gave to the apostles has split thousands of times. Jesus entrusted his disciples to establish His church:

And so I say to you are Peter, and upon this rock I will build "my" church, and the gates of the netherworld shall not prevail against it.[278]

Did you notice in the passage that Jesus said "my church"? Do you understand that this passage does not mean to build *your* church? There is only one church that Jesus gave to man. Man's division has created all the other churches. Today there are over thirty thousand registered Christian churches. Some of the many different Christian church denominations are the following: Episcopal, Lutheran, United Methodist, Pentecostal, Presbyterian, Assemblies of God, Anglican,

---

[276] Don Henley and Danny Koltchmar, "Dirty Laundry" (1982).
[277] John 11:33, National Conferences of Bishops, the New American Bible (Wichita, KS: Devore &Sons, 1981), p. 1154.
[278] Matthew 16:18, the New American Bible, p. 1035.

Nazarene, Baptist, Methodist, United Church of Christ, Evangelical, Mennonite, Congregational, Disciples of Christ, Mormon, Seventh-Day Adventist, Jehovah's Witness, Salvation Army, Church of Brethren, Unitarian, United Episcopal Church, World Wide Church of God, Hara Krishna, Christian Covenant Fellowship, United Church of Canada, Orthodox Anglican Church, Evangel Friends (Quakers), Wesleyan, Calvary Chapel, Grace Brethren, Celtic Apostolic Church of North America, Christian Holiness, Church of Religious Science — just to name a few. Can you get to heaven if you practice the faith and doctrine of any of these churches? Absolutely! But Jesus only started one church—His church! Just as Adam deviated from God's plan in the beginning, we continue to follow Adam's formula with just about everything else in life: not God's plans, but man's plan!

Christianity now has a cafeteria plan to fit just about everyone's requirements. If you do not like what one church has to offer, just keep shopping until you find the one that has the desired outcome you are looking for. In the name of Christianity, man cannot even agree on the "true word of Jesus Christ." It is sad that church members who sing and praise God one day will spit fire and brimstone at another church the next day. If we sling mud and insults and cannot agree to the meanings of Jesus's teachings, no wonder we are so pathetic and dysfunctional in the home (have you watched *Jerry Springer, Jersey Shore, Bride Wars, Real Housewives, The Bachelor/Bachelorette, My Super Sweet 16, Wife Swap, My Teenage Wedding*, and any MTV programs just to name a few? Ugh! Imagine how man would truly be if we were all unified in the true church of Christ. I contemplate that Jesus would say, "You humans have made progress, but in the wrong areas. In the two thousand years since I last left you, you are still lost, frightened, afraid, misplaced, and damaged, and you have not understood My message of peace, love, and forgiveness."

Another way of summarizing what I believe Christ would say to us is *The Paradox of Our Age* by the Dalai Lama:

> *We have bigger houses, but smaller families; more conveniences, but less time; we have more degrees, but less sense; more knowledge but less judgment; more experts, but more problems; more medicine,*

> *but less healthiness. We've been all the way to the moon and back, but we have trouble crossing the street to meet the new neighbor. We built more computers to hold more information, to produce more copies than ever but we have less communication. We have become long on quantity but shot on quality. These are times of fast food but slow on digestion; Tall man but short character; steep profits but shallow relationships. It is a time when there is much in the window, but nothing in the room.*[279]

Ten years after my wife divorced me, I did not understand why the pain from her sting was still lingering. What was it about my divorce that led me to abandon faith and hope, to seek a restless chance and gamble to end my life, to hide in shame from my brothers and friends, to lash out at the world with the venom of hate? To find that answer, I had to go back to the book of Genesis and look at the relationship Adam and Eve had with God. Out of love for man, God established a relationship with Adam and Eve. God invited His creation to His love—it was not forced. God's love has no boundaries, no limitations, and no restrictions. Adam and Eve were free to move deeper into their relationship with God: to live in God and have God live in them. However, Adam and Eve became selfish and independent. Independence from God is pride. Pride is sin, and sin is death. I was prideful in my relationship to God and my ex-wife. God told me a thousand times to tell my ex-wife the truth. My prideful decision was my downfall and the death of my marriage and my ex's love.

> *Court not death by your erring way of life, nor draw to yourselves destruction by the works of your hands. Because God did not make death, nor does he rejoice in the destruction of the living.*[280]

Adam and Eve chose death from God. They chose to rely on their own judgments instead of relying on God's grace and goodness.

---

[279] Dalai Lama, *The Paradox of Our Ages*, www.dalailama.com/the-dalai-lama (2013).
[280] Wisdom 1:12–13, National Conferences of Bishops, the New American Bible (Wichita, KS: Devore & Sons, 1981), p. 680.

Remember the song "My Way" by Frank Sinatra? Well, Adam and Eve were saying the same thing: "I did it my way." That's really what sin is!

Only pure love and goodness can reside in heaven with God. Once Adam and Eve sinned, they became insecure to one another and were detached from God. It's so very painful to be separated from God's love, especially once they bathed in the immense joy, happiness, exhilaration, and grace that God originally offered. All things that are not virtuous and righteous are dreadful and revolting, and only honorable and worthy souls were permitted to reside in the garden of Eden. Adam and Eve were sinful, so they were banned from the garden. They would not be allowed back into the kingdom until atonements were completed with the shedding of the blood from Jesus Christ. The connection to God's grace could only be reestablished with the new covenant—Jesus Christ. The new covenant was absolute and sealed with the spilling of the blood of Jesus. God's great and merciful heart gave mankind a second chance.

Like Adam and Eve, my divorce separated me from the love of my wife and my children. For a time, I was bathed in happiness and joy; I had children, I had a family—I had unity. For a time, I had it all. I was residing in my garden of Eden. My sin separated me from the love of my children and my wife. In my situation, my wife chose not to give me a second chance. She rejected me. Rejecting me meant rejecting everything I stood for—my heart, mind, and soul. Rejection is such a bitter pill to swallow. If you feel rejected, remember God was rejected first with the sin of Adam and Eve. Jesus too was rejected many times and even in his hometown:

> *He came to Nazareth, where he had grown up and went according to his custom into the synagogue on the Sabbath day. At first, they were amazed at the gracious words that came from his mouth. Later when the people in the synagogue hard this, they were all filled with fury. They rose up, drove him out of town, and led him to the brow of the hill on which their town had been built to hurl him down headlong. But he passed through the midst of them and went away.*[281]

---

[281] Luke 4:16–29, the New American Bible, pp. 1099–1100.

Jesus was also rejected with a simple kiss.

My ex-wife did not offer me a second chance, nor did she truly see my heart. However, God did, and He will continue to hold out hope for all men until the bitter end.

The Lord doesn't see things the way you see them. People judge by outward appearance, but the Lords looks at the heart. (1 Samuel 16:7)

In 1997 Billy Graham told a pack-filled stadium in Tampa, "If you believe that Jesus died for your sins, you can live forever with Him in heaven. No matter what has happened in your past, that free gift is offered to you."[282] Remember Jesus's invitation to the two thieves on the cross; one rejected Him and the other accepted Him.

Jesus said to him, "I am the way and the truth and the life. No one comes to the Father except through me. If you know me then you will also know my Father."[283]

God gives us the intellect to know Him, then the freedom to choose to love and serve Him. God's will is never coerced, influenced, compelled, intimidated, or persuaded. His love for us permits free will— to freely choose Him or independence. As all men who came before me, I too am a sinner. At times I still struggle between the goodness of God's love and the depravity of this fallen world. It is a constant battle between good and bad. I may fall short of my goals today, but I pray that tomorrow I am a better man than I was yesterday. When I was in high school, I read a poem by Pearl Yeadon McGinnis that I can still recall, and it is so fitting to this topic: "I have no yesterdays, time took them away. Tomorrow may not be, but I have today." Proverbs 27:1 is another good reminder that our time here is very short to get it right with God:

"Boast not of tomorrow, for you know not what any day may bring forth." In other words, take care of today for it is presumption for

---

[282] www.billygraham.com.
[283] John 14:6, National Conferences of Bishops, the New American Bible (Wichita, KS: Devore &Sons, 1981), p. 1158.

any of us to believe that we will be around tomorrow to rectify mistakes made today or yesterday.[284]

The pain and sorrows we feel today may be gone tomorrow and replaced with everlasting happiness, joy, ecstasy, elation, bliss, and love—if you allow God to steer your choices in the direction that He can utilize for His goodness and greatness. God will always be there in those times when you need to make an emergency 9-1-1 phone call. But He also wants to be a part of your joy, elations, wonders, marvels, and happiness. God even wants to go for a ride with you—even when you are going to get a snowball.

Throughout Jesus's short ministry, there was not a day that someone was asking something of Jesus. The Gospel is full of requests: the cleansing of a leper, the healing of a centurion's servant, the cure of Peter's mother-in-law, the healing of the Gadarene demoniacs, the healing of a paralytic, a woman with a hemorrhage, the healing of two blind men, and the healing of a mute person—just to name a few. In all of those requests, Jesus was moved to pity, and He so often heard,

> *"Lord, if you wish, you can make me clean." He stretched out his hand, touched him, and said "I will do it; be clean."*[285]

> *Courage, child, your sins are forgiven.*[286]

> *You may go as you have believed, let it be done for you.*[287]

> *"Son of David, have pity on us." Jesus said to them, "Do you believe that I can do this?" "Yes Lord," they said to him. Then he touched their eyes and said, "Let it be done for you according to your faith."*[288]

---

[284] Proverbs 27:1, the New American Bible, p. 658.
[285] Matthew 9:28–29, the New American Bible, p. 1022.
[286] Ibid., 9:2, p. 1021.
[287] Ibid., 8:13, p. 1020.
[288] Ibid., 9:27–28, p. 1022.

> *Then Jesus said to her in reply, "O woman, great is your faith! Let it be done for as you wish."*[289]

Each and every time Jesus granted a request, essentially, He was telling you "As you wish," that "I love you."

> *The world is full of many promises, Lord. So many gurus and life coaches and therapists promise to show you the way to peace and wholeness. But can they forgive sins? Only you can reach into the depths of my soul; only you can see even deeper than I can; only you can heal me and cleanse me and give me a new start. I don't want to hinder you by stubbornly sticking to my own desires and plans if you are leading me along new paths. Your will, Lord is beyond my comprehension; your plan is greater than I can imagine.*[290]

So, please take my humble advice from a hard and painful lesson learned. If you are ready and willing to reconnect and reestablish your bond, your love, and relationship with God, just ask Jesus. But be still, patient, and be sure to listen for His reply, "As you wish."

Things to ponder alone or with a group:

- What about this story caught your attention, and why?
- How often do you say to a stranger, "As you wish"?
- How often do you say to God, "As you wish"?
- Have you ever been rejected? What did you do about it?
- Have you ever rejected someone? Why do you think you did that?
- Did you ever tell someone you are sorry for rejecting that person?
- Do you actively take part in gossip and/or spread it yourself? Do you support the entertainment gossip industry by subscribing to their products?
- Why do we like to see the downfall of those who are struggling?

---

[289] Ibid., 15:28, p. 1033.
[290] Fr. John Bartunek, *The Better Part* (Hamden, CT: Circle Press, 2007), p. 132.

CHAPTER 16

PFLT

By the time Jesus began his public ministry, the Jewish people were under Roman occupation since the second century BC. Roman procurators such as Pontius Pilate were authorized with the powers of taxation, judiciary, and military powers. Autonomy in religious affairs was still a privilege, as long as their subjects paid their heavily imposed taxes. As procurator, Pilate had the right to appoint the high priests and control the undertaking of their office. Placating the Romans, Herod the Great remained in power as long as he cooperated as a pawn. Although King Herod built architectural wonders and masterpieces, his Jewish subjects feared and loathed his ruthless behavior. Herod eliminated all of his political rivals, including his children; imposed additional burdensome taxations; brought pagan advisors into his court; and slaughtered the legislative body of the Hasmoneans (tribal dynasty of Judea), while altering the Sanhedrin (supreme religious council) into a puppet society. Torture and death were always lurking around the corner. Crucifixions were a weakly message to all to showcase that the Romans had the power and the control. The Romans did not invent crucifixion, but they perfected it.

The most common methods of killing a condemned man in the Roman Empire are hanging, burning him alive, beheading, placing him inside a bag full of scorpions then drowning him, and crucifixion. As terrible as the first four might be, the last is considered the worst by far. Even though crucifixion is practiced regularly through-out the Roman Empire, it is a death so horrible that it is forbidden to execute Roman citizens in this manner. In AD 70 the Romans burned Jerusalem to the ground and leveled the city.

Thousands were eventually nailed to the cross during the siege, so many that the Romans ran out of wood. Trees had to be logged and carried to Jerusalem from miles away in order to accommodate the tremendous number of crucifixions.[291]

For the average citizen living in Palestine, life was extremely hard. For the vast majority, everyday life was focused on survival. Food was the main essential of life that came from crops and livestock.

The common professions of the inhabitants of Jerusalem were widely known. As found in rabbinical writings, they were bakers, butchers, shoemakers, moneychangers, farmers, perfumers, and artisans who sold souvenirs to pilgrims. Certain professions were looked on with contempt. The Mishna (Qidushin 4:14) gave a list: the donkey driver, the camel driver, the sailor, the coachman, the shepherd, the shopkeeper, the doctor and the butcher. (Ketubot 7:10) included in its list the collector of dog dung, specialists in copper or bronze, and tanners. (Sanhedrin 25) contained a different list: the dice player, the usurers, the organizers of pigeon contests, and the dealer in products from the sabbatical year, the shepherd, the tax collector and the publicans. No father wanted to teach these trades to his son.[292]

Life was better for men and boys than it was for the women and girls. While the husbands were charged with providing lodging, food, clothing, and fulfilling conjugal obligations, it was the duty of the females to obey the man, make the meals, draw the water, feed the

---

[291] Bill O'Reilly, *The Last Days of Jesus* (New York City, NY: Henry Holt & Company, 2014), pp. 47, 214.
[292] Fr. Frederick Manns, OFM, *Every Day in the Life of Jesus*.

children, grind the grain, spin the wool, and even wash the feet of their husbands. Adultery was punishable by death. However, if the husband contracted leprosy, the woman had equal rights to petition for divorce. Beggars were never lacking in Jerusalem, in particular at the outer gates of the temple.

This chapter begins with a little history into everyday life in Jerusalem. For the average citizen under Roman occupation, life was not easy and was worth little.

> *Life expectancy was less than forty years, and far less if you happen to anger the Roman power that were. An excellent description of the time was written by journalist Vermont Royster in 1949: There was oppression—for those who were not the friend of Tiberius Caser… what was man for but to serve Caesar? There was persecution of Men who dare think differently, who heard strange voices or read strange manuscripts. There was enslavement for those who did not have familiar visage.*[293]

As horrible as life was, the taxation placed upon the people by the Romans and King Herod made life even more wearisome.

> *Outrage against Rome has been building for decades. The people have been levied with tax after tax after tax. Herod Antipas is a lover of luxury, and he uses some of these taxes to rebuild Sepphoris and finance his own lifestyle. The more luxury Herod wants, the higher the taxes climb. Actual money is scarce. Every adult male has to pay an annual half-shekel to the temple in coin. Farmers have no way of avoiding the taxes. The hated taxman is always on hand when they arrive at their destinations to sell their goods. Fishermen have it no better. They are levied special rights fees for permission to drop their nets or dock in a port and are required to give up a portion of their daily catch. Each year the people must journey to*

---

[293] Bill O'Reilly and Martin Dugard, *Killing Jesus* (New York City, NY: Henry Holt and Company, 2013), p. 3.

their birthplace for the census count, so the Roman emperor would know exactly how much money he would make from the people.[294]

Jesus begins his ministry here, in Jerusalem, at a time when the people are desperately looking for salvation—not spiritual salvation but rather military deliverance. The Jews were praying for a leader who would change the scene to offer everlasting liberation as a nonviolent revolutionary preaching a different message of *peace, forgiveness, love,* and *truth*. Therefore, this chapter is broken down into four segments explaining the message and interpretation of PFLT.

PEACE

Peace is a noun meaning *harmony* and *agreement*. It is synonymous with the words *accord, amity, cessation, friendship, love, order, truce, treaty, reconciliation, union,* and *unity*. The Bible has a plethora of verses and stories regarding peace in both the Old and New Testament:

> *David went out to meet them, and said to them, "If you come peacefully to me to help me, my heart shall be united with you; but if you betray me to my adversaries, since there is no wrong in my hands, may the God of our fathers look on it and decide."*[295]
>
> *Glory to God in the highest, and on earth peace among men with whom He is pleased.*[296]
>
> *Peace I leave with you; my peace I give to you. Not as the world gives do, I give to you. Do not let your hearts be troubled or afraid.*[297]

---

[294] Bill O'Reilly, *The Last Days of Jesus* (New York City, NY: Henry Holt & Company, 2014), pp. xx, 48, 49.
[295] 1 Chronicles 12:18, National Conferences of Bishops, the New American Bible (Wichita, KS:Devore & Sons, 1981), p. 359.
[296] Luke 2:14, the New American Bible, p. 1095.
[297] John 14:27, the New American Bible, p. 1159.

> *Finally, brethren, rejoice, be made complete, be comforted, be like-minded, live in peace; and the God of love and peace will be with you.*[298]

Peace is a word that has different meanings to many different people. If one is suffering from war, then peace is freedom or a cessation of fighting. A homeless person may believe that peace is when he finds shelter and his next meal, while another suffering physical pain from disease believes peace is when the pain subsides. Therefore, peace may be just a state of mind meeting the immediate needs of any individual in any given circumstances. I believe that peace is an internal tranquility and harmonious feeling or emotion overcoming any conflict resolution—an environment of contentment, satisfaction, and happiness. Remember the sign at my friend Liz's Diner: "Peace—it does not mean to be in a place where there is no noise, trouble, or hard work. It means to be in the midst of those things and still be calm in your heart."

> *There is only one way under the sun by which man can attain harmony, that is to say health, prosperity, peace of mind—salvation, in the true sense of the word—and that is by bringing a radical and permanent change for the better in his own consciousness.*[299]

> *God truly wants us to live in peace, happiness, and harmony. Not just in a physical manner but mostly in a spirit that is flowing abundantly in our hearts, minds, bodies, and souls. It was part of His plan from the moment He created us. But through sin, God's plan is altered. Sin is everything but peace. Peace is freedom from anxiety, worry, and distraction. To live in peace means placing trust in God and if you trust in God then you are free from distractions, worry, and anxieties. If you are not at peace, then you are worrisome. Worry is sin for sin is not trusting God. If you are worry about your illness and weakness you cannot have peace of mind. If you are nervous and anxious you cannot have*

---

[298] 2 Corinthians 13:11, the New American Bible, p. 1267.
[299] Emmet Fox, *Sermon on the Mountain* (San Francisco: Harper, 1934), p. 128.

tranquility sensation of the Divine Love—peace of heart. If you're angry and spiteful, gossip and criticize, you cannot have balance and harmony in your prayers—peace of soul. "We have no rights to accept anything less than freedom and harmony and joy, for only with these things do we glorify God and express His will which is our raison d'etre. It is our most sacred duty, out of loyalty to God Himself, to refuse to accept anything less than all-round happiness and success, and we shall not be following out the wishes and instructions of Jesus if we do accept less.[300]

Peace is a gift of God's love that can transform a wounded soul to a life of fullness and freedom. Jesus's nonviolent message to the world is that we live in accord and conformity with our brothers and neighbors in spite of the different languages we speak, the clothes we place on our backs, the religions we practice, the customs and traditions we honor, and the color of our skin. God wants unity, friendship, truce, and order. Peace is an expression of God's love and grace bringing healing and completeness to our estranged lives filled with broken interpersonal relationships, struggle and pain, hatred and separation. "The Son of man came to seek and to save what was lost."[301]

Peace is synchronization and balance with God's will and love for us. To live in God is to live in serenity. Only when we are open to the call of God do we receive the gift of peace. In the New Testament, the Gospels have a beautiful story committed to topple the Roman authorities and Matthew, a tax collector employed by the Romans. Both are united as disciples of Christ to live and learn and show themselves as examples of peacemakers. Earlier I wrote about Jake DeShazer in the chapter "God Is Calling You." Even though Jake DeShazer was a prisoner of war for forty months, kept in solitary confinement, tortured, and starved to the brink of death, he too found peace.

---

[300] Emmet Fox, *Around the World* (San Francisco: Harper, 1958).
[301] Luke 19:10, National Conferences of Bishops, the New American Bible (Wichita, KS: Devore & Sons, 1981), p. 1124.

> *Once he found peace in God, death was no longer a threat to him. Jake later returned to Japan, a hated enemy of his, to "tell the Japanese about Jesus because he was so filled with peace and love of God.*[302]

Earthly peace is not just a vision of something far off in the future. Peace is attainable today even in the middle of strife and mayhem. To find this peace, man must turn away from violence, bitterness, hatred, and sin and seek the kingdom of God first. Instead, man is filled with uncertainties, bewilderment, and apprehension. Worrying about tomorrow, man fails to live in the present while fretting on past mistakes. We look for greener pastures across to our neighbors' lawn when all we have to do is pull the weeds in our own yards. We spend hours exploring better communications equipment but fail to consult the wisdom of our spouses and loved ones. We are troubled over the failing economy and possibility of losing a job, but we spend money like there is no tomorrow to keep up with the Joneses. We leave Sunday worship only to yell and flip off the driver in front of us for taking his time. We look to self-help books, antidepressants, and advice columns for esteem dysfunctions instead of relying on the goodness of God's grace and love. Is this a peaceful existence? No! Have you ever noticed that the news media rarely show good-hearted stories but rather stories of chaos, fighting, stealing, killing, and man at his worst? It's sad that daytime talk shows will air episodes of people fighting and tearing their lives apart all for the sake of rating and profits.

Man may desire peace, but his actions dictate otherwise. The brutal veracity is that for thousands of years, man has showed his inability to obtain peace by his constant conquering, invading, disputing, arguing, enslaving, killing, and imposing his will on others. We air out our anger and resentment on public television shows and in magazines; we scream at our spouses, children, coworkers, employees, and strangers; and we kill each other in the streets, workplace, schools, movie theaters, hospitals, and entertainment concerts. In the name of peace, man points nuclear

---

[302] Craig Nelson, *The First Heroes* (Viking Penguin, 2002), p. 336.

weapons at one another's countries, builds walls around cities, draws imaginary lines marking off territory borders, places blockades, and signs treaties. In the name of peace, man established a United Nations to hash out conflicts in a "civilized manner." Then once a year we honor an individual whom we believe inspired a noble effort to acquire and preserve peace by giving him/her the Nobel Peace Prize. We as a species yearn for peace, but if we cannot even initiate a two-minute dialogue with a stranger in an elevator, how will we ever establish dialogue in the neighborhood, much less the world? How can we talk to one another about peace if we can't put our cell phones down at the dinner table? Living in alienation from one another's neighbor, and countries, only reinforces the internal war going on within our conscience and soul. Exploiting and decimating our earthly home and neighbors fuel the continued separation from God's plan for world peace.

To me, world peace will exist when there are no armed conflicts, when no race is trying to exterminate, convert, and impose a belief, doctrine, policy, or dogma onto another culture that is believed to be inferior because of religion, color, and ethnicity. Subversion and chaos must be replaced with serenity and tranquility. I believe that this level of peace is not attainable. Just watch any news outlook, and it is all about pandemonium. But if by some large miracle it transpires, it is unlikely that it could be sustained for an extended period of time. Man has a pattern of repeating bad behavior. *Shalom* is an antiquated word that is often used as a greeting in the Middle East. It means, "May you live in anticipation of the day when God makes things whole again."[303]

With all humility and gentleness, with patience, bearing with one another the unity of the spirit through the bond of peace let us make room for each other's faults because we love.[304]

God invites you to his discipleship as a peacemaker. Beyond our personal lives, this invitation is to include community, friends, family, and

---

[303] www.webster.com.
[304] Ephesians 4:2–4, National Conferences of Bishops, the New American Bible (Wichita, KS: Devore & Sons, 1981), p. 1281.

the nation as a whole. In the garden of Gethsemane, Jesus was showed the sins of all mankind: both past and future. Jesus knew that the price of everlasting peace and the salvation of man would cost the spilling of His blood. Facing a slow and agonizing death on the cross, Jesus refused to save Himself. His ministry for three years was a message of peace, and to Jesus, death was worth the price to obtain everlasting peace.

Someday I think the world should have a "ride-a-donkey day." In the days of Palestine, the donkey was the animal of the poor. Kings rode horses to signify his colossal power and authority. When a king wanted to show humbleness and meekness, let's say after conquering a country, the king would ride into the city upon a donkey to symbolize peace. In retrospect, the donkey or ass was then transferred into a symbol of kingship. Around 520 BC, the prophet Zechariah foretold the mightiest King of kings, Jesus, riding into Jerusalem upon a donkey: "See, your king shall come to you; a just savior is he, Meek, and riding on an ass, on a colt, the foal of an ass."[305] In Mark 11:1–11, Jesus fulfills this Old Testament prophecy.

> He said, "Go into the village and you will find a colt tethered on which no one has ever sat. Until it and bring it here. If anyone should say to you, 'Why are you doing this?' Reply, 'The master has need of it.'" So, they brought the colt to Jesus and put their cloaks over it. And he sat on it. Many people spread their cloaks on the road, and others spread leafy branches that they had cut form the fields. Those preceding him as well as those following him kept crying out, "Hosanna! Blessed is he who comes in the name of the Lord! Blessed is the kingdom of our father David that is to come! Hosanna in the highest!"[306]

Jesus purposely enters riding on a donkey proclaiming peace rather than a king preparing for war.

In his book *Medjugorje* by Wayne Weible, the author revels a conversation between Father Svetozar and Ivanka, one of the visionaries:

---

[305] Zechariah 9:9, the New American Bible.
[306] Mark 11:1–11, the New American Bible, p. 1080.

Father Svetozar: *What are the messages?*
Ivanka: *Peace, conversion, fasting, penance, prayer.*
Father Svetozar: *Which is the most important?*
Ivanka: *Peace.*
Father Svetozar: *Why Peace?*
Ivanka: *When everyone in the world is at peace, everything is possible.*[307]

"GIVE ME LOVE"
by George Harrison

Give me love
Give me love
Give me peace on earth Give me light.
Give me life
Keep me free from birth.
Give me hope
Help me cope, with this heavy load
Trying to, touch and reach you with,
Heart and soul.
Ommmmmmmmmmmmm Mmmmy lord…
Please take hold of my hand, that I might understand you, my lord.[308]

FORGIVENESS

Wikipedia defines *forgiveness* "as the process of concluding resentment, indignation or anger as a result of a perceived offense, difference or mistake, and ceasing to demand punishment or restitution." The *Oxford English Dictionary* defines *forgiveness* as "to grant free pardon and to give up all claim on account of an offence or debt." The Bible is very clear on the importance of forgiveness as shown in the following passages:

---

[307] Wayne Weible, *Medjugorje: The Message* (Brewster, MA: Paraclete Press, 1989), p. 65.
[308] George Harrison, "Give Me Love," *Living in the Material World* CD (1973).

They refused to listen, and they did not remember your wondrous deeds which you had performed among them; so, they became stubborn and appointed a leader to return to their slavery in Egypt. But you are a God of forgiveness, Gracious and compassionate, Slow to anger and abounding in loving kindness; and you did not forsake them.[309]

Then Peter asked,

"Lord, if my brother sins against me, how often must I forgive him? As many as seven times?" Jesus answered, "I say to you not seven times but seventy-seven times."[310]

But so that you may know that the Son of Man has authority on earth to forgive sins.[311]

He breathed on them and said to them, "Receive the Holy Spirit. Whose sins you forgive are forgiven them and whose sins you retain are retained."[312]

Jesus Christ was so moved with love and compassion that He chose to forgive the offense—to heal the afflicted heart before healing the physical ailment. Even while being nailed to the cross, Jesus was thinking more about the salvation of man than Himself:

Father, forgive them; for they do not know what they are doing.[313]

Mother Teresa is quoted as saying, "If we really want to love, we must learn how to forgive." Just moments before being guillotined, King

---

[309] Nehemiah 9:17, National Conferences of Bishops, the New American Bible (Wichita, KS: Devore & Sons, 1981), p. 421.
[310] Matthew 18:21, the New American Bible, p. 1039.
[311] Matthew 9:6, the New American Bible, p. 1021.
[312] John 20:22–23, the New American Bible, p. 1167.
[313] Luke 23:24, the New American Bible, p. 1132.

Louis XVI is quoted as saying, "I pardon the authors of my death."[314] Awaiting her death, Queen Maria Antoinette writes to her sister asking her to forgive her son:

> *"I have to speak to you of one thing which is painful to my heart, I know how much pain the child must have caused you, forgive him."*[315] *As she writes on, the Queen forgives her enemies and reaffirms her faith; "I die in the Catholic Apostolic and Roman religion, that of my fathers, that in which I was brought up, and which I have always professed. Having no spiritual consolation to look for, not even knowing whether there are still in this place any priests of that religion, I sincerely implore pardon of God for all the faults which I have for a long time addressed to Him, to receive my soul into His mercy. I beg pardon of all I have known, and especially of you my sister, for all the vexations, which, without intending it, I may have caused it. I pardon all my enemies the evils that they have done me."*[316]

Forgiveness is an incredible gift from God; it is the ability to let go and move on. Forgiveness is for you, the one who forgives—the forgiver. We are all empowered with the grace to forgive. To forgive does not mean we forget the offense, nor does it mean we have to trust the one we forgave; it simply means healing thyself. To forgive releases the forgiver from all that will keep you from being whole, from the anger that destroys joy and prevents you from loving. Forgiving reestablishes you in God's grace.

Forgiving is an internal question. It is about choice and power. If one chooses to release the power, the control, he/she is free to move about in life and spirit. But those who refuse to give up the power may suffer somber consequences. Rejecting forgiveness is succumbing to pride and vanity. The foundation of Satan's sham is to hold on to anger, bitterness, antipathy, and resentment. If you do that, then you are in a position not

---

[314] Ann Coulter, *Demonic* (New York: Crown Forum, 2011), p. 113.
[315] Ibid., p. 113.
[316] Ibid., pp. 123–124.

to forgive the offender. The inability to forgive fools you to believe you are now entitled to vindication from your betrayer. But Jesus teaches forgiveness is the understanding of finding internal peace, tranquility, and harmony. Forgiving is a journey. To actually forgive someone may take time, but one must start moving in that direction. The pain may be felt over and over; and forgiveness in your heart, mind, and soul may have to take place over and over until such time the memory has washed away. Forgiving takes courage; holding grudges takes weakness. When pain and hurt remains in our memory, our memory controls us. But if we let go of those pain and hurt, memory no longer controls us. In other words, forgiveness allows us to release the painful memory.

> *When you feel hurt because someone has been ungrateful for your kindness, it shows that you have been looking for gratitude, and this is a great mistake. The true reason for helping another is our duty to help others insofar as we can do wisely or because it is an expression of love. Of course, love will not be remembering, if we wish, that in some other way the deed would surely be recognized. The very fact that one is looking for gratitude means that he is putting the other person under a sense of obligation, and that person will probably get this subconsciously and resent it strongly, as such a thing is highly repugnant to human nature. Do good deed and then pass on, neither expecting nor wishing for personal recognition.*[317]

Peace and forgiveness go hand in hand. You cannot have one without the other. If you want peace in your heart and soul, you must forgive; and in forgiving, you will release your sullenness, and that emancipation will give you peace. In the Catholic Church, just before receiving the Blessed Eucharist, the priest will say, "Let us offer peace to one another." The meaning of this statement implies that before receiving the body and blood of Jesus, you must go to your brother with whom you might have a grievance and make peace with him. This is the perfect time to forgive any transgressions against you and a time to ask for clemency

---

[317] Emmet Fox, *The Sermon on the Mount* (San Francisco: Harper, 1934), p. 113.

from the people you've slighted. Only then can you receive the spiritual nourishment for the soul with a clear heart and mind.

> *If you bring your gift to the altar and there recall that your brother has anything against you, leave your gift there at the altar, go first and be reconciled with your brother, and then come offer your gift.*[318]

Three modern powerful examples illustrating forgiveness that made national news are Pope John Paul II, Ronald Cotton, and Eva Mozes. In 1983, Pope John Paul entered the prison in Rome to offer forgiveness to his assassin Mehmet Ali. Just because he was pope, this did not make the act to forgive this person trying to kill him any easier; on the contrary—though he was pope, John Paul was still a man with human emotions. Reading his autobiography, Pope John Paul had to devote much time in prayer to reach that crucial moment to let go of the hurt and acrimony he harbored toward Mehmet Ali. However, Pope Paul forgave his unknown attacker shortly after being shot: "Still conscious on the ride to Gemelli Hospital, the pope looked at Father Dziwisz and told him explicitly that he had forgiven his assailant."[319] As President Reagan lay on a stretcher in the emergency room fighting for his life after an assassin's bullet lodged in his lung and near his heart, he prayed to forgive John Hinckley: "Lying on the operating table, the president began to pray for the soul of the "mixed up young man" who had just shot him.[320]

Ronald Cotton is not a famous man—far from it. In fact, he served eleven years in prison after being found guilty of raping Jennifer Thompson, a twenty-two-year-old college student in 1984. In 1995 Ronald was exonerated and released from prison because his DNA did not match those of the attacker. In 1997 Ronald and Jennifer met after a guilt-ridden Jennifer asked for forgiveness. Not only did Ronald forgive

---

[318] Matthew 5:23–24, National Conferences of Bishops, the New American Bible (Wichita, KS: Devore & Sons, 1981), p. 1015.
[319] Paul Kengor, *A Pope and a President* (Wilmington, DE: ISI Books, 2017), p. 248.
[320] Ibid.

Jennifer for her false accusation, they formed a friendship and wrote a book about their story entitled *Picking Cotton.*

For two weeks in 1944, Eva Mozes lay near-death in a hospital barrack at the Auschwitz death camp, feverish and covered with egg-size welts because the notorious Dr. Josef Mengele injected something into the tenyear-old as part of his notorious experimentation on twins. Because Eva was expected to die, no one was allowed to treat or feed her. To get water, she had to muster all of her strength to crawl to a faucet at the other end of the building. She and her twin, Miriam, survived. A half century later, Eva —now Eva Mozes Kor—did something that might seem unthinkable: she forgave the Nazis, even though her parents and two older sisters had perished at Auschwitz.

> *The act of forgiveness gave me back the power that was taken away from me as a victim. As long as we hold on to the anger, those who victimized us still have a hold on our lives.... You don't forgive because the perpetrator deserves it. You do it because you, the victim, deserve the right to be free again.*[321]

> *If you forgive others their transgressions, your heavenly Father will forgive you. But if you do not forgive others, neither will your Father forgive your transgressions.*[322]

Does God say try to forgive them? No, He commands to "forgive them"! Another thing, Jesus is also stating forgiving is provisional to how we forgive one's transgression. "If we refuse to have a gracious and forgiving attitude toward those who have hurt us, then God says He cannot have a gracious attitude toward us. That's a shocking thing to think about, but again, these are Jesus's own words. He seems to be saying that God's forgiveness toward us is released as we exhibit forgiveness toward others. And be sure you do not ask for justice for if we want God to give us real justice, we're going to be condemned too.

---

[321] "John Pope," *Times Picayune* newspaper (September 9, 2012).
[322] Matthew 5:23–24, National Conferences of Bishops, the New American Bible (Wichita, KS: Devore & Sons, 1981), p. 1015.

God is trying to tell us that we are all guilty. So, if we want real justice, we don't skip away to heaven while the Son of Sam and Hitler go to hell. We all go to hell. Apart from God's grace, we are all guilty. But wait, God says if we can be honest about our guilt, then He'll forgive us! He offers grace, not justice. Jesus is the One who paid for our sins. So, there is justice. But Jesus paid the price so that justice can be served. And we walk away scot-free, because of what He did—and emphatically not because of us being so wonderful."[323]

There is no sin that God will not forgive if one is truly sorry. God will even forgive Satan. Yes, you read this right! Here is a fascinating question Segatashya (the boy who met Jesus) asked Jesus and Jesus's replies:

Segatashya: Jesus, you tell us love our enemies…even when our enemies seem to be evil, sinful, and harm us. But didn't God fight a war against Satan and cast him into hell? You tell us that Satan is our greatest enemy and that we must fight against him, against his temptations. Will you please explain how on the one hand you can tell us to love our enemies, when, on the other hand, it seems obvious that you hate Satan?

Jesus: My child, I do not hate Satan—on the contrary, it is Satan who hates me. If Satan would repent and sincerely ask God to forgive his sins, then Satan would be forgiven, and he would be allowed back into heaven. But for that to happen, Satan must repent sincerely from his heart.

Segatashya: Yes, Lord, I understand. But because Satan is the great liar, it will be difficult for him to ever confess from the heart.

Jesus: As I told you, Satan would be forgiven if he could find it in his heart to apologize to God. But to this day, Satan has not found the courage or the sincerity to say he is sorry and seek God's forgiveness. Satan will never apologize.[324]

---

[323] Eric Metaxas, *Everything You Always Wanted to Know about God (but Were Afraid to Ask)* (Ventura, CA: Regal Publishing, 1982), pp. 166–173.

[324] Immaculee Ilibagiza, Steve Erwin, *The Boy Who Met Jesus* (New York City: Hay House Inc., 2011), pp. 106, 107, 108.

There are a few words that humans sometimes find hard to express. One being "I love you," and the other is "I am sorry." When you go to your church and tell God how sorry you are for your sinful transgressions, you in return will hear—through the ministry of Christ's Church and by the power of God through the chosen priests—actual words of God as He gives you absolution. Speaking through the priest, he recites, "I absolve you from your sins." God's love is greater than any sin. Three good psalms to consider when thinking about the forgiveness of God:

Psalm 51:19, *"My sacrifice, O God, is a broken spirit; a broken and contrite heart; you, God, will not despise"*[325]

Psalm 130:3–4, *"If thou, O Lord, should mark iniquities, Lord, who could stand? But there is forgiveness with thee."*[326]

Psalm 103:8–13, *"The Lord is merciful and gracious, slow to anger and abounding n steadfast love. He will not always chide, nor will he keep his anger forever. He does not deal with us according to our sins, nor requite us according to our iniquities. For as the heavens are high above the earth, so great is his steadfast love towards those who fear him; as far as the east is from the west, so far does he remove our transgression from us. As a father pities his children, so the Lord pities those who fear him."*[327]

In his book *The Better Part*, Father John Bartunek explains, "The crux of the Our Father is forgiveness. Jesus realizes that linking God's forgiveness of our own sins with our forgiveness of those who offend us is a hard doctrine. That's why He reemphasizes it after he's finished teaching the words of this prayer. Why does he put this difficult condition on our forgiveness? Simply put, because unless we forgive those who offend us, God can't forgive us. Forgiveness requires

---

[325] Psalm 51:19, National Conferences of Bishops, the New American Bible (Wichita, KS: Devore & Sons, 1981), p. 577.
[326] Psalm 130:3–4, the New American Bible, p. 624.
[327] Psalm 103:8–3, the New American Bible, p. 607.

humility—from both directions. Basically, humility means recognizing that you are not God, and when we refuse to forgive someone, we are forgetting precisely that. A refusal to forgive is passing judgement on the offender and that is placing oneself in God's place. Only God can see into the secret recesses of the human heart and only God has the right to pass judgement. Refusing to forgive is acting like God, elevating oneself above the offender. The throne of judgement has only enough room for one judge at a time, either oneself or God. This attitude, then, simply outs God, shutting the door on Him and so the merciful, forgiving God is left standing outside in the cold, unable to bring his forgiveness."

Summing up forgiveness, Emmet Fox writes,

> *Setting others free means setting you free, because resentment is really a form of attachment. It is a cosmic truth that it takes two to make a prisoner, a prisoner and a jailer. There is no such thing as being a prisoner on one's own account. Moreover, the jailer is as much a prisoner as his charge. When you hold resentment against anyone, you are bound to that person by a mental change. A cosmic tie to the thing that you hate ties you.*
>
> *The one person perhaps in the whole world whom you most dislike is the very one to whom you are attaching yourself by a hook that is stronger than steel. Is this what you wish? Is this living? Remember, you belong to the one thing with which you are linked in thought, and at some time or other, if the tie endures, the object of your resentment will be drawn again into your life, perhaps to work further havoc. No one can afford such a thing; and so, you must cut all ties by a clear act of forgiveness. You must lose him and let him go. By forgiveness you set yourself free. You save your soul. And because the law of love works alike for one and all, you help to save his soul too.*[328]

---

[328] Emmet Fox, *Around the World* (San Francisco: Harper, 1931), p. 4.

LOVE

You know when I said I knew little about love? That wasn't true. I know a lot about love. I've seen it. I've seen centuries and centuries of it, wars. Pain and lies. Hate...you could search to the furthest reaches of the universe and never find anything more beautiful. So yes, I know love is unconditional. But I also know it can be unpredictable, unexpected, uncontrollable, unbearable and strangely easy to mistake for loathing, and...what I'm trying to say is...I think I love you! My heart...it feels like my chest can barely contain it. Like it doesn't belong to me anymore. It belongs to you. And if you wanted it, I'd wish for nothing in exchange. No gifts. No goods. No demonstrations of devotion. Nothing but knowing you loved me too. Just your heart, in exchange for mine.[329]

Jesus at any time could have exhibited his divinity and kingship forcing peace on to His subjects. But then that is not love and free will. Fasting in the desert for forty days, Jesus refused to declare His kingship, turn stones into bread, or call his legions of angels to save Him. Rather than submit to temptations from the prince of darkness, Jesus rejected Satan and stayed on the path of His Heavenly Father's plan of powerlessness and submission. Faced with torture and death, Jesus continued to refuse all means to rescue Himself. Instead He fulfilled His love for mankind with His death on the cross rather than give into the bitterness of those who hated Him:

You who would destroy the temple and rebuild it in three days, save yourself if you are the Son of God. The scribes and elders even mocked him saying: he saved others, but he cannot save himself. So, he is the king of Israel! Let him come down from the cross now, and then we will believe him.[330]

---

[329] Neil Gaiman, *Stardust* movie quote (2007).
[330] Matthew 27:40, National Conferences of Bishops, the New American Bible (Wichita, KS: Devore & Sons, 1981), p. 1060.

No! Jesus would stay the course feeling every fiber of pain inflicted upon His precious body and trusting in God alone. His death on the cross highlights the full extent of His love. Love was part of his three-year ministry in accordance with His Father's will by not forcing others to accept Him or His teachings. Man is capable of love because it already exists with God. Our ability to love is renewed by our experience of being loved. As peacemakers, we are called to love even in times that we do not feel very loving. Often it is through the execution of loving acts that loving emotions and passion can build up inside of us. Love reaches out to people not with all the answers but with experience of fear and hurt and understanding the process of what it takes to heal. Man was created to be loved, and to live as if you were unloved is an imperfection, and God's love has no imperfections.

> *If I have all faith so as to move mountains but do not have love, I am nothing. If I give away everything I own, and if I hand my body over so that I may boast but do not have love, I gain nothing.*[331]

Jesus fulfilled the prophecies because He loved. He came into being to teach man about His Father's love. Jesus's answer to hate, abhorrence, and detestation is love.

> *And the Word became flesh and made his dwelling among us. When pressed by the Pharisees regarding which commandment is the greatest, He said, "You shall love the Lord, your God, with all your heart, with all your soul, and with all your mind."*[332] *This is the greatest and the first commandment. The second is much like it: "You shall love your neighbor as yourself."*[333]

Jesus did not say we have to like our neighbors; there are many people that I know that offend me, and I do not like them. But that is not what Jesus is teaching here. He is saying *we have to* love our

---
[331] 1 Corinthians 13:2, the New American Bible, p. 1244.
[332] John 1:14, the New American Bible, p. 1137.
[333] Matthew 22:36–39, the New American Bible, pp. 1047–1048.

neighbors. In *Jesus: His External Legacy*, author Jon Kennedy explains love is to "reach out and love someone who, by your standards, is unlovable, and you'll begin approaching the Kingdom-of-God lifestyle." Father John Bartunek writes,

> *When we are stuck in our sins or wallowing in selfcenteredness, the good deeds of others agitate us; they prick our conscience. We try to stamp them out. We try to minimize them. Instead of rejoicing in goodness wherever we find it, we resent it, and we rejoice instead in our neighbor's fall, since it brings them down to our level. Christ is never like that with us. The more we experience his unquenchable generosity towards us, the more it will purify our stinginess and free us to love our neighbors as he does.*

And in the midst of horrific suffering, Jesus's enduring love invites everlasting hope. Then the good thief said,

> "We have been condemned justly, for the sentences we received correspond to our crimes, but this man has done nothing criminal. Jesus, remember me when you come into your kingdom." He replied to him, "Amen, I say to you, today you will be with me in Paradise."[334]

I love the story of Jesus on the cross speaking with the good thief. Let's take a look at it. Jesus is in immense pain both physical and mentally. He is on the verge of dying, and He is more interested in the suffering man next to Him than He is about His own condition. With barely any breath left in His lung, Jesus is listening to a sinner asking for forgiveness. Even as He is dying, Jesus is looking for lost souls to bring back into His kingdom. "I tell you today you will be in paradise!"

> *The way of love, upon which you may step at any moment—at this moment if you like—requires no formal training, permit, has no entrance fee and no condition whatever. You need no expensive laboratory in which to train, because your own daily life and*

---

[334] Luke 23:24–42, the New American Bible, p. 1132.

your ordinary life surroundings are your laboratory. You need no reference library, no professional trainings; no external acts of kind. All you need is to begin steadfastly to reject from your mentality everything that is contrary to the law of love. You must build up by faithful daily exercise the true Love Consciousness. Love will heal you. Love will comfort you. Love will guide you. Love will illumine you. Love will redeem you from sin, sickness, and death, and lead you into the promise land. Say to yourself: My mind is made up; I have counted the cost; and I am resolved to attain the goal by the oath of love. Others may pursue knowledge, or organize great enterprises for the benefit of humanity, or scale the austere heights of asceticism; but I have chosen the path of Love. My own heart is to be my workshop, my laboratory, my great enterprise, and love is to be my contribution to humanity.[335]

In 1 Corinthians 13 1:13, Saint Paul writes,

If I speak in human and angelic tongues but do have love, I am a resounding gong or a clashing cymbal. If I have all faith so as to move mountains but do not have love, I am nothing. If I give away everything I own, and if I hand my body over so that I may boast but do not have love I have gain nothing. Love is patient. Love is kind. It is not jealous, [love] is not pompous, it is not inflated, it is not rude, it does not seek its own interests, it is not quick-tempered, it does not brood over injury, it does not rejoice with the truth. It bears all things, believes all things, hopes all things, and endures all things. Love never fails. If there are prophecies, they will be brought to nothing; if tongues, they will cease; if knowledge it will be brought to nothing. For we know partially, and we prophesy partially, but when the perfect comes, the partial will pass away. When I was a child, I used to talk as a child, think as a child, reason as a child; when I became a man, I put aside childish things. At present we see indistinctly, as in a mirror, but then face to face. At present I know

---

[335] Emmet Fox, *Around the World* (San Francisco: Harper, reprinted 1992), p. 356.

partially; then I shall know fully, as I am fully known. So, faith, hope, love remain, these three; but the greatest of these is love.[336]

Jesus teaches man to love not as with a feeling but love with a behavior. There is a big difference. Love is an emotion. You can have the feelings of love but it's not a feeling. Love is not a feeling according to God's definition of love. And I think maybe God would know, since He is love…and invented the whole concept of it. According to the Bible, love is a behavior. I might not feel loving toward you, but if I behave lovingly toward you, I'm doing what God says to do when He says to "love one another." If I treat you as I would want to be treated, I'm treating you in a loving way. That's the way that God treats us, and that's the way He want us to treat everyone else—including one's enemies. Remember love according to God is not a feeling it's a behavior. Behavior is not involuntary. It's volitional, to be exact. So, behavior is an act of the will. So, you can't force yourself to feel love towards someone, but you can obviously force yourself to behave lovingly toward him or her. Our feelings are often out of sync with God's will. But God says to us that we do not have to act on those feelings. We can and should act in a way that's in accordance with God will.[337]

Jesus intentionally walked into the arms of his betrayer, he didn't resist arrest, he didn't defend himself at the trial—it was clear that he was willingly subjecting himself to what you've described as a humiliating and agonizing form of torture. What could possibly have motivated a person to agree to endure this form of punishment? Doctor Alexander Metherell searched for the right words. "Frankly, I don't think a typical person could have done it. Jesus knew what was coming and He was willing to go through it, because this was the only way he could redeem us—by serving as our substitute and

---

[336] 1 Corinthians 13:1–13, National Conferences of Bishops, the New American Bible (Wichita, KS: Devore & Sons, 1981), p. 1244.

[337] Eric Metaxas, *Everything You Always Wanted to Know about God (but Were Afraid to Ask)* (Ventura, CA: Regal Publishing, 1982), pp. 90–94.

paying the death penalty that we deserve because of our rebellion against God. That was his whole mission in coming to earth. So, when you ask what motivated Him, well...I suppose the answer can be summed up in one word—and that word would be love."[338]

Miracle Max: Hey! Hello in there. Hey! What's so important? What you got here that's worth living for? *[presses on Westley's chest to force the air back out]*

Westley *[faintly]*: Truuueee...looovvveee...

Inigo Montoya *[excited]*: True love! You heard him! You could not ask for a more noble cause than that.

Miracle Max: Sonny, true love is the greatest thing in the world. Except for a nice MLT—mutton, lettuce, and tomato sandwich, where the mutton is nice and lean and the tomato is ripe. They're so perky, I love that. But that's not what he said! He distinctly said "to blave." And, as we all know, "to blave" means "to bluff," huh? So, you're probably playing cards, and he cheated—

Valerie *[popping out from another room]*: Liar! LIAR! LIAAAR!

Miracle Max: Get back, witch!

Valerie: I'm not a witch, I'm your wife! But after what you just said, I'm not even sure I want to be *that* anymore!

Miracle Max: You never had it so good.

Valerie: "True love!" He said, "True love." Max! My God—

Miracle Max: Don't say another word, Valerie.

Valerie *[to the others]*: He's afraid. Ever since Prince Humperdinck fired him, his confidence is shattered.

Miracle Max: Why'd you say that name? You promised me that you would never say that name!

---

[338] Lee Strobel, *The Case for Christ* (Grand Rapids, MI: Zondervan, 1998), pp. 209, 210, 212.

GOD AND FREE WILL

Valerie: What, *Humperdinck? Humperdinck. [Begins chasing Max around the house.] Humperdinck.* Oooh, oooh, *Humperdinck*!

Miracle Max *[holding his hands over his ears]*: I'm not listening!

Valerie: True love, life expiring, and you don't have the decency to say why you won't help!

Miracle Max: Nobody's hearing nothing!

[Valerie continues repeating Humperdinck *at Max]*

Inigo Montoya *[simultaneously]*: This is Buttercup's true love! If you heal him, he will stop Humperdinck's wedding.[339]

"CHRISTMAS SONG"
by Dave Matthews

She was his girl; he was her boyfriend
She'd be his wife and make him her husband
A surprise on the way, any day, any day
One healthy little giggling dribbling baby boy
The wise men came, three made their way
To shower him with love
While he lay in the hay
Shower him with love, love, love
Love, love, love
Love, love was all around

Not very much of his childhood was known
Kept his mother Mary worried
Always out on his own
He met another Mary who for a reasonable fee,
less than reputable was known to be.
His heart full of love, love, love

---

[339] Rob Reiner, William Goldman, *Princess Bride* movie quote (1987).

Love, love, love
Love, love was all around

When Jesus Christ was nailed to his tree
Said "oh, Daddy-o, I can see how it all soon will be
I came to shed a little light on this darkening scene
Instead I fear I've spilled the blood of our children all around"
The blood of our children all around
The blood of our children's all around
So I'm told, so the story goes
The people he knew were
Less than golden hearted
Gamblers and Robbers
Drinkers and Jokers, all soul searchers
Like you and me.
Like you and me
Rumors insisted he soon would be
For his deviations
Taken into custody
By the authorities less informed than he.
Drinkers and Jokers all soul searchers
Searching for love, love, love
Love love, love
Love, love was all around

Preparations were made
For his celebration day
He said "eat this bread and think of it as me
Drink this wine and dream it will be
The blood of our children all around
The blood of our children's all around
The blood of our children all around
Father up above, why in all this hatred do you fill
Me up with love, love, love
Love, love, love

Love, love was all around
Father up above, why in all this anger do you fill
Me up with love, fill me love, love, love
Love, love, love all you need is love you can't buy me love
Love, love, love
Love, love
And the blood of our children's all around[340]

TRUTH

Let your yes mean yes and your no mean no! Anything more is from the evil one.[341]

In simple words, if you are a truthful person, you will be reliable regarding the truth you speak; therefore, no one should have doubts. In 1969, Pope Paul VI told his new bishop: "Error makes its way because truth is not taught. We must teach the truth, repeat it, not attacking the ones who teach errors, because that would never end—they are so numerous. We have to teach the truth."[342] Cardinal Gagnon writes, "He told me truth has a grace attached to it. Anytime we speak the truth, we conform to what Christ teaches and what is being taught us by the Church. Every time we stand up for the truth, there is an internal grace from God that accompanies that truth…He said that error does not have grace accompanying it. It might have all the external means, but it does not have the grace of God accompanying it."[343]

The Bible is filled with stories regarding the meaning of truth. To cite just a few:

---

[340] Dave Matthews, "Christmas Song," *Remember Two Things* CD (1997).
[341] Matthew 5:37, National Conferences of Bishops, the New American Bible (Wichita, KS: Devore & Sons, 1981), p. 1016.
[342] Thomas Langan, *The Catholic Tradition* (St. Louis: University of Missouri Press, 1998), p. 371.
[343] Ibid.

We saw his glory as of the Father's only son, full of grace and truth.[344]

And you will know the truth, and the truth will make you free.[345]

Therefore Pilate said to Him, "So you are a king?" Jesus answered, "You say correctly that I am a king. For this I have been born, and for this I have come into the world, to testify to the truth. Everyone who is of the truth hears my voice."[346]

Jesus answered him, "If I have spoken wrongly, testify to the wrong; but if I have spoken rightly, why do you strike me?"[347]

The opposite of truth is a lie, a falsehood—a fib.

Lies are one of the easiest places to run to. They give you a sense of safety, a place where you have to depend only on yourself. But it's a dark place. Lies are a little fortress; inside you can feel safe and powerful. Through your little fortress of lies you try to run your life and manipulate others. But the fortress needs walls, so you build some. These are the justification for your lies. You tell lies not to protect her but to protect yourself because you are afraid of having to deal with the emotions you might encounter both from her and in yourself. You lie to protect yourself. What if she does not forgive me? Ah, that is the risk of faith and truth.[348]

God is bigger than lies. Jesus taught us to live in God—pure love, pure truth. Truth demands obedience, discipline, and transparency to God's love. Truth forces man to look into his soul and admit his sins, weaknesses, and insecurities. Truth requires change, and people are afraid of change. Even if one lives in chaos, chaos is the comfort zone.

---

[344] John 1:14, National Conferences of Bishops, the New American Bible (Wichita, KS: Devore & Sons, 1981), p. 1137.
[345] Ibid., 14.6, p. 1158.
[346] Ibid., 18:37, p. 1164.
[347] Ibid., 18:23, p. 1163.
[348] W. P. Young, *The Shack* (Newbury Park, CA: Windblown Media, 2008), p. 189.

Change requires trust, and trust is submission, and submission is giving up control.

> *Where did this man get all this? What is this wisdom that has been given to him? What deeds of power are being done by his hands? Is not this the carpenter, the son of Mary and brother of James and Joseph and Judas and Simon, and are not his sisters here with us?' And they took offense at him.*[349]

Jesus spoke the truth in His own town to people who knew Him to be from a righteous man, and yet even they took offense.

> *In Judaism you needed the testimony of two witnesses so witness A could witness the truth of witness B and vice versa. But Jesus witnesses to the truth of his own sayings. Instead of basing his teaching on the authority of others, he speaks on his own authority. He begins his teachings with the phrase "Amen I say to you," which is to say, "I swear in advance to the truthfulness of what I'm about to say."*[350]

In 2009 at the Miss USA Pageant, Miss California, Carrie Prejean, spoke what she felt was her truth when asked by a judge if gays should be allowed to marry. Her reply set off a national firebomb. "Well, I think it's great that Americans are able to choose one or the other. Um, we live in a land that you can choose same-sex marriage or opposite marriage, and you know what, in my country and in, in my family, I think that I believe that a marriage should be between a man and a woman. No offense to anybody out there. But that's how I was raised, and that's how I think that it should be between a man and a woman."[351] Why did this controversy explode and express outrage among people? Carrie's statement was immediately met with swift anger and criticism. Many felt that her statement went against popular liberal culture and political

---

[349] Matthew 13:54–57, National Conferences of Bishops, the New American Bible (Wichita, KS: Devore & Sons, 1981), p. 1031.
[350] Lee Strobel, *The Case for Christ* (Grand Rapids, MI: Zondervan, 1998), p. 146.
[351] Ann Coulter, *Demonic* (New York: Crown Forum, 2011), p. 251.

correctness that a man and woman can marry any one they want to even if it is of the same sex despite what the morality of religious orders and beliefs dictate. MSNBC's talk show host Keith Olbermann and Michael Musto from the *Village Voice* tried to demolish Miss Prejean's wholesome reputation night after night on this program. They called her stupid, compared her to an Italian suppository, and made suggestions that she needed fat from her butt injected into her brain. God's truth does not define political correctness. Truth never is pretentious.

Little sixteen-year-old Justin Bieber also felt the sting of speaking the truth. An international culture pop singer from Canada, Justin was "denounced as a jerk" after airing his views regarding premarital sex and abortion in a *Rolling Stone* interview. "Bieber told the interviewer he believed you should just wait until you're in love to have sex. But most risky for his singing career, he said I really don't believe in abortion because it's like killing babies. Bieber was promptly ridiculed by the coven on *The View*. MSNBC's Beltway blog bravely derided Bieber in an anonymous item intended to teach Justin about keeping his mouth shut with reporters. It wittily said, 'Dear Biebs: You are simply adorable when talking about girls and music but talking politics with Rolling Stone is not a wise move. We know you're just a 16-year-old Canadian, but that's all the more reason you shouldn't be pontificating about American politics, abortion and rape.'"[352] Why can't a sixteen-year-old pontificate his beliefs that are keeping with the teachings of Christ? No one else will! These two individuals used courage to showcase God's glory. The outrage against them was because they were right and spoke according to God's teaching rather than the false promises and seduction of this world.

They are the people who hear the Word, but worldly anxiety, the lure of riches and the craving for other things intrude and choke the word, and it bears no fruit.[353]

---

[352] Ibid.
[353] Emmet Fox, *Around the World* (San Francisco: Harper, 1992), p. 13.

I can use a statement from *The Shack* by Paul Young that may help to explain the odd reaction to Carrie Prejean's and Justin Bieber's comments.

> *Most emotions are response to perceptions—what you think is true about a given situation. If your perception is false, then your emotional response to it will be false too. So, check your perceptions, and beyond that check the truthfulness of your paradigms—what you believe. Just because you believe something firmly doesn't make it true. The more you live in the truth, the more your emotions will help you see clearly. But even then, you don't want to trust them more than me [that is—God].*[354]

Jesus Christ spoke the truth, and He challenged the authority to submit to change. And for that, He was crucified. Jesus was willing to die for His principles, for his principles were the Word, and the Word is God. Rejecting His death was to give in to a lie, and Jesus is unadulterated and pure truth. With the exception of Judas, all the apostles believed in the truth, and with the exception of John, all were put to death for their belief in the truth. I heard Tim Tebow on the radio say, "If you do not have enemies, then you are not standing up for something righteous." Throughout the Gospels, Jesus stood up for truth and what's righteous, and He indeed made many enemies.

> *The first main aspect of God is Life. God is not just living, nor does God give life, but God is life. Where God is, there is life. The second main aspect of God is Truth. God is not truthful but Truth itself, and wherever there is Truth, there is God. There are many things that are relatively true at certain times and places only, but God is absolute Truth at all times and in all circumstances. As soon as we touch God, who is the absolute, relative thing disappear. Over the century's mankind has attempted to bend the truth, sway the truth, change and deny the truth so that it will conform to meet man's ideology at the time. Despite what man wants, the Truth*

---

[354] W. P. Young, *The Shack* (Newbury Park, CA: Windblown Media, 2008).

will always be protected by the power of the Holy Spirit. Truth is constant—it never changes, transform, amends or waiver. Truth is the same in the past, the present, and the future. Truth is honest, sincere, genuine and pure.

Jesus Christ summed up this truth, taught it completely and thoroughly, and above all, demonstrated it in His own person. Most of us now can glimpse intellectually the idea of what it must mean in its fullness. To accept the Truth is the great first step, but not until we have proved it in doing is it ours. Jesus proved everything that He taught, even to the overcoming of death in what we call the resurrection. By surmounting every sort of limitation to which mankind is subjected, He performed a work of unique and incalculable value to the race and is therefore justly entitled the Savior of the world.[355]

Let's look at two facts of logic between God and truth. Fact number 1: what is true is also factual, accurate, and correct; and what is real is authentic, genuine, and actual. Fact number 2: God is the Creator of all that is real, and therefore, what is real has its beginning, foundation, and origin in God. If the origin of what is real is in God, then God is also the origin of truth. We believe this to be true because in John 14:6, Jesus says, "I am the way and the truth and the life." This truth, which is Jesus, came from God, was sent into the darkness of the world for the salvation and everlasting life of man. Once we learn the truth, we must commit ourselves to the truth and be on constant defense, for the lies and delusion a darken and fallen world will try and deceive you of all that is true.

Lieutenant Kaffee: I want the truth!

Colonel Jessup [*shouting*]: You can't handle the truth!

Colonel Jessup: Son, we live in a world that has walls, and those walls need to be guarded by men with guns. Who's going to do it? You?

---

[355] Emmet Fox, *Around the World* (San Francisco: Harper, 1999), pp. 79 and 365.

You Lieutenant Weinberg? I have a greater responsibility than you can possibly fathom. You weep for Santiago and curse the Marines—you have that luxury. You have the luxury of not knowing what I know: that Santiago's death, while tragic, probably saved lives, and that my existence, while grotesque and incomprehensible to you, saves lives. You don't want the truth because deep down, in places you don't talk about it, at parties, you want me on that wall, you need me on that wall. We use words like *honor*, *code*, and *loyalty*. We use them as the backbone of a life trying to defend something. You use them as a punch line. I have neither the time nor the inclination to explain myself to a man who rises and sleeps under the blanket of the very freedom I provide and then questions the manner in which I provide it. I would rather you just said thank-you and went on your way. Otherwise, I suggest that you pick up a weapon and stand a post. Either way, I don't give a damn what you think you are entitled to.[356]

Things to contemplate alone or with a group:

- What about this story caught your attention, and why?
- How would you put PFLT in order? Is peace needed first, or should forgiveness be placed first?
- Should you be truthful or tell a lie if you know you will hurt someone's feelings?
- Do you speak the truth despite not following pop culture's view?
- Why is it so hard to forgive?
- Have you asked forgiveness from all that you have harmed?
- Does forgiving mean forgetting?
- Who is in the greatest need of love from you?
- Does love mean liking the person?
- How can you bring peace to another?
- Is there dissension in your family that you can bring the message of PFLT?

---

[356] Aaron Sorkin, Rob Reiner, *A Few Good Men* movie quote (1992).

CHAPTER 17

SUPERSTAR

I was fourteen years old when the movie version of the rock opera *Jesus Christ Superstar* appeared in 1973. Having been very familiar with the Broadway record (*records* are now called CD), I could not wait to see the movie. The night the movie premiered, the band director from the University of Southwest Louisiana invited my father to sit with the band to watch the football game and the band's halftime performance. My father had several of his high school band students in USL band. I wanted to go to the game, but I also wanted to see the movie. So, after the halftime show was over, my parents and I left the stadium and raced to the theater that had a 9:00 p.m. showing. Forty-six years later I am still belting out the songs to *Jesus Christ Superstar*. I had to wait thirty years to see the actual traveling Broadway production when it played New Orleans in 2003. When my son Dominic went to Cap 21 training in New York City, *JCS* was playing on Broadway. Because of me, he too was very familiar with the musical. I convinced him to go to the production. Afterward viewing the musical, Dominic was very impressed with the production. Now when he and I are together in a car, and he asks me what I want to listen to, I tell him *JCS*! Recently he has gotten tired of me asking him to "put it on." He now yells back, "No, Dad! I don't want to hear that again!" I missed agitating him with that request!

Jesus Christ Jesus Christ
Who are you?
What have you sacrificed?
Jesus Christ Jesus Christ
Who are you?
What have you sacrificed?
Jesus Christ Superstar
Do you think you're what they say you are?
Jesus Christ Superstar
Do you think you're what they say you are?[357]

History is full of people claiming they hear a message from God while others claim they are a "god." However, no other man could back up the truth quite like the superstar Jesus. In the book *Life of Christ* by Bishop Fulton J. Sheen, he explains the passing of the litmus test this way:

> *Reason dictates that if any one of these men actually came from God, the least thing that God could do to support His claim would be to pre-announce His coming.... If God sent anyone from Himself, or if He came Himself with a vitally important message for all men, it would seem reasonable that He would first let men know when His messenger was coming, where He would be born, where He would live, the doctrine He would teach, the enemies He would make, the program He would adopt for the future, and the manner of His death. By the extent to which the messenger conformed to these announcements, one could judge the validity of his claims... Socrates had no one to foretell his birth. Buddha had no one to pre-announce him and his message or tell the day when he would sit under the tree. Confucius did not have the name of his mother or his birthplace recorded, nor were they given to men centuries before he arrived so that when he did come, men would know he was a messenger from God...There were no predictions about Buddha,*

---

[357] Andrew Lloyd Webber, Tim Rice, *Jesus Christ Superstar* (1971).

Confucius, Lao-tze, Mohammed, or anyone else; but there were predictions about Christ.[358]

In his other book *Your Life Is Worth Living*, Bishop Sheen puts it like this:

If anyone is coming from God with a revelation for our reason and strength for our will, reason is going to impose certain test. If God is going to send someone to this earth certainly the least, He can do is to let us know. This requirement will do away with the idea of any individual suddenly appearing upon the stage of History and saying, "I am God," or I have a message from God. Buddha, Confucius, Lao-tze, Mohammed, Mark, Brahmans, witch doctors, Hindu philosophers, university professors, anyone you please and the founder of the latest cult! Stand there, we want to ask you questions: Buddha, did anyone ever know you were coming? Confucius, was the place of your birth prophesied? Socrates, did anyone foretell you would die of hemlock juice? Did any one of your mothers know you were coming? Is there a single one of you who can pinpoint to a historical record in which it was foretold where you would live, where and how you would die, what your character would be, the manner of your teaching, the kind of enemies you would provoke, and evoke by the dignity of teaching? Now, one steps out of the ranks. What is your name? My name is Jesus Christ.[359]

Only Jesus Christ is foretold in the Bible: prophesied in the Old Testament and validated in the New Testament. Some of the Old Testament prophecies are as follows: "He will be the offspring of a woman and defeat Satan" (Genesis 3:15); "He will not have any of his bones broken" (Exodus 12:46); "He will not decay in the grave" (Psalm 16:10); "He will be forsaken by God, mocked, by people, and have his clothing divided by the casting of dice" (Psalm 22:1–8); He will be

---

[358] Bishop Fulton J. Sheen, *Life of Christ* (New York: Doubleday, 1997), pp. 1–3.
[359] Bishop Fulton L. Sheen, *Your Life Is Worth Living* (Schnecksville, PA: St. Andrew's Press, 2014), pp. 38–39.

rejected by a friend" (Psalm 41:9); "He will ascend into heaven" (Psalm 47:5); "He will be born of a virgin" (Isaiah 7:14); "He will perform miracles" (Isaiah 35:5–6); "He will be spat on and beaten" (Isaiah 53:6); "Be silent as a lamb" (Isaiah 53:7); "Burial by a rich man" (Isaiah 53:9); "He will be alive during the slaughter of Bethlehem's children" (Jeremiah 31:15); "He will enter Jerusalem by riding a donkey" (Zechariah 9:9) "He will be betrayed for thirty pieces of silver, which will later buy a potter's field" (Zechariah 11:12–13); "He will be pierced" (Zechariah 12:10).[360] Psalm 22 was written about one thousand years before the birth of Jesus while Isaiah 53 was written about seven hundred years before Jesus's birth.

> Daniel 9:24–26 *foretells that the Messiah would appear a certain length of time after King Artaxerxes I issued a decree for the Jewish people to go from Persia to rebuild the walls in Jerusalem. That puts the anticipated appearance of the Messiah at the exact moment in history when Jesus showed up. Is it possible that Jesus merely fulfilled the prophecies by accident? Maybe he's just one of many throughout history who have coincidentally fit the prophetic fingerprints. "Not a chance came," Lapides response. The odds are so astronomical that they rule them out. Someone did the math and figured out that the probability of just eight prophecies being fulfilled is one chance in one hundred million billion! The probability of fulfilling forty-eight prophecies was one chance in a trillion, trillion, trillion, trillion, trillion, trillion, trillion, trillion, trillion, trillion, trillion, trillion, and trillion. The odds alone say it would be impossible for anyone to fulfill the Old Testament prophecies. Yet, Jesus—and only Jesus throughout all of history —managed to do it.*[361]

---

[360] The American Bible Society, *Bible Prophecies: Faith, History and Hope* (New York: Time Inc., 2009).

[361] Lee Strobel, *The Case for Christ* (Grand Rapids, MI: Zondervan, 1998), pp. 197, 198, 200.

Continuing on, Bishop Sheen writes,

> *A second distinguishing fact is that once Jesus appeared, He struck history with such impact that He split it in two, dividing it into two periods: one before His coming, the other after it. Buddha did not do this, nor did any of the great Indian philosophers. Even those who deny God must date their attacks upon Him, A.D. so and so, or so many years after His coming.*[362]

Today the politically correct indication is now recorded as *BCE* (Before Common Era) and *CE* (Common Era). To add to this topic, Jon Kennedy writes in his book *Jesus, His External Legacy*,

> *Though there has been efforts, for some years to redefine the western calendar as divided between b.c.e. (before common era) and c.e. (Common era) rather than b.c. (before Christ) and a.d. (Anno Domini, or year of our Lord), there can still be little doubt about the dividing line between the "before" and "after"; it is the approximate birth of Jesus, the God whose incarnation marks, for Christians, the watershed between lost and found, between law and grace, old and new, and the world that was perishing and the world being renewed.*[363]

In his third fact, Bishop Sheen concludes Jesus is separated from every other leader because

> *every other person who ever came into this world came to live. He came into it to die. Death was a stumbling block to Socrates—it interrupted his teaching. But to Christ, death was the goal and fulfillment of His life; the goal that He was seeking…the story of every human life begins with birth and ends with death. In the*

---

[362] Bishop Fulton J. Sheen, *Life of Christ* (New York: Doubleday, 1997), p. 7.
[363] Ibid., p. 7.

Person of Christ, however, it was his death that was first and His Life that was last."[364]

A fourth distinguishing fact from the Bishop is

Christ did not fit, as the other world teachers do, into the established category of a good man. Good men do not lie. But if Christ was not all that He said He was, namely, the Son of the living God, the Word of God in the flesh, then He was not "just a good man"; then He was a knave, a liar, a charlatan and the greatest deceiver who ever lived. If he was not what he said He was, the Christ, the Son of God, He was the anti-Christ. If He was only a man, then He was not even a "good" man.[365]

Jesus clearly distinguished Himself from all of the prophets and from Confucius, Buddha, Muhammad, Lao Tzu, etc. by actually claiming to be God and the Son of God. No one else has this claim. In his book *The Better Part*, Father John Bartunek writes, "Jesus Christ makes more 'I' statements than any other world's great religious figures, and we shouldn't overlook this. Buddha pointed to the Four Noble Truths, Mohammad to the words he received from Allah, and even Moses drew his people's attention to their covenant with God and the Ten Commandments, but Jesus Christ never tires of calling men to himself: 'I am the way, the truth and the life (John 14:6); I am the vine (John 15:5); I am the light of the world (John 8:12) and in this passage: Follow me…I came to call sinners (Luke 5:32). Jesus Christ is the cornerstone (Acts 4:11), the one foundation upon which the house of salvation is built (1 Corinthians 3:11)." Here are some other "I" statements of Jesus: "I am the light of the world"[366] (John 8:12); "Before Abraham was, I am" (John 8:59); "I came from God and am here; I did not come on my own but He sent me." (John 8:42)[367]

---

[364] Ibid., p. 7.
[365] Ibid., p. 7.
[366] John 8:12, the New American Bible, p. 1149.
[367] Ibid., p. 1150.

While those quotes are beautiful, my two favorite "I" quotes from Jesus are so powerful, they strike fear into the hearts and souls of his enemies.

"Whom are you looking for?" They answered him, "Jesus the Nazorean." Jesus answered to them "I am." When He said to them "I AM," they turned away and fell to the ground.[368]

Wow! Why would they fall to the ground over two little words: "I am"? What were they afraid of? After all, Jesus was surrounded by a "large crowd with swords and clubs."[369] But here is the best one of the two. Jesus is in the presence of a frustrated Caiaphas, who cannot understand why Jesus is silent to all of the false allegations brought against Him.

The high priest said to him, "I order you to tell us under oath before the living God, 'Are you the Messiah, the Son of the Blessed One?'" Then Jesus answered, "I am."[370]

Caiaphas is so shocked that he tears his garments and yells, "Blasphemy!"

Jesus didn't just claim to be God—he backed it up with amazing feats of healing, with astounding demonstrations of power over nature, with transcendent and unprecedented teachings, with divine insights into people, and ultimately with his own resurrection from the dead, which absolutely nobody else had been able to duplicate. The resurrection was the ultimate vindication of his identity.[371]

---

[368] John 18:5–6, p. 1162.
[369] Matthew 26:47, Stephen J. Hartdegen, OFM, the New American Bible (Catholic Bible Press,1987), p. 1108.
[370] Mark 14:61, Stephen J. Hartdegen, OFM, the New American Bible (Catholic Bible Press, 1987),p. 1138.
[371] Lee Strobell, *The Case for Christ* (Grand Rapids, MI: Zondervan, 1998), pp. 159, 170.

In addition to all of the miracles that Jesus performed to prove His authority, He forgives sins. This was mind-blowing to the Jewish authority, for they knew and understood that only "Yahweh" can forgive sins. More mind-blowing news? On two separate occasions, the crowds gathered around Jesus heard the booming voice of God when God spoke, "This is my beloved Son whom I am well pleased. Hear Him." This can be found at the baptism of Jesus by John at the Jordan River (Matthew 3:17). At the Transfiguration of Jesus (Matthew 17:5), Peter, James, and John also heard God say, "This is my beloved Son whom I am well pleased. Listen to Him."

Still having some minor doubts of His "star power"? That's okay. Let's take a look at how His death makes Jesus shine the brightest. For over three years Jesus was gaining a reputation throughout Judea. He was all the buzz and the talk of the town and the hot gossip during the festival of Passover in Jerusalem. Jerusalem was filled with hundreds of thousands of pilgrimages and several thousand highly trained Roman soldiers. The city had the feel and atmosphere of a huge Mardi Gras carnival celebration. At the height of the celebration, Jesus enters the city riding on a donkey as a symbolic triumphant and peaceful king. Jerusalem explodes with exhilaration. The visiting pilgrimages came out in droves; maybe ten to fifteen people deep to see the man everyone was talking about. They hailed Him, tried to touch Him, brought their children to Him, and waved palm branches as if He was king. The news even reached King Herod, and he too was filled with great anticipation to meet this man. Five days later, this Jesus was dead and buried. Those who hailed Him earlier witnessed His frail, scourged, and unrecognizable, battered body, dragging a heavy cross upon his shoulder throughout the city to "the place of the skull" to be crucified. In other words, there were hundreds if not thousands of witnesses.

What a startling blow it must have been to all those who looked forward to Jesus as the Savior of Israel. His death surely must have been a high topic of discussion throughout the city. His death was surely a high topic of discussion among the temple leaders! So much a discussion that the temple principals asked Pilate to have guards placed at His tomb to prevent the body from being stolen by His disciples and proclaim that He has risen. They even went so far as to seal the tomb. Roman guards were not just any solider. They were highly trained centurions. They were the best of the best. Failure to carry out their duties could result in severe punishment or death. So, guarding the tomb of Jesus was something they did not take lightly. After all that happened the day before, these pagan men would have been on high alert! Surely, they discussed among themselves the strange and unexplained events that occurred on that Friday. As soon as Jesus died,

> *the veil of the sanctuary was torn in two from top to bottom. The earth quaked, rocks were split, tombs were opened, and the bodies of many saints who had fallen asleep were raised.*[372]

And then what happened? Sunday morning, there were neither guards nor a dead decomposing body of a man that died three days earlier! All that was left was a broken seal, a rolled-backed door, the burial cloth of Jesus, and a couple of angels hanging around.

> *And behold there was a great earthquake; for an angel of the Lord descended from Heaven, approached, rolled back the stone, and sat upon it.*
>
> *His appearance was like lightning and his clothing was white as snow. The guards were shaken with fear of him and became like dead men.*[373]

The Roman guards were so frightened that they were paralyzed by fear to move a muscle! After Jesus leaves the tomb, the soldiers go running to the city to tell their superiors what had happened. They had to be bribed to keep silent:

> *Some of the guards went into the city and told the chief priests all that had happen. They assemble with the elders and took counsel;*

---

[372] Matthew 27:51–52, p. 1060.
[373] Ibid., 28:1–4, p. 1062.

GOD AND FREE WILL

then they gave a large sum of money to the soldiers, telling them you are to say his disciples came by night and stole the body while they were asleep. And if this gets to the governor ears, we will satisfy him and keep you of trouble.[374]

What a huge cover-up! However, the silence of the centurions would not remain still for very long, for the holy women were about to spread wonderful and amazing news.

Mary Magdala came to the tomb early in the morning while it was still dark and saw the stone was removed from the tomb.[375]

Notice there is no mention of any guards, and the seal had been broken because the tomb was open.

Entering the tomb, the women were terrified. The angels said: "Do not be afraid! I know you are looking are seeking Jesus the crucified. He is not here, for he has been raised just as he said; Come and see the place where he lay. Then go quickly and go and tell his disciples. He has been raised from the dead, and he is going to Galilee, there you will see him."[376]

So off she runs to tell Peter and the other apostles. They don't believe her because women at that time were not credible witnesses. So, Peter and John dashed off to the tomb, and John arrived first. After Peter arrived,

they enter the tomb and saw the burial clothes there, and the cloth that had covered his head, not with the burial cloths but rolled up in a separate place.[377]

---

[374] Ibid., 28:11–14.
[375] John 20:1, p. 1166.
[376] Matthew 28:1–8, pp. 1061–1062.
[377] John 20:6–7, the New American Bible, p. 1166.

If His apostles were going to risk stealing the body by overpowering centurions, would they take the time to take off the burial cloths, much less "roll it up"? No, they would not! They would have hurried up as fast as they could to get out of a dangerous situation with the body. In any case, the apostles were not trained soldiers; they could not have defeated Roman centurions! Keep in mind the apostles were nowhere to be found. That Thursday night they ran for the hills as Jesus was arrested. They were scared to death that the Romans and temple guards were going to arrest them as well! They disobeyed, denied, and deserted Jesus, and they went into hiding.

The Bible goes on to say that after His resurrection, Jesus spends the next forty days with His apostles and His disciples. In other words, again there were a lot of witnesses to seeing the resurrected Jesus! Jesus then ascends to the heavens with over five hundred people witnessing this miraculous event. Words of Jesus's resurrection surely would have spread throughout Jerusalem like a fast-acting plague!

Paul writes in 1 Corinthians 9:1, "Am I not an apostle? Have I not seen Jesus our Lord?" And he says in 1 Corinthians 15:8, "Last of all he appeared to me also." Paul continues, "Christ appeared to Cephas, and then to the twelve. After that, he appeared to more than five hundred of the brothers and sisters at the same time, most of whom are still living though some have fallen asleep. Then he appeared to James, then to all the apostles." The book of Acts is littered with references to Jesus's appearances. The apostle Peter was especially adamant about it. He says in Acts 2:32, "God has raised this Jesus to life, and we are all witnesses of it." In Acts 3:15, he repeats, "You killed the author of life, but God raised him form the dead. We are witnesses of this." He confirms to Cornelius in Acts 10:41 that he and others "ate and drank with him after he rose from the dead." And in Acts 13:31, "For many days he was seen by those who had traveled with him from Galilee to Jerusalem."[378]

---

[378] Lee Strobel, *The Case for Christ* (Grand Rapids, MI: Zondervan, 1998), pp. 247, 254.

	Jesus	Mohammed	Buddha	Confucius	Lao-Tze	Prophets
Predicted	Yes	No	No	No	No	No
Conceived by the Holy Spirit	Yes	No	No	No	No	No
Performed miracles	Yes	No	No	No	No	Some but only through God
Raised people from the dead	Yes	No	No	No	No	One did through God's power
Claimed to be God	Yes	No	No	No	No	No
Died	Yes	Yes	Yes	Yes	Yes	Yes
Resurrected and witnessed ascension into heaven	Yes	No	No	No	No	No
Incarnated	Yes	No	No	No	No	No

The asking price to transform the world and save the world from our sins cost God the blood of His Son. Satan met his defeat at the cross, but he was most severely trounced at the empty tomb. At His death and resurrection, Jesus offered everlasting salvation by restoring the broken relationship man had with God. Now all things are possible because of Him. Jesus Christ truly is a *superstar*—and in a category of His own. I do not believe that anyone can sum up His stardom better than Bishop Sheen, but Laurie Beth Jones gives it all her best:

Jesus is one of the most revered and misrepresented figures in history. His life has inspired saints and incited riots. His image, which we have only reconstructed since there were no cameras in his time, decorates and sanctifies some of the most beautiful buildings in the world. His name is used for both cursing and blessing. Some people who sing it in churches on Sunday are afraid to mention it at work on Monday. People who claim to be his representatives have committed some of the most heinous acts against humanity. Religions have sprung up around him, nations have been divided, cultures have been delineated, and families have been torn apart. Cleary this man has had an impact on history.[379]

Recently I opened an email addressed to me but delivered from an unknown source. The subject simply said, "No Mere Man." In Groom, Texas, just outside of Amarillo, an artist sculptured the passion of Christ out of metal. The creator of this email took pictures of this man's artwork and attached a message to each picture. Here are the quotes from the pictures. (I'm sorry that I cannot give credit to the creator of the incredible metal art, to this email, and the attached pictures, but these are what the photos state:

Jesus Christ:

- In biology He was born without normal conception
- In poverty He was born. He had no wealth, no servants, yet millions and millions call Him Master, Lord, Savior, King, and God
- In chemistry He turned water into wine
- In physics He disproved the law of gravity by walking on water and ascending to heaven
- In economics He disproved the law of diminishing returns by feeding five thousand men with two fishes and five loaves of bread
- In medicine He cured the sick, the lame, and the blind without administering a single dose of drug
- In history He is the Alpha and the Omega, the beginning and the end

---

[379] Laurie Beth Jones, *Jesus: Life Coach* (Nashville, TN: Thomas Nelson, Inc., 2004), pp. xvii.

- In government He said that His kingdom is not of this world and that He shall be called wonderful counselor and prince of peace In religion He said that no one comes to the Father except through Him
- He had no degree, yet he is called Teacher
- He provided no medicine, yet He was a healer
- He had no army, yet kings feared Him
- He won no military battle, yet He conquered the world
- He committed no crime, yet He was crucified
- He was buried in a tomb, yet He rose from the dead and lives among us today at the right hand of God

Everything we just read about Jesus should be enough to authenticate his divinity and his kingship. But there is so much more! Remember reading in the Gospel of John where John writes that if everything about Jesus were recorded, the book of record would be enormous. There are many references in the Old Testament referring to Jesus as a superstar (i.e., King). In the New Testament, Matthew refers to Jesus as *King* fourteen times while Mark has six, Luke has five, and John has fourteen. There are many other references to the divinity of Jesus: John 1:1, "The word was God"; John 1:14–15, "Glory of Father's only son"; John 8:19, "If you knew me you would know my father"; John 10:30–33, "The father and I are one." Many times my students would question me for references of Jesus other than the Bible. My reply is that there are many nonbiblical or religious historical books referring to Jesus and Christians. Here are a few.

Flavius Josephus, a Jewish historian (AD 37–101) living around the time of Christ and recording for the courts of numerous Roman emperors wrote this about Jesus:

> *About this time lived Jesus, a man full of wisdom, if indeed one may call him a man. For he was the doer of incredible things, and the teacher of such as gladly received the truth. He thus attracted to himself many Jewish people and many Gentiles. He was the Christ. On the accusation of the leading men of our people, Pilate*

condemned him to death upon the cross; nevertheless, those who had previously loved him still remained faithful to him. For on the third day he again appeared to them living, just as, in addition to a thousand other marvelous things, prophets sent by God had foretold. And to the present day the race of those who call themselves Christians after him has not ceased.[380]

Flavius Josephus recorded this tribute to Jesus in a time when Rome considered Christianity an unlawful religion.

Lucian of Samosata writes in *The Death of Peregrinus:*

The Christians, you know, worship a man to this day—the distinguished personage who introduced their novel rites, and was crucified on that account.... These misguided creatures start with the general conviction that they are immortal for all time, which explains the contempt of death and voluntary selfdevotion which are so common among them; and then it was impressed on them by their original lawgivers that they are all brothers, from the moment that they are converted, and deny the gods of Greece, and worship the crucified sage, and live after his laws. All this they take quite on faith, with the result that they despise all worldly goods alike, regarding them merely as common property.[381]

Around AD 221, Julius Africanus refers in his writings about a man named Thallus, who wrote a manuscript in AD 52 about how darkness fell upon the city around midday when the man Jesus was martyred:

Thallus, in the third book of histories, explains away this darkness as an eclipse of the sun—unreasonably, as it seems to me (unreasonably, of course, because a solar eclipse could not take place at the time of

---

[380] Jon Kennedy, *Jesus, His External Legacy* (New York City, NY: Fall River Press, 2010), p. 126.
[381] Ibid., p. 23.

the full moon, and it was at the season of the Paschal full moon that Christ died).[382]

So, what exactly is it about this God-man that makes Him a superstar? I have previously admitted how big a fan I am to the musical *Jesus Christ Superstar*. I have always been drawn to the second verse in the song "Superstar": "If you'd come today, You could have reached a whole nation. Israel in 4 BC had no mass communication." No mass communication, yet Jesus was able to deliver his message to over five thousand people (those who ate were about five thousand men, not including women and children[383]) without a massive stage, no microphone, or a television screen the size of the one in the Dallas Cowboys Stadium (159 feet x 71 feet = 11,289 sq. feet). Over two thousand years ago, Jesus started His ministry with twelve ordinary men in a time in the world that had no "mass communication." Today, in the year 2019, it is estimated there are 2.1 billion Christians worldwide. Can any celebrities match that status or attention? Nope!

Subsequently, how powerful was His voice to speak to such a crowd? What drew people to Him? What was it about Jesus that people wanted to be near Him? Touch Him? Cut a hole in the roof to lower a sick friend down to Him? Leave their former life and follow Him? Crawl on their knees to atone to Him? Bring their children to Him? Order their servants to bring messages to Him? Provide drink of water to Him? Pour expensive ointment on Him? Line the road with palm branches for Him? And die for Him? And die for Him they did! It can be said that those who encountered Jesus were sincerely and authentically changed.

> *The people of the Roman Empire initially thought this new Jewish sect curious, and then bizarre, then fair game for use in sports spectacles in their coliseums, and, finally, a threat, as their growth in numbers and unflagging loyalty to Christ made Jesus more beloved and worshipped by more people than the current Caser.*[384]

---

[382] Ibid., p. 23.
[383] Matthew 14:21.
[384] Jon Kennedy, *The Everything Jesus Book: His Life, His Teachings*.

> Shortly after the apostle Stephen was martyred "about 2000 suffered martyrdom during this persecution in Judea."[385]

> The martyrdom of thousands in the first three centuries of the church who were willing to face death rather than burn incense to Caesar or pagan idol, is the strongest evidence for the truth of the claims of the New Testament. Men who had recently been afraid to be seen with Jesus when He hung on the cross of dead and that his victory had procured their own hope for life beyond death.[386]

In AD 112, Tacitus writes in his book *Annals*,

> The emperor Nero hence to suppress the rumor that he was responsible for starting the great fire of Rome persecuted the Christians falsely charged with the guilt, and punished with the most exquisite tortures, the persons called the Christians who were hated for their enormities. Christus, the founder of the name was put to death by Pontius Pilate.[387]

Eusebius of Caesarea was a Roman historian (AD 263–339) who wrote in the *Ecclesiastical History (of the Church Book 5)*; it has a copy of an account from a Christian survivor that proclaims the Christians were being persecuted in AD 177 during the reign of Marcus Aurelius. One such story is about a young girl named Blandina, who stated, "Yes, I am," when asked by the governor if she was a Christian. Upon her profession of faith, Blandina was then whipped, beaten, and tortured. She was finally killed by a beast in the arena. An eyewitness to her death reports, "When we were all afraid, and her earthly mistress (who was herself facing the ordeal of martyrdom) was in agony lest she should be unable to make a bold confession of Christ because of bodily of weakness, Blandina was filled with such power that those who took it

---

[385] Ibid., p. 147.
[386] Ibid.
[387] Eric Metaxas, *Everything You Always Wanted to Know about God (but Were Afraid to Ask)* (Ventura, CA: Regal, 1982), p. 16.

GOD AND FREE WILL

in turns to subject her to every kind of torture from morning to night were exhausted by their efforts and confessed themselves beaten—they could think of nothing else to do to her. They were amazed that she was still breathing, for her whole body was mangled and her wounds gaped; they declared that torment of any kind was enough to part soul and body, let alone a succession of torments of such severity. But the blessed woman, wrestling magnificently, grew in strength as she proclaimed her faith, and found refreshment, rest and insensibility to her sufferings in uttering the words: "I am a Christian; we do nothing to be ashamed of."[388]

> When Jesus was crucified, his followers were discouraged and depressed. The Jesus movement was all but stopped in its tracks. Then, after a short period of time, we see them abandon their occupations, regathering and committing themselves to spreading a very specific message—that Jesus Christ was the Messiah of God who died on the cross, returned to life, and was seen alive by them. And they were willing to spend the rest of their lives proclaiming this, without any payoff from a human point of view. It's not as though there were a mansion awaiting them on the Mediterranean. They faced a life of hardship. They often went without food, slept exposed to the elements, and were ridiculed, beaten, imprisoned. And finally, most of them were executed in torturous ways.[389]

Dying for Jesus:

- Peter: Crucified upside down around AD 64 in Rome
- Jude: Clubbed to death then beheaded
- James the Great: Executed by sword by Herod Agrippa I, AD 44
- James the Less: Crucified then sawed in half after his death
- Andrew: Crucified on a diagonal X-shaped cross
- Philip: Crucified around AD 54

---

[388] WorldPress.Com, tdhigg 01 (August 4, 2012).
[389] Lee Strobel, *The Case for Christ* (Grand Rapids, MI: Zondervan, 1998), p. 266.

- Bartholomew: Flayed alive (skinned) then crucified and beheaded
- Thomas: Killed by a spear around AD 72
- Matthew: Axed to death
- Simon the Zealot: Sawed in half around AD 74
- Matthias (replaced Judas): Stoned and beheaded
- John: The only one who died of old age

According to the ICC (International Christian Concern), a human rights organization for religious freedom, this world continues to persecute Christians. Here are some 2011–2016 headlines across the world taken from the ICC website:

- Removal of Cross from Army Chapel in Afghanistan Stirs Controversy
- Mobile Networks Told to Ban "Jesus Christ" from Airwaves (Pakistan)
- Nigeria Militants Kill Children of Christian Convert
- Rimsha Masih, 11-year-old Christian girl charged with blasphemy by Islamic cleric in Islamabad, Pakistan
- Christians in Nepal Attacked as Constitutional Deadline Nears
- Chinese Special Agents Detain Distributor of Christian Documentary
- Philippines: No Breakthrough in Murder Investigation of Catholic Missionary
- Hundreds of Hardline Indonesian Muslims Rally Against Church on Sunday
- At the 2012 Democratic Convention, the crowd booed when the word *God* was placed back into the platform
- A suicide bomber drove his SUV loaded with explosives into a Catholic Church during Sunday morning service, killing 7 and severely injuring over 100 in Kaduna, Nigeria, on October 29, 2012.
- 2014: Isis radical groups are beheading and even crucifying Christians in Iraq and Syria

- 2014: Meriam Yehya Ibrahim, a 27-year-old Christian Sudanese mother that was eight months pregnant was condemned to death by hanging for having left her Islam faith. After succumbing to international protest, Meriam was released after spending two months in prison
- 2017: Thousands of Christians are still being slaughtered and killed by ISIS or ISIS (Islamic State of Iraq)
- 2019: China cracking down on Christianity by destroying hundreds of Christian churches
- 2019: Pastor Bryan Nerren of Tennessee arrested in India for violating Foreign Exchange Management Act—in simplicity, preaching Christianity.
- 2019: Islamic state terrorists kill 11 Christian hostages on Christmas Day to avenge the deaths of their leaders in Iraq and Syria

Why do men, women, and children believe and die for Jesus? Because He is God incarnate. Though He is not the Father, He is the second person of God in the Trinity—He is also the Son of God. Jesus is sinless and so pure that He radiates goodness, wholesome, honesty; but more importantly, Jesus radiates life and love. Can you imagine today—with emails, twentyfour-hour cable network news, texting, twittering, Facebook, and YouTube—how fast the first miracle of Jesus would have traveled globally? But, on the other hand, I wonder…with all our advanced technology, would people today really believe the miracles of Jesus, or would they doubt Him believing this was nothing but special effects created from Pixar! It probably was a good thing that Jesus came into being when He did. To mass a following of 2.1 billion followers would probably be difficult today even with our high-tech modern communication system.

Regarding this topic, T. S. Eliot sums it up very nicely in John Bartunek's book *The Better Part*:

> In culture more and more dominated by information and mass media, this is perhaps the greatest danger of all. The constant

flow of images, ideas, opinions, advertisements, chats, noise, music, entertainment, news, and everything else can, if we let it, create such a quantity of traffic in our minds that we become unable to savor truth, even on the off chance that we recognize it amidst the din. The same mind we use all day long, the one we fill with idle chatter and sensationalized news and everything else—that's the same mind we bring to prayer. Unless we put a fence around what we attend to in our minds, unless we practice self-mastery and discipline in our thoughts, the graces of God constantly sends us will bounce onto the top of the beaten track and sit there, easy picking for the devil.

Jesus is a superstar even if He did not perform all His miracles because He came into our being so that we may know the Father. It was never about Him, but always about the Father. His miracles were to catch the people's attention while showing the glory of the Father. The miracles were not publicity stunts, for that would be vanity. No, they were to show the power of God. Many times, after performing a miracle, Jesus gave strict instructions not to disclose the healing to anyone. Often Jesus refused to perform a miracle and instead was relying to showcase His authority and divinity by forgiving sins. The chief priests and elders approached Jesus and said,

> "*By what authority are you doing these things? And who gives you this authority?" Jesus relied; "I shall ask you one question, and if you answer it for me, then I shall tell you by which authority I do these things. Where was John's baptism from? Was it heavenly or human origin?" They discussed this among themselves and said "if we say of heavenly origin, they will say to us, 'then why did you not believe him?' But, if we say, of human origin, we fear the crowd for they all regard John as a prophet." So, they said to Jesus in reply, "we do not know." He himself said to them, "neither shall I tell you by what authority I do these things."*[390]

---

[390] Matthew 21:23–27, National Conferences of Bishops, the New American Bible (Wichita, KS: Devore & Sons, 1981), p. 1044.

Jesus spoke the "Word" not as a scribe or a Pharisee would but only as God can. He was accused by the religious elite as receiving his power from the prince of darkness himself—Beelzebub. Being God, Jesus was able to know what they are thinking and said this to them:

> *Every kingdom divided against itself will be laid waste, and no town or house divided against itself will stand. And if Satan drives out Satan, he is divided against himself; how then, will his kingdom stand? And If I drive out demons by Beelzebub, by whom do your own people drive them out? But if it is by the Spirit of God that I drive out demons, then the kingdom of God has come upon you.*[391]

Jesus came into being so that He could become the new Adam and establish His church as the new Eve. His kingdom was not of this world, but His kingship was of this world.

> *My kingdom does not belong to this world. If my kingdom did belong to this world, my attendants would be fighting to keep me from being handed over to the Jews. But as it is, my kingdom is not here.*[392]

Jesus connected with everyone from rich to poor. He often chose to intermingle with the lower class of society like the thieves, tax collectors, prostitutes, sick, ill, outcasts, downtrodden, undeserving, uneducated, and the illiterate. They too have a place in His kingdom. Jesus was just as comfortable eating with the wealthy as He was eating in the house of a poor person. Let's look at the story of Zacchaeus:

Accordingly to Luke, Zacchaeus is the chief tax collector in the town of Jericho (a tax collector was regarded as a great sinner). He is detested by the people, for he is employed by the Romans, and he is part of the corruption—scheming off the collected taxes and becomes rich. In addition, Luke says Zacchaeus is short in stature; most likely the villagers ridicule his height to show their contempt for him. As the

---

[391] Ibid., 12:24–28, p. 1027.
[392] John 18:36, the New American Bible, p. 1163.

story goes, Zacchaeus hears Jesus is approaching, and he cannot view Him, for the crowd is large. So, Zacchaeus climbs a sycamore tree so that he can get a glimpse of this miracle worker he has heard so much about. Whatever the crowds think of Zacchaeus, he does not let that deter him from seeing the Master. Then something amazing happens: Jesus sees Zacchaeus and calls out to him, "Zacchaeus, hurry up and come down, for I must stay at your house today!" The crowd and His disciples grow angry at Jesus dining with a sinner, but Zacchaeus stands his ground and is not affected by their resentments. Luke then tells us that before Jesus tells Zacchaeus anything, Zacchaeus knows what he must do, and he makes amends to Jesus. Jesus is overjoyed by Zacchaeus's enthusiasm to obtain salvation. Zacchaeus went out on a limb to secure his salvation.

Jesus's new teachings were outside of the box, not in keeping with the norms of the scribes and Pharisees:

It would be harder for a rich man to enter His Father's Kingdom than for a camel to walk into the eye of a needle.[393]

He approached women at a time when women were not too been seen or heard. They were property! He told them they too were included in His salvation plan. Jesus challenged the religious authority, taught openly in the towns and the temple, criticizing the scribes and Pharisees, calling them hypocrites. He was unafraid of their authority or the power of the Romans. He preached forgiveness and to turn your cheek when struck—offering the other cheek as well. He told his audience to pray and love your enemies rather than hate them. He was not politically correct.

To love your enemies, bless them that curse you, do good to them that hate you and pray for them which despitefully use you and persecute you.[394]

---

[393] Matthew 19:23, the New American Bible, p. 1041.
[394] Ibid., 5:43–46, p. 1061.

But most of all, what really set Himself apart from all other men? What really made Him a superstar was His incredible loving heart, His capacity to accept all men with all their sins, and His proficiency to give compassion, mercy, and forgiveness.

Jesus knew the truth of our situation. He knew that we needed saving, that we were not okay. But it's not as if He was happy about it. It broke His heart…it still breaks His heart. Because He knows that even though He reaches out to us, even though He died for us, many of us just won't accept His offer of salvation. He really does see us for who we are. He knows that without Him, without God, we are naturally inclined to darkness. That's why He came to save us; to offer Himself to us. He communicated with a balance between truth and love and grace. He was the perfect balance between truth, love and grace. He told an adulterous woman, "Go and sin no more," but He did it in a way that was obviously full of love and grace. Jesus said to the woman, "Where are those accusers of yours"? And she said they had left. And then Jesus said to her, "Neither do I condemn you; go and sin no more." So obviously Jesus hadn't taken lightly what the woman had done. He called it a sin. He didn't humiliate her. But He did called her sin out. Rather than stoning her as the law of Moses ordered, Jesus showed grace and love toward her. That's what was so new and shocking. He immediately offered her grace and love and forgiveness. That's not something we see in the other religious authority figures. They would have stoned her!

He was the ultimate communicator. He cared about being understood. And He didn't speak at them; he tried to communicate, telling stories and answering questions, there was something beautiful and compelling about Him. Jesus was the whole package. He said things that were true, but He said them in a way that was true too. The love and the grace were part of the truth. It wasn't just information. There's more to truth than mere information and facts. He communicated in a way that was challenging. It challenged the hearer to really pay attention—to think outside the box, to look deeper. To get the real meaning of what Jesus said or did one had to really pay attention. One had to think with one's heart. Jesus is far clever than we are…And in a way that's the point…he taught us that we cannot outsmart

God. He tells us that we will fail each time we try. He told us to be simple and innocent in our approached to God; to be humblethe way a child approaches thing. Jesus taught us to be humble and trusting and innocent, the way a child is—only then can we perceive truly. In a sense, that's what listening with one's heart means.[395]

Jesus was and still is the most straightforward, honest, and loving human being that ever walked on this earth. He was a straight shooter; you always knew where He stood. Never did He speak from both sides of his mouth. At times He was patient; at times He was soft-spoken. At times he was moved to tears and cried. Many times, He was perturbed; and one time, He yelled and screamed and turned over the money tables. He did this not to scare you but to tell you like it is. Jesus was also amazed. Only in this manner could we then fully understand our genuine circumstance. Thereby, we come to realize that Jesus wants us to approach Him with all our brokenness, with all our heartaches and troubles and sins. Only then on bended knees we can then ask Him for help. Jesus wants to be the person to fix things; He is not counting on us to be perfect before we approach Him. All we must do is say yes to Him when He asks us, "Will you follow Me? Do you believe?"

Reiterating Bishop Sheen, C. S. Lewis sums up Jesus's stardom from his writing in *Mere Christianity*:

---

[395] Eric Metaxas, *Everything You Always Wanted to Know about God (but Were Afraid to Ask)* (Ventura, CA: Regal, 1982), pp. 132–135.

To make the claim, if not true, either indicates madness or a lie, and if either of those are true of Him he couldn't possibly have been a great moral teacher.[396]

In the Old Testament, God showed his identity to Moses via a shadow; otherwise, Moses would have died by directly gazing upon God's face. "Moses said let me see your Glory. He answered I will, but my face you cannot see for now man sees me and still lives. When my glory pass you may see my back but my face is not to be seen."[397] But in the New Testament, Jesus shows three apostles His true identity by shining like a star. "While He was praying his face changed in appearance and his clothing became dazzling white" (Luke 9:29). Mark 9:2–3 records, "And he was transformed before them and his clothes became dazzling white, such as no fuller on earth could bleach them."[398] According to the mystic venerable Anne Catherine Emmerich, Jesus showed Mary and Joseph His true identity at birth: "I saw our Redeemer as a tiny child, shinning with a light that overpowered all the surrounding radiance."[399] "On the carpet before Mary lay the newborn Jesus in swaddling-clothes, a little child, beautiful and radiant as lightning."[400] Father John Bartunek declares, "He lifts his veil cloaking his divinity and His disciples became awake and afraid. If a passing glimpse of Jesus's splendor fills them with amazement, just imagine how easy it would have been for Him to win all of Palestine to His cause if He had fully unveiled His divinity."[401]

---

[396] Jon Kennedy, *Jesus, His External Legacy* (New York, NY: Fall River Press, 2010), p. 22.

[397] Exodus 34:18–23, American Bible (Nashville, TN: Catholic Bible Press, 1987), p. 84.

[398] Stephen J. Hartdegen, the New American Bible (Nashville, TN: Catholic Bible Press, 1987), pp. 1129 and 1161.

[399] Venerable Anne Catherine Emmerich, *The Life of the Blessed Virgin Mary* (Charlotte, NC: Tan Books, 2013), p. 198.

[400] Ibid., p. 199.

[401] Father John Bartunek, *The Better Part* (Hamden, CT: Circle Press, 2007), p. 622.

When Jesus took His last breath as a man and yielded His soul to God, the earth shook, wept, and moaned. "The veil of the Temple was torn in two from top to bottom; the earth quaked, the rocks split; the tombs opened, and the bodies of many holy men rose from the dead and appeared to a number of people. Meanwhile, the centurion, together with the others guarding Jesus, seeing the earthquake and all that was taking place and they were terrified and said, in truth this was the Son of God."[402] Just moments earlier, there were many mocking and taunting Jesus, jeering and laughing at Him to perform a superstar act by coming down from the cross. Now they were on their knees frightened as Jesus's stardom shone. "The Cross on which the innocent Jesus was cruelly executed is the place of utmost degradation and abandonment. Christ, our Redeemer, chose the Cross to bear the guilt of the world and to suffer the pain of the world. So, He brought the world back to God by his perfect love. The disciples, who before had lost all hope came to believe in Jesus' Resurrection because they saw Him in a different way after His death, spoke with Him and experienced Him as being alive."[403]

For the next forty days, Jesus remained among them. He appeared and disappeared! He walked through walls! To some He broke bread while others He walked about; still, to a few He waited on the shore while cooking. To one special person, He allowed the fingers of that man to probe His wounds. The many meetings with the risen Jesus ended with five hundred people witnessing His ascension into the heavens. All of this leaves no doubt to His being the only true *superstar*. The empty tomb on Easter Sunday places Jesus into a class all His own—a superstar, the likes of which this world has never seen before or ever since. Well, that is, until his second coming!

---

[402] Ibid., p. 326.
[403] Rev. John Trigilio Jr., PhD, and Rev. Kenneth Brighenti, PhD, *Youth Catechism of the Catholic Church* (San Francisco, CA: Ignatius Press, 2010), p. 68.

"SUPERSTAR"
from *Jesus Christ Superstar*
Andrew Lloyd Webber

Every time I look at you I don't understand
Why you let the things you did
Get so out of hand
You'd have managed better
If you'd had it planned
Now why'd you choose such a backward time
And such a strange land?

If you'd come today
You could have reached a whole nation
Israel in 4 B.C.
Had no mass communication

Jesus Christ
Jesus Christ
Who are you? What have you sacrificed?
Jesus Christ
Jesus Christ
Who are you? What have you sacrificed?
Jesus Christ
Superstar
Do you think you're what they say you are?
Jesus Christ
Superstar
Do you think you're what they say you are?

Tell me what you think
About your friends at the top
Now who do you think besides yourself
Was the pick of the crop?
Buddha was he where it's at?

Is he where you are?
Could Mohamed move a mountain or was that just PR?
Did you mean to die like that?
Was that a mistake or
Did you know your messy death would be a record breaker?[404]

Things to contemplate alone or with a group:

- What about this story caught your attention, and why?
- Has any religious leader ever been foretold besides Jesus Christ?
- Beside Jesus, do you know of any miracles performed by any other religious leader?
- Beside Jesus, do you know of any other religious leader that was raised from the dead and witnessed ascending into the heavens?
- Why are celebrities given titles as superstar?
- Why do people flock to current magazines for the latest gossip rather than reach for a Bible?
- Celebrities have massive followers. Can they give you peace and everlasting life?
- Can you list the other individuals raised from the dead listed in both the Old and New Testaments?

---

[404] Andrew Lloyd Webber, Tim Rice, *Jesus Christ Superstar* (1971).

CHAPTER 18

OPEN DOOR POLICY

When I moved away to New Orleans to attend nursing school, I often spoke to my classmates and my new friends in New Orleans about growing up in Abbeville, Louisiana. To those who inquired about my whereabouts, I often compared Abbeville to the 1960 television show *The Andy Griffith Show*. The fictional town of this show is a small rural North Carolina community called Mayberry, where everyone knows one another, attend church regularly, sing in the church choir, have little or no crime, and nobody locks their doors until nighttime. Like Mayberry, Abbeville is also a small rural community located in Cajun country of Southwest Louisiana. Not only did we know most of the people in town, we also knew everyone living in our school and neighborhood—right down to the parents, grandparents, children, boyfriends, girlfriends, and family pets. My family attended church regularly and then some. My father at one time directed the church choir with my mother playing the piano. My six older brothers and I all participated singing in the church choir and some of us served as altar boys. On Sunday afternoons, my parents often played volleyball for hours with members of our church parish along with the teachers and coaches from Mount Carmel Elementary and Vermilion Catholic High School. In summertime, I rode my bike by myself to and from baseball practice at Comeaux Park—about five miles from my house. After practice or the games, I would return safely on my bike usually into the early night. At nighttime, we chased and caught fireflies. During the school years, I walked to and from school with my friends, and yes—even when it rained or was cold.

I also had more than one set of parents. In fact, I had about twenty-fiveplus sets of parents! My neighborhood was so tightly entwined that all the kids in the neighborhood were practically raised by all the parents. We were praised, scolded, and disciplined by all of them. Knowing all the kids in the neighborhood led to endless games of kick the can, hide-and-seek, basketball, and football games. My brother Robert and I along with our friends PJ and Byron invented slow-motion football. The rules of football applied to this game, but you had to play it as if the TV camera of the NFL were filming it in slow motion. When I was playing varsity football as a freshman on our high school team, we introduced this concept of playing slow-motion football to the entire team. There we were on a Thursday afternoon, just after football practice, marching up and down the football field—playing slow-motion football with twenty-two high school football players!

My parents' kitchen was unofficially identified as the free local coffeehouse for many of my parents' friends. My mother—famous for her brownies, cinnamon rolls, and coffee cakes—always had large quantities of the goodies packed in Tupperware on the counter or in the freezer ready for anyone and all to eat. In addition, the twenty-quart coffeepot was always hot and full. And if it was ever empty, everyone knew where the coffee was stored. I cannot begin to count the numerous times that I walked into our house and found my friends' parents sitting around our table enjoying coffee, baked treats, and great conversation. The funny thing about this is that many times my parents were not even home! Tony and Evelyn Fontana's front door was always open, and they welcomed neighbors, friends, family, and strangers into their home. During football seasons, Saturday morning was an especially busy time around the kitchen table as coaches and friends stopped over for coffee, smokes, and goodies while rehashing the Friday night football game highlights. It was during this time that my father received his firsthand account concerning his son's performance at the previous night game. As the band director of Abbeville High School Wildcats, my father was obligated to watch other kids play football on Friday nights. Many times, the Saturday morning "quarterback sessions" lasted into the early afternoon as we then gathered around the TV to watch the Fighting Tigers of LSU.

Sports were not the only conversation held at the kitchen table. My parents were very involved in our church parish marriage counseling program. I tell you those sessions were most daunting. I usually bolted from the house when those couples seeking marital advice came over. Prayer meetings were also held for a couple of hours at our home usually on a Wednesday night. In addition to all this ongoing activity, my mother would seek out the less fortunate from time to time and have them over for Sunday dinner. Those less fortunate seeking refuge from hurricanes were also invited. At my parents' funerals, there was countless praise and gratitude expressed to my brothers and me from many of the recipients who were welcomed to my parents' table due to their unofficial open door policy.

> *The story of Noah and the ark yields some interestingly analysis as a type of Christ. The ark itself is a type of Christ! God gave Noah every detail of how it was to be built, from its dimensions to its purpose in protecting Noah and his family from the judgment that awaited the rest of the world. Likewise, God planned every minute detail of how Jesus would redeem God's people; not a single detail was left to man. As the big boat brought earthly salvation for Noah, so Christ brings external salvation for all who believe in Him. As the ark but had one door, so Christ is the door to God—He is the only way we can gain forgiveness for our sins and come to the Father.*[405]

Like my parents, Jesus has an open door policy. His invitation is to everyone that hears His words, repents, believes, and seeks salvation. After Jesus gave His "it's easier for a camel to pass through the eye of a

---

[405] Jerry MacGregor and Marie Prys, *1001 Surprising Things You Should Know about the Bible* (New York, NY: Fall River Press, 2002), p. 67.

needle than for one who is rich to enter the kingdom of God"[406] speech, the apostles were greatly astonished and asked, "Lord, who then can be saved?"[407] In *Acts 16:30–31*, Paul was asked by a jailer, "Sirs, what must I do to be saved?" And he said, "Believe in the Lord Jesus and you and your household will be saved."[408] The New Testament has around 175 passages referring to Jesus as the Savior, salvation, and/or being saved. In other words, salvation is the invitation to Jesus's open door. Some of the many passages that validate Jesus's invitation to be saved are the following:

- John 11:25: "Jesus said unto her, I am the resurrection, and the life: he that believeth in me, though he were dead, yet shall he live."[409]
- John 14:6: "Jesus said unto him, I am the way, the truth, and the life: no man cometh unto the Father, but by me."[410]
- John 6:40: "And this is the will of him that sent me, that everyone which seeth the Son, and believeth on him, may have everlasting life: and I will raise him up at the last day."[411]
- Mark 1:15: "And saying, the time is fulfilled, and the kingdom of God is at hand: repent ye and believe the gospel."[412]
- John 3:3: Jesus answered and said unto him, Verily, verily, I say unto thee, except a man be born again, he cannot see the kingdom of God.[413]
- John 3:16: "For God so loved the world, that he gave his only begotten Son, that whosoever believeth in him should not perish, but have everlasting life."[414]

---

[406] Matthew 19:24, National Conferences of Bishops, the New American Bible (Wichita, KS: Devore & Sons, 1981), p. 1040.
[407] Ibid., 19:25, p. 1041.
[408] Acts 16:30–31, p. 1192.
[409] John 11:25, the New American Bible, p. 1154.
[410] Ibid., p. 1158.
[411] Ibid., p. 1146.
[412] Mark 1:15, the New American Bible, p. 1066.
[413] John 3:3, the New American Bible, p. 1140.
[414] Ibid., p. 1141.

- First Timothy 1:15: "This is a faithful saying, and worthy of all acceptation, that Christ Jesus came into the world to save sinners; of whom I am chief."[415]
- Acts 26:18: "To open their eyes, and to turn them from darkness to light, and from the power of Satan unto God, that they may receive forgiveness of sins, and inheritance among them which are sanctified by faith that is in me."[416]
- Romans 10:13: "For whosoever shall call upon the name of the Lord shall be saved."[417]
- First Corinthians 3:11: "For other foundation can no man lay than that is laid, which is Jesus Christ."[418]
- Galatians 3:26: "For ye are all the children of God by faith in Christ Jesus."[419]
- Luke 12:31–32: "Seek the kingdom of God, and all these things shall be added to you. Do not fear, little flock, for it is your Father's good pleasure to give you the kingdom."[420]

To enter the kingdom of God, one must enter through the open door provided by Jesus. Contemporary thinking and teaching have many believing that all will be saved and enter the kingdom of God. But Jesus begs to differ on that, and He has explicitly stated so in the Gospels. Although the invitation is sent out to everyone, Jesus says to

> *enter through the narrow gate; for the narrow gate is wide and the road broad that leads to destruction, and those who enter through it are many. How narrow the gate and constricted the road that leads to life. And those who find it are few.*[421]

---

[415] 1 Timothy 1:15, the New American Bible, p. 1307.
[416] Acts 26:18, the New American Bible, p. 1203.
[417] Romans 10:13, the New American Bible, p. 1221.
[418] 1 Corinthians 3:11, the New American Bible, p. 1223.
[419] Galatians 3:26, the New American Bible, p. 1273.
[420] Luke 12:31–32, the New American Bible, p. 1115.
[421] Matthew 7:13–14, the New American Bible, p. 1019.

Here are a few other passages Jesus provides a warning to mankind that everyone will not enter through the open door:

- Matthew 3:12: "He will clear his threshing floor and gather his wheat into his barn, but the chaff he will burn with unquenchable fire."[422]
- Matthew 7:19: "Every tree that does not bear good fruit will be cut down and thrown into the fire[423]
- Matthew 7:26: "Everyone who listens to these words of mine but does not act on them will be like a fool who built on sand. The rain fell, the floods came, and the winds blew and buffeted the house and it collapsed and was completely ruined."[424]
- Matthew 26:41: "Then he will say to those on his left, depart from me, you accursed, into the external fire prepared for the devil and his angels."[425]
- Romans 2:12–13: "All who have sinned without the law will also perish without the law, and all who have sinned under the law will be judged by the law. For it is not the hearers of the law who are righteous before God, but the doers of the law who will be justified."[426]

In *Matthew 11:28*, Jesus summons all to enter his kingdom: "Come to me, all you who labor and are burdened and I will give you rest."[427] The invitation from Jesus is not sent to just a select few but rather Jesus is sending it to all men. Jesus proclaimed throughout His ministry that anyone who accepts Him would not be rejected. Jesus is not asking for perfection; He is asking for repentant sinners. By entering the open door of Jesus Christ, God will reveal to you His truth—a path that will bring you to ultimate freedom: "If you remain in my word, you will truly be

---

[422] Ibid., p. 1012.
[423] Ibid., p. 1019.
[424] Ibid., p. 1019.
[425] Ibid., p. 1056.
[426] Romans 2:12–13, the New American Bible, p. 1212.
[427] Matthew 11:28, the New American Bible, p. 1026.

my disciples, and you will know the truth and the truth will set you free."[428] In *John 10:7–9*, Jesus is the open door:

I say to you that I am the gate for the sheep. All who came [before me] are thieves and robbers, but the sheep did not listen to them. I am the gate. Whoever enters through me will be saved and will come in and go out and find pastures.

A thief comes only to steal and slaughter and destroy. I came so that they might have life and have it more abundantly.

William Holman Hunt has a famous painting titled *The Light of the World*. In this painting, Jesus is outside of an unopened door and looks as if He is about to knock. Very noticeable in the picture is the absence of outside handles. The door can only be opened from inside. Therefore, the painting is telling the story of *Revelation of John 3:20*.

Behold, I stand at the door and knock. If anyone hears my voice and opens the door [then] I will enter his house and dine with him, and he with me.

Even today, Jesus is standing outside of your door, waiting patiently for the person on the inside (you and I) to open the door. The question here is, will you open the door and invite Him in?

So, what is the moral of this short story? To be just like the many friends of Tony and Evelyn Fontana: have an understanding that the door is always open to friendship, companionship, brotherhood, sharing, and love. If one enters the open door of Jesus's kingdom, one will find the joys of everlasting life.

Igor: You know, I'll never forget my old dad. When these things would happen to him…the things he'd say to me.

Dr. Frederick Frankenstein: What did he say?

---

[428] John 8:31–32, the New American Bible, p. 1150.

Igor: "What the hell are you doing in the bathroom day and night? Why don't you get out of there and give someone else a chance?"[429]

Things to contemplate alone or with a group:

- What about this story caught your attention, and why? What does it take for you to open your door to Christ?
- Is your door to Christ closed, and if so, why is it closed?
- Does Jesus know where the coffee is stored in your home?
- Have you ever invited Jesus to have coffee with you?

---

[429] Mel Brooks, *Young Frankenstein* movie quote (1974).

CHAPTER 19

OH YEAH, A CONCLUSION

It has been ten long years since my daughter left for Italy and I began writing this book. I've changed it a thousand times. I cannot honestly say what motivated me to write. Maybe I began to write because it gave me something to do and to take my mind off from my worries while my daughter traveled the Italian countryside. Maybe I had too much idle time and I began writing out of boredom; maybe I wanted to show my children Dominic and Alissa who God is and how He interacts in our lives. Perhaps I was writing to prepare for my annulment process. Whatever the reasons were, I really want to use this opportunity to showcase my weaknesses, failures, struggles, obstacles, and success to highlight God's glory in my life. Despite all my setbacks, I am not angry or bitter. All my adversaries have brought me to where I am right now in my life, and for that I am a better husband, father, brother, and friend than I ever was yesterday. I am proud to say that I depend on God more than I ever did in the past sixty years of my life. I want you all to know that it has truly been an honor and privilege to share my prodigal story for you. If I can help change your life and have you avoid my mistakes, my sufferings, failures, sins, and challenges in my life, this book will have been worthwhile!

God has finally lifted me out of the desert and rewarded me with wonderful graces. He reintroduced to me an incredible lady named Joni Santapadra, who I dated thirty years ago. After we both were granted

OH YEAH, A CONCLUSION

annulments, we were married May 17, 2019, two years after reconnecting. For our honeymoon, we spent ten incredible days exploring the Holy Land. I have to recommend that all Christians make a pilgrim to the Holy Land. Once there, it all comes together. No more speculations. You can visibly see the hills and roads that Jesus walked. Take a boat ride on the Sea of Galilee. Touch the site where Jesus was born as well as the tomb of the risen Christ. See the house of Mary where she said yes to God at the Annunciation, and follow in the footsteps of Jesus carrying His cross. And so much more. The Bible becomes alive!

In addition to my new marriage, I have inherited three bonus children that my two children embraced as their own siblings. We moved into a beautiful three-story home and have a total of four dogs—a standard poodle, a miniature greyhound, a Siberian husky, and a fun-loving Pomsky named Luna, which I gave to Joni as a wedding present. Joni thinks Luna is her dog, but she really is my dog! I am back in school pursuing my lifelong dream of becoming an athletic trainer. I am taking several prerequisite classes at a local college, and I hope to be enrolled in the University of Arkansas athletic trainer master's program very soon. Joni and I usually attend Our Lady of the Lake Catholic Church and are regular worshipers at the adoration chapel on Monday afternoon. I am also back teaching CCD to tenth graders. Paula, my former wife, and I are no longer at war with each other. We often interact and have functions together, usually when Dominic is back in town.

I hope that you understand that God must be the center of your life no matter what life throws at you. And when I say *life*, it's really God throwing it at you! God may give you health or sickness, wealth or poverty, fame or shame, and even let you be single, divorced, or married. He may send you a straight path with little or no discomfort, or you may get a rocky crooked road over a mountain. Whatever the case may be, God is giving you free reign to choose your destiny. That's the beauty of His love. He loves us so much that we can write our own ending. We can accept His love or reject it. Either way we choose, God will always love us and respect our decision. However, there is only one way to hear Him say, "Come you are blessed by my Father, inherit the kingdom prepared for you from the foundation of the world."[430]

Throughout my tribulations, I often read *2 Corinthians 12:8–10* for consolation and contemplated what was Paul's thorn in his side and what did he mean by "my power works best in weakness":

> *Three different times I begged the Lord to take it away. Each time he said, "My grace is all you need. My power works best in weakness." So now I am glad to boast about my weakness, so that the power of Christ can work through me. That's why I take pleasure in my weakness and in the insults, hardships, persecutions and troubles that I suffer for Christ. For when I am weak then I am strong.*[431]

I can tell you from my past experiences when I was suffering, there were times I did not feel my weakness and pain was sufficient for the day. I freely admit I asked to have the thorn in my side removed. However, I truly tried to find the power of God in my low state of existence. According to Coach Lombardi, weakness is being number 2. The Marines even had a logo saying, "Pain is weakness leaving the body." As a registered nurse for thirty-six years, I have witnessed my share of people suffering with pain both physically and mentally. Today's society views pain as a weakness, burden, liability, and/or problem. But to God, He celebrates weakness. For to Him, weakness signifies a transformation of the heart.

In this chaotic and ever-changing world, it is hard to keep up with all the advanced communication technology we have at our fingertips. With communication satellites, laptop computers, and wireless cell phones, all it takes is the click of a button, and we are free to search the entire world for answers to our many questions. In a nanosecond, surfing the net can allow us to cross over distant continents and establish dialogue with thousands of people in a foreign land. With

---

[430] Matthew 25:34, National Conferences of Bishops, the New American Bible (Wichita, KS: Devore& Sons, 1981), p. 1054.

[431] 2 Corinthians 12:8–10, the New American Bible, pp. 1265–1266.

GPS (global positing system), we can even determine a physical precise position, navigate from one location to another, track and monitor personal movement. All this advanced technology to stay in constant communication, and yet we fail at listening to the free and simple words of God and embracing His love. How can we hear God trying to talk to us if we drowned Him out with all the noisemakers we have. God deeply wants us to be happy and at peace. God is good to all souls that seek His unconditional love; there are no strings attached! All that God wants is a sincere heart that is open to His love and His will. *Joel 2:12–13* reaffirms this:

> *Yet even now, says the Lord, return to me with your whole heart, with fasting, and weeping, and mourning; rend your hearts, not your garments and return to the Lord your God. For gracious and merciful is he, slow to anger, rich in kindness, and relenting in punishment.*[432]

God is eternal, almighty, loving, true, pure, holy, and good. God is not alone. He did not create man to keep Him company. Created in His image, we are fashioned for His glory, not for ours. Over the millennia, God has repeatedly showed man that He can be trusted. He has always kept his covenants with man despite the many times man has broken his side of the agreements. God has made many covenants with man: Adam and Eve, Noah, Abraham, Moses, and David, among others. The final covenant God has made is to each one of us that believes and has faith in Jesus, repents, receives baptism, and keeps the commandments. In other words, everyone that chooses Christ will inherent the kingdom of God and will be called His holy people. To prove this covenant, God sacrificed His only begotten Son for *our* benefit, not for His. It's ironic and sad that the greatest thing man desires is to love and to be loved, yet we reject the very God that is love:

> *Come to me all you who labor and burdened, and I will give you rest. Take my yoke upon you and learn from me, for I am meek*

---

[432] Joel 2:12–13, the New American Bible, p. 948.

and humble of heart; and you will find rest for yourselves. For my yoke is easy and my burden is light.[433]

In *Mark 13:31*, it is written: "Heaven and earth will pass away, but my words will not pass away."[434] The world will pass, but the *Word* will speak for an eternity. We are free to believe and live as we wish. We can choose unrepentant lives, or we can enrich our fellow man; we can give to the poor or steal from the rich; we can love our enemies or hate our brothers; we can treat our neighbors as we wish to be treated, or we can selfishly hoard our gifts; we can believe in God or rebut His words; we can strive for world peace, or we can inflict sorrows; we can plant the seeds of everlasting life, or we can choke the existence; all in all we have the choice—it's free will.

As I conclude this book, I want you to know that throughout the Bible, there are many characters that I can truly relate and identify with. At times in my life I associated with the following:

- John the Baptist: Preaching in the wilderness about the coming Messiah, the Savior Jesus. I truly love talking about Jesus and our Eternal Father. I will refuse no one who wants to hear the words of God. I preach the Word teaching CCD class, to my recovery room coworkers, and whenever someone asks me too. I often pray with sick and dying patients.
- Martha: Being so busy with her task at hand instead of realizing that God is in front of her eyes. How many times am I like that? A gazillion!
- Mary Magdalene: I cannot count the many times I crawled on my knees humbling myself seeking peace and forgiveness while reaching out to touch just His foot, for I was not worthy to gaze upon His loving face. So many times, I wished I were at His tomb that Easter Sunday.
- Lazarus: There were so many times in my life that I was just as dead as Lazarus. I have been dead spiritually, emotionally, and

---

[433] Matthew 11:28–30, the New American Bible, p. 1026.
[434] Mark 13:31, the New American Bible, p. 1084.

mentally; and it took Jesus saying to me, "Come out," to have life abundant.
- Peter: I have heard a thousand times that I have an arrogant personality. I can be just like Peter—stubborn, strong, assertive, boastful, and prideful. I faltered when I asked Jesus to command me to walk on the water by His side. I have denied Jesus more than three times. I can rush into things without thinking, waving a sword in my hand ready to fight. I have heard the cock crow more than three times in my sinful life.
- Thomas: At my weakest point in life, I too wanted Jesus to prove Himself to me. I wanted Jesus to let me put my fingers in His side, to see with my eyes rather than by faith.
- Paul: I have persecuted Christ with my sins, and at times, it took me getting knocked off my horse to come back to God. I've been knocked of my horse so many times that the horse doesn't want to carry me anymore. Like Paul, I have traveled far (Guatemala and Mexico) and close (my own community) distances to preach the Word of God.
- Daniel: I pray that my faith is so strong in God that I can feel secure and peace even when surrounded by the lions of this fallen world.
- The bad thief: In my darkest moments in life, I too am guilty of yelling and cursing at God, just like the bad thief hanging on the cross. I too blamed everyone for my problems in life.
- Satan: I've been seduced by his lies and taken a bite of the forbidden fruit. My pride was and has been greater than God. I place myself above Him so many times.
- Judas: I betray Jesus when I sin. I was greedy in my life. David: I hope and pray that I too am a man that God is so in love with and that my heart is a heart that God is after.
- The good thief: I always come to the realization that I am a sinner responsible for my sins as I hang on my cross. I know beyond doubt in my heart, mind, and soul that Jesus suffered and died for all our sins—mine included. Every day, I too ask

Jesus with faith in my heart to "remember me in His kingdom at the hour of my death."

- The good Samaritan: I have taken part in many medical mission trips to Guatemala and Mexico serving the poorest of the poor in those countries. I assist and help street people as often as I can. I give comfort to those in the hospital. I try to see Jesus in all humans. I hear those words all the time: "What you do for others, you have done for Me."
- Job: If I truly had to pick one individual that I truly can associate, relate, and identify with—it's Job! For the past fifteen years, my life has mimicked that of Job's. I lost my wife, my friends, my business, my home, my job, and my finances. I had to declare chapter 13 bankruptcy protection and borrow money from my brothers to pay the attorney. At times I was so broke I had to dig up pocket change to get gas in my car. I was devastated when my only companion, my faithful Siberian husky, Chester, died. I went through many grueling months fighting and suffering through severe depression and battled with thoughts of suicide. I had to fight extreme loneliness for at times I worked alone, exercised alone, lived alone, and went to church alone. But in the end, I rose out of the ashes, and today I have received many wonderful blessings.

There is a very old saying: "You can lead a horse to water, but you can't make it drink." I can apply this saying to all of us when Jesus told the woman at the well, "Whoever drinks the water I shall give will never thirst."[435] Jesus will always lead us to the water and offer us a cup to drink, but the decision to drink will not be forced. Jesus loves us that much! The decision to drink from His cup is yours and yours alone. Until the world passes away, there will always be a struggle between the goodness and temptations and false illusions of this world. However, there are only two choices in life and in every situation we encounter: God's way or your way. I can tell you from experience that if you

---

[435] John 4:14, the New American Bible, p. 1142.

choose the self-serving ways of this materialistic and immoral world, the gratifications acquired will only be short-lived, and you will fall flat on your face just like I have. But if you choose God's way, the reward of righteousness and eternal glorification will let you see and touch the face of God forever. Adam and Eve chose to selfserve, but Mary, Joseph, and Jesus did not! When the archangel Gabriel appeared to Mary and told her that she has found favor with God and that she would bear the Son of God in her womb, Mary could have said no, but she did not! She accepted God's invitation to serve as his handmaid even though she did not know His entire plan for her. Joseph, a righteous man, wanted to divorce Mary quietly when he found out that she was with child. But after a dream from God, Joseph also accepted the invitation of God even though he too did not fully understand God's plan. Can you imagine what could have happened to mankind had Mary and Joseph refused God's invitation? What if Mary wanted to abort her fetus, the Savior of the world? Mary could have said no! But Mary said yes!

- Be it done unto me according to Your word.
- For God, who is mighty, has done great things for me.
- And through her faith, salvation came to a world starved for love.

In *Luke 11:14–26*, Jesus clearly denotes in this parable the place where humans make daily decision is the human heart.

> Each day we make thousand of decisions. Every decision is based on a criterion, a goal. If the criteria and goals are in harmony with the true goal of human existence and with Christ's kingdom, those decisions will be good and thus will contribute to individual and social well-being. The devil wants to stir up selfish motives and self-centered attitudes, so that our decisions will be made as if we were God and everything depended only on ourselves. Christ, through his teachings and His grace, through our conscience and the inspiration of the Holy Spirit, wants to stir up noble and true motives. But neither the devil nor Christ will make our decisions for us. We can

GOD AND FREE WILL

make the most from Christ's grace (especially through prayers and the sacraments) to obtain forgiveness and be strengthened in virtue, but as long as we remain on this earth, we will still have to make our own decisions, and we will still be influenced by temptation as well as grace. Life on earth is a mission and adventure, but its also an ongoing battle.[436]

Before I end this book, I must say, in a small way I feel a little sad. Reading and reediting this book over the past ten years was like having a private conversation with God. It brought me solitude and peace. For eight of the past ten years, I was alone, and in a way, writing was my way of having company with God. It took my loneliness away. I would look forward to the next time I sat at my computer and open this file and talked with God. I usually wrote during the night or early in the morning. In many ways it was if I was at the adoration chapel at Our Lady of the Lake in Mandeville, Louisiana, where I live. I think I'm going to miss my time with God. Well, to solve this problem, I guess the only thing I can do is start on book number 2.

God is great all the time! I hope and pray that my story has given you many things to contemplate regarding your life with God and your free will. I hope and pray that you too say yes! Free will is a daily battle; sometimes it is also an hourly battle to say no to the world and yes to God. Right now. I chose God!

The Grandson: Grandpa…maybe you could come over and read it again to me tomorrow.

Grandpa: As you wish.[437]

---

[436] Father John Bartunek, *The Better Part* (Hamden, CT: Circle Press, 2007), p. 647.

[437] Rob Reiner, *Princess Bride* movie quote (1987).

GOD AND FREE WILL BIBLIOGRAPHY

1. Anne Catherine Emmerich, <u>The Dolorous Passion Of Our Lord Jesus Christ</u> (El Sobrante, CA: North Bay Books, 2003) pp. 43–53

2. Jerry Rankin, <u>In the Secret Place</u> (Nashville, Tenn: B&H Books. 2009) pp. 28–29

3. Father John Bartunek, <u>The Better Part</u> (Hamden, CT; Circle Press. 2007) pp. 393

4. Blessed Anne Catherine Emmerich, The Life of Jesus Christ & BiblicalRevelations (Charlotte, North Carolina. Tan Books. 2004) pp. 2

5. Alissa Fontana, LSU Health Science Application Letter 2010

6. Erick Metaxas, <u>Everything you Always wanted to Know About God but were Afraid to Ask</u> (Ventura, CA: Regal. 1973) pp. 153.

7. Jon Krakauer, <u>Where Men Win Glory</u> pp. 137–138

8. National Conferences of Bishops, The New American Bible (Wichita, Kansas: Devore & Sons, 1981) pp1141

9. Anne Catherine Emmerich, <u>The Dolorous Passion Of Our Lord Jesus Christ</u> (El Sobrante, CA North Bay Books, 2003) pp.43–53

10. National Conferences of Bishops, The New American Bible (Wichita, Kansas Devore & Sons, 1981) pp1337

11. Ibid., p. 1156.

12. Ibid., p. 1085

[13] Ibid., p. 1157.

[14] Eric Metaxas, <u>Everything You Wanted to Know About God but was Afraid to Ask</u> (Ventura, CA: Regal. 1973) pp. 153.

[15] National Conferences of Bishops, The New American Bible (Wichita, Kansas Devore & Sons, 1981) pp1129

[16] Ibid., pp. 1132.

[17] Bishop Fulton L. Sheen. Your Life Is Worth Living. (Schnecksville, Pa. St. Andrew's Press. 2014). Pp 166–167

[18] Steve Koren, Mark O'Keefe, Steve Oedekevk. Bruce Almighty movie.Universal Pictures. 2003

[19] National Conferences of Bishops, <u>The New American Bible</u> (Wichita, Kansas Devore & Sons, 1981) pp. 1384.

[20] Bishop Fulton L. Sheen. Your Life Is Worth Living. (Schnecksville, Pa. St. Andrew's Press. 2014). Pp 154–155

[21] Ibid. pp 154–155

[22] Eric Metaxas, <u>Everything You Wanted to Know About God but was Afraid to Ask</u> (Ventura, CA: Regal. 1973) pp. 153.

[23] Dr. Lorraine Day, <u>What was God's Purpose in Creating Humanity, from Her online paper, Why Did God Create Human Beings into a Universe Already Heavily Contaminated With Sin</u>; 2006

[24] Genesis 1: 26–27, National Conferences of Bishops, <u>The New American Bible</u> (Wichita, Kansas. Devore & Sons, 1981) pp. 9.

[25] Ibid., pp.. 782.

[26] Ibid., Genesis 2:7. P 9

[27] Rev John Trigilio Jr. Phd; Rev Kenneth Brighenti, Phd., <u>Youth Catechism of the Catholic Church</u> (San Francisco, CA: Ignatius Press 2010) pp. 45.

[28] Genesis 2:17; Genesis 1: 26–27, National Conferences of Bishops, <u>The New American Bible</u> (Wichita, Kansas: Devore & Sons, 1981) pp. 9.

[29] Ibid., Genesis 2:16 p. 9

[30] Ibid; 3: 1–6 p.10

31   Ibid 3:4

32   Eric Metaxas, <u>Everything You Always Wanted To Know About God But Were Afraid To Ask</u> (Ventura, CA: Regal. 1973) pp. 153.

33   Genesis 3:16 National Conferences of Bishops, The <u>New American Bible</u> (Wichita, Kansas: Devore & Sons, 1981) pp. 9.

34   Dr. Lorraine Day, <u>What was God's Purpose in Creating Humanity, from Her online paper, Why Did God Create Human Beings into a Universe Already Heavily Contaminated With Sin</u>; 2006

35   Genesis 3:6 National Conferences of Bishops, <u>The New American Bible</u> (Wichita, Kansas: Devore & Sons, 1981) pp. 9.

36   Bishop Fulton L. Sheen. <u>Your Life Is Worth Living.</u> (Schnecksville, Pa. St. Andrew's Press. 2014). Pp 160–161

37   Erick Metaxas, <u>Everything you Always Wanted to know about God but was afraid to Ask</u> (Ventura, CA; Regal 1981) pp. 155–159

38   Genesis 3:7 National Conferences of Bishops, the <u>New American Bible</u> (Wichita, Kansas: Devore & Sons, 1981) pp. 9.

39   Ibid. Genesis 3:21–24. pp. 11.

40   Ibid Genesis 3:16–19. p. 10.

41   Ibid., Genesis 3:14–15, pp. 10 Ibid John 10:10, pp. 1152

42   Ibid John 10:10, pp. 1152

43   Ibid. Isaiah 59:2. Pp 796

44   Ibid. Deuteronomy 30:19, pp. 189

45   Ibid. 1 Acts 20:32. pp. 1197

46   Ibid. Joshua 24:15. Pp 215.

47   Ibid. Genesis 3:19, pp. 10

48   Ibid Romans 5:12–19

49   St. Augustine

50. Dr. Lorraine Day, What was God's Purpose in Creating Humanity, from Her online paper, Why Did God Create Human Beings into a Universe Already Heavily Contaminated With Sin; 2006

51. Luke 4:1–12 National Conferences of Bishops, the New American Bible (Wichita, Kansas: Devore & Sons, 1981) pp. 1099

52. Ibid: Luke 22:32–39. Pp.1130

53. Ibid, Acts 9:3–5. Pp.1181

54. Ibid. Exodus 3:2–6, pp 60

55. Ibid. Matthew

56. James Martin, SJ, Jesus (Harper One. New York, New York. 2014) pp.39

57. Craig Nelson, The First Heroes (New York City, New York: Viking Penguin: 2002) pp. 304, 305, 327, 328

58. Ibid328

59. Immaculee Ilibagiza, Left to Tell (New York, New York: Hay House) pp. 3.

60. Ibid. pp 70

61. Ibid., pp. 78–79

62. Ibid., p. XIV

63. Tony Dungy, Quiet Strength (Carol Stream, Illinois: 2007). Pp. 289.

64. Ibid. pp288

65. Life without Limb.com

66. Ibid.

67. Immaculee Ilibagiza, The Boy who met Jesus (Carlsbad, California. Hay House, Inc 2011) pp. 77–78

68. Ibid. pp

69. Ibid. pp 120

70. Ibid. pp 112–113

GOD AND FREE WILL BIBLIOGRAPHY

71   Akiane Kramari Foreli Kramarik, <u>Akiane</u> (Nashville, Tennessee. Thomas Nelson 2006) pp.7

72   Ibid. pp 2–8

73   Ibid. pp.37–38

74   2 Peters 1:10 National Conferences of Bishops, <u>the New American Bible</u> (Wichita, Kansas: Devore & Sons, 1981) pp. 1099

75   Ibids., Matthew 22:1–14. Pp. 1046–1047

76   Ibids., Mark 10:17–22. Pp 1079

77   Fr. John Bartunek, <u>The Better Part</u> (Hamden, CT: Circle Press; 2007) pp. 295.

78   1 Kings 11–13. National Conferences of Bishops, <u>the New American Bible</u> (Wichita, Kansas: Devore & Sons, 1981) pp. 1099

79   Bob Dylan, <u>Gotta Serve Somebody</u>; Slow Train Coming Album. 1979

80   Wizard of Oz movie quote. Produced by MGM. 1939

81   Ibid

82   George Lucas. Empire Strike back movie quote 1980

83   James 4: 7 National Conferences of Bishops, <u>the New American Bible</u> (Wichita, Kansas: Devore & Sons, 1981) pp. 1099

84   Ibids., Revelation12:10–12. Pp. 1384

85   Ibid., Genesis 1:31pp. 9

86   Rev John Trigilio Jr. Phd; Rev Kenneth Brighenti, PhD., <u>Youth Catechism of the Catholic Church</u> (San Francisco, CA: Ignatius Press 2010) pp. 49– 52.

87   Ibid., pp. 48.

88   Genesis 3:10 National Conferences of Bishops, <u>the New American Bible</u> (Wichita, Kansas: Devore & Sons, 1981) pp. 1099

89   Ibid: Romans 14:23 pp 1225.

90   Poltergeist movie quote: 1982

91   Matthew 6:19–21 National Conferences of Bishops, <u>the New American Bible</u> (Wichita, Kansas: Devore & Sons, 1981) pp. 1018

92. Ibid., Matthew 5:43–48. Pp1016

93. Ibids. Matthew 6:22–23. Pp 1018

94. St. John Chrysostom

95. St. Augustine

96. Romans 5:21 National Conferences of Bishops, <u>the New American Bible</u> (Wichita, Kansas: Devore & Sons, 1981) pp. 1216

97. Leon Bloy

98. Hermann Hesse

99. Matthew 7:13–14 National Conferences of Bishops, <u>the New American Bible</u> (Wichita, Kansas: Devore & Sons, 1981) pp. 1019

100. Mother Teresa of Calcutta, www.life-changing-inspirational-quotes.com

101. Wizard of Oz movie quote. MGM Studio. 1939

102. Darth Vader-s answer are taken from Star War 1977 movie quote

103. Rocky Balboa movie quote. Written by Sylvester Stallone. 2006

104. 2 Corinthians 4:7–10 National Conferences of Bishops, <u>the New American Bible</u> (Wichita, Kansas: Devore & Sons, 1981) pp.1256

105. Fr. John Bartunek, Inside the Passion (West Chester, PA: Ascension Press:2005) pp. 112

106. John 15:13 National Conferences of Bishops, <u>the New American Bible</u> (Wichita, Kansas: Devore & Sons, 1981) pp.1160

107. Ibid Matthew 6:25–34. Pp1018

108. Ibid. Mark 15:21. Pp 1087

109. Fr. John Bartunek, Inside the Passion (West Chester, PA: Ascension Press: 2005) pp. 121

110. Luke 8:40–48. National Conferences of Bishops, <u>the New American Bible</u> (Wichita, Kansas: Devore & Sons, 1981) pp. 1108.

111. Ibids. Mark 2:1–12. Pp 1067

112. My Cousin Vinny movie quote. Written by Dale Launer. 1998

[113] Luke 5:12–16 National Conferences of Bishops, <u>the New American Bible</u> (Wichita, Kansas: Devore & Sons, 1981) pp.1101

[114] Ibis. Matthew 25:35 pp 1054

[115] Ibis. Psalm 69:21. Pp. 586.

[116] Ibis. Psalm 52. Pp. 577

[117] Ibis. John 4–42. Pp. 1142–1143

[118] Ibis. John 8:4–10. Pp. 1149.

[119] John Mayer. <u>Dreaming with a Broken Heart.</u> 2010

[120] Genesis 6: 5–20 National Conferences of Bishops, <u>the New American Bible</u> (Wichita, Kansas: Devore & Sons, 1981) pp.62–63

[121] Wizard of Oz movie quote. MGM Studio. 1939

[122] Mel Brooks, Spaceballs movie quote. 1987

[123] National Oceanic and Atmospheric Administration (NOAA) website

[124] Matthew 24: 15–28. National Conferences of Bishops, <u>the New American Bible</u> (Wichita, Kansas: Devore & Sons, 1981) pp.1051–1052

[125] Ibis. Matthew 6:19–21. Pp1018 &Mat thew 6:10–21

[126] Ibd. 7–12. Pp1018

[127] Luke 6:27–36 National Conferences of Bishops, <u>the New American Bible</u> (Wichita, Kansas: Devore & Sons, 1981) pp.1103

[128] Wizard of Oz movie quote. MGM Studio. 1939

[129] James 2:17–18 National Conferences of Bishops, <u>the New American Bible</u> (Wichita, Kansas: Devore & Sons, 1981) pp.1344

[130] Ibids. Genesis. 19:12. Pp24

[131] Ibids. Matthew 24: 36–44 pp. 1052–1053

[132] Jerry Rankin, <u>In the Secret Place</u> (Nashville, Tenn.: B&H Books: 2009) pp. 162–163

[133] Led Zeppelin, <u>When the levee break.</u>, Led Zeppelin IV album, 1971

134 Princes Bride movie quote, Rob Reiner director, 1987

135 John 21:24, National Conferences of Bishops, the New American Bible (Wichita, Kansas: Devore & Sons, 1981) pp. 1168

136 Ibis. Matthew 11:4–5. Pp. 1025.

137 Rev John Trigilio Jr. Phd; Rev Kenneth Brighenti,Phd.,Youth Catechism of the Catholic Church (San Francisco, CA: Ignatius Press 2010) pp. 66

138 Bishop Fulton L. Sheen. Your Life Is Worth Living. (Schnecksville, Pa. St. Andrew's Press. 2014). Pp 41–44

139 Matthew 13:38–39 National Conferences of Bishops, the New American Bible (Wichita, Kansas: Devore & Sons, 1981) pp. 1028

140 Ibid. Mark 14:32–34. pp 1084

141 Ibid. 35–37. pp 1084

142 Ibid. Matthew 10:1 pp. 1023.

143 www.CharleneRichard.com. 2013

144 Luke 3: 46–47 National Conferences of Bishops, the New American Bible (Wichita, Kansas: Devore & Sons, 1981) pp. 1097

145 Fr. John Bartunek, The Better Part (Handen, CT: Circle Press: 2007) pp74

146 Immaculee Ilibagiza; Our Lady of Kibeho. (Hay House Inc. New York City; 2008) pp xiii–xvi

147 Bruce Almighty movie quote, written by Steve Koran, Mark O'Keefe &Steve Oedkerf. 2003

148 Romans 8:28 National Conferences of Bishops, the New American Bible (Wichita, Kansas: Devore & Sons, 1981) pp. 1219

149 Ibids. John 11:4. Pp.1153

150 Ibids. John 11:33 pp. 1154

151 Ibid 11:22–27 pp. 1154

152 Isaiah 53:1–12 National Conferences of Bishops, the New American Bible (Wichita, Kansas: Devore & Sons, 1981) pp. 792

GOD AND FREE WILL BIBLIOGRAPHY

[153] Matthew 26:38 Ibids. pp1056

[154] Luke 22:44 Ibid pp 1130

[155] Lee Strobel. <u>The Case For Christ</u>(Grand Rapid, Michigan. Zondervan. 1998) pp. 209, 210, 212

[156] John 19:30 Ibid. Pp.1165

[157] Rev John Trigilio Jr. Phd; Rev Kenneth Brighenti, Phd., <u>Youth Catechism of the Catholic Church</u> (San Francisco, CA: Ignatius Press 2010) pp. 67

[158] Saint Pio of Pietrelcina

[159] 2 Cor 12: 9 National Conferences of Bishops, <u>the New American Bible</u> (Wichita, Kansas: Devore & Sons, 1981) pp. 1256

[160] Ibid. 2 Tim 4:17. Pp 1317

[161] Letter to the Editor, Abbeville Meridional Newspaper. Sept 1988

[162] Luke 11:13 National Conferences of Bishops, <u>the New American Bible</u> (Wichita, Kansas: Devore & Sons, 1981) pp. 1113

[163] John Bartunek, the Better Part (Circle Press: Hamden, CT: 2007) pp.247

[164] Rev John Trigilio Jr. Phd; Rev Kenneth Brighenti, Phd., <u>Youth Catechism of the Catholic Church</u> (San Francisco, CA: Ignatius Press 2010) pp. 67

[165] 1 Peter 2:21 National Conferences of Bishops, <u>the New American Bible</u> (Wichita, Kansas: Devore & Sons, 1981) pp.1350

[166] Ibis. Matthew 2: 16; pp 1011

[167] Ibis. Luke 2: 34. Pp 1096

[168] Ibis Matthew 24:9 Pp 1051

[169] Ibis Colossians 1:24. Pp 1294

[170] The Piera Prayer Book (Hickory Corners, Michigan. 1972) pp5

[171] Lee Strobel. <u>The Case For Christ</u> (Grand Rapid, Michigan. Zondervan. 1998) pp. 152, 153, 154

[172] Crusaders at Our Lady of Fatima (Lancaster, California)

[173] Matthew 5:45 National Conferences of Bishops, the New American Bible (Wichita, Kansas: Devore & Sons, 1981) Pp 1016

[174] List of Wars & Anthropogenic Disasters by estimates Death toll, Wikipedia. 2013

[175] Rev John Trigilio Jr. Phd; Rev Kenneth Brighenti,Phd., Youth Catechism of the Catholic Church (San Francisco, CA: Ignatius Press 2010) pp. 67

[176] Darius Rucker, If I had Wings (Learn to Live CD). 2008

[177] All quotes and information taken from the website: http://www.des.emory.edu/mfp/OnFailing.html

[178] All quotes and information taken from the website: http://www.des.emory.edu/mfp/OnFailing.html

[179] Sarah Ban Breathnach, A Man's Journey to Simple Abundance (Press Book: 2000). pp.277.

[180] Ibid

[181] www.huffingtonpost.com/steve-jobs-standford commencement address 2013

[182] Matthew 16:13–14 National Conferences of Bishops, the New American Bible (Wichita, Kansas: Devore & Sons, 1981) pp.1034–1035

[183] Ibid Matthew 26:38. Pp. 1056

[184] www.footprint-in the sand.com

[185] www.motherteresa.org

[186] Galatians 3:26 National Conferences of Bishops, the New American Bible (Wichita, Kansas: Devore & Sons, 1981) pp.1273

[187] Ibid 4:6 pp. 1273

[188] Ibid Mark 2:16–17. Pp.1067

[189] Dr. Ian Barnes, The Historical Atlas lf the Bible (Chartwell Books: New York, New York 2006). Pp.257–258

[190] Fr. John Bartunek, The Better Part (Circle Press; Hamden, CT:2007).Pp.361

[191] Matthew 21:31–32 National Conferences of Bishops, the New American Bible (Wichita, Kansas: Devore & Sons, 1981) pp.1045

GOD AND FREE WILL BIBLIOGRAPHY

[192] Ibid Luke 1:31. Pp. 1093

[193] Ibid John 6:35. pp.1146

[194] Ibid John 7:40–43. pp. 1148–1149

[195] Ibid Matthew 16:13–16. Pp.1034–1035

[196] Ibid Matthew 3:17. Pp. 1013

[197] Saint Peter Chrysologus

[198] Mark 10:46–52. National Conferences of Bishops, the New American Bible (Wichita, Kansas: Devore & Sons, 1981) pp.1080

[199] Seinfeld TV show season 7; "The Maestro Script"

[200] History of the World Part I movie quote, Mel Brooks writer. 1981

[201] Matthew 5:17–19 National Conferences of Bishops, the New American Bible (Wichita, Kansas: Devore & Sons, 1981) pp.1015

[202] Ibid Colossians 3:5. Pp.1296.

[203] Dani Johnson, Spirit Driven Success (Worldwide distribution 2009) pp71 &72

[204] Steven Koren, Mark O'Keefe, Steve Oedekerk, Bruce Almighty movie quote, 2003

[205] Matthew 26:65 National Conferences of Bishops, the New American Bible (Wichita, Kansas: Devore & Sons, 1981) pp.1057

[206] 6 Ibid. Deuteronomy 6:11 Pp. 167

[207] Rev John Trigilio Jr. Phd; Rev Kenneth Brighenti, Phd., Youth Catechism of the Catholic Church (San Francisco, CA: Ignatius Press 2010) pp. 198–199

[208] Exodus 20:12 National Conferences of Bishops, the New American Bible (Wichita, Kansas: Devore & Sons, 1981) pp.75

[209] www.searchquotes.com/search/st_john_Chrysostum

[210] Rev John Trigilio Jr. Phd; Rev Kenneth Brighenti, Phd., Youth Catechism of the Catholic Church (San Francisco, CA: Ignatius Press 2010) pp. 198–199

[211] Deuteronomy 6:16 National Conferences of Bishops, the New American Bible (Wichita, Kansas: Devore & Sons, 1981) pp.167

212 Ibid 1 Samuel 2:30. Pp.245

213 Steve Gordon, Arthur movie quote, 1981

214 Genesis 4:5 National Conferences of Bishops, <u>the New American Bible</u> (Wichita, Kansas: Devore & Sons, 1981) pp.11

215 Ibid Exodus 21:22 Pp. 76

216 Emmet Fox, <u>Around the Year</u>

217 1 Corinthians 6:19 National Conferences of Bishops, <u>the New American Bible</u> (Wichita, Kansas: Devore & Sons, 1981) pp.1236

218 Rob Reiner, Princess Bride movie quote.1987

219 John Patrick Shanley, <u>Moonstruck</u> movie quote, 1987

220 Mark 10:11–12 National Conferences of Bishops, <u>the New American Bible</u> (Wichita, Kansas: Devore & Sons, 1981) pp.1079

221 Ibid. Genesis 2:24 Pp. 10

222 Ibid Pp.10

223 Ibid Matthew 19:6 Pp1040

224 Leviticus 20:10 Ibid Pp. 113

225 1 Corinthians 7:39 Ibid Pp.1238

226 Ibid. 7:10:11. pp1236

227 Proverbs 6:12–14. Ibid Pp. 639

228 Matthew 18:8–9 Ibid Pp. 1038

229 Mark 10:9 Ibid. Pp. 1078

230 Ephesians 5:22–23. Ibid. Pp.1283

231 Hebrews 13:4 Ibid. Pp.1339

232 Malachi 2:14–16. Ibid Pp.993

233 1 Corinthians7:10–11 Ibid. Pp.1237

234. Rev John Trigilio Jr. Phd; Rev Kenneth Brighenti, Phd., <u>Youth Catechism of the Catholic Church</u> (San Francisco, CA: Ignatius Press 2010) pp. 198–199

235. Proverbs 15:5 National Conferences of Bishops, <u>the New American Bible</u> (Wichita, Kansas: Devore & Sons, 1981) pp.646

236. Proverb 19:9 Ibid. Pp.651

237. Malachi 3:5 Ibid Pp 993

238. Matthew 7:1–2 Ibid. Pp. 1018

239. John 14:6. Ibid Pp. 1158

240. Rev John Trigilio Jr. Phd; Rev Kenneth Brighenti, Phd., <u>Youth Catechism of the Catholic Church</u> (San Francisco, CA: Ignatius Press 2010) pp.251

241. Proverb 6:25–29 National Conferences of Bishops, <u>the New American Bible</u> (Wichita, Kansas: Devore & Sons, 1981) pp.639

242. Matthew 5:27 Ibid. pp. 1016

243. Immaculee Ilibagiza, <u>Our Lady of Kibeho</u> (Hay House, Inc. Carlsbad, CA: 2008). Pp.118.

244. Jeff Dunham, <u>Melvin the Superhero</u>. YouTube. 2013

245. Matthew 5:17–20. National Conferences of Bishops, <u>the New American Bible</u> (Wichita, Kansas: Devore & Sons, 1981) pp.1015

246. Matthew 22:34–40. Ibid. pp. 1047

247. Kevin Bisch, <u>Hitch</u> movie quote. 2005

248. Luke 3:23, National Conferences of Bishops, <u>the New American Bible</u> (Wichita, Kansas: Devore & Sons, 1981) pp.1097

249. Ibid. pp. 1098

250. www.johnlocke.biography.com

251. Eric Clapton, <u>Change the World</u>, 1999

252. Proverbs 3:5 National Conferences of Bishops, <u>the New American Bible</u> (Wichita, Kansas: Devore & Sons, 1981) pp.636

253. Luke 10:38–41. Ibid. pp. 1112

254 Oswald Chamber, My Utmost For His Highest (Discovery House: Grand Rapids, Michigan: 1922) pp. 1

255 Exodus 33:18–19. National Conferences of Bishops, the New American Bible (Wichita, Kansas: Devore & Sons, 1981) pp.88

256 John 11:41–42. Ibid. pp. 1154

257 Rob Reiner, The Princess Bride movie quote. 1987

258 John Patrick Stanley, Moonstruck movie quote. 1987

259 Matthew 13:45–46. National Conferences of Bishops, the New American Bible (Wichita, Kansas: Devore & Sons, 1981) pp.1031

260 Steven K. Scott, The Richest Man Who Ever Lived (Doubleday: 20060)PP.10

261 Don Henley, Danny Koltchmar, Dirty Laundry lyrics. 1982

262 John 11:33. National Conferences of Bishops, the New American Bible (Wichita, Kansas: Devore & Sons, 1981) pp.1154

263 Matthew 16:18. Ibid. pp1035

264 Dalai Lama, The Paradox of Our Ages (www.dalailama.com/the-dalailama)2013

265 Wisdom1:12–13 National Conferences of Bishops, the New American Bible (Wichita, Kansas: Devore & Sons, 1981) pp.680

266 Luke 4:16–29. Ibid. pp. 1099–1100

267 1 Samuel 16:7. Ibid. pp 257

268 www.billygraham.com

269 John 14:6. National Conferences of Bishops, the New American Bible (Wichita, Kansas: Devore & Sons, 1981) pp.1158

270 Proverbs 27:1 Ibid. pp. 658

271 Matthew 9:28–29 Ibid. pp1022

272 Ibid. 9:2 pp 1021

273 Ibid. 8:13 pp 1020

274 Ibid. 9:27–28 pp1022

GOD AND FREE WILL BIBLIOGRAPHY

275 Ibid 15:28. Pp. 1033

276 Fr. John Bartunek, The Better Part (Circle Press. Hamden, Ct: 2007) pp132

277 Bill O'Reilly, The Last Days of Jesus (Henry Holt &Company. NYNY.2014) pp 47,214

278 Fr. Frederick Manns, O.F.M., <u>Every day in the Life of Jesus</u>

279 Bill O'Reilly, Martin Dugard, Killing Jesus (Henry Holt and Company: NYNY: 2013) pp. 3

280 Bill O'Reilly, The Last Days of Jesus (Henry Holt &Company. NYNY.2014) ppXX, 48, 49

281 1 Chronicles 12:18 National Conferences of Bishops, <u>the New American Bible</u> (Wichita, Kansas: Devore & Sons, 1981) pp 359

282 Luke 2:14 Ibid. pp.1095

283 John 14:27 Ibid. pp.1159

284 2 Corinthians 13:11. Ibid. pp.1267

285 Emmet Fox, Sermon on the Mountain (Harper: San Francisco: 1934). pp.128

286 Emmet Fox, Around the World (Harper. San Francisco 1958)

287 Luke 19:10. National Conferences of Bishops, <u>the New American Bible</u> (Wichita, Kansas: Devore & Sons, 1981) pp 1124

288 Craig Nelson, The First Heroes (Viking Penguin 2002) pp 336

289 www.Webster.com

290 Ephesians 4:2–4 National Conferences of Bishops, <u>the New American Bible</u> (Wichita, Kansas: Devore & Sons, 1981) pp 1281

291 Zechariah 9:9 Ibid. pp.

292 Mark 11:1–11 Ibid. pp. 1080

293 Wayne Weible, <u>Medjugorjel The Message</u> (Paraclete Press: Brewster, Massachusetts:1989). Pp.65

294 George, Harrison, <u>Give me love</u> lyrics. Living in the Material World CD. 1973

295 Nehemiah 9:17. National Conferences of Bishops, the New American Bible (Wichita, Kansas: Devore & Sons, 1981) pp421

296 Matthew 18:21 Ibid. pp. 1039

297 Matthew 9:6 Ibid. pp 1021

298 John 20:22–23 Ibid. pp.1167

299 Luke 23:24 Ibid. pp.1132

300 Ann Coulter, Demonic (Crown Forum, New York. 2011) pp. 113

301 Ibid. pp113

302 Ibid. pp. 123–124

303 Emmet Fox, the Sermon on the Mount (Harper: San Francisco: 1934).Pp.113

304 Matthew 5:23–24 National Conferences of Bishops, the New American Bible (Wichita, Kansas: Devore & Sons, 1981) pp1015

305 Paul Kengor, A Pope and A President (Wilmington, Delaware; ISI Books. 2017) pp.248

306 Ibis

307 John Pope. Times Picayune Newspaper. September 9, 2012

308 Matthew 5:23–24 National Conferences of Bishops, the New American Bible (Wichita, Kansas: Devore & Sons, 1981) pp1015

309 Eric Metaxas, Everything You Always Wanted to Know About God (Regal Publishing. Ventura, CA. 1982). Pp166–173

310 Immaculee Ilibagiza, Steve Erwin, The boy who met Jesus (Hay HouseInc. New York City. 2011)pp.106,107,108

311 Psalm 51:19 National Conferences of Bishops, the New American Bible (Wichita, Kansas: Devore & Sons, 1981) pp577

312 Psalm 130:3–4. Ibid. pp.624

313 Psalm 103:8–3. Ibid. pp607

314 Emmet Fox, Around the World (Harper: San Francisco: 1931) pp4

315 Neil Gaimear, Stardust movie quote. 2007

[316] Matthew 27:40. National Conferences of Bishops, the New American Bible (Wichita, Kansas: Devore & Sons, 1981) pp1060

[317] 1 Corinthians 13:2 Ibid. pp. 1244

[318] John 1:14. Ibid. pp. 1137

[319] Matthew 22:36–39 Ibid. pp. 1047–1048 [320] Luke 23:24–42. Ibid. pp. 1132.

[321] Emmet Fox, Around the World (Harper: San Francisco. Reprinted 1992). Pp. 356

[322] 1 Corinthians 13:1–13 National Conferences of Bishops, the New American Bible (Wichita, Kansas: Devore & Sons, 1981) pp1244 [323] Eric Metaxas, Everything You Always Wanted to Know About God (Regal publishing,. Ventura, CA: 1982). Pp.90–94.

[324] Lee Strobel. The Case For Christ (Grand Rapid, Michigan. Zondervan. 1998) pp. 209, 210, 212

[325] Rob Reiner, William Goldman, Princess Bride Movie quote. 1987

[326] Dave Matthews, Christmas Song., Remember Two Thing, CD. 1997

[327] Matthew 5:37 National Conferences of Bishops, the New American Bible (Wichita, Kansas: Devore & Sons, 1981) pp1016

[328] Thomas Langan, The Catholic Tradition (University of Missouri Press:St Louis. 1998). Pp. 371

[329] Ibid.

[330] John 1:14. National Conferences of Bishops, the New American Bible (Wichita, Kansas: Devore & Sons, 1981) pp1137

[331] Ibid. 14.6. pp1158

[332] Ibid 18:37. Pp 1164

[333] Ibid. 18:23. Pp1163

[334] W.P. Young, The Shack (Windblown Media: Newbury Park, CA: 2008) pp189

[335] Matthew 13:54–57 National Conferences of Bishops, the New American Bible (Wichita, Kansas: Devore & Sons, 1981) pp1031

336. Lee Strobel, The Case For Christ (Zondervan: Grand Rapids, Michigan. 1998). pp146

337. Ann Coulter, Demonic (Crown Forum, New York: 2011) pp 251

338. Ibid.

339. Emmet Fox, Around the World (Harper: San Francisco: 1992). Pp. 13

340. W.P. Young, The Shack (Windblown Media: Newbury Park, CA: 2008)pp

341. Emmet Fox, Around the World (Harper: San Francisco. 1999). Pp 79 & 365

342. Aaron Sorkin, Rob Reiner, A Few Good Men, movie quote. 1992

343. Bishop Fulton J. Sheen, Life of Christ (Doubleday. New York: 1997) pp. 1–3

344. Bishop Fulton L. Sheen. Your Life Is Worth Living. (Schnecksville, Pa. St. Andrew's Press. 2014). Pp 38–39

345. The American Bible Society, *Bible Prophecies: Faith, History and Hope*, New York: Time Inc., 2009

346. Lee Strobel, The Case For Christ (Zondervan: Grand Rapids, Michigan. 1998). pp 197, 198, 200

347. Bishop Fulton J. Sheen, Life of Christ (Doubleday. New York: 1997) pp.7

348. Ibid. pp 7

349. Ibid. pp. 7

350. Ibid. pp. 7

351. John 8:12 Ibid. pp. 1149

352. Ibid. pp. 1150

353. Mark 14. Ibid. pp.1086

354. John 18:5–6. Pp. 1162

355. Lee Strobell, *The Case For Christ* (Grand Rapid, Michigan: Zondervan 1998) pp159,170

356. Matthew 27:51–52. National Conferences of Bishops, the New American Bible (Wichita, Kansas: Devore & Sons, 1981) Pp. 1060

357. Ibid. 28:1–4. Pp.1062

358. Ibid. 28.11–14. pp/

359. John 20:1. Ibid Pp. 1166

360. Matthew 28: 1–8. Ibid. Pp. 1061–1062

361. John 20:6–7. Ibid. pp.1166

362. Lee Strobel, *The Case For Christ* (Grand Rapid, Michigan: Zondervan 1998) pp 247, 254

363. Laurie Beth Jones, Jesus, Life Coach (Thomas, Nelson, Inc. Nashville,Tenn.: 2004) pp. xvii

364. Jon Kennedy, Jesus, His External Legacy (Fall River Press, New York, NY. 2010). Pp126

365. Ibid. pp23

366. Ibid. pp. 23

367. Ibid. pp 31

368. Ibid. pp. 147

369. Ibid. pp. 147

370. Eric Metaxas, Everything You Always Wanted To Know About God (Regal. Ventura, Ca. 1982). Pp. 16

371. World Press.Com, by tdhigg 01; August 4, 2012

372. Lee Strobel, *The Case For Christ* (Grand Rapid, Michigan: Zondervan 1998) pp266

373. Matthew 21:23–27. National Conferences of Bishops, the New American Bible (Wichita, Kansas: Devore & Sons, 1981) pp 1044

374. Ibid 12:24–28. Pp1027

375. John 18:36 Ibid. pp. 1163

376. Matthew 19:23 Ibid. pp. 1041

377. Ibid. 5:43–46. Pp.1061

378. Eric Metaxas, Everything You Always Wanted to Know About God (Regal. Ventura, CA. 1982). Pp132–135

379. Jon Kennedy, Jesus, His External Legacy (Fall River Press, New York,NY. 2010). Pp.22

380. Father John Bartunek, The Better Part (Circle Press. Hamden, Ct 2007).Pp.326

381. Rev John Trigilio Jr. Phd; Rev Kenneth Brighenti, Phd., <u>Youth Catechism of the Catholic Church</u> (San Francisco, CA: Ignatius Press 2010) pp.68

382. Andrew Lloyd Webber, Tim Rice, <u>Jesus Christ Super Star</u>, lyrics, 1971

383. Jerry MacGregor, Marie Prys, <u>1001 Surprising Things You Should Know About the Bible</u> (Fall River Press; New York, NY. 2002). 67

384. Matthew 19:24 National Conferences of Bishops, <u>the New American Bible</u> (Wichita, Kansas: Devore & Sons, 1981) pp 1040

385. Ibid. 19:25. Pp1041

386. Acts 16:30–31. Ibid pp.1192

387. John 11:25 Ibid. pp. 1154

388. Ibid. pp. pp.1158

389. Ibid. pp. 1146

390. Mark 1:15. Ibid. pp. 1066

391. John 3:3 Ibid. pp. 1140

392. Ibid. pp. 1141

393. 1 Timothy 1:15. Ibid. pp. 1307

394. Acts 26:18. Ibid. pp. 1203

395. Romans 10:13. Ibid. pp. 1221

396. 1 Corinthians 3:11 Ibid. pp. 1223

397. Galatians 3:26 Ibid. pp. 1273

398. Luke 12:31–32. Ibid. pp. 1115

399. Matthew 7:13–14. Ibid. PP. 1019

[400] Ibid. pp. 1012

[401] Ibid. pp. 1019

[402] Ibid. pp. 1019

[403] Ibid. pp. 1056

[404] Romans 2:12–13. Ibid. pp. 1212

[405] Matthew 11:28. Ibid. pp. 1026

[406] John 8:31–32 Ibid. pp. 1150

[407] Mel Brooks, Young Frankenstein, movie quote. 1974

[408] Matthew 25:34 National Conferences of Bishops, <u>the New American Bible</u> (Wichita, Kansas: Devore & Sons, 1981) pp. 1054

[409] 2 Corinthians 12:8–10 Ibid. pp. 1265–1266

[410] Joel 2:12–13 Ibid. pp. 948

[411] Matthew 11:28–30. Ibid. pp. 1026

[412] Mark 13:31 Ibid. pp. 1084

[413] John 4:14 Ibid. pp. 1142

[414] **<u>Spirit & Song 1&2.</u>** OCP Publications. NE Hassalo Publication, Or. 2005.

[415] Rob Reiner, Princess Bride movie quote. 1987

ABOUT THE AUTHOR

My name is John Lawrence Fontana. I live in Covington, Louisiana, with my wife and four dogs. I am the father of five children. I am a retired registered nurse with thirty-six years of clinical experience working in trauma and emergency room, wound care, hyperbaric recovery, and medical sales. I served in the US Army Reserve and Louisiana National Guard as an Army nurse. I am currently in college studying toward a master's degree in athletic training. I have taught CCD (Confraternity of Christian Doctrine) for our Lady of the Lake Catholic Church in Mandeville, Louisiana, to public school tenth graders for over ten years.

www.ingramcontent.com/pod-product-compliance
Lightning Source LLC
LaVergne TN
LVHW091659070526
838199LV00050B/2213